OPERATION BARBAROSSA

OSPREY
PUBLISHING

OPERATION BARBAROSSA

THE GERMAN INVASION OF SOVIET RUSSIA

ROBERT KIRCHUBEL

First published in Great Britain in 2013 by Osprey Publishing,
Midland House, West Way, Botley, Oxford, OX2 0PH, UK
43-01 21st Street, Suite 220, Long Island City, NY 11101, USA
E-mail: info@ospreypublishing.com

Osprey Publishing is part of the Osprey Group

A CIP catalogue record for this book is available from the
British Library

ISBN: 978 1 78200 408 0
E-pub ISBN: 978 1 4728 0471 6
PDF ISBN: 978 1 4728 0470 9

Typeset in Adobe Garamond Pro and ITC Machine
Cartography by The Map Studio and Boundford
Index by Alan Thatcher
Originated by PDQ Digital Media Solutions, UK
Printed in China through Worldprint

13 14 15 16 17 18   10 9 8 7 6 5 4 3 2 1

Osprey Publishing is supporting the Woodland Trust, the UK's
leading woodland conservation charity, by funding the
dedication of trees.

www.ospreypublishing.com

AUTHOR'S NOTE

This book is written to the glory of God. It is meant to be the
single-volume operational history of Operation *Barbarossa* for a
new generation. I want to express my lasting gratitude to my
wife Linda and our three sons for their forbearance during my
discussions, reading, writing, wargaming, and vacation detours
concerning military history. None of my books would have been
as successful without the invaluable assistance of my editing
team of Joe Wilson and Gary Komar. Gary provided much of
the basic data for many of the new sidebars. Thanks also to the
Interlibrary Loan Departments at the libraries of San Joaquin
County (California), California State University, Fresno, and
Purdue University. Lastly, I appreciate the decade-long support
of Osprey, which had faith in an unpublished author, especially
the backing of Marcus Cowper, who was "present at the
creation" of my Campaign series trilogy and who is the
godfather of the present volume. Kate Moore and her team have
been a pleasure to work with.

CONTENTS

PREFACE

This consolidation includes over 90 percent of the original Campaign trilogy text previously published by Osprey. New material includes updates from recent scholarship, clarifications, additional maps, photographs, graphics plus sidebars to address topics not covered in detail elsewhere. Those familiar with the Campaign series know that Osprey has a successful formula which specifies a book's organization, the length of any given section, and the number of supporting graphics. The need to put a lot of information onto fewer than 100 pages challenges an author to balance all the many components of modern warfare — especially in a gigantic campaign like *Barbarossa*. The present volume, however, allows me to write more expansively. Furthermore, Operation *Barbarossa* and the Nazi–Soviet War in general were among the most politicized and ideologically charged in modern history. Therefore this expanded volume has allowed me to put politics and ideology in their proper and prestigious positions.

Another major objective of this book is to present *Barbarossa* in a more understandable manner for an audience perhaps not comfortable or familiar with it. Unfortunately some of the campaign's features that make it so fascinating to me can make it inaccessible to or unpopular with others: its chaos, complexity, massive scale, twists and turns, to name just a few. In terms of activity, chronology, geography, personalities, units, and other measures *Barbarossa* experienced constant peaks and valleys which can be hard to follow or make sense of.

Significant combat by major units could be widely separated by time and distance. On the face of it, it may not be easy to see the relationship between events at opposite ends of the calendar or map. Immediately after the German invasion there was no longer a solid frontline running between the Baltic and Black Seas; often gaps of dozens of miles developed with nothing to fill them but a thin cavalry screen or a single division. Likewise, massive casualties during *Barbarossa* make *Band of Brothers* type micro-histories difficult; one would have trouble finding a company of von Kleist's panzer group where more than 50 percent of the men survived the five months from Poland to Rostov.

I have organized this narrative along the lines suggested by the German Federal Military Archives (BA-MA) and Soviet historians. Therefore this narrative is more thematic and less purely chronological. German sources for the new organization are the various *Schlacht- und Gefechtsbezeichnungen* at www.bundesarchiv.de/findbuecher/ma/.../index.htm while the Soviet sources are from David Glantz, *Colossus Reborn*, Tables 3.1 and 3.6. With that in mind, I have split *Barbarossa* into four stages rather than the usual three. I have included introductions and summaries for each stage to help tie them together. A key innovation of this volume are the engagement and battle matrices in the Appendix. I encourage the reader to refer to them when reading the corresponding combat narrative.

As I have written before, the book's title is "Operation *Barbarossa*," not "The Soviet Defense of the Motherland." In considerable part this is due to the fact that I speak and read German, therefore any non-English sources I used were in that language rather than Russian. Despite that, however, I believe that I have been true to the historian's responsibility to maintain impartial objectivity and have described events as facts warrant. In about 1980, as a US Army armor officer in Germany, I sat on my tank alongside a country road during a pause in the usual autumn maneuvers (REFORGER – Return of Forces to Germany). An old Ostheer veteran came over to me and struck up a conversation. Describing *Barbarossa*, he said *"Dass war eine' Leistung!"* – "That was quite a performance!" While I still agree with him, in the final analysis the Nazi–Soviet War ended clearly as a tremendous Allied victory.

Finally, I am not usually one to make positive references to Field Marshal Bernard Montgomery, but I have to agree with his first rule of war: do not march on Moscow.

OPPOSITE PAGE:
Irresistibly Forward (Unaufhaltsam vorwärtz) by Walter Gotschke (gouache, 1941). Austrian-born Gotschke painted auto-racing scenes both before and after World War II. He painted advertisements for Daimler-Benz until the war put a halt to commercial auto production. Between July and October 1941 he accompanied one of Hoepner's panzer regiments as a war artist. (Library of Congress)

CHRONOLOGY

1940

June 2 Hitler tells von Rundstedt about Eastern campaign.

June 18 Halder sets up Eastern Front Study Group.

July 31 Hitler briefs generals on his intent to invade USSR.

August 5 Marcks completes his *Operationsentwurf Ost*.

August 7 OKW completes *Aufbau Ost*.

October–May 1941 Luftwaffe aerial reconnaissance over the USSR.

Mid-October Stalin redirects Soviet main defensive effort from Moscow to the Ukraine.

November 12–13 Molotov visits Berlin.

November 28–December 3 and 7 Paulus hosts *Barbarossa* wargames.

December 5 Hitler approves basic plan in conference with von Brauchitsch and Halder.

December 17–20 *Barbarossa* logistical wargames.

December 18 Führer Directive 21 issued.

December 23–January 13, 1941 Kremlin command conferences and wargames; another shake-up within Soviet High Command.

1941

January 31 *Aufmarschanweisung* published, adds Rumania to *Barbarossa* planning.

February 20 Göring creates Luftwaffe planning staff for *Barbarossa*.

March 30 Hitler describes *Barbarossa* to 250 generals as a "struggle of two world views."

April 6 German leaders begin Balkans campaign.

May 23 Soviets call up 1905–18 year-group reservists, establish martial law.

May 30 Mussolini establishes a corps for action in the USSR although German leaders have not officially told Italy about *Barbarossa*.

May 25–27 Finnish chief of staff visits OKW.

June 6 Commissar Order issued.

June 12 Kriegsmarine begins mining Baltic.

June 14 Hitler clarifies *Barbarossa* objectives to Wehrmacht leaders: Leningrad, the Ukraine, Donbas, and Caucasus. Moscow is not included.

June 20 Rumanians first officially briefed on *Barbarossa*.

June 22 *Barbarossatag*; Soviet Military Districts become Fronts. Churchill makes speech in support of USSR.

June 22–30 Battle for fortress Brest.

June 23 Stavka created.

June 23–25 Boldin's counterattack at Grodno.

June 24 LVII Panzer Corps captures Vilnius.

June 24 First Panzer Group passes through Sixth Army; Kirponos' counterattacks begin.

June 24–29 Battle of Raseiniai, XLI Panzer Corps against 12th Mechanized Corps.

June 24 Japanese Army and Navy leaders decide "not

to intervene in the German-Soviet War for the time being."

June 26 LVI Panzer Corps captures Dünaburg bridgehead.

June 27 Unattributed bombing brings Hungary into war.

June 28–29 20th and 18th Panzer Divisions close Minsk Kessel.

June 29–July 6 Mountain Corps Norway's first attack across Litsa River.

June 29 1st Mountain Division enters L'vov.

June 30 Hoth and Guderian confer. OKH directs von Bock to advance on Smolensk.

June 30 Sobennikov replaces Kuznetsov as commander of the Northwest Front.

July 1 XXXVI Corps and Finns attack at Salla.

July 2 Operation *Munich* crosses Rumanian border.

July 2 Emperor Hirohito decides against attacking the Soviet Union and for striking South Asia and the Pacific instead.

July 3–27 Von Kluge commands Fourth Panzer Army.

July 4 3rd Panzer Division captures Dnepr bridge at Rogatchev.

July 7 13th Panzer Division reaches Berdichev.

July 8 20th Panzer Division captures Dvina bridge at Ulla.

July 9 Piadyshev takes command of LOG.

July 9 14th Panzer Division takes Zithomir.

July 10 Voroshilov arrives at Northwest Direction; Finns attack in Karelia north of Lake Ladoga.

July 10 13th Panzer Division reaches Irpen River, 10 miles from Kiev, rest of III Panzer Corps close behind; Stavka creates Strategic Direction.

July 12 Stavka orders Timoshenko to organize counterattacks toward Bobruisk and prepare defense of Mogilev.

July 13 Kirponos begins counterattacks against Zithomir Corridor.

July 13–17 Mountain Corps Norway's second attack across Litsa River.

July 14 6th Panzer Division achieves bridgehead over the Narva River.

July 14–18 11th Army counterattacks against LVI Panzer Corps at Soltsy.

July 15 7th Panzer Division captures Yartsevo, isolating Smolensk.

July 15 26th Army counterattacks at Kanev into First Panzer Group's rear.

July 16 29th Motorized Division enters Smolensk, completing "loose" encirclement.

July 17 XI Corps crosses Dniestr River.

July 17–27 Battle for Mogilev after Soviets frustrate initial German attempts to lever River Dnepr.

July 19 Führer Directive 33 issued.

July 20 10th Panzer Division occupies Yelnia.

July 21–22 Luftwaffe initiates bombing of Moscow.

July 21 Hitler visits Army Group North headquarters.

July 21 Rumanians cross Dnestr; XLVIII Panzer Corps reaches Monastyrishche near Uman.

July 23 Supplement to Führer Directive 33 issued.

July 23 Soviet forces counterattack at Monastyrishche.

July 23–August 7 Timoshenko mounts counteroffensive – Group Kachalov.

July 24–27 Timoshenko mounts counteroffensive – Groups Kalinin and Khomenko, plus Gorodovikov's cavalry raid.

July 27 Seventeenth Army breaks free of Stalin Line, heads for junction with First Panzer Group.

July 29–31 Timoshenko mounts counteroffensive – Group Maslinnikov.

July 30 Führer Directive 34 published.

July 30 Sixth Army's first direct assault on Kiev.

July 31 Finns attack in Karelia south of Lake Ladoga.

August 3 IX Army and XXIV Panzer Corps encircle Roslavl.

August 3 16th Panzer and 1st Mountain Divisions link up at Pervomaysk, closing Uman pocket.

August 5 Stalin relieves Zhukov as chief of staff.

August 5 German leaders consider battle for Smolensk to be over.

August 7 26th Army renews attacks at Kanev.

August 8 Uman fighting over; Rumanians close on Odessa; Sixth Army's second attack on Kiev.

August 8–10 German general offensive on Luga River begins.

August 10 Stavka gives up Dnepr River line.

August 11 Soviets begin general offensive around Yelnia.

August 12 Supplement to Führer Directive 34 issued; 11th, 27th, 34th, 48th Armies attack Sixteenth Army at Staraya Russa.

August 16 First Rumanian assault on Odessa.

August 19 XXIV Panzer Corps plus VII and XIII Army Corps capture Gomel.

August 19 LVI Panzer Corps counterattacks to Staraya Russa.

August 19 LSSAH takes Kherson; 9th Panzer Division gains bridgehead at Zaporozhe.

August 20 Seventeenth Army wins Dnepr bridgehead at Kremenchug.

August 22 Hitler issues *Denkschrift* ending High Command debate.

August 23 5th Army retreats behind Dnepr.

August 24 Sixth Army reaches Desna.

August 26 LVII Panzer from Army Group Center captures Velikie Luki.

August 26 XVII Corps takes Chernobyl; Tyulenev replaced.

August 28 Tallinn falls to XLII Corps.

August 29 Vyborg taken by Finnish IV Corps.

August 30 OKH issues order for Kiev Kessel.

August 31 Red Army abandons right bank of Dnepr.

September 1 XXXVI Corps and Finns unite at Allakurtti.

September 2 Von Brauchitsch and Halder visit Army Group North headquarters.

September 6 Soviets re-occupy Yelnia. Hitler issues his Directive 35.

September 7 XIII, XLIII, and XXXV Army Corps capture Chernigov.

September 7 Sensing impending doom at Kiev, Kirponos requests permission to give up Desna Line.

September 8 Finns reach Svir River; XXXIX Panzer Corps captures Shlisselburg encircling Leningrad.

September 8–20 Mountain Corps Norway's third attack across Litsa River.

September 9 Zhukov arrives in Leningrad; XLI Panzer Corps renews assault toward Krasnogvardeysk.

September 9 Stalin approves Desna move; von Rundstedt orders Eleventh Army to attack Crimea.

September 10 Stavka instructs forces before Moscow to transition to defense.

September 10 Sixth and Second Armies (Army Group Center) link up; 3rd Panzer Division reaches Romny; XLVIII Panzer Corps shifted to Kremenchug.

September 11 Stalin fires Budenny, Timoshenko becomes commander of Southwest Direction.

September 12 Von Schobert killed at Berislav.

September 13 XXIV Panzer Corps takes Lokhvitsa; XLVIII Panzer Corps fighting for Lubny.

September 14 Amphibious assault on Muhu Island.

September 14 3rd and 16th Panzer Divisions link up at Lokhvitsa, completing Kiev encirclement.

September 15 German forces assault Saaremaa Island.

September 16 XLI Panzer Corps occupies Strelnya, 8th Army cut off from Leningrad.

September 16 XXIX Corps' final assault on Kiev begins.

September 17 Stalin permits evacuation of Kiev; von Manstein takes over Eleventh Army.

September 20 Kirponos killed escaping Kiev.

September 22 German High Command issues directive on starvation of Leningrad.

September 23 Soviet 9th and 18th Armies begin Sea of Azov battle.

September 24 Kiev fighting dies down; LIV Corps begins first assault at Perekop (until 28th).

September 25 Frontlines around Leningrad essentially solidify for duration of siege.

September 25 Von Rundstedt orders First Panzer Group to counterattack behind Soviets at Melitopol.

September 29 Oktyarbrsky suggests to Stalin that Odessa be abandoned.

September 30 and October 2 Army Group Center begins Operation *Typhoon*.

October 1 Finnish VII Corps takes Petrozavodsk.

October 1 First Panzer Group attacks toward Melitopol.

October 2 Rumanians renew assault on Odessa.

October 5 Panzer Groups become Panzer Armies.

October 7 7th and 10th Panzer Divisions close Viazma Kessel. Beginning of *rasputitsa* and first snowfalls.

October 7 XIV Panzer Corps and LSSAH meet at Berdyansk and close Melitopol pocket.

October 8 XLVII Panzer Corps and LIII Army Corps close Bryansk Kessel.

October 8, 9, and 19 Soviets issue various directives on defense of Moscow.

October 10 Hoth replaces relieved ("ailing") von Stülpnagel.

October 11–16 First battle of Mozhaisk line ends in stalemate. Town of Mozhaisk falls on 19th.

October 12 Attack of Hiiumaa Island.

October 13 Kaluga falls to German forces.

October 14 1st Panzer Division enters Kalinin.

October 15 Soviets abandon Odessa at night.

October 16 XXXIX Panzer Corps begins attack toward Tikhvin.

October 18 LIV Corps launches second attack at Perekop (through 26th).

October 21 OKH orders Army Group South to Stalingrad and Maikop.

October 24 Sixth Army takes Kharkov.

October 26 Von Leeb visits the Führer's Headquarters.

November 8 Tikhvin falls to German forces.

November 9 Timoshenko briefs Stalin on Rostov attack plan.

November 12 52nd Army counterattacks at Volkhov.

November 13 Halder hosts conference of Ostheer chiefs of staff at Orsha.

November 14 and 16 Zhukov launches pre-emptive attacks against Army Group Center.

November 15 Von Bock's left wing begins Operation *Volga Reservoir*.

November 15 Finnish Group "F" links up on Kandalaksha axis.

November 16 Eleventh Army reaches Kerch.

November 18 Guderian launches final assault south of Moscow.

November 19 4th Army launches attack to recapture Tikhvin.

November 20 III Panzer Corps reaches Rostov.

November 22 Klin falls to German forces.

November 25 17th Panzer Division reaches Kashira – Guderian's farthest advance.

November 25 56th Army launches counterattack at Rostov.

November 27 Timoshenko counteroffensive opens along entire First Panzer Army salient.

November 28 Von Kleist orders III Panzer Corps out of Rostov.

November 30 Von Rundstedt approves retreat to Mius River.

December 1 Von Rundstedt resigns; von Reichenau named replacement.

December 2 Hitler visits Army Group and Panzer Army headquarters.

December 5 Soviets initiate general winter counteroffensive.

December 6 Finnish II Corps and Group "O" take Medvezh'yegorsk.

December 7 German forces evacuate Tikhvin.

INTRODUCTION

"This is not the Second World War, it is the Great Racial War (grosser Rassenkrieg)*"*

Hermann Göring, October, 1942

Nazi Germany's invasion of the Union of Soviet Socialist Republics (USSR) on June 22, 1941, Operation *Barbarossa*, has no equal in military history. By nearly any measure – numbers of combatants involved, physical scope, hatred, and ruination – the Nazi–Soviet War was immense. It is doubtful whether humankind will ever again see another battlefield with 6 million men, tens of thousands of artillery pieces, armored vehicles, and aircraft arrayed against each other on a single day. Timothy Snyder accurately called *Barbarossa* "…the beginning of a calamity that defies description."[1]

German Führer Adolf Hitler achieved strategic, operational, and tactical surprise against an amply forewarned Soviet Premier Josef Stalin. Rapacious panzer groups, supported overhead by the Luftwaffe, recorded daily advances of 30 and 40 miles or more. The bulk of the Wehrmacht marched on foot behind, closing off pockets of many hundreds of thousands of Red Army captives. On the campaign's first days Nazi Propaganda Minister Josef Goebbels demurred at showing the German people maps of the USSR while some Germans wondered if prior to launching *Barbarossa* Hitler had even seen such a map. Significantly, the German people had little enthusiasm for the endeavor.

While the Soviet Union's immense landmass was obvious to anyone looking at a globe of the earth, the resilience of the Communist government, the toughness of the Red Army soldier and the ultimate wisdom of its leadership's conduct of the war came as an unexpected shock to the invaders and many observers. Hitler's initial opinion that Germany need only "kick in the door and the whole rotten structure will come crashing down" was not unreasonable given the collapse of the Tsarist and Provisional governments at the end of the Great War. Additionally the Red Army's poor performance against Poland in 1919–20, against other opponents prior to 1941, and during the Spanish Civil War gave no indication of its real capabilities. From the very start the vicious border battles demonstrated to the Wehrmacht in the field, if not to its leaders behind

---

1   Snyder, *Bloodlands*, p.155.

Within hours of the German invasion opening, American political cartoonist Theodor Geissel ("Dr Seuss") recognized that the war in the East would be a far different matter from Hitler's earlier invasions. Note that Italy is portrayed in the middle of the Führer's wall of trophies as a road-kill skunk. (Ralph Ingersoll Collection)

the front, that *Barbarossa* would not be as easy as previous campaigns. Many Soviet soldiers, cut off behind the advancing enemy in huge encirclements did not give up but either fought to the death or joined civilians to form partisan bands. By the time the first freezing weather hit in October, the Wehrmacht was greatly weakened and still far from achieving most of its objectives. But the unbroken string of massive encirclement victories up to that point kept alive the German High Command's hubris that allowed them to think they would succeed and later continued well into the autumn to convince them that they could ultimately win the war.

While Hitler and many in his professional military staff had a rosy view of the invasion's projected results many top Germans had their doubts. To those on the scene in 1941, *Barbarossa*'s ultimate outcome was far from clear at any point prior to December. The Wehrmacht's blitzkrieg – the combination of flexible mission-style orders, mechanization, airpower, and communications – won victory after victory. Each blitzkrieg segment was purposefully very brief since that was the only type of war Germany could ever hope to win. Having vanquished the French, the world's "best army" the year before, Germany had unshakeable confidence in its armed forces bordering on imprudent arrogance.

However, as in 1812, when after each defeat the Tsar's army remained intact, the Soviet military did not exhibit signs of total collapse in 1941. Neither did an alternative to the Communist system present itself. First

Hitler and then Stalin called for a total war of extermination and national survival. Both men put their nations on the horns of dilemma where being party to mass murder was the lesser of two evils. Both wanted and got a war of hate. They exhorted their troops to fight without mercy, to harden themselves and to intimidate their enemies. The loser would be tied to a criminal regime: as the war turned out, the German officer corps would live and die with Hitler and Nazism.

An SdKfz 10 prime mover half-track towing a 37mm PAK through a burning village. The death and destruction of *Barbarossa* rivaled that of the Thirty Years War. (HITM)

Interestingly, only in the two dictators' minds did the political and military strategy of either country coalesce. Both men made the worst miscalculations of their political careers regarding *Barbarossa*: Hitler in thinking he could win, Stalin in thinking he could "trust" Hitler to abide by the terms of their 1939 treaty. The war on the Eastern Front, and, it might be argued, the opening five months which are presented here, sealed the fate of Hitler's Third Reich and determined the outcome of World War II in Europe.

The Road to *Barbarossa*

Homer's *Iliad* begins and ends on the eve of battle and is centered on Achilles' anger. Likewise, the *Barbarossa* story opens with preparations for the campaign and closes as Stalin initiated his general winter counteroffensive and revolves around Hitler's obsession with exterminating "Jewish-Muscovite Bolshevism."

War between Germans and Russians in 1941 was not pre-ordained. For nearly 150 years, from the end of the Seven Years' War in 1763 until the decade prior to World War I, the two peoples had been at peace. The pinnacle of their cooperation came during the final stages of the wars against Napoleon. In this context, relations during the reign of Wilhelm II (r.1888–1918) can almost be seen as an anomaly. Within a year of the Versailles Treaty, the new Weimar Republic and Soviet Union rediscovered their earlier common interests as codified by the 1922 Rapallo Treaty and 1926 Berlin Treaty. Through March 1934 Hitler even considered accommodation with the USSR. However, during the mid-1930s, the extremes of totalitarianism made continuing this cozy relationship impossible as each dictator consolidated power at home.

The *Barbarossa* Campaign

Stage I
Front line
Encirclements

Stage II
Front line
Encirclements

Stage III
Front line
Encirclements

Stage IV
Front line
Encirclements

N

WHITE SEA

Murmansk

Archangel

FINLAND

SWEDEN

Lake
Onega

Lake
Ladoga

Helsinki

Leningrad

ESTONIA

Pskov

LATVIA

Riga

Dvina

Volga

BALTIC SEA

LITHUANIA

Kalinin

Moscow

Königsberg

Smolensk

Minsk

Bryansk

SOVIET UNION

Rokitno
Marshes

Warsaw

GERMANY

GOVERNMENT-
GENERAL

Kursk

Lvov

Kiev

Karkov

Don

SLOKAKIA

Dnepr

Donets

HUNGARY

Dnestr

UKRAINE

Odessa

Rostov

ROMANIA

Sevastopol

BLACK SEA

0   200 miles
0   200km

Germany

S.J. Lewis described *Barbarossa* as "the only war Hitler ever wanted." Hitler had numerous reasons for launching *Barbarossa*: to carry out threats he had made since writing *Mein Kampf* 20 years earlier, to fulfill expansionist desires of the army, industry, and the bureaucracy as well as to remove any remaining British hope of continental assistance. In the first case, a basic tenet of Nazism, supported by the traditional German elites, held that the vast lands to Germany's east were its for colonization and economic exploitation. Therefore Hitler attacked the USSR for ideological, strategic, and economic reasons. As if to validate V.I. Lenin's designation of Fascism as Communism's main threat, Hitler wrote in *Mein Kampf* that the Nazis "have finished with the eternal German striving toward the south and west of Europe and we are now directing our gaze at the lands in the east." The Führer saw Bolshevism as the most extreme form of "international Jewry" and set forth plans for a New Order in *Mein Kampf* and even more in his second book of 1928.

Although greater Germany was not overpopulated in 1923 when he first began to write *Mein Kampf* or 1941, Hitler sought *Lebensraum* (space to live), a euphemism for exploited human and natural resources combined with radicalized colonial notions reminiscent of Charlemagne's warrior-farmers.[2] In his vision, Aryan racial superiority plus this Lebensraum would then lead to a final showdown with the British Empire and the United States and, ultimately, German world domination (with a little help from Japan and other smaller allies). Just days after taking power, on February 3, 1933, Hitler told skeptical Reichswehr leaders of his desire to rebuild the army and conquer Lebensraum in the east. Likewise, on February 28, 1934, he told senior Army and SS leaders that he sought "short, decisive and crushing

During a pause in their advance eastward, men of a panzer unit watch a flight of Ju 87B Stukas land at an improvised airfield. While such an open landscape might be familiar to a Russian or North American, it was psychologically overwhelming to the Germans. (HITM)

---

2   Unfortunately for Nazi settlement policies, Germans showed no enthusiasm for moving to newly conquered Lebensraum, while during the late 1930s Germans living in Central and Eastern Europe returned to Germany in soaring numbers.

actions, first against the west, then to the east." Introducing the new Four-Year Plan on September 4, 1936, Herman Göring told Germany's top leaders "the showdown with Russia is inevitable."

The Führer looked for "accomplices wherever and whenever they could be of use to him." For the first years of the Third Reich, Hitler tried the expedient of enlisting Poland as a satellite against the USSR. When Warsaw would have none of it, Hitler reversed himself, "temporarily set aside his anti-Bolshevik fixation" and made a bargain with Stalin.[3] For his part, Stalin wanted to prevent the elimination of the world's only Socialist state by appeasing Hitler much as Britain and France had done before him. Therefore, after years of antagonism, following the initiative of the pragmatic German Foreign Minister, Joachim von Ribbentrop, on August 38, 1939, Nazi Germany and the Soviet Union shocked most of the world by signing a Nonaggression Pact. Hitler said the pact was "misunderstood by many [Nazi] party members" and had to reassure Italian dictator Benito Mussolini that the agreement was only a temporary move. Almost 19 years to the day after Lenin's representative in Berlin first suggested that Germany and the USSR divide Poland between them, the two dictatorships indeed partitioned Poland for the fourth time in 200 years. The Führer put his newly purchased freedom of action, represented by this disposable "tactical maneuver," to good use, crushing all opposition in non-Russian Europe in the months prior to *Barbarossa* – all with the Soviet leader's tacit approval.

Since Britain believed Stalin's purges had fatally weakened the Red Army it depended on a strong Poland to Germany's east. The Nazi–Soviet Pact so stunned Britain that it would not fight for Poland's existence one week later (although it did declare war on Germany). Abandoned by east and west, bordered on three sides by the Reich and outclassed in every military category, Poland fell to German arms at the Bzura River after just two weeks. With Britain and its allies still in shock, Hitler moved quickly and in April 1940 overran Denmark in a matter of hours and after a tense struggle prevailed in Norway, basically in the Royal Navy's backyard. The world was in for an even bigger shock the following month when Hitler invaded France and the Low Countries. British and French moves played right into the German leadership's hands, but Hitler's trepidation saved the former from real disaster by allowing the men of the British Expeditionary Force to escape destruction at Dunkirk.

---

3   Muller and Ueberschar, *Hitler's War*, pp.9–11.

When, less than a month after France's capitulation, on July 19, 1940, the United Kingdom rebuffed the Führer's half-hearted peace offer (actually an arrogant "call to reason"), Hitler just as half-heartedly began the Battle of Britain. He cared little for this project, nor were the Luftwaffe or Kriegsmarine anywhere close to ready for a complex cross-Channel invasion. General of Artillery Alfred Jodl, Operations Chief of Oberkommando der Wehrmacht (OKW, Supreme High Command of the German Armed Forces) admitted that English "stoic equanimity" would carry them through the bombing and that there was no indication that German bombardment would cause their collapse.

Hitler soon lost sight for the main reason for the aerial assault, to prime Great Britain for invasion, while aerial and naval realities caused constant delays in Operation *Sealion*, so by mid-winter the continued aerial assault represented mainly a convenient cover story for *Barbarossa*'s preparations.[4] As Germany was even less capable of bringing her military forces to bear on the United States, the Führer settled on attacking the Soviet Union as the best way to defeat the Anglo-American maritime powers; in reality all three enemies were physically invulnerable to Nazi Germany.

Indeed, even before the height of the Battle of Britain, Hitler had instructed the Wehrmacht to plan for an invasion of the USSR. The first inkling most senior Wehrmacht, Army, and Navy leaders had of his intentions came at a secret meeting at the Berghof on July 31.[5] To his thinking, with the Red Army emasculated by Stalin's purges and with Russia's resources at his disposal, the Reich would be America's equal. Although the majority would eventually toe the line, almost to a man Germany's senior military leadership initially counseled Hitler against attacking. This was especially true in Jodl's staff, which

A German machine-gun crew silhouetted against the eastern sky. The man in front has an MG34 while his comrades lug ammo cans, spare barrels, etc. Imagine marching and fighting across 1,000 miles over five months, carrying your entire life on your back. (Nik Cornish at www.Stavka.org.uk)

---

4   Thanks to Bletchley Park intercepts, by mid-January 1941 the British concluded that the Wehrmacht had already cancelled *Sealion*.

5   Presumably Luftwaffe leaders were busy with the air war against Britain.

raised "a chorus of objections." Göring's subsequent opposition must have been the harshest blow: Hitler told the Reichsmarschall, "Why don't you stop trying to persuade me to drop my plans for Russia. I've made up my mind."

Hitler thought that Britain required "one more demonstration of our military might" to acknowledge German dominance of the continent. Likewise, he made fuzzy linkages between the "Jewish Anglo-Saxon warmongers" and the "Jewish rulers of Bolshevik-Muscovite Russia." Both factors combined to push Hitler toward a violent confrontation with the Soviet Union. Thanks to their commercial treaty of February 1940, however, Stalin was able to control the flow of certain raw materials important to Germany's war effort.[6] By the summer of 1940 a dangerous situation had developed: the USSR's industries required many of the same commodities for the Red Army's rearmament program that Germany did. Hitler could not force Stalin to act as Germany's long-term supplier and it was against this background that the slide toward *Barbarossa* accelerated.

The final straw came in November, 1940: first, Franklin D. Roosevelt won re-election as US President, thus ruling out American isolationism for much longer; and then Soviet Foreign Minister V.M. Molotov paid a return visit to Berlin. Any pretense of long-term Nazi–Soviet cooperation vanished. Molotov, initially wanting to continue appeasing Germany, attempted to talk specifics, but Hitler tried vaguely to redirect the USSR. It was an open secret in the capital that Hitler expected to score a diplomatic coup: he would offer Stalin a free hand against the British Southwest Asian possessions in exchange for German dominance of Central and Eastern Europe and the Mediterranean. Molotov, however, had no intention of accepting Hitler's plans and came to Berlin with his own agenda, even resurrecting Soviet interests in Finland.

At this point Nazi–Soviet relations hit rock bottom as Molotov flexed Soviet economic muscle and Hitler sensed impending blackmail. Historians have linked the Führer's final decision to launch *Barbarossa* with Molotov's visit. Hitler needed to decide once and for all if Stalin's wider aims clashed or coincided with his own. In fact he considered the talks with Molotov a charade, simultaneously telling his staff that "preparations for the East are to be continued."

Hitler believed that continuing British resistance had emboldened the USSR and, enraged by this rebuff, formalized the plans for Operation

---

6   Since mid-1940 the United States had been doing exactly the same thing to Japan.

Barbarossa within a month of Molotov's departure. In early January 1941 Nazi economists told Hitler that Russian resources "…would liberate us from every economic worry." For his part, Stalin no longer harbored any illusions about the ultimate future relationship with Nazi Germany, although he disastrously underestimated the imminence of the threat.

After nearly two decades of Nazi ranting about a Jewish-Bolshevik conspiracy and making demands for Lebensraum, with an overheated German economy constantly threatening a domestic crisis in addition to the growing impossibility of an invasion of Britain, Hitler signed the *Barbarossa* directive on December 18. In the spring of 1941 he put his personal imprint on the character of the impending Eastern campaign with three policy documents which highlighted the central racial-political foundation of *Barbarossa*.

A firing squad shoots Soviet citizens into a half-full mass grave. Murder was part and parcel of German occupation polices, especially in the east. Contrary to the myth of the Nazis' "industrialized killing," most of their killing was done like this: up close and personal. (From the fonds of the RGAKFD in Krasnogorsk via Stavka)

The first was the March 13, 1941 publication of an annex to the operations order in which Hitler rejected army administration of occupied areas, instead turning these duties over to Nazi Party and police organs. Reichsführer-SS Heinrich Himmler received "special tasks," including the creation of *Einsatzgruppen*, Special Task Forces, that would follow the army to round-up and murder Jews, Communists, and other enemies of the *Volk*, or German people. Hitler augmented this annex on May 13 with his Decree on Military Justice, relieving military commanders of responsibility for prosecuting their own soldiers as war criminals; and again on June 6, with the better-known Commissar Order. These documents can be considered the beginning of a second Nazi revolution: henceforth Germany's conduct of the war took on a new and darker complexion.

Two other Nazi programs also require mention here. One is the short-term Hunger Plan overseen by Göring, meant to starve "many tens of millions" of Slavs and Jews in order to feed Germans. The other is Himmler's *Generalplan Ost* (General Plan East) a long-term (*c.*30 year) plan to colonize Central and Eastern Europe and exterminate or expel many, if not most indigenous peoples. Anyone who minimizes or ignores the connection between *Barbarossa* and Nazi racial eliminationist policy misses Hitler's primary reason for prosecuting World War II.

The Führer famously told the Reichstag on the sixth anniversary of the Nazis' ascension to power, January 30, 1939, and repeated many times afterward, "If the international Jewish financers … again succeed in plunging the nations into a world war the result will be … the annihilation of the Jewish race throughout Europe." Operation *Barbarossa* is where Nazi expansionism and anti-Semitism converged. Taken together with these general occupation practices and its brutal treatment of Soviet POWs (an army responsibility), the spring of 1941 marks the date when Germany began to sink irretrievably toward Auschwitz.

By the summer of 1941 all of continental Europe, with the exception of the USSR, was Axis, Axis-occupied, or neutral (and in many cases leaning toward Germany). Between the outbreak of war in 1939 and June 1941 the weaknesses and failings of its opponents had concealed the shortcomings of Germany's own military forces. The assumption, validated in previous campaigns, was that blitzkrieg would only face an enemy's forces in being and that no opportunity would be given for the enemy to recover or rebuild. Nazi domestic authority and German victories preceding *Barbarossa*, all attributed to Hitler's genius, undermined any lingering German military opposition to the dictator. With his military and political position assured, *Barbarossa* was carried out according to the Führer's wishes.

The Soviet Union

According to the Soviet interpretation of the Great War's beginnings, Russia had been tricked into attacking Imperial Germany in support of the Western Capitalists and had come out the big loser in 1918. Optimally Stalin would join any subsequent war only after comprehensive peacetime preparations and on his own terms. This meant waiting out the "self-laceration of Capitalism and its Fascist afterbirth" on the Western Front. But Germany's lightning victory in the spring of 1940 wrecked that hope.

In 1939 Stalin's primary concern remained establishing "socialism in one country." He strengthened the USSR by expanding the military and by ruthlessly and brutally developing Soviet industry with successive Five-Year Plans (the USSR was in the midst of the third plan in 1941). He created an entirely new resource and industrial base deep in the Ural region beyond the range of any potential enemy. Output of numerous strategic materials was only slightly higher than Germany's, but the Soviet growth rate was much greater.

In June 1941 the USSR was militarily relatively weaker but politically much stronger than its Tsarist predecessor had been in August 1914. Granted, Stalin's ruthless purges had decapitated its military in 1937–38, the Five-Year Plans were losing momentum, and by 1941 any potential continental allies had succumbed to the German steamroller. However, paramilitary organizations had trained over 13,000,000 snipers, radiotelephone operators, horsemen, vehicle drivers, pilots, and parachutists. The Red Army grew to 5,000,000 men by the eve of *Barbarossa*. Significantly, the efforts of the Second and Third Five-Year Plans, which focused on heavy industry, were concentrated in the eastern regions of the USSR so that by 1940 37 percent of its steel, 35 percent of its coal, and 25 percent of its energy production came from areas the German forces never reached.

A hopeful prewar Soviet poster boasts "The borders of the USSR protect all the Soviet people." Even after the Wehrmacht had overrun most of Europe the blitzkrieg's violence came as a shock to the USSR. (NARA)

In the summer of 1939 Stalin went along with Hitler's Nonaggression Pact. Britain and France had sacrificed Czechoslovakia the year before to buy a few months' peace; the USSR sacrificed Poland for the same purpose. The Soviet leader's opinion of the pact was little different from Hitler's; indeed Stalin admitted at the Yalta Conference that the pact was "not serious." While one of Hitler's intentions was that the pact should spread distrust and chaos among his enemies, Stalin sought time and stability to continue his vast restructuring of the Soviet Union. Ruthlessly consolidating

Soviet riflemen in hasty defensive positions. In one of the infrequent examples of good German intelligence they anticipated Soviet defensive capabilities, but even this did not prepare them for *Barbarossa's* harsh realities. (NARA)

power, Stalin purged some 25,000 officers from his military during the 1930s. Over 8,000,000 Soviet citizens were in jail at any one time from 1937–53, and of those 1,000,000 died each year. Stalin took his final step to power on May 5, 1941 when he added the title of Soviet Premier to that of Communist Party Chairman.

In line with the secret protocols of the Molotov–Ribbentrop Nonaggression Pact of September 23, 1939 and exploiting Germany's distraction with war in the west, Stalin diddled behind Hitler's back and occupied Estonia, Latvia, Lithuania, and Rumanian Bessarabia as part of the "Expansion of the Fraternal Family of Soviet Nations." In this instance, as well as at Khalkin Gol in 1939, in the occupation of eastern Poland in September 1939, and in his war against Finland in the winter of 1939–40, Stalin showed no hesitation in using the Soviet military. He levered economic power as well and, in seeking commercial arrangements with Stalin to circumvent the British naval blockade, Hitler became dependent on a very dangerous business partner. Stalin knew Hitler could not field his huge army without Soviet resources.

Therefore by late 1939 and throughout 1940, Soviet aggression matched that of Germany. Commenting in his diary, Goebbels wrote, "That's our price for Russia's neutrality." The Western Allies saw Stalin as Hitler's willing partner, so they helped Finland fight against the USSR and contemplated a treaty with Turkey over the Straights. After the fall of France, Britain put its

A 37mm Pak 36 and crew crushed by Soviet tanks. Although still used in large numbers during *Barbarossa*, 37mm guns were practically useless against Soviet tanks, especially at the long ranges common in the USSR. (NARA)

own far-fetched schemes into high gear by sending Royal Navy squadrons and submarines into the Black Sea, violating Soviet airspace with reconnaissance aircraft and making plans to bomb Caucasus and Baku oil facilities from Iraq (plans they would dust off in 1942 as the German forces neared both places). All these moves only made Stalin more mistrustful of the British as *Barbarossatag* (*Barbarossa* Day) approached.

Red Army failings during the 1939–40 Winter War were legion and only by applying overwhelming violence and numbers did the USSR finally prevail. While Hitler's war machine swept all before it, Soviet weaknesses were an embarrassment. With Stalin's moves in eastern Poland, Finland, and the Baltic States the Red Army's frontlines were shorter, requiring fewer units to garrison them. Yet the Red Army largely squandered the advantages of this buffer zone by abandoning its fortifications 200–400 miles behind it and through its imprudent forward deployment. This surge westward also created distance from its already-inadequate logistical support and demonstrated the Stalinist military dilettantism that plagued Soviet operations well into *Barbarossa*.

On the eve of war with Germany, the Soviet military was not in good shape. Like Mussolini's military, the Red Army had modernized too early, and by 1941 much of its equipment was effectively obsolete. In the early 1930s the Red Army had been at the forefront of mechanized warfare doctrine but nearly a decade later its attitudes were reactionary. During the Great Purge Stalin arrested and tried 9,506 army and air force officers (most were executed) and expelled a further 14,684 from service (although subsequently he reinstated many). The purges hit the higher ranks worst. The victims also tended to be the most experienced and farsighted of the Red Army's officer corps. The continuing executions and imprisonment plus political interference from the commissars undermined the morale of the remnants. The lessons of Germany's blitzkrieg victories were not effectively digested and applied to the Red Army while fear of provoking Hitler further limited corrective action.

Meanwhile, Stalin appeared to be blissfully ignorant of the impending war. His first foray into military leadership, as a top political officer in the Ukraine during the young Soviet Union's 1920 defeat by Poland, had ended in failure. The undisputed fount of all domestic and foreign policy and military decision-making (indeed much like Churchill and Roosevelt), he was not the first world leader to misjudge Hitler. Within the Soviet hierarchy he had many equally unprepared accomplices in state, party, diplomatic, and military circles. However, his much criticized signing of the Nonaggression Pact with Hitler in 1939 and the Economic Accord the following January kept the USSR out of the pan-European war for nearly two years. The Neutrality Pact negotiated with Japan on April 13, 1940 was equally significant. While the Soviet High Command had to keep a wary eye on the 39 divisions, 1,200 tanks, and 2,500 aircraft of Japan's Kwantung Army in Manchuria during the first half of *Barbarossa*, Stalin's staff could be reasonably sure that they only had to plan for a one-front war.

The key issue is not whether the USSR noticed Nazi preparations, but what it did with information received. Soviet generals informed Stalin of Hitler's July 31, 1940 meeting within days. Soviet rail passengers traveling through occupied Poland could not but see and report the massive military buildup. Numerous Luftwaffe reconnaissance aircraft crashed inside the USSR, their camera films full of photos of Soviet military facilities. Stalin's diplomats and spies, the British and others flooded Soviet intelligence agencies with detailed information of Germany's ongoing preparations. Like the Germans, the Soviet leaders had a long time to prepare for *Barbarossa*.

Stalin made three critical errors of judgment that led directly to his nation's strategic, operational, and tactical surprise: 1) he believed that Germany was too dependent on Soviet resources to attack; 2) he was further convinced that Hitler would not attack while the Anglo-American maritime powers remained intact on Germany's Atlantic flank; and 3) he thought that any invasion would be preceded by an ultimatum as had occurred with Czechoslovakia and Poland

and indeed at the beginning of World War I. Nazi Germany had its *Führerprinzip*[7] and the USSR its cult of personality. Institutional forces in each country and their respective philosophies contributed directly to the nature of *Barbarossa*.

On the day before the invasion, People's Commissar for Internal Affairs L.P. Beria wrote to Stalin, agreeing with his master that, "Hitler is not going to attack us in 1941." Although Stalin was surprised by the timing, the axis of the main attacks, and the ferocity of *Barbarossa*, in fact he had in all probability expected an eventual German invasion. By signing the pact with Hitler, by providing Germany with natural resources and strategic materials, and by sacrificing much of Central and Eastern Europe, Stalin hoped to improve the USSR's position before war between the two states erupted. As N.I. Khrushchev pointed out in 1956, this was a near-fatal assumption. Approximately half an hour after German preparatory air and artillery fire began General G.K. Zhukov called the dictator with news of the attack. He asked "Did you understand what I said, Comrade Stalin?" Silence. "Comrade Stalin, do you understand?" At last Stalin understood.

German Operational Developments

Operational planning is where strategic intent would be translated into orders executed at the army group and army levels. It is therefore appropriate to look in detail at the three subordinate theatres of *Barbarossa*'s main front:

Army Group North

The battlefields portrayed here long possessed military significance for the Germans and the peoples of Eastern Europe. Here the Teutonic Knights sought to Christianize the heathen via the edge of the sword, the Prussians under David von Yorck abandoned Napoleon to join Tsar Alexander, and the Freikorps battled Bolsheviks after World War I. Finland represented a prize historically coveted by both Sweden and Russia.

Army Group North's Field Marshal Wilhelm *Ritter* von Leeb had not been tested in either the German conquest of Poland in 1939 or the assault on France and the Low Countries a year later. He had neither led panzer formations nor worked with his senior commanders prior to June 1941. While Army Group North's operational area might be the smallest of those assigned to the three German army groups, so were its forces. The terrain between East Prussia and Leningrad was some of the worst encountered by

---

7   This refers to the German doctrine that the Führer's word was absolute and that ultimate responsibility lay with him.

N

XXXXX
Baltic

Riga

XX
6

XX
48

Baltic

XXXX
8

Jelgava

LATVIA

Jekelopils

XX
126

Livani

Divina

XX   XX
28   7

XX
202   Musa Pasvalys

XXX

Dünaburg

auliai

XX
11

Panevezys

Tytuveniai

Baisogala

LITHUANIA

Utena

einimi

XX
64

XX
2

Ariogala   Kedainiai

Ukmerge

Dubysa

Neveži

XXXX
4
1/6

XX   XXXX
29   11   11

XX
84

Neris

XX
179

XX
8

Vilnius

XX
5 (-)

Kaunas

XX   XX
33 (-)   23 (-)   126

XXX
3

III
126

XX
5

XX
22

XX
128

▲

XX
184

III
23

BALTIC
XXXXX
WESTERN

the Ostheer (the German Army in the East), and possessed a transportation infrastructure that was at best primitive. Army Group North's primary objective, Leningrad – a city of 3,000,000 souls – had ideological and economic significance for both sides. However, at no time did Hitler provide von Leeb with the resources necessary to conquer it.

In the extreme north, German *Gebirgsjäger* (mountain troops) battled futilely toward Murmansk across frozen tundra. Both climate and terrain in this region were alien to the German forces, earning them the thinly disguised contempt of their Finnish allies and Soviet enemies alike. Disjointed Axis command and control created numerous liabilities; von Leeb's main front fell under the Oberkommando des Heeres (OKH, or Army High Command), Finnish Marshal Carl Mannerheim commanded his country's effort northwest of Leningrad, while the Oberkommando der Wehrmacht (OKW, or Armed Forces High Command) controlled Axis operations near the Arctic Circle. To compound German problems, Finland's military ambitions did not really extend beyond regaining territory lost to the Soviet Union in 1939–40; Mannerheim proved unwilling to cross much beyond the 1939 boundary in order to link up with von Leeb. German logistics, intended for a brief blitzkrieg, naturally failed in a sustained war of attrition.

Soviet arrangements were not markedly better. At the highest level, the Northwest Front suffered from weak leadership; its commander, Lieutenant General F.I. Kuznetsov, proved completely incapable. His successor, Marshal K.E. Voroshilov, demonstrated heroic leadership, but poor managerial skills. As with all Red Army forces on June 22, the Northwest Front defended exposed and ill-prepared positions; the relative security of the Stalin Line defenses had been left behind during the Soviet land-grab of 1939–40.

The Northern Front under Lieutenant General M.M. Popov, guarding Leningrad and the Finnish border, gave a better account of itself. Popov exploited Finland's limited war aims around Leningrad and allowed a skillful subordinate, Lieutenant General V.A. Frolov, to frustrate the Axis in the far north.

After the shock of the campaign's first few days wore off, Luftwaffe elements enforced their will on the Soviet forces only with substantial reinforcement, and the size of the Finnish area of operations dissipated the small Luftwaffe effort there. Throughout *Barbarossa* German soldiers repeatedly shot at their Luftwaffe comrades because they saw German aircraft so seldom that they assumed any aircraft to be Soviet. On the other hand, the Red Army Air Force soon recovered to represent a persistent threat to the invaders. At sea the large and prestigious Red Banner Baltic Fleet remained

Two columns of troops with entirely different fates. On the left, walking toward the camera, are Germans on their way to the front. On the right, walking away, are Soviets on their way to captivity. (Nik Cornish at www.Stavka.org.uk)

passive against the relatively small Kriegsmarine and Finnish naval elements in the Baltic Sea. However, Soviet Northern Fleet elements constantly harassed the German forces in the Arctic Ocean and its littoral.

Army Group Center

The Nazis' decisions concerning Moscow are among the most hotly debated aspects of World War II. Stalin's capital never figured prominently in Hitler's concept of *Barbarossa*. It was not an initial objective; that prestige went to destroying the bulk of the Red Army west of the Dvina and Dnepr. Neither was Moscow the ultimate geographic objective of the invasion, which was the Archangel–Astrakhan line. After all, the Wehrmacht had essentially defeated both Poland and France before either Warsaw or Paris had fallen; the capture of the capital cities merely represented political formalities. Clearly, many German generals thought differently, principal among them being Army Chief of Staff Colonel General Franz Halder. Below the Führer and Halder stood operational leaders of armies and corps who, with their soldiers on the ground, simply wanted clear and firm guidance from above.

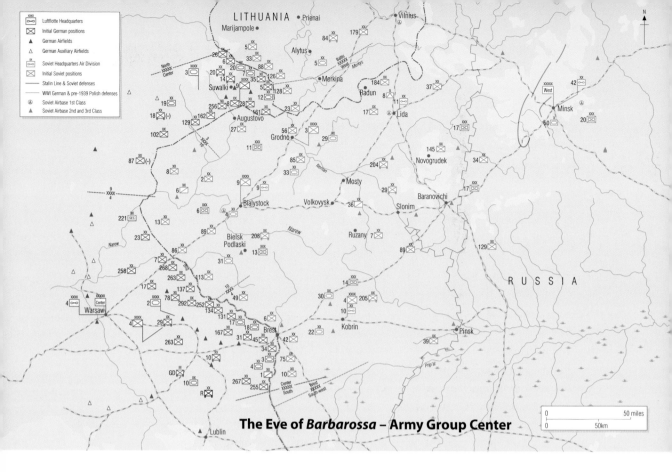

The Eve of *Barbarossa* – Army Group Center

Field Marshal Fedor von Bock would lead Army Group Center, the *Schwerpunkt* or decisive element of the *Barbarossa* plan, toward Moscow. The German forces attacked generally along the relative high ground that divided the watersheds of the Dvina and Dnepr rivers – the same route followed by Napoleon in his fateful 1812 invasion. Von Bock had proved himself in Germany's earlier blitzkrieg campaigns, and was well resourced; his command comprised the Fourth and Ninth Armies and two armored groups, plus the Luftwaffe's premier close air support (CAS) formation.

After Stalin's central European land grab in 1939–40, the Red Army in Poland stood closer to Berlin than to Moscow. However, the bulk of the Western Special Military District (WSMD – "Special" meaning that it could supposedly fight without substantial reinforcement) occupied dangerously exposed positions in the Bialystok salient between East Prussia and occupied southern Poland. Since the acquisition of these territories had represented the high point of Soviet interwar foreign policy, Stalin insisted that Colonel General D.G. Pavlov, commanding WSMD, fight hard to keep them. One of the few Soviet veterans of the Spanish Civil War to survive Stalin's purges, Pavlov's command was a secondary front, since the dictator expected the

German forces' main blow to fall in the Ukraine. Von Bock outclassed Pavlov in every way, and, although Bolshevik theorists had predicted the Second Imperialist War since the days of Lenin, the unleashing of *Barbarossa* achieved total surprise against Pavlov, as against his fellow commanders elsewhere.

Army Group South

At 0100hrs on Sunday, June 22, 1941 Army Group South issued codeword "Wotan," indicating *Barbarossa* would begin as planned in little more than two hours. The German Army's senior officer, Field Marshal Gerd von Rundstedt, commanded 55 divisions plus numerous brigades and other smaller units along a front of more than 800 miles. His headquarters, under Chief of Staff General of Infantry Georg von Sodenstern, had proved itself in France. Von Rundstedt managed the Reich's version of coalition warfare, with Hungarian, Italian, Rumanian and Slovakian formations under command. With the largest operational area of any army group, yet only one panzer group, his men had four difficult tasks: 1) destroying Red Army units to their front; 2) capturing the Ukrainian capital of Kiev and the Dnepr River crossings; 3) seizing the Donets Basin (Donbas); and 4) opening the route to the Caucasus oil region. Of the three army groups, von Rundstedt's came closest to accomplishing its assigned missions.

Facing Army Group South were the Kiev Special Military District and Odessa Military District, which at the start of the war became the Southwest and Southern Fronts respectively. Commanded by Lieutenant General M.P. Kirponos, the Southwest Front especially was well led, and had some of the Red Army's best equipment and other benefits accrued from Stalin's belief that the south would be the Germans' main theater. Along the Black Sea coast Lieutenant General I.V. Tyulenev commanded the new Southern Front (originally the 9th Independent Army). Taking liberties with Stalin's orders not to make provocative gestures prior to June 22, both military districts had coordinated with NKVD Border troops and dispersed their aircraft. Soviet forces under their command offered a more skillful defense of the frontier than did the fronts facing Army Groups North and Center. Counterattacking as Red Army assets allowed and withdrawing to successive defense lines, they put von Rundstedt behind schedule.

Only when robbed of any operational freedom by Stalin's orders did true disaster hit Soviet defenders south of the Rokitno Marshes. Finally, in mid-September, and only with the cooperation of Army Group Center, von Rundstedt's forces achieved dramatic success. In the encirclement at Kiev,

The Eve of *Barbarossa* – Army Group South

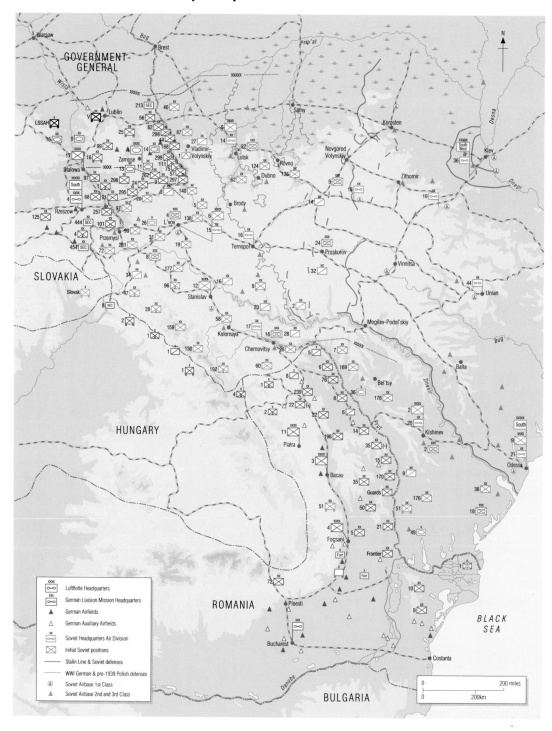

two-thirds of a million Soviet troops surrendered in history's greatest single military victory. For the first and only time in World War II German forces in the field outnumbered those of the USSR. Stalin's High Command somehow plugged the resulting massive gap and resistance stiffened once again. Meanwhile, Hitler bled off mechanized forces from Army Group South for the attack on Moscow, German logistics foundered in the Ukrainian steppes, weather once more delayed von Rundstedt's advance, and his troops reached the limit of their endurance. By November, the Donets River in the north, temporary possession of Rostov in the center, and the siege lines around Sevastopol in the Crimea represented Army Group South's high water mark. Soon after, the Soviet forces counterattacked along the entire front. By then, however, none of the senior commanders remained in their posts – Hitler had accepted von Rundstedt's resignation, Kirponos died at Kiev, and Tyulenev went to the rear severely wounded. Army Group South's plunge into the great agricultural and industrial El Dorado of the Ukraine would supposedly satisfy all of the Third Reich's desires.

German myth holds that the Holy Roman Emperor Frederick I Barbarossa lies sleeping under Kyffhäusser Mountain in the southern Harz, ready to heed his nation's emergency call. The elderly emperor drowned in 1190 leading the Second Crusade through present-day Turkey. Hitler renamed his eastern crusade from *Otto* to *Barbarossa*, "imparting to it an epic, archaic, even redemptive aura."[8]

The stage was set for history's greatest campaign. Fringe historians continue to perpetuate unsubstantiated rumors that Stalin was preparing for his own pre-emptive attack. The Red Army General Staff naturally had contingency plans for an attack against Germany, but there is no evidence that these had any effect on German planning. As with Hitler's every aggressive act since the fairy-tale wars of the Rhineland, Austria, and Czechoslovakia, *Barbarossa* was purely a war of conquest: however the ending would be radically different.

---

8   Hagen, *German History in Modern Times*, p.32.

OPPOSING PLANS

German Plans

A bittersweet soldiers' one-liner, equal parts cleverness and accuracy, holds that there are two types of military plans: those that won't work and those that might work. Except in over-determined hindsight, it is difficult to decide into which category *Barbarossa* falls. Flushed with victory after crushing France, Hitler had wanted to invade the USSR in autumn 1940 – an ambition vigorously opposed by his generals. This disagreement, and logistical weakness and delays, convinced Hitler to postpone the assault until the following spring. The dominating role of logistics was underlined on July 21, 1940 when the army commander-in-chief, Field Marshal Walther von Brauchitsch, told Hitler that only 80–100 divisions would be required to subdue the Soviet troops – a number in fact largely dictated by what the Reichsbahn (the German national railroad network) could move and sustain, rather than a realistic estimate of fighting forces needed.

According to international common opinion, shared by Hitler and the Wehrmacht, a war against the USSR would be quick and easy. The German leadership had nearly 11 months to plan *Barbarossa*, much longer than for their earlier campaigns. However, their hard-marching army did not have the capacity simultaneously to penetrate the Soviet lines and to conduct huge encirclements much beyond the frontier – indeed, it is questionable if even a fully-motorized force, like the US Army in 1944–45, could have done what the Wehrmacht expected of the Ostheer in *Barbarossa*. In addition, the Nazi "philosophy" of racial and martial superiority which exaggerated Germany's prowess while minimizing that of its enemies, combined with insufficient resources and poor staff work, would ensure a difficult campaign.

Barbarossa's planning suffered from curious effects harkening back to the German experiences in the east during the Great War. Then, as later, a single division could successfully take on two or three Russian divisions. Still, war in the East had been no easy proposition; in 1915, when the Central Powers made their greatest advance in that theater, losses were 1.25 times greater than those

in the West. Although Ludendorff's defensive line ultimately stretched from
Finland to the Crimea, the German forces and their Habsburg allies had
ample experience with Russian weather and terrain. They knew their own
manicured forests were nothing like the common eastern wildernesses
(referred to as the *Urwald*). German and Austrian soldiers lived with Russian
filth, vermin, disease, and poverty. Ironically, terrible roads and poor
communications had been a major cause of Russian failure in 1914–17.
Evidently these lessons were lost on Wehrmacht leaders a generation later.[9]

As indications of his confidence in his own military abilities and the
importance of the ideological struggle against Communism, Hitler put his
mark on *Barbarossa's* operational details like no previous campaign. Taking
into account the Army's and Luftwaffe's short striking ranges, the plan
eschewed deep operations and settled on a line formed by the Dvina and
Dnepr rivers for its initial goal. As happened in Poland and the West, the
Soviet commanders' forward deployment played into the German forces'
hands. Writing after the war former Field Marshal Friedrich Paulus recreated
the contemporary mood of the German leadership: "tremendous vigor of
National Socialist policy, then at its zenith" and "complete confidence born
of the victory in the Western campaign." He went on to say that "experts
declared [Hitler's] previous victories impossible." The Wehrmacht would
again prove them wrong in 1941. While many of Hitler's generals questioned
Barbarossa as an indirect attack on Britain, they were enthusiastic about
building a blockade-proof Reich.

As stated, Hitler began thinking of an Eastern campaign before France
had even formally surrendered. Initial planning began with the rushed (four
days), poorly researched assessment of the Red Army's strength by Lieutenant
Colonel Eberhardt Kinzel's Fremde Heere Ost staff (FHO – Foreign Armies
East). German intelligence knew very little about their future enemy despite
ten years' efforts. In addition, every Abwehr (counterintelligence) agent in
the USSR had been turned. They underestimated the overall size of the Red
Army while overestimating the number of units in the western military
districts. All subsequent plans were based on the weak cornerstone of Kinzel's
inadequate and faulty analysis that the Wehrmacht would take to its grave.
This junior officer and his small overworked staff also had responsibility for
the armies of Scandinavia, the Balkans, China, Japan, and the United States
(Kinzel subsequently committed suicide in 1945). The Gestapo, answerable

---

9   Among others, the following senior German generals served in Russia during World War I:
    von Rundstedt, Kesselring, von Manstein, von Mackensen, and Halder.

German Plans

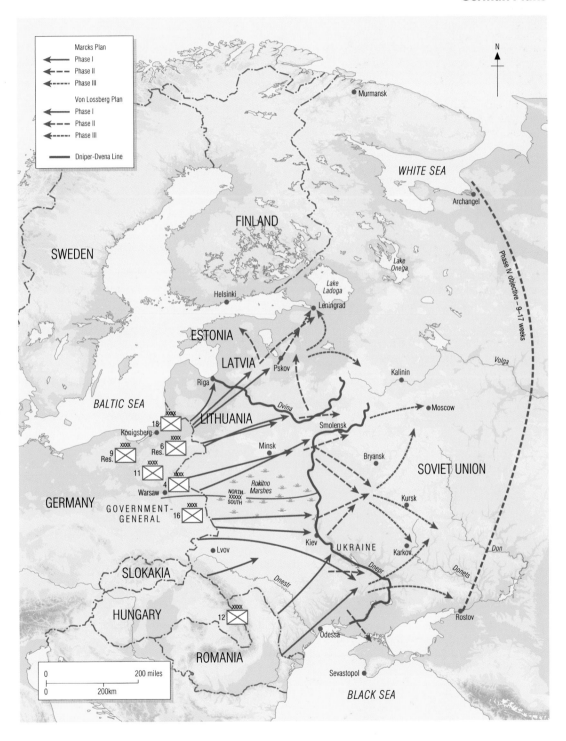

Marcks Plan
- → Phase I
- →-- Phase II
- →··· Phase III

Von Lossberg Plan
- → Phase I
- →-- Phase II
- →··· Phase III

── Dniper-Dvena Line

N

SWEDEN

FINLAND

WHITE SEA

Murmansk

Archangel

Lake Onega

Lake Ladoga

Helsinki

Leningrad

Phase IV objective — 9–17 weeks

ESTONIA

LATVIA

Pskov

Kalinin

Volga

Riga

BALTIC SEA

LITHUANIA

Dvina

Smolensk

Moscow

18

Königsberg

6 Res.

Minsk

Bryansk

SOVIET UNION

9 Res.

11

Warsaw

Rokitno Marshes

Kursk

GERMANY

GOVERNMENT-GENERAL

16

NORTH XXXXX SOUTH

4

Kiev

UKRAINE

Karkov

Lvov

SLOKAKIA

Dnestr

Dnepr

Donets

Don

HUNGARY

12

Rostov

Odessa

ROMANIA

Sevastopol

BLACK SEA

| 0 | | 200 miles |
| 0 | | 200km |

A Red Army soldier crawls to surrender to a Panzer IV and attendant Landsers. The barn is well built and undamaged, a valuable refuge in the coming winter. (HITM)

for political intelligence, added another layer of inaccuracies by predicting the Soviet state's collapse within weeks. Although just days into *Barbarossa* Hitler began to hedge his bets by saying that he might not have begun the campaign if he had known the real strength of the USSR, it is difficult to see an intelligence estimate (or anything else, for that matter) dissuading him from a campaign he had been anticipating for nearly 20 years.

With the German military focused in the summer of 1940 on the Battle of Britain and Operation *Sealion*, on July 4, 1940 Army Chief of Staff Colonel General Franz Halder put generals Georg Küchler and Erich Marcks to work planning the Eighteenth Army's defense of the East. Their planning turned offensive two weeks later when Hitler told Halder, "*Stalin kokettiert mit England*" (Stalin flirts with England). By the end of July, Marcks' plans neared completion. Following Kinzel he assumed "… the Russians no longer possess the superiority of numbers they had in the World War…" On July 29, he flew to Halder's headquarters in Fontainebleau where the army chief of staff succeeded in shifting Marcks' emphasis from the Ukraine to Moscow. Marcks completed his *Operationsentwurf Ost* (Operational Draft East) on August 5,

1940. In general he divided the invading force into three army groups in two main bodies, north and south of the Rokitno Marshes with Moscow as the ultimate objective. Marcks' plan had three phases: 1 – the initial three-week 250-mile push to the Dvina–Dnepr line; 2 – an intermediate phase between two and four weeks consisting of a logistical pause and possible advance up to 100 miles; and 3 – final drives lasting from three to six weeks on Leningrad, Moscow, and the deep Ukraine. Presumably the war would be won at that point, so phase 4 would be the last month of tidying up the front and establishing winter defenses along the Volga.

Hitler wanted the OKW involved so on July 29, he told Jodl to prepare a plan also. Another lieutenant colonel, Bernhard von Lossberg, wrote the OKW plan largely on his own initiative with some input from Jodl. He also required only one month to create his *Aufbau Ost* (Buildup East). He completed an additional *Operationsstudie Ost* (Operational Study East) on September 15, 1940. He included Rumania

General Erich Marcks wrote OKH's plan for *Barbarossa* then commanded the 101st Light Division. Shrapnel cost him his left leg on June 26, 1941. He died three years later commanding the LXXXIV Corps at St Lô. (NARA)

more fully in his plan and assumed a vigorous Soviet forward defense followed by an 1812-type fighting withdrawal. Both OKH and OKW assumed the bulk of the Red Army would be destroyed in phase 1 and envisioned the Schwerpunkt against Stalin's capital. Since von Lossberg started his plan five weeks later than Marcks and as Jodl was closer than Halder to Hitler – both in thinking and proximity – we can assume the former plan was more in line with Hitler's concept. Von Lossberg's main contribution was to clarify Hitler's thoughts with regard to *Barbarossa*'s later phases, specifically the turns north and south preparatory to the assault on Moscow and flexibility in subsequent operations that would prove the most controversial features of the campaign. The drafting of the plans for history's greatest invasion had thus devolved on one major general – the lowest general rank in the Heer (Army) – and two lieutenant colonels. All had drafted their plans based on the same questionable information so independent analysis and checks and balances were nonexistent. Neither the Marcks/OKH nor the von Lossberg/OKW plans doubted the Wehrmacht's ability to successfully overthrow the Soviet Union.

This is especially true considering the unreasonable six-, eight-, or ten-week assumptions about *Barbarossa's* expected length. Also, the massive size of the eastern theater clearly had a significant effect and dramatically decreased German weapon densities. They could count on one panzer per 29 square miles in the West; in the East this fell to one panzer per 112 square miles. Above the battlefield the ratio plummeted from one aircraft per 2 square miles in 1940 to one in 95 during *Barbarossa*.

Realizing that Germany would not only seek to secure the Ukraine's natural resources but also to put as much distance as possible between the Red Army and Rumanian oil, Stalin concluded the main effort would come in the south. Judging from his actions, Hitler as well as many German economic and military leaders, the Abwehr, and the army's own Military Geography Department concurred. Planners in the OKH's operations staff favored giving weight to Army Group South in order to counter the Soviet main effort there. In fact, increased Soviet activity in the Ukraine in the winter of 1940–41 caused the German leadership concern over operations in the south. However, Moscow beguiled many army leaders, most significantly Halder. Further, it seems that the German army chief of staff was especially susceptible to the arrogance that affected the entire Wehrmacht after the defeat of France.

Halder gave General Paulus, Oberquartiermeister I as of September 3, the tasks of de-conflicting the competing OKH and OKW courses of action and further developing the Marcks plan. Paulus finished this work in just two weeks, presenting his own "Foundations of the Russian Operation" at the end of October.[10] After the war Paulus admitted that he had approached the problem "from the purely military point of view" – not a ringing endorsement of his own job performance and emblematic of poor-to-nonexistent German strategic thinking.

Between November 28 and December 7, 1940 he hosted *Barbarossa* wargames. Von Brauchitsch told participants to expect "a hefty border fight" lasting some four weeks, after which the remainder of the USSR would be occupied against only "weak resistance." As a result of these simulations Paulus insisted on creating an 11-division OKH reserve. He also attached an infantry corps to each panzer group mainly to assist with breakthrough operations. Not surprisingly, the wargames confirmed the primacy of the Moscow axis and a three-week phase 1 was followed by a logistical pause of the same length. They centered on the Baltic States and Leningrad, and less

---

10   Unfortunately for historians, OKH/OKW primary source documents from this critical autumn and winter timeframe seem not to be available.

Simulating *Barbarossa*

Prussian-German commanders and staffs had been wargaming since the 17th century. The simulations' main goals were to exercise plans, bring likely problems to light, identify friction points, rectify potential mistakes, and allow senior commanders to meet and work with their subordinates. Wargames either had no instructions or else very loose rules, so as to intentionally avoid "even the slightest semblance of regimentation" and allow for full intellectual freedom. The OKH carried out strategic simulations from November 29 to December 3, 1940 as well as on December 7.

Army Group South conducted Planspiel *Otto* over four days between January 20 and February 5, 1941 at its headquarters in a luxury hotel in St Germain en Laye, downstream from Paris (in a *Planspiel* commanders brainstorm the plan). Participants were mainly colonels and lieutenant colonels under the supervision of Army Group Chief of Staff Lieutenant General Georg von Sodenstern. Field Marshall von Rundstedt was present throughout while General Halder attended the last day only. The plan assumed a larger army group than historically present since the Balkan invasion lay in the future; forces in Rumania included two German armies and a panzer corps.

This arrangement gave Army Group South the double-envelopment capability found in Army Group Center, the highly coveted *Zangenangriff* (literally "fang attack," encirclement battle) against Soviet forces in Galicia and Bessarabia. In the *Otto* wargame the attackers were roughly handled by Soviet defenses but did close a *Kessel* (cauldron, or pocket) near Proskurov. In his concluding remarks von Sodenstern enumerated some special issues: questions of surprise, creating the Schwerpunkt, cooperation between Army and Luftwaffe units, and the daring of the leadership disposed far in the enemy's depth and maneuvering without fear of threatened flanks. He sided decisively with the acting panzer group commander, especially concerning the latter's freedom of action.

Operation *Marita* against Greece and Yugoslavia plus the backward Rumanian infrastructure that limited the size of German units stationed there changed the situation. With forces halved and panzer units removed altogether the Proskurov encirclement was off. However, *Otto* did accurately anticipate the furious counterattacks launched by Soviet mechanized corps and the disrupting influence of the 5th Army in and around the Rokitno Marshes.

The Second Army carried out a *Kriegsspiel* at the Park Hotel in Munich from March 10 to 13 under the eye of commander Colonel General von Weichs. As a *Kriegsspiel* it had a more familiar format, alternating Red (German) and Blue (Soviet) sides. Another interesting point is the simulation's start date: May 20. Since it took place well before German operations in the Balkans it shows that *Barbarossatag* was a moving target.

Significantly Leningrad is never mentioned in the wargame. Army Group North weighted its attacks to the right flank and was much more oriented on Moscow and supporting von Bock. This backfired on the German troops as "the Soviets" (played by Wehrmacht officers) took advantage of the relative paucity of von Leeb's forces on the left and recaptured Riga in a surprise counteroffensive. After taking Dvina River bridgeheads the German troops stalled for nearly two weeks. German units took heavy losses and even requested three days' rest barely a fortnight into the campaign. *Barbarossa* in the north was going so poorly that the German leaders even considered employing chemical weapons (*Geländevergiftungen*).

In his closing remarks von Witzleben warned against micromanaging subordinates in a way that stifled their initiative. But the Second Army's wargame must have disappointed all concerned. Army Group North had lost Riga, was stalemated along the middle Dvina, and was stalled around Minsk. Army Group North took many remedial measures which paid dividends during *Barbarossa*. Once across the Dvina the panzers no longer wheeled southeast toward Minsk but made for Leningrad. Gone were conservative German movement rates: instead of infantry marching 60 miles in six days it advanced 150 miles in ten days; instead of panzers going 90 miles in six days they covered over 200 miles in less than 100 hours. But the fact that von Leeb and members of his staff chose not to attend the simulation can only be seen as a lost opportunity.

A rubber raft, in this case a *"Grosser Flossack,"* used to cross the Ukraine's many rivers. The troops appear to be *Gebirgsjäger* with the soldier in front carrying a Panzerbüchse 39, the infantry's standard antitank weapon. Its 7.92mm round proved ineffective against most Soviet tanks. (NARA)

on Moscow. Prophetically, the wargames indicated that clearing the Baltic States would take much time and impact Army Group Center operations. Even at this early planning stage von Rundstedt asked for units from Army Group Center to attack southward into the rear of Soviet forces attempting to escape from Kiev.

Army Commander Field Marshal Walther von Brauchitsch and Halder briefed Hitler on the wargames' outcome on December 3. The Führer approved the basic plan. Significantly, however, he added a prophetic comment, declaring Moscow "not so very important." For the next nine months Hitler continually emphasized destruction of the Red Army in the field over capturing Moscow.

Von Lossberg wrote the first draft of Führer Directive 21 on December 12, the Luftwaffe added its details on the 16th; it went to Hitler the next day and became official on the 18th. Although it mentioned numerous geographic objectives, Moscow among them, it clearly identified *Barbarossa's* main goal as the destruction of the Soviet military. All preparations for *Barbarossa* were to be completed by mid-May. A series of logistical wargames were held from December 17 to 20, after Hitler signed the Directive! The Wehrmacht believed its logistics nearly failed in France because the Western theater was so large and therefore required serious reworking for *Barbarossa*. These wargames confirmed the requirement for a logistics pause at the Dvina–Dnepr rivers. Finally, these simulations proved that if the Soviet military was not destroyed west of that line, the abysmal infrastructure further east meant the German forces probably would not succeed against even weak resistance.

OKH published its operation order, *Aufmarschanweisung Ost* (Deployment Directive East), on January 31, 1941.[11] While Führer Directive 21 can be considered a strategic overview of *Barbarossa*, *Aufmarschanweisung Ost* represented the campaign's actual operational nuts and bolts. The directive's introduction mentioned Moscow as an objective of von Bock's men only *after* resistance in northern "Russia" had been broken. Specific instructions for Army Group Center did not mention the Soviet capital. Six or seven months later many German generals feigned surprise and righteous indignation when Hitler held them to this prioritization of *Barbarossa's* objectives.

One threat identified by FHO on February 12 consisted of Red Army forces that could retreat to relative safety east of the Rokitno Marshes, only to later attack the flanks of German thrusts making for Moscow or Rostov. This draft study anticipated perfectly the July and August controversies. Fearing dilution of his pet effort against Moscow, Halder deleted these references from the final version presented to Hitler on January 21, demonstrating how far his subterfuge would go to subvert the German staff system.

Operational staffs created detailed directives and operation orders during the following winter and spring. However, the German leaders' traditional emphasis on operations hamstrung the planning for personnel, military intelligence, and logistics, especially given the unrealistic assumptions about *Barbarossa's* expected length – of between six and ten weeks only.

---

11   In the German staff system a directive (*Weisung*) did not have the force of an order (*Befehl*).

Further, the German leadership expended a lot of energy planning for *Barbarossa*'s logistical requirements although these efforts bore little fruit. Hermann Göring correctly predicted in February 1941 that logistics would "endanger the entire operation." The staff assumed that the roads and railroads west of the Dvina and Dnepr rivers would be superior to those east of that line; but this was true only in a very relative sense, and movement capability became a limiting factor as soon as the German troops crossed the border. Logistics were also one main reason for locating *Barbarossa*'s Schwerpunkt in the center: German rail connections from the Reich to East Prussia and occupied Poland – which also offered better staging areas for a potential attack on the Moscow axis – were superior to those farther south in Hungary and Rumania.

The German Air Force completed its plans for *Barbarossa* on February 20. The Luftwaffe possessed the same concepts of *Vernichtungskrieg*, *Auftragstaktik*, and Schwerpunkt as the army.[12] It also shared the army's weakness of having very junior officers plan such a massive undertaking as *Barbarossa*: this task fell on Major Rudolf Loytved-Hardegg and three subordinate officers. These men provided sealed orders to Luftwaffe crews that were to be opened only eight hours prior to H-Hour!

Consistent with the Luftwaffe's main war-fighting doctrine, Regulation 16, *Luftkriegsführung* (1935), air superiority was its first priority. The Luftwaffe sought first to destroy the Red Army Air Force (especially its most modern equipment) and its supporting ground operations. Assisted by Lufthansa pilots gathering data during civilian flights over the USSR, the German leaders had very good intelligence on Soviet dispositions. They named their *Barbarossatag* assault the *Grosses Wecken* (Great Reveille). However, owing to range and payload limitations, the Luftwaffe could not attack the Soviet aviation industry effectively. After gaining air superiority the Luftwaffe would shift to flying CAS missions for the army – its primary mission.

On the last day of April, Hitler officially set Operation *Barbarossa*'s start date for June 22. Some historians falsely believe Germany's Balkan invasion fatally delayed the launching of the campaign. Von Lossberg wrote that Hitler always planned to conquer Greece prior to *Barbarossa*.

---

12 *Auftragstaktik* refers to doctrine of giving subordinates broad "mission type" guidance rather than very specific orders; Schwerpunkt refers to the main, overriding objective – capture this or defend that at all costs; *Vernichtungskrieg* is the doctrine of victory by destroying an enemy's forces in the field, as opposed to capturing its capital, a certain hilltop, etc.

Indeed, invading the Balkans was discussed at the Führer conference of December 5. The main causes for deferring *Barbarossa*'s start date from May 15 to June 22 were incomplete logistical arrangements and an unusually wet winter that kept Central European rivers at full flood until late spring. Besides, to have started much earlier would have only meant that *Barbarossa* began during the infamous *rasputitsa* (spring and autumn rainy season, "time without roads").

Differences between Hitler and his generals and between OKH and OKW were discounted by the German High Command's expectation that their Russian campaign would be short. With near-unanimity they assumed *Barbarossa* would begin with the quick elimination of the Red Army followed by a series of marches and then a brutal occupation. The planned final assault on Moscow was predicated on the two northern army groups cooperating to capture Leningrad and Kronshtadt before wheeling southeast. However, the planned one-two punch never occurred.

Barbarossa suffered from a liability common to other Wehrmacht operations, namely the absence of a unifying strategic objective. The entire plan appears to be a combination of operational-level solutions to a war with the USSR; strategy was relegated to the realm of wishful thinking. Traditionally directed at enemy forces rather than geographic objectives, the German forces therefore chased a moving target with mission accomplishment accordingly hard to judge. This "strategy," undermined by weaknesses in the vaunted German general staff system, lop-sided emphasis on operations over personnel, intelligence, and logistical concerns, tweaking wargame results until they fit pre-conceived notions, and relegating bad news to the category of "inconvenient truths" met its match in the USSR.

Planners for *Barbarossa* have been variously described as suffering from "unbounded hubris" and "sublime inattention to logistical realities," but the *Führerprinzip* then ascendant in Nazi Germany allowed no warnings, only optimism. It suspended reality, made the impossible feasible, and substituted faith and will power for numerical strength and technological superiority. In a system that had thrived on risk ever since Frederick's most audacious oblique maneuvers in the 18th century and with men who believed the bigger the risk the more they liked it (witness the Schlieffen Plan), *Barbarossa* represented the ultimate risk. The German forces would have to get every break possible if they were to make good on Hitler's boast to turn the Volga River into his Mississippi.[13]

13　Snyder, *Bloodlands*, p.160.

Army Group North

Leningrad, unlike Moscow, was one of *Barbarossa*'s strategic objectives from the very first. Regarding Army Group North, Marcks wrote "north of the main group of forces [aiming for Moscow] a strong group advances through the Baltic States to Leningrad and takes the base of the Russian Fleet." He anticipated the advance on the axis Dünaburg–Pskov–Leningrad. Von Lossberg likewise, planned to annihilate the Red Army west of the Dvina River, and called for German troops in Norway and the Finns to cut the Murmansk railroad and to cooperate with forces advancing from East Prussia to encircle Leningrad.

General Paulus' wargames demonstrated that if Eighteenth Army was strengthened at the expense of the Sixteenth, the Army Group Center flank would be vulnerable to Soviet counterattacks. Threats to their common boundary did indeed cause constant friction between the two army groups. The wargames also established the need for intermediate objectives on the army group's right shoulder, near Velikie Luki or Lake Il'men, preparatory to an assault on Leningrad. Propitiously they confirmed the requirement for the loan of some Army Group Center panzers if von Leeb hoped to conquer the city. At the December 5 meeting between Hitler, von Brauchitsch, and Halder, the Führer stressed, "We must strive to encircle the enemy forces in the Baltics. Therefore the Moscow Army Group must be so strong that it can turn significant portions to the north." Ironically Hitler dashed Army Group North's chances of success when he failed to heed his own advice.

The *Aufmarschanweisung* confirmed the primacy of encircling the Red Army west of the Dvina, leading with a strong right and the Schwerpunkt along the axis Dünaburg–Opochka–Leningrad. Field Marshal von Leeb's main goals were: 1) destroy the Red Army holding the Baltic States; 2) neutralize Kronshtadt; 3) capture Leningrad; and 4) link up with the Finns.

Army Group North's plan for reaching Leningrad, 500 miles away, went generally as follows: Hoepner's Panzer Group would punch through the Soviet's frontier defenses and make for the Dvina crossings near Dünaburg, from there aiming toward Opochka. Depending on Leningrad's defenses, Hoepner would either advance due north or swing northeast. The Eighteenth Army would clear the Baltic region and be prepared to take the islands off Estonia's coast. The Sixteenth Army had responsibility for securing the boundary with Army Group Center.

Ironically, Army Group North suffered the most severe impact from the Balkan operation; when Hitler dispatched the Twelfth Army against Yugoslavia and Greece in April 1941 he moved the Eleventh from OKH Reserve and sent it south to Rumania. Only five of 21 divisions (none mechanized) from the Eleventh ever reappeared on von Leeb's order of battle, despite his desperate need for them.

Motorized infantry run to catch up with an SdKfz 251 half-track on the way out of a Russian village. German mechanized and motorized infantry rode to battle, but fought dismounted. (HITM)

Army Group Center

In a plan where the big money was on the panzer groups, Army Group Center had a distinct advantage by having two. In contrast to the other two army groups whose frontages expanded enormously from the campaign's first day, von Bock's axis of advance was anticipated to basically remain the same width from Poland to Moscow. Army Group Center even "benefited" from an unexpectedly weak opponent: Kinzel's analysis of the Red Army overestimated Soviet infantry facing it by 40 percent while underestimating enemy armored and mechanized forces by 70–80 percent.

Army Group Center's first mission was to destroy the Red Army forces in Belorussia. Panzer groups on the flanks represented von Bock's main punch, with infantry armies marching in between. After creating an initial Kessel at Minsk, Army Group Center's operational goals were Vitebsk and Orsha (the Dvina–Dnepr line), to be followed by a three-week logistical pause for the "railroad advance." The outer wings would then swing wide and meet again to create another pocket at Smolensk. Victory was universally defined as destruction of the Red Army west of the Dvina and Dnepr.

Except in the mind of Franz Halder, a few other generals, and some postwar critics, Moscow represented merely an operational objective, not the strategic key to a total German victory. The overview portion of the OKH *Aufmarschanweisung* mentioned Moscow as von Bock's objective only after resistance in the North had been broken, and specific instructions for his army group did not mention the Soviet capital. A major adjustment occurred on March 8, 1941 when Hitler directed that 1) an infantry corps be detailed for security duty on the army group's right, bordering the Rokitno Marshes (to help maintain contact with Army Group South); and 2) *Barbarossa*'s entire strategic reserves would follow von Bock. These formations, generally under Second Army, quickly became a *de facto* part of Army Group Center, so that OKH ceased to have any reserves worthy of the name. The folly of such high-risk behavior, launching an invasion like *Barbarossa* without strategic reserves, cannot be overstated.

While acknowledging the benefits to the defense of numerous rivers, Colonel General Hermann Hoth's own *Aufmarschanweisung* urged that his Third Panzer Group go "eastwards fast and without looking back," to wreak havoc on enemy command and control, reinforcements, and logistics. Third Panzer Group would initially be under Ninth Army control. Colonel General Heinz Guderian hoped to reach Minsk with his Second Panzer Group in five or six days; this formation initially came under Fourth Army, which also had the missions of defending against a surprise Soviet invasion to the west, and helping close off any encirclements. After taking Smolensk, both strategic and operational leaders anticipated that Army Group Center would turn north toward Leningrad.

Army Group South

Führer Directive No. 21 gave von Rundstedt three to four weeks to reach Kiev and the Dnepr crossings. He would then turn south to trap enemy forces against the Black Sea with the Caucasus oil region his ultimate

destination. At *Barbarossa*'s start, Army Group South massed in the cramped space between the Rokitno Marshes and the Carpathian Mountains. The impact of Red Army elements lurking in and east of the marshes on Army Group South's northern flank remained a significant threat to its operations throughout *Barbarossa*'s first three months.

Von Rundstedt wanted to create a German–Hungarian force based on the Seventeenth Army, but Hitler distrusted Hungary and forbade any formal contact between the two militaries. However, the *Aufmarschanweisung* did add Rumania to von Rundstedt's area of responsibility. The ensuing 200-mile wide Hungarian gap between Axis forces in occupied Poland and Rumania created numerous security, logistical and command and control problems.

Army Group South's original plan envisioned a double envelopment during phase 1, employing First Panzer Group in the north and Twelfth Army coming out of Rumania. Hitler soon decided against this course of action,

A busy scene, complete with a halted Panzer III and a convoy led by a quad 2cm *Flakvierling* cannon mounted on an SdKfz 7/1 half-track, followed by trucks, motorcycles, staff cars, and other vehicles. (HITM)

and besides, in April he ordered Twelfth Army to invade Yugoslavia and Greece. As discussed above Eleventh Army took over duties in Rumania but combined forces there would not be ready by June 22 so would attack later, giving *Barbarossa* its staggered start in the far south. Therefore von Rundstedt would initially fight mainly a frontal war, punctuated by occasional penetrations and relatively small encirclements.

These factors, along with relatively weaker friendly forces and stronger Soviet forces, and a larger area of operations, combined to create difficulties for Army Group South. Additionally, von Rundstedt contended with a subtle prejudice within the Wehrmacht dating back to World War I when primarily Austria, not Germany, fought in the Ukraine.

Soviet Plans

On August 23, 1939 Stalin created conditions to eliminate the Polish buffer and give the USSR a common border with Germany for the first time since 1918. At the same time he pursued an active foreign policy to replace Poland with an expanded Soviet Union that within a few months included eastern Poland, the Baltic States, and Bessarabia.[14]

For at least a dozen years prior to *Barbarossa* the USSR vacillated between defensive and offensive strategies. By the late 1930s it built fortified regions along the border behind which the Red Army would mobilize, fend off any attack, and then launch a general offensive (collectively the Germans called the Fortified Regions the Stalin Line). In the Soviet experience static fortifications had been quite effective when used against them by the Finns; they attributed the apparent failure of the Maginot Line to specifically French weaknesses.

The avalanche of murder known as the Great Purges began in May 1937 with the execution of Marshal M.N. Tukhachevsky, the Red Army's brightest star in the early 1930s. Stalin used Soviet military leaders to expose traitors and saboteurs, not to improve the Red Army. Despite being severely weakened by these purges, thanks to its extensive and effective spy network the USSR learned of *Barbarossa* soon after Wehrmacht leaders did. With the advantage of this forewarning, initially, the Soviet military planned to defend critical axes of advance using the fortified regions. That plan ceased to be workable when the Soviet Union extended its borders west in 1939–40.

---

14   Bessarabia is a region in Eastern Europe between the former USSR and Rumania bounded by the Dniestr River in the east and the Prut River in the west.

A favored weapon since the Russian Civil War, the armored train proved to be a useful tool given the huge distances and poor roads in the Soviet Union. This example mounts T-34/76 tank turrets. (Elukka)

The decision to deploy defending units so far forward also robbed the Red Army of room to maneuver, a traditional Russian strength, by placing them right under the Germans' guns. As Red Army chief of staff and member of the Military Soviet from 1926–34, Tukhachevsky had focused on defending the Ukraine and the twin "capitals" of Moscow and Leningrad. By 1940, however, much had changed and the German blitzkrieg campaigns had turned the military world on its head. While Stalin acted the good neighbor to assuage Hitler, Soviet military thinkers put Tukhachevsky's offensive doctrines on hold until they had found a way to halt the blitzkrieg. Red Army planning became more defensive – if only for the first few weeks of a future war.

The Soviet leadership had a long time to prepare for *Barbarossa* and was contemptuous of Poland, which had been surprised by Germany despite years of increasing tensions prior to 1939. Since then, from their vantage point on the war's sidelines, the Soviet High Command had watched Hitler dismember Poland, France, and numerous smaller opponents, yet they developed no workable plan to counter the blitzkrieg. The Red Army began planning in earnest immediately following Hitler's "secret" July 31, 1940 meeting. Sensing that an upcoming conflict would be a war of attrition, with resource-poor Germany aiming for the resource-rich Ukraine, on October 5, 1940 Stalin ordered the main Soviet defensive effort redirected south and away from the Moscow axis. This course of action ignored the fact that communications in occupied southern Poland and Rumania were too poor, and the Balkans too insecure, for that area ever to support the deployment *Barbarossa*'s Schwerpunkt forces.

The new southern orientation became Mobilization Plan 1941 (MP 41) on October 14 and was further refined over the next six months. This commitment to an inherently and, in fact excessively, offensive approach was not the USSR's only error: in addition, although the Soviet leaders knew Hitler had ordered the number of panzer divisions doubled, they did not know that in order to achieve this the number of panzers per division had been halved. Further, the "1941 Plan for the Defense of State Borders" assumed Germany would need 10–15 days to finalize its invasion preparations. However, Stalin preferred to look the other way as the Wehrmacht made ready for 11 months. One observer called Hitler the only man Stalin ever trusted. Soviet military intelligence failures complimented the dictator's wishful thinking. The Red Army over-estimated German strength at 260 divisions, 10,000 panzers, and 15,000 aircraft (real numbers: 150, 3,300, and 2,510 respectively). Unfortunately for them, 500,000 untrained recruits and reserve armies sent to the front in the weeks prior to *Barbarossatag* could not stave off disaster.

Soviet planning forged ahead when Stalin summoned the Politburo and military leaders to a ten-day conference in Moscow starting on December 23, 1940. Wargames followed immediately, with General G.K. Zhukov teamed with 21 other generals to simulate an attack on WSMD, against Pavlov and 28 other generals. From January 2 to 6, Zhukov led the "Germans" out of Prussia and Poland, and these maneuvers exposed the vulnerability of Pavlov's four armies to encirclement. When roles were reversed, Zhukov easily parried Pavlov's mechanized attack into Germany – causing the Soviet leadership to question the wisdom of its strategic "Red Folder" plans for a counteroffensive into Germany, but not with sufficient vigor.

In simulating the south, Kiev Special Military District commander Zhukov led the German troops and won as expected; after all the Soviet High Command had seriously neglected defensive doctrine. In the second

simulation Zhukov successfully defended the Ukraine and even launched a limited attack into Hungary and Rumania. His successes and high-visibility roles confirmed the primacy of the south in Red Army calculations. Results of wargames in December and January of 1941 painted a gloomy picture. On January 13 Stalin asked "Who won here?" None of his generals answered satisfactorily. The next day, after the wargames' conclusion, Stalin made Zhukov Red Army Chief of Staff, effective two weeks later. Stalin and Zhukov nevertheless delayed making substantive changes in Soviet deployments for weeks.

When Zhukov took over as chief of staff he had less than five months to implement a realistic defensive strategy and minimize the offensive mindset. Through April he updated MP 41 during a series of high-level conferences. Under the new plan the USSR would create 344 divisions of 7.85 million men, 6.5 million of them facing Germany. They retained the need to hold the border, followed by an active defense followed in turn by a counteroffensive. This tactic consisted of allowing the panzers to slip east then destroying each

Red Army riflemen advance with the support of a Maxim M1910 machine gun (left) and 50mm M1940/1941 mortar (right). The defense of the USSR ultimately depended on men like these. (HITM)

Soviet riflemen and T-34 tank in the attack. Losses suffered by poorly conceived and executed attacks conducted as part of the Soviet strategy of the active defense meant any mobile counterattack forces would not be available later in the campaign.

spearhead individually. His "Plan for the Defense of the State Frontier" issued the month before *Barbarossa* advocated a defense followed by an attack into the Reich's rear areas. Military Districts readied plans by April and distributed them to subordinate armies in May. Corps commanders were permitted to look through the plans, to familiarize themselves with their general outline, but not to keep copies.

Even the USSR's best general could not work defensive miracles in less than five months. His State Defensive Plan 41 (DP 41) stated "that the Red Army would begin military operations in response to an aggressive attack." While remaining on the strategic defensive it would unleash operational offensives that might penetrate into the Reich; the Soviets were also aware of the potential panzer thrusts' lack of mutual support and vulnerable flanks.

Fatefully, Zhukov's plans also called for the forward deployment of 237 out of 303 divisions – a high number. However, the opening of the *Barbarossa* offensive on June 22 came too soon for the revised MP 41 and DP 41 to take effect. On that date the Red Army was deployed as follows: first echelon (6–30 miles deep) – 57 divisions; second echelon (30–60 miles) – 52 divisions; third echelon (60–240 miles) – 62 divisions. This positioning of so much of the Red Army in forward areas played into the German forces' hands.

The Soviet Union was finally actively preparing for war. By spring Zhukov convinced Stalin to mobilize 500,000 reservists and send them directly to front-line units. At about the same time he and Defense Commissar Marshal S.K. Timoshenko learned of *Barbarossa*'s final plans.

The Baltic Special and Leningrad Military Districts

Initial Red Army planning in the north assumed that Leningrad would only be threatened from Finland and that German thrusts would aim for Moscow. By November 18, 1940 the Soviet High Command learned of the existence in German planning of a supporting attack heading for Leningrad. A defensive plan from that date identified an attack axis through Pskov and also anticipated the Finns advancing via Vyborg against Leningrad. Responsibility for defending the Pskov–Ostrov approaches to Bolshevism's birthplace shifted to the Baltic Special Military District (BSMD) from the Leningrad Military District. Unfortunately for the Soviet forces, neither headquarters gave the issue its full attention.

Such plans as did exist identified two phases of defensive fighting: first at the frontier and along the Dvina River; second on the Riga–Pskov–Luga–Novgorod line. This took advantage of natural obstacles like the Velikaya and Luga rivers, as well as marshes and forests in the area. A later plan, dated May 15, 1941, maintained the Leningrad Military District's responsibility for defending Leningrad and the Murmansk rail line. The same plan gave the BSMD the mission to halt the enemy between Riga and Vilnius and hold the Baltic Islands. The "Leningraders" would accomplish their assigned mission. Their comrades on the East Prussian border would not.

The Western Special Military District

The Soviet leaders' sanguine assumptions about war with Germany, borne out by the outcome of their wargames, matched those of the German commanders about theirs. Red Army defenses were revealed to be only one echelon deep and lacking reserves, but these facts did not trouble the national leadership. Napoleon probably would have called Pavlov, the WSMD commander, "an unlucky general." When Stalin shifted the Soviet emphasis from the Moscow axis to the Ukraine Pavlov lost the status and resources of the main defensive effort.

Significant forces still occupied the massive Bialystok salient, ripe for von Bock's picking; WSMD occupied a 270-mile front, most of it along this treacherous bulge. According to John Erickson, Pavlov's main contribution to his defensive capability during the months before *Barbarossa* was to tweak a few unit dispositions, in the process weakening the line and depriving his forces of reserves of their own. This was most noticeable on the very axis that Guderian would use, but it was approved by the Soviet High Command.

The WSMD issued its Order 008130 on March 26, 1941, ordering all units to achieve full strength by June 15, but resources fell far short of good intentions. It is very likely that in the minds of Stalin and Zhukov WSMD existed as a sacrifice to the blitzkrieg; by February 1941 they may already have been thinking that the Reserve Front might fight the main defensive battle along the pre-1939 frontier and the Stalin Line. Pavlov's bad luck would continue.

The Kiev Special and Odessa Military Districts

The Soviet High Command knew the Germans' Schwerpunkt stood north of the Rokitno Marshes, yet Stalin insisted their emphasis remain in the south. The latter theater played a prominent role in Soviet planning from a desire to ensure continued dominance of the Ukrainian people, retain the region's resources and industry, and maintain a power base close to the Balkans. To that end, Zhukov dispatched the 19th Army from the Northern Caucasus to Tserkov (south of Kiev) and the 16th Army from Transbaikal to Shepetkovka in central-western Ukraine.

Despite Zhukov's changes, no Red Army formations were fully prepared for the coming onslaught, the future Southwest and Southern Fronts included. Kirponos' forces deployed too far forward in the first operational echelon, within 30 miles of the frontier. Bearing in mind its dearth of transport, the Soviet infantry would move slower than the panzers attempting to bypass them, inviting disaster. Divisions within the many mechanized corps in the Ukraine were often based 100 miles apart from one another. Stalin Line fortifications in the south, approximately the second operational

The commander of a T-26 light tank surrenders to the command "Hände hoch!". (Podzun)

echelon, generally ran between the pre-1939 frontier and the Dnepr. This massive river marked the boundary of Kirponos' strategic echelon. Aware that German forces in Rumania were separated from any support by Hungary, the Red Army planned to attack Hitler's ally once the initial assault had been blunted. Included in these offensive plans were naval aviation raids against the Ploesti oil fields and amphibious attacks on Rumanian islands in the Danube delta.

As a testimony of Kirponos' good judgment, Soviet border guards fell under military command only in his KSMD. Further in accordance with prewar plans, he prepared a counteroffensive into the Reich, allocating two shock groups of three mechanized corps each, totaling 3,700 tanks for the purpose. The violence of von Rundstedt's assault overwhelmed these plans, however. As a final indication of the Ukraine's importance, on June 22 Stalin sent his best general, Zhukov, directly to the Southern Front's headquarters to coordinate its defense.

OPPOSING ARMIES

German Forces

National Leadership

Mercifully for mankind, throughout two world wars Germany's national leadership showed very little strategic aptitude. Neither the Kaiser and his generals nor the Führer and his showed much understanding of the wider world beyond Germany's immediate frontiers. The OKW was theoretically a Department of Defense-type organization but was intentionally kept weak in accordance with Hitler's leadership style.[15] It managed to coordinate neither national political, military, and economic objectives, nor Germany's four armed services: Heer (Army), Kriegsmarine (Navy), Luftwaffe (Air Force), and Waffen-SS.

Personalities at the top played critical roles. Hitler flaunted his lack of formal military training and operated primarily on intuition. In view of the racial, cultural, and national importance he placed upon *Barbarossa* he set his imprint on that campaign more than any other, completely eclipsing every other member of the leadership. As a military leader Luftwaffe commander Hermann Göring was an unqualified buffoon although he played a much bigger role in *Barbarossa* through his various economic positions and titles than he did in actual Luftwaffe operations; Kriegsmarine commander Erich Raeder never played more than a marginal role in what was mainly a land and air war; and Heinrich Himmler of the SS was militarily irrelevant in 1941.

Senior German army leaders were uniformly ineffectual. As professional head of the army, von Brauchitsch peaked on November 5, 1939 when he stood up to Hitler and vetoed an autumn 1939 invasion of France. Completely unable to duplicate that feat later, he slipped farther into the shadows over the next two years, finally retiring at the end of *Barbarossa* for health reasons. His chief of staff, Halder, worked tirelessly to subvert the German war effort and advance his

---

15   While Wehrmacht translates to "armed forces," in common usage it can refer to the army alone.

own agenda until replaced in September 1942. Supposedly Hitler's primary military adviser as chief of OKW, Field Marshal Wilhelm Keitel was a mere toady of the Führer who failed his subordinates and his nation at every turn. The OKW operations chief, General of Artillery Alfred Jodl, practically worshipped Hitler to the point where he lost all objectivity (Jodl skipped lieutenant general when Hitler promoted him to full general). Generals in charge of the armaments industry, personnel replacements, and logistical sustainment of the fighting front doubtless worked hard but never rose to the level of difficulty required by *Barbarossa*.

Doctrine

German success prior to *Barbarossa* rested on the weakness and disorganization of its enemies and the blitzkrieg. The vast extent of the USSR and the internal cohesion of the Communist state negated the former advantage, but the latter would still dominate land combat. The blitzkrieg was never a doctrine in the sense of a system of theories and practices spelled out in German military manuals. The phrase seems to originate in attempts by contemporary Western theorists to define Wehrmacht techniques in Poland and, later, the West. At the highest levels it was executed in discrete steps, isolating its victims and destroying them one by one; it is therefore more proper to speak of a blitzkrieg campaign than of a blitzkrieg war. This technique gave resource-poor Germany a way to fight a war on the cheap – or so it thought.

The German military commanders concentrated on *Waffenkrieg* (the operational level of war) and tactics. What written doctrine they did have, *Truppenführung* (Part I was unclassified and published in 1933), discussed leadership techniques the world would come to recognize as blitzkrieg, but made very little mention of armored warfare or CAS. Once on the field of battle German officers applied this theory in combination with the independent *Stosstrupp* infiltration tactics of World War I, with General Hans von Seeckt's theories of combined arms, the meeting engagement, and the Schwerpunkt, all wedded to the internal combustion engine and the radio in order to create the blitzkrieg.

Arguably the strength of the German Wehrmacht peaked on June 21, 1941. The army's manpower stood at 3.8 million, up from 115,000 when Hitler took power. Although to a lesser degree than its Red Army adversary, it was an army still in transition. Since the physical isolation of Britain and America (Germany's assumed next victims) made them less vulnerable to blitzkrieg tactics, Hitler told von Brauchitsch to disband 35 divisions after

A hasty divisional officers' conference takes place surrounded by a variety of vehicles (clockwise from top): an SdKfz 251 half-track, SdKfz 263 eight-wheel command vehicle, a Horsch Pkw staff car, motorcycle, and Flak gun mounted on a Krupp L2H143 "Schnauzer." (HITM)

the fall of France, but on June 30, 1940 in fact only stood down 17. Others were reclassified as *Urlaubsdivisionen* (furlough divisions) whose soldiers reported to the war industries since Germany already suffered from a shortage of qualified manpower.

Subsequent re-expansion negated the army's planned modernization, stretching limited resources. On August 21 Hitler reduced the amount of infantry in each panzer division. He also halved the number of panzers in each division, thereby doubling the number of divisions, but never corrected this supposedly temporary expedient of slashing the divisions' panzer strength. Manpower and material shortages throughout the Third Reich meant that units varied in organization, strength, and equipment according to when they were created.

A German Pack Wireless Type d2 for company–battalion–regiment communications. Radios gave the Germans an advantage in command and control. During all of *Barbarossa* they captured only 149 radios from the Soviets, who relied excessively on the telegraph. (NARA)

OPPOSITE PAGE:
A convoy of trucks carrying *Bautruppen* (construction personnel) and boats for a pontoon bridge. German forces were provided with everything they thought they would need, from truckloads of beans and bullets to the telegraph poles required to string new communication lines. The failures of the logistic system lay in its inability to deliver materiel reliably to the frontlines. (HITM)

All of the Ostheer can be divided into two groups; a small motorized elite and the vast bulk of marching and horse-drawn troops. When, after the victory in France, Hitler doubled the number of panzer divisions he robbed the German infantry of much of its motor transport in the process. As a result, lessons learned in the earlier campaigns, for example the benefits of motorizing both antitank guns and artillery forward observers, could not be applied to *Barbarossa*.

During *Barbarossa*, corps' and armies' tables of organizations changed at a confusing rate. Large numbers of non-divisional units made up corps and higher echelon formations. These combat support or combat service support units often doubled the number of men in a corps beyond those simply assigned to divisions. Together the synergistic effect of all the forces in a corps greatly multiplied its combat power beyond that of the divisions alone; by task-organizing these assets, the commander built his Schwerpunkt, reinforced success, or plugged holes in his lines.

ARMY GROUP NORTH

	Mtn Corps Norway	Army Group North	Eighteenth Army	I Inf Corps	XXVI Inf Corps	Pz Group Four	XLXI Pz Corps	LVI Pz Corps	Sixteenth Army	II Inf Corps	X Inf Corps	XXVIII Inf Corps
Artillery			2 2/3**	6*	1		4*	1	2*	6**	3	3
StuG				1						1		2
Nebelwerfer							3			2		
Eng/ Construction		2	2	2	2		2	3	3	2	2	2
Eng/Pioneer				1	1	1	1	1	1***	4		3
Lt/Med Flak			2	2/3	1/3		2		2			
Hvy Flak												
LW Flak						3	3	2	3			
Inf/Machinegun	3		2		1							
Pak	1				2/3	1		1				

ARMY GROUP CENTER

	Army Group Center	Ninth Army	VIII Inf Corps	XX Inf Corps	Pz Group Three	V Inf Corps	VI Inf Corps	XXXIX Pz Corps
Artillery			14*	7*				3*
StuG			1	1		2		
Nebelwerfer			2					3
Poison Gas NW	1		1					
Eng/Construction	2	3	5	2		2	4	
Eng/Pioneer	1	2	3***	1		1	3	1
Lt/Med Flak	1/3	1	1 2/3				2/3	1
Hvy Flak		1						2 2/3
LW Flak		5			1/3			
Inf/Machinegun								
Pak		1						1 1/3
Reconaissance								
Flamethrower Pz								

ARMY GROUP SOUTH

	Army Group South	Seventeenth Army	IV Inf Corps	XLIX Mtn Corps	LII Inf Corps	Sixth Army	XVII Inf Corps	XLIV Inf Corps
Artillery		1	7*/**	2		1*	2	3*
StuG			1					
Nebelwerfer								1/3
Poison Gas NW	1							
Eng/Construction	4	9	1	1	1	4	3	2
Eng/Pioneer			1	2		1***	1	
Lt/Med Flak	1/3	1 1/3	1/3	1/3		1 1/3	1/3	1/3
Hvy Flak		1				1		
LW Flak		3				3		
Inf/Machinegun	1				1			
Pak					1			
Flamethrower Pz			1					

LVII Pz Corps	Fourth Army	VII Inf Corps	IX Inf Corps	XIII Inf Corps	XLIII Inf Corps	Pz Group Two	XII Inf Corps	XXIV Pz Corps	XLVI Pz Corps	XLVII Pz Corps
3*	2*	5*/**	4*		4*	2*	6*	3*		4*
		1	1				2			
							1 2/3	1		2
							1			
	3	3	3	2	3		3			
1	1	2			1		2	1	1	1
		1/3	1/3		1 1/3	2	1 1/3			
	2						1			
3	5						7			
							1			
							1	1		1
								1		
										1

Pz Group One	XIV Pz Corps	III Pz Corps	XXIX Inf Corps	XLVIII Pz Corps	Eleventh Army	XI Inf Corps	XXX Inf Corps	LIV Inf Corps
1		9*	2*	6*		2	2	4
		1		1	2/3	1/3		
		1		1 2/3				
		2	2	2	1			
1		2	1	3***	3	1		
2/3		1	1/3	1/3	1 1/3			
6				1	3			
1		1				1		

Infantry

Sixty of the 73 officers of Infantry Regiment 12 (31st Infantry Division), photographed in April 1941 at Kutno in occupied Poland. By December the regiment would be on its fourth commander since the start of the campaign; its losses would also include the two majors shown here, two of the three captains, one of the five physicians, and 27 of the 56 lieutenants. (Podzun)

Despite the dominant position occupied by armored divisions in many military histories, it was the infantry that bore the brunt of the Nazi–Soviet War. The Ostheer suffered 300,000 killed during *Barbarossa* – the equivalent of one regiment per day – and most of them were infantrymen, the *Landser*s. Except for the few who rode to battle with armored or motorized divisions the vast majority marched. Many considered the constant marching worse than the sporadic fighting. Regardless of how they got into combat, the infantry all fought on foot.

Most German soldiers carried a Mauser Kar98k 7.92mm bolt-action rifle with five-round magazines. German designers adapted the same ammunition to an automatic weapon when they created the excellent MG34, giving the infantry squad its own general purpose machine gun. John English calls the MG34 the "most advanced machine gun of its time."[16] After the Western campaign many squad leaders were armed with 9mm MP38 and MP40 machine-pistols. Based on observations made during the Spanish Civil War, the Landsers had learned how to defeat enemy tanks in individual combat. But they could not rely solely on individual acts of bravery to win a campaign of this nature.

---

16   English, *On Infantry*, p.89.

Despite the German infantry's prestige, within the Wehrmacht it lost the manpower battle to the SS, Luftwaffe, and Panzertruppen. Further dilution occurred when the best infantry divisions were transformed into mechanized units. Therefore, with its modernization stillborn, the infantry of 1941 looked like that of 1939 (or 1914 for that matter). According to S.J. Lewis, the better infantry divisions were those of the earlier mobilization waves: 1st (26 divisions), 2nd (16), 4th (14), 5th (4), and 7th and 8th (24) waves. Infantry leaders had suggested many improvements based on their experiences in Poland and France, but few were implemented in time for *Barbarossa*. In fact, two days before the campaign began, army inspectors judged 73 infantry divisions to be of "reduced offensive strength and mobility."

German infantry formations were organized along triangular lines (a division of three regiments, each with three battalions, etc). They depended heavily on horses, which the German soldiers discovered could not be pushed as hard as men, but needed regular water, food, and rest. Not far into campaign, small, hardy *panje* horses, native to Poland and Russia, met many of the infantry's logistics needs. As early as June 22 it became obvious that war in the USSR would be much harder than that in Poland or France. The 111th Infantry Division noted roads rendered impassable by rain as early as June 24, while clouds of dust rose from the bone-dry steppe a day later. One company commander wrote: "the roads and the day belonged to the Germans. But the forests and the night belonged to the Russians."

Artillery

In modern warfare artillery usually causes the most destruction – in both offense and defense. German artillery had been highly developed at the end of the Great War but had not progressed markedly by 1941. The German artillery branch expanded from seven regiments in 1927 to over 100 in 1940. During that period it concentrated on swift movement, rapid fire control adjustment, and combined-arms operations. Another modern innovation was to equip forward observers with radios.

At the lowest level infantry platoons were equipped with 50mm and 82mm mortars. The campaign in the West had made clear that the former were too small to be effective. Excellent 105mm infantry guns and 150mm howitzers served as the backbone of divisional and corps artillery throughout World War II. Corps and army echelon support artillery provided additional heavy artillery assets, usually deployed at critical points. Very heavy-caliber weapons were 210mm, 240mm, and 305mm cannons, howitzers, and

The forward observer for a light field howitzer battery – perched atop a haystack, with "scissors" binoculars – searches for targets, while his radio operator below relays instructions. Quick communications and accurate fire adjustment somewhat compensated for the relatively smaller German artillery branch. (MHI)

mortars. The indirect fire weapons of infantry divisions, corps, and armies were generally horse-drawn while mechanized units possessed vehicle-towed or self-propelled artillery pieces. *Nebelwerfer* ("smoke projector") rocket launchers, demoralizing multi-barreled weapons, were generally found at corps level. These 150mm weapons threw an antipersonnel round over 7,600 yards. Army Groups Center and South possessed poison-gas *Nebelwerfer* battalions, but uncommon Nazi restraint prevented their use.

Each army group possessed super-heavy artillery consisting of K5 "Bruno" (280mm) railroad guns plus some one-off variants. A single gun required two trains to move and operate and could send a 561-pound projectile up to 37½ miles. These were mainly used to reduce massive fixed fortifications of the kind found at Brest or Sevastopol.

Antitank artillery (Pak) was stretched to the limit against Red Army tanks. German 37mm guns were useless against the new Soviet models, the 50mm gun only slightly better. Larger-bore artillery, normally used for indirect fire, frequently operated to good effect against tanks over open sights. In addition to helping keep the Red Army Air Force at a distance, army and Luftwaffe large-caliber Flak (antiaircraft artillery), most notably the 88mm, were the Landser's best hope of defeating Soviet armor. However, in the first half of 1941 when the Royal Air Force stepped up attacks on Germany, Hitler ordered 15,000 army Flak guns held back to guard the

Reich. The charts above show how sparsely Flak units were distributed. Often only one or two batteries covered an entire corps area; clearly only high-value targets could be protected in these cases. Finally, Germany only partially adopted the infantry-support tank (the 75mm short-barrel PzKpfw IV) used by other nations and instead employed the *Sturmgeschütz* (StuG or assault gun), which was employed in the infantry-support role. During *Barbarossa* most StuG consisted of the same short-barrel 75mm gun mounted on a PzKpfw III chassis.

Panzers

German mechanization, especially in the form of tanks, was cutting-edge in the 1930s. The German Army experimented with armored warfare at their Grafenwöhr training area and during autumn maneuvers prior to 1932. Panzers gained essential political support during Guderian's famous demonstration in 1933, the year that Hitler came to power. In 1935 the first three panzer divisions were established, and two years later one of them made its debut at the autumn maneuvers. The German Army also created its first panzer corps in 1935; the panzer branch had come into its own and from that point forward became a truly operational weapon.

The loader of a 105mm artillery piece. Artillery fire exceeded that of previous Wehrmacht campaigns by a massive margin. Artillery ammunition was the largest single commodity in the German logistics system. (NARA)

The new panzers epitomized much of Germany's success during the first part of World War II. Panzer divisions usually had two to three panzer battalions, five infantry battalions (four truck or half-track mounted, one on motorcycles), and three artillery battalions. Motorized infantry divisions, which often combined with the panzers to create a panzer corps, consisted of seven infantry, three to four artillery battalions, and occasionally a panzer battalion.

A panzer battalion usually included three companies of PzKpfw IIIs and one company of PzKpfw IVs. Light panzers, such as the PzKpfw II, were most numerous but had been intended primarily as a stopgap measure pending the introduction of the PzKpfw III and IV. The Ostheer also fielded many captured tanks, including the Czech tank designated PzKpfw 38(t) in German service. They were well-built, reliable and roughly equivalent to the

37mm PzKpfw III: the 8th Panzer Division having 118 on its order of battle. The older and smaller Skoda 35(t)s were obsolete in 1941, although the 6th Panzer still possessed 155 of them. Captured French tanks were unsuited to German doctrine and were generally passed on to Germany's allies.

Despite impressive performances in 1939–40, one-quarter of all the German tanks employed in the West in 1940 had been lost – a total of 683. In 1941, when the Wehrmacht still relied upon modestly updated versions of prewar designs that were at least equal to the great bulk of even older Soviet types, the Red Army was receiving a new and superior generation of tanks in the form of the T-34 medium and KV heavy designs. These made their mark during *Barbarossa's* first days and German inferiority in production capacity would soon prove equally significant.

Barbarossa's armored formations were concentrated in the panzer groups. As "groups" these did not have the full complement of engineer, artillery, signals, and other support units associated with a numbered army. After the panzer groups became panzer armies between October 1941 and January 1942 they gained these assets.

Logistics

Barbarossa suffered from weak logistics from its earliest days as planners tried unsuccessfully to wish away monumental logistics problems. It is doubtful that if Germany had fielded larger forces its logistics system could have supported them. Planners assumed the Ostheer would live off the land, in much the same way as had Napoleon's armies in 1812. This is essentially what happened in fact, and the German commanders were quite successful at improvisation. OKH wargames recommended a logistics pause less than a month into the operation. The German forces would indeed slow down to allow supplies to catch up but relentless Soviet counterattacks would give them no "pause" while continuous defensive combat also puts a massive strain on support. Logisticians based *Barbarossa's* ammunition usage on the highest expenditures in the campaigns in the West – a flawed assumption. Separate and redundant supply systems for the army, Luftwaffe, and individual allies added further problems.

The chaotic internal administration of the Nazis spilled over into the sustainment arena. Wehrmacht agencies operated the railroads while the *Grosstransportraum* (figuratively a bridge between railroads and units) and the *Aussenstelle* (a higher-level depot system) reported to the army's Quartermaster General – none accountable to the operational commander.

In one example, Army Group North was supposed to receive 34 supply trains per day but never got more than 18, and achieving even that figure was rare. Non-standard vehicles created supply and maintenance nightmares; one artillery regiment fielded 69 different vehicle types.

In a theater of war with very few paved roads and where most other roads alternated between chocking dust and glutinous mud depending on the weather, rail transport was especially important. Soviet railroads had to first be cleared of Red Army units, and then German specialists converted the rail system to one they could use. Not only did the Germans have to change the rail gauge, a simple but manpower-intensive job, but Soviet signal facilities required modernization, Russian water stations were too far apart for smaller German locomotives and German coal had to augment the poor-quality Russian coal. German logistics plans also assumed taking some rail lines and rolling stock intact, something not always possible due to over-zealous Luftwaffe "train busters."

The *Grosstransportraum,* the truck transport between the railheads and the armies and forward to tactical units, was stretched to the limit. Poor convoy discipline caused further, self-inflicted hardships. A normal infantry

An SS private and *Unterscharführer* attempt to cross a swollen stream with their field kitchen ("Goulash cannon"). Cooked food might be a luxury where campaign planners figured living off the land was good enough for the Ostheer. (NARA)

Regauging railroads in the USSR was labor-intensive and time consuming. Decades earlier, when developing their rail network, the Russians modeled theirs on American and Canadian examples, where continental distances were more similar than those in France or Germany. (Nik Cornish at www. Stavka.org.uk)

division had 942 vehicles (not counting motorcycles) and 1,200 horses. Often augmented with hundreds of panje horses, these beasts carried many supplies. As the Ostheer moved east and numbers of POWs mounted, many of these men volunteered to drive wagons, care for horses, handle supplies, and prepare food. At times these *Hiwis* (volunteers) numbered up to 2,000 per division, or one-fifth of its strength. However, partisans represented a constant threat to rail lines, bridges, rearward communications, and support infrastructure throughout the Nazi occupation of the USSR.

Two special army formations present in *Barbarossa* deserve mention:

Infantry Regiment Grossdeutschland (GD): This elite army formation began as a Berlin guard company with ceremonial duties; by the war's end it had grown into a complete mechanized corps. Its name, meaning Greater Germany, indicated that its soldiers were chosen from all over the country rather than from a specific *Wehrkreis*[17] as with most of the army. In 1941 it was much stronger than its official designation suggested; GD had three infantry battalions, each with three line companies, a machine-gun company, and a heavy company. A fourth battalion grouped a light infantry gun, an

---

17   Military District – one of 17 army administrative divisions of Germany who were responsible for milization, recruiting, etc.

antitank, a heavy infantry gun and an assault gun company; reconnaissance, pioneer, signal, and Flak companies made up the 5th Battalion; and the regiment also had an artillery battalion and a logistics column.

Lehr Brigade (Motorized) 900: In order to keep army branch-of-service schools current with developments in the field, instructors needed combat experience; so the Replacement Army commander agreed to requests from these schools to create a unit to participate in *Barbarossa*, so long as this did not compromise their primary instruction mission. The brigade's organization was unsatisfactory, since minimizing the impact on the schools outweighed the need to create an efficient fighting unit. Lehr Brigade (mot) 900 consisted of a headquarters, two battalions from the Döberitz Infantry School, one each panzer (using captured French tanks) and antitank battalions from the Wünsdorf Panzer School, an artillery battalion, and an assault gun battery from the Jüterbog Artillery School, plus medical and logistics support. Its supposed three-month deployment in fact lasted until March 1942, by which time it had been worn down to two companies and a few heavy weapons.

Luftwaffe

The Luftwaffe entered *Barbarossa* using the same Bf-109s, He-111s, Ju-52s, and Ju-87s (with some modifications) as it used during the Spanish Civil War. After the costly Battle of Britain the Luftwaffe entered *Barbarossa* on June 22, 1941 with fewer aircraft than it had for the Western campaign 13 months earlier. Führer Directive 21 gave the Luftwaffe three concurrent missions: 1) defend Germany, its allies and occupied territories; 2) continue the war against England and its shipping; and 3) attack the Soviet Union. Luftwaffe strength was thus dissipated over the continent of Europe (and, soon, north Africa). More than 1,500 aircraft were employed in these secondary theatres while the Luftwaffe simultaneously tried to rule the skies over the world's largest theater of war. It employed many obsolete aircraft that were considered good enough to confront the even more antiquated equipment of the Red Army Air Force. Further, no less than half of its transport aircraft had been lost on Crete during the German invasion of the island in the weeks immediately prior to *Barbarossa*. Lastly, despite the efforts of von Richthofen and others, German air-ground coordination was still rudimentary.

Even with the astounding destruction meted out to the Red Army Air Force during *Barbarossa*'s opening days, the Luftwaffe did not have the strength to fly both air-superiority and CAS missions so the Soviet airpower rapidly bounced back. The same miserable conditions on the ground with

A Bf 109F of II/JG-53 Pik
As (Ace of Spades) on an
Estonian airfield alongside the
burnt-out shell of a Red Army
Air Force Polikarpov fighter.
Except when reinforced by VIII
Fliegerkorps, Luftflotte 1 was
another formation trying to
fight *Barbarossa's* northern tier
on a shoe-string, much to the
Army's frustration. (HITM)

which the army had to contend created boggy airfields and prevented the forward movement of maintenance, supply, and communications assets. Furthermore, the Luftwaffe underestimated the situation in the air in three critical ways: 1) they evidently did not realize that most of the Soviet aircraft destroyed during *Barbarossa's* first days were obsolete; 2) while they destroyed a great number of aircraft many of the pilots survived; and 3) they misjudged the recuperative powers of the Soviet aircraft industry.

The air component in the north, Luftflotte 1, was smallest of those supporting the army groups. It possessed 592 aircraft, with 453 of those in an airworthy condition on June 22. Luftflotte 5 in Norway contributed little (just 200 aircraft) considering its huge area of operations. In the north the Red Army Air Force outnumbered the Luftwaffe nearly 3:1 in bombers, over 7:1 in fighters, and nearly 4:1 overall. Against these Army Group North had only three Flak regiments assigned. Airborne forces made a brief appearance in the Leningrad area. After recovering from its losses on Crete, the 7th Flieger Division fought on foot around Shlisselburg from mid-September until mid-December.

Luftflotte 2 supporting Army Group Center represented the largest air component with two *Fliegerkorps*, II and VIII, plus the I Flak Corps. Including VIII Fliegerkorps (see below) Field Marshal Albert Kesselring counted two fighter, one Zerstörer, two bomber and one Stuka *Gruppen* plus reconnaissance and transport units. He commanded 1,367 aircraft, of which 994 were operational on *Barbarossatag*. The I Flak Corps had two Flak regiments. The operational area of Luftflotte 2 measured 180 miles wide by 600 miles deep.

Von Richthofen's elite VIII Fliegerkorps had to move from Greece and Yugoslavia to Suwalki after the Balkan campaign, so 600 of its vehicles and 40 percent of its aircraft were unavailable on *Barbarossatag*. At its peak the VIII Fliegerkorps consisted of 87 twin-engine medium bombers, 50 Ju-87B Stukas and 26 Henschel Hs-123 biplane dive-bombers, 22 Messerschmitt Bf-110 twin-engine fighters, and 66 Bf-109 single-engine fighters. However, von Bock did not always have VIII Fliegerkorps flying overhead in support of his army group; as a strategic asset higher headquarters moved it throughout the theater in order to create an aerial Schwerpunkt.

Army Group South air operations suffered from a number of handicaps: it was not the German main effort and so not fully resourced, it had no Stukas and many of its air assets were committed to the defense of Rumania's oil fields. In all von Rundstedt could count on the aerial support of 887 aircraft, 694 of which were operational on June 22. Luftflotte 4's CAS came from two Gruppen of Ju-88s and one fighter *Gruppe* fitted with ground-attack sights and ordnance mounting points. Seven *Gruppen* of Bf-109s provided fighter cover while the II Flak Corps, including the elite General Göring Regiment, mainly protected First Panzer Group's spearheads.

A truck-mounted 20mm Flak 38 takes on a Soviet column. The truck's white "K" stands for von Kleist's First Panzer Group. An entire Luftwaffe Flak corps accompanied von Kleist. (NARA)

In April V Fliegerkorps deployed from the Channel coast to southeast Poland. It flew in support of the Sixth and Seventeenth Armies and von Kleist's panzers. It covered an area 200 miles wide at the start and ultimately 900 miles deep, reaching all the way to Rostov. The IV Fliegerkorps moved from France to Rumania in May. From there it supported the southern flank, initially against Bessarabia and the Crimea. Its front was approximately 350 miles wide and 300 miles deep.

German Flak forces deployed 239 heavy and 135 medium and light batteries in the east on *Barbarossatag*. These numbers represented respectively only 20 percent and 15 percent of Germany's total, with the mass of the remainder defending the Reich in the west.

Each Axis ally had its own air force. Rumania contributed approximately 350 front-line aircraft, Finland 300, Italy 80, and Hungary an additional 50.

Waffen-SS

In the bizarre polycracy of Nazi Germany fiefdoms competed for power. Around the time of *Barbarossa*, Reichsführer Heinrich Himmler's personal army eclipsed Göring's Luftwaffe as the hyper-politicized darling of the Wehrmacht. Two SS divisions fought in Army Group North: Totenkopf and

The crew of an SS 37mm Pak 36 cross a stream in their Krupp L2H 43 "Schnauzer" truck. Maintenance and supply for the bewildering number of non-standard vehicles from all over Europe multiplied the Wehrmacht's logistical woes. (NARA)

Polizei. Totenkopf was essentially a motorized infantry formation. Polizei, foot infantry, consisted of mobilized policemen. It received recognition as an SS division in 1942. Division Nord, another ad hoc organization, fought in Finland with very uneven results. It was the Army of Norway's only motorized formation.

SS Division Reich in Army Group Center began as a collection of SS-Standarten (regiments) during the Polish campaign. These were united as the SS-Verfügungs Division for France and then renamed "Reich" on February 25, 1941. During *Barbarossa*, Reich was a motorized division made up of three motorized infantry regiments, an artillery regiment, and more than the usual number of assigned battalions.

Von Rundstedt's army group included two SS formations – Leibstandarte SS Adolf Hitler (LSSAH) and SS Motorized Division Viking. Like all SS units in 1941 they consisted of volunteers drawn from among the best of German manpower. The LSSAH grew out of Hitler's personal bodyguard and was commanded by the Führer's crony, Josef "Sepp" Dietrich. Starting in 1940 it grew from a regiment into a brigade and finally a division, although this reorganization was incomplete on *Barbarossatag*. Viking was a full division, originating with Standarte Germania. Its uniqueness came from its Scandinavian and Western European volunteers. Regiment Nordland hailed largely from Denmark and Norway while Westland was made up of Dutch and Flemish volunteers.

In addition to these Waffen SS formations, security units such as Einsatzgruppen and Polizei units under SS command followed close behind the army groups to pursue the Nazis' genocidal policies of summary execution on racial and political grounds.

Justice, Nazi occupation style: Soviet citizen hanged from a telephone pole for some now unknown reason and left for all to see as life in the town goes on. (Corbis)

Kriegsmarine

While the German Navy's primary mission was to fight the Royal Navy, it had much in common with its Soviet counterpart: in their national-strategic schemes, both were subordinated to the army and air force; both underwent accelerated development in the 1930s, and both stressed undersea warfare, especially using submarines and mines. Kriegsmarine ships operating in the Baltic usually consisted of three to four light cruisers, five U-Boats, 30–40 fast patrol boats, plus numerous minelayer/sweepers and sub-chasers. The Finns contributed two heavy monitors, four gunboats, five submarines, and six patrol boats. However, coordination between the two navies was weak.

The Navy was not fully integrated into the *Barbarossa* plan; sea transport in the Baltic came as an afterthought and an all-out naval effort was not considered necessary. The Germans began mining the Gulfs of Finland and Riga on June 12. Other Kriegsmarine missions included preventing the Red Banner Fleet from escaping from the Baltic and from launching amphibious operations. In the south, the German Navy was essentially absent from the Black Sea.

Other Nationalities

In addition to lacking certain key natural resources, for which it was at least partly dependent on the Soviet Union, Germany had other weaknesses which Hitler sought to offset to some degree with the Tripartite Treaty of September 27, 1940 between Nazi Germany, Fascist Italy, and Imperial Japan. Intended to build an anti-Soviet coalition and warn the US to keep out of Europe, the Pact of Steel only gave "the image of Axis solidarity."[18]

Hitler did not, however, include his more senior Italian and Japanese allies in *Barbarossa's* planning, preferring instead to rely on his smaller Eastern European allies. Interestingly, centuries of hostility meant that the Hungarians and Rumanians hated each other as much as their common Soviet foe. Another planning headache for the German High Command was keeping their two antagonistic allies from serving side-by-side. Reliability, both at home and on the battlefield, and logistics would remain a constant problem for all of Germany's allies. In reality, the German leaders had very little faith in the fighting abilities of any of their allies, even the Finns.

---

18   Erickson and Dilks, *Barbarossa*, p.87.

Austria

While fully absorbed into the Greater German Reich in 1938, Austria had its own identity and military traditions. Numerous Wehrmacht units had Austrian origins and Austrian personnel. On April 1, 1936 Austria had thrown off the post-World War I Treaty of St Germain and instituted its own universal military service laws. Its forces grew from barely 20,000 men in six brigades to over 60,000 in seven infantry and one fast/mobile division plus two aviation regiments by the time of the *Anschluss* with Germany. Its Bundesheer officially became part of the Wehrmacht on April 1, 1938 and Austrian formations were subsumed into the German military.

Finland

Finland's distance from Germany gave it a measure of independence from Hitler's influence yet it still wanted to recover lost territories and gain some advantage in the new European order so obvious in the spring of 1941. As part of the restructuring of Europe's power structure in 1809 by Napoleon,

Axis commanders in Finland; von Falkenhorst and Mannerheim. The Finnish border with the USSR was two-thirds as long as the main front from Memel to the Black Sea. However, the theater was doomed as a strategic backwater plagued by complicated command relationships and few mutual objectives. (Ediciones Dolmen)

Finland became a Russian grand duchy and for the next 100 years the Finns strained under the Russian yoke. During the Russian Civil War (1917–22), with the help of a German army corps, forces under Marshal Mannerheim won Finnish independence. In the Winter War of 1939–40 the Soviet Union took its revenge. Stalin launched the Red Army against Finland and, despite an inept performance from the Soviet forces and heroic resistance by the Finns, the result was inevitable. Finland lost 23,000 killed and 45,000 wounded, and had to evacuate 420,000 people from lands ceded to the USSR, approximately 10 percent of its territory. So while Stalin secured Leningrad he created a dangerous enemy. On the other hand, Hitler's tepid support for Finland during the Winter War frequently left lingering doubts in the minds of the small nation's leadership.

Axis-Allied Dictators

Ion Antonescu, 1882–1946, Rumanian Marshal

The Rumanian dictator served as defense minister under King Carol II. In 1940, in that position, he proved incapable of halting the loss of Bessarabia and Northern Bukovina to the USSR or Dobruja to Bulgaria or Transylvania to Hungary. In September of that year Carol abdicated in favor of his son Michael, and Antonescu was named *Conductor* (Leader) in the National Legionary State established jointly with the Fascist Iron Guard movement. In January 1941 Antonescu eliminated the Iron Guard with Hitler's help (after a debate within the Nazi hierarchy as to which side Germany would back). A German military mission to Rumania soon followed, supposedly to train the Rumanian military, protect the oil fields, and prepare for *Barbarossa*.

Cavalry officer Antonescu served in staff positions during World War I and was personally decorated for bravery by King Ferdinand. When he was nominated as military attaché to France in 1920, the French objected, describing him as "vain, chauvinistic, and xenophobic." Conversely, Hitler praised his "breadth of vision" and called him a "real personality." Antonescu was an avowed anti-Communist and anti-Semite. With the German Eleventh Army, he led the Rumanians across the Prut River, "liberated" Bessarabia, and invested Odessa. His inept and wasteful siege of that Black Sea port cost 100,000 lives, basically the flower of Rumania's prewar military. Thereafter Rumanian forces helped subdue

the Crimea. The following year the battles of Stalingrad caused another 150,000 Rumanian casualties.

Suffering from undisclosed medical problems, Antonescu withdrew from active public politics but still led Rumania and supported Germany. As Red Army forces overran the Ukraine he possibly tried to negotiate a deal with the Western Allies. A royal coup on August 23, 1944 overthrew and arrested Antonescu. After the war a People's Tribunal convicted him of crimes against peace and treason and executed him on June 1, 1946.

Miklos Horthy, 1868–1957, Admiral and Regent of the Kingdom of Hungary

An officer in the Austro-Hungarian Navy, Horthy served as prewar naval aide-de-camp to Emperor Franz Josef, won a minor naval engagement at Otranto and ended World War I commanding the navy. He was declared Regent (or "Protector") and Head of State in 1920 following the brief Hungarian Socialist Republic. Horthy served as head of state in a parliamentary republic until the Depression caused Hungary to move toward extreme conservatism.

Wedged between Hitler to the west and Stalin to the east, anti-Communist Horthy favored the former. Horthy refused to participate in the dismemberment of Czechoslovakia but Hitler gave Hungary the southern portion of Slovakia anyway. Horthy joined the Anti-Comintern Pact in February 1939 and withdrew from the League of Nations two months later. In

In August 1940, the USSR once more massed troops on the Finnish border, making new demands on Finland which Molotov amplified during his Berlin visit. Therefore both Germany and Finland discovered expedient reasons to reorient their relationship. Shortly thereafter a member of Göring's staff made the first secret contacts. Both Führer Directive 21 and the *Aufmarschanweisung* allowed Finland a modest role in *Barbarossa*. The first tentative talks between German and Finnish military planners followed in the winter and spring of 1941. Hitler wanted Finnish assistance in three main areas: pressure on Leningrad, help against the Arctic ports and the Murmansk railroad, and raw materials – especially the nickel mines at Petsamo. Eager to avenge losses suffered during the Winter War, Finland agreed to most of the German expectations. However, Finland was not at

August 1940 Hitler rewarded Hungary with northern Transylvania taken from Rumania. On June 27, 1941 Horthy declared war on the Soviet Union. Eighteen months later, 200,000 poorly equipped troops of the Hungarian Second Army suffered 84 percent casualties during the Soviet's Stalingrad counteroffensive. At this point Horthy's already-lukewarm support of Hitler became downright tepid.

In April 1943 Hitler demanded that Horthy take tougher measures against Hungary's 800,000 Jews; Horthy complied with Hitler's demands as little as possible. In June, Horthy refused Hitler's request for Hungarian reinforcement to Russia. Months later Hungary actively schemed to bail on the Axis cause. Goebbels recorded in his diary in September 1943, "As regards the possibilities of treachery by other satellite states, Horthy would like to desert us, but the Führer has already taken the necessary precautions against this."

In March 1944 Horthy pleaded with Hitler to recall Hungarian troops fighting the USSR and to cease using Hungary as a base for military transport. When Hitler threatened occupation, Horthy decided to allow German troops to occupy Hungary. He also accepted Hitler's demand to hand over Jews to the SS. However under pressure from the Western Allies, in August Horthy replaced the pro-Nazi ministers, stopped Jewish deportations, then announced Hungary's withdrawal from the Axis and broadcast his intention to seek peace. Forced to resign in favor of the Fascist Arrow Cross Party leader, Horthy was promptly arrested and taken to Germany as a "guest of honor" until liberated by American troops in May 1945. The following December Horthy was released from Nuremberg to exile in Portugal where he wrote his memoirs.

Jozef Tiso, 1887–1947, President of Slovakia

A Roman Catholic priest who, following a short stint as a military chaplain in World War I, became involved in separatist Slovak politics. Tiso rose through the Slovak People's Party (founded by another priest) until, upon the death of the party's leader in 1938, he was in charge. In March 1939 as the Nazis destroyed Czechoslovakia Tiso arrived in Berlin to be blackmailed by Hitler: either submit to German "protection" or be partitioned between Hungary and Poland.

Slovakia contributed one corps-sized group to *Barbarossa*. Tiso's anti-Semitism seemed to mesh nicely with Hitler's and Tiso deported tens of thousands of Jews to their death. Hitler occupied Slovakia in October 1944 following the failed national uprising and the Red Army conquered the country in the following year. Tiso technically served as president until 3 April although the Slovak Republic had basically ceased to exist months earlier. He was tried and in April 1947 hanged for collaboration with Nazi Germany.

war and Helsinki crawled with foreign diplomats. Partly as a result, Hitler kept Finland out of serious planning until late May 1941. Finland's limited goals for World War II were: freedom from Soviet intimidation, reliable sources of food, and restoration of the 1939 borders.

Prior to the Winter War the Finnish Amy had not exceeded 200,000 men in nine operational divisions armed with World War I-era weapons. For *Barbarossa* it mobilized nearly 475,000 troops in 16 divisions and three independent brigades supplied with more modern German ordnance. Equipment, from helmets to tanks, came from every army in Europe – making for a logistical disaster. Between the Winter and Continuation Wars,[19] 105mm and 120mm artillery and associated antitank forces benefited from new German weaponry. Finland fielded one tank battalion that was part of the 1st Jäger Brigade (light troops mounted on bicycles in summer) plus seven platoons of British and captured Soviet tanks. Divisions were relatively small and usually commanded by a colonel. A principal strength was the individual Finnish soldier and his familiarity with the extremes of fighting in the heavily forested far-north theater. By the end of 1941 Finland had suffered 75,000 casualties.

Hungary

Hitler lacked faith in Hungary as a result of its weak support during the crises of 1938 and 1939. Therefore he forbade most military contacts prior to *Barbarossa*. In the spring of 1941 Hungary volunteered to conduct mopping-up operations in Yugoslavia behind advancing German troops, alarming the USSR and linking Hungary to the Reich. In recognition of German assistance at the Vienna Award of August 1940 in regaining territory lost in the Trianon Treaty of 1920, Hungary contributed a small contingent to *Barbarossa*. Hungary formally joined the Axis war effort on June 27, 1941 after supposedly being bombed the day before by the Red Army Air Force (in reality possibly by Rumanian aircraft).

In 1941 the Hungarian Army counted 29 divisions, each of which had only one regular regiment during peacetime. The army was well-trained and competent but lacked modern equipment and was not equal to the rigors of World War II combat. For *Barbarossa* it contributed a 24,000-strong Fast Corps of two motorized and one cavalry brigades (largely using requisitioned civilian vehicles for mobility) under Lieutenant General F. Szombathely and a

---

19   Finnish names for wars against the USSR respectively from November 30, 1939 to March 13, 1940 and June 25, 1942 to September 19, 1944.

like number of marching troops. Armored forces consisted of 81 indigenous Toldi tanks, mounting only a 20mm gun. Hungarian air contingents flew mostly second-rate German (He-112s) and Italian (Fiat C.R. 42s) machines. Hungarian forces first saw action on July 9 but played a steadily declining role. They tried to remove the Fast Corps from the fighting in early September but Hitler refused permission. By November, obsolete weapons, high losses and a lack of enthusiasm led the Fast Corps to be withdrawn from the active front.

A Hungarian general talks on a field phone while a German liaison officer looks on. The Germans usually attached liaison officers to the commanders and headquarters of their allies, both to help and give advice, but also to keep an eye on the allies' activities. (Nik Cornish at www.Stavka.org.uk)

Italy

In terms of preparedness the Italian Army had peaked in the mid-1930s and by World War II it was both trying to catch up with the other major European powers and in the middle of another reorganization. At fewer than 10,000 men its divisions were small and the same can be said of its under-gunned artillery, outdated armor and insufficient support echelons. Hitler left Germany's closest ally out of *Barbarossa*'s plans; he wanted Italy to concentrate on the Mediterranean. Nevertheless, Benito Mussolini created the Italian Expedition Corps in Russia (CSIR), eventually under the command of 57-year-old General Giovanni Messe, a former aide-de-camp of King Victor

Emmanuel III and one of the few competent Italian generals to emerge from the previous Albanian and Greek operations. Although technically taking orders from the Italian High Command in Rome, it was seldom actually commanded by Messe and initially came under the operational control of the German Eleventh Army. Italian Air Force units were subordinated to local Luftwaffe headquarters.

The CSIR consisted of two infantry divisions, the 9th Pasubio and 52nd Torino, and one "cavalry-motorized" division, the 3rd Principe Amedeo Duca d'Aosta. The former had two infantry and one artillery regiments plus the normal assortment of support troops. Duca d'Aosta counted two cavalry, one Bersaglieri (fast light infantry), and one motorized artillery regiments in addition to support troops. The CSIR included the 30th Corps Artillery Group. The Italians called their infantry units "auto-transportable," which the Germans wishfully misinterpreted as "motorized." This misnomer frustrated the Germans and upset the Italian troops, who marched everywhere! A mere battalion of L6/40 light tanks made armored operations difficult.

Altogether CSIR numbered 62,000 officers and men, 960 artillery pieces, and 670 antiaircraft and antitank guns, plus 5,500 wheeled vehicles (many commercial) and 4,600 horses and mules. Individual Italian soldiers were undeniably brave but shared none of the German soldiers' crusading spirit. Italian officers had minimal contact with their troops and each company possessed only six to eight NCOs. Torino's commander, Brigadier General Ugo de Carolis, died in December fighting along the Mius River as part of First Panzer Army; the Germans posthumously awarded him the Knight's Cross. Of the CSIR's 62,000 troops, over 8,700 became casualties during *Barbarossa* (half of those were killed in action) and barely 4,000 ever returned to Italy.

Rumania

The defeat of France, its traditional patron, and its fear of the USSR pushed Rumania into the German fold. Rumania put its entire military at Germany's disposal for *Barbarossa* – the only Axis ally to do so. The country suffered approximately 100,000 casualties during *Barbarossa* alone. In the summer of 1940 the country was in dire straits; Stalin seized Bessarabia, former allies France and Britain were either crushed by Germany or struggling for self-preservation, and finally Hitler and Mussolini awarded large tracts of her territory to Bulgaria and Hungary.

Huge petroleum reserves and a lengthy border with the USSR made Rumania indispensable to the Reich. The Ploesti oil fields provided one-half of Germany's needs. Occupying Bessarabia put Soviet forces only 100 miles

Battlefield Conditions

The northern theater began in Lithuania, basically the edge of the North European Plain, which has many wetlands and mixed forest regions. Latvia is heavily forested while Estonia is nearly one-quarter swampland. Two large lakes, Peipus and Il'men, dominated the center of the combat zone and the many watercourses that feed them create a swampy morass. Further east are the Valdai Hills which were not significantly higher than other terrain encountered during *Barbarossa* (c.1,100 feet elevation) but contain the headwaters of the Dvina, Dnepr, and Volga rivers. The interior of the theater consisted of terrain and vegetation that could be considered worst for mechanized warfare but ideal for partisan operations.

Leningrad was the most remarkable manmade feature in the Army Group North area. Famously made by slave labor under Peter the Great from drained swampland on the site of an old Swedish fortress on the Neva River delta, St Petersburg (Petrograd during World War I) was the Russian capital from 1712 to 1918. In 1941 its population was 3 million but the ravages of the 900-day siege cut that number by 80 percent two years later. To the city's east is Europe's largest lake, Ladoga, which became Leningrad's lifeline during the siege. The barrier represented by the Gulf of Finland, Leningrad, and Lake Ladoga prevented the German and Finnish armies from ever linking up.

Belorussia has no natural frontiers, and for centuries the native population had resisted Mongol, Kievan, Lithuanian, Polish, Russian, German, and Soviet masters. The theater of war covered here literally and figuratively divided the western USSR. To the north lay the lake district, where Scandinavian ice sheets had scoured out the thin layer of earth; to the south were the Rokitno Marshes and other poorly drained areas. In between, marking the farthest advance of the glaciers, lay deposits that created the drainage divide along the line Grodno–Minsk–Smolensk–Valdai Hills. The contemporary highway and rail lines followed this traditional commercial

and invasion route (called the Post Road in Napoleonic times). Roughly parallel routes ran from Latvia through Vitebsk and Rzhev (in 1941, Hoth's area), and from Brest through Gomel and Bryansk (Guderian's area).

This River Gate represented the ridgeline's crowning feature – basically the relative high ground (in reality, only approximately 600 feet in elevation) – between Vitebsk and Orsha and centered on Smolensk. Hoth described this feature as being approximately 42 miles wide: enough room for three armored divisions to maneuver. The lobe pattern representing the glacier's margin also had military significance – for example, in the northward jut of the Berezina River.

Some words on Ukrainian geography: south of the Rokitno Marshes mentioned above the soil was fine and humus-rich, producing particularly nasty mud that evaporated slowly. The *rasputitsa* ensued numerous times each spring and autumn as temperatures rose and fell and roads alternately turned into quagmires or froze solid. The Ukraine lacked the vast forests found north of the marshes. It did contain numerous large rivers, the Dnepr being over a mile wide in many places. Interestingly, these rivers did not constitute a significant tactical barrier but hamstrung logistics – operations east of the Dnepr caused German rear echelon troops constant headaches. The western Ukraine began rising elevations toward the Hungarian highlands.

Kiev was the Ukraine's capital and largest city with a prewar population of under 400,000. To the east, near Kharkov and in the Donets Basin (Donbas), centered on Stalino, stood huge industrial and mining enterprises. The same could be found on the great bend of the Dnepr River at Dnepropetrovsk, Krivoi Rog, and Zaporozhe. Nikolaev on the Bug River was a large inland naval base. These resource areas were key objectives in Hitler's economic concept of the war and they would see brutal urban fighting throughout *Barbarossa* and indeed the entire Nazi–Soviet War.

Field Marshal von Brauchitsch (center) and Marshal Antonescu (left) enter a car as staffers look on. During *Barbarossa* the Rumanian proved to be a staunch ally if not quite a stellar commander. (Nik Cornish at www.Stavka.org.uk)

away from the wells and refineries. Both main authors of *Barbarossa*, Marcks and von Lossberg, believed that the country was essential for attacking Odessa and the Crimea plus defending Ploesti. In November 1940, Rumania signed the Tripartite Agreement and soon German Army and Luftwaffe personnel in Rumania numbered 63,000. However, the German High Command formally briefed the Rumanians on *Barbarossa* only two days prior to the start of operations.

Rumanian military reorganization on the German model took place amid political turmoil. The Rumanian army had previously concentrated on defensive doctrine using French methods where infantry and especially artillery benefited. German offensive doctrine and techniques were unfamiliar to the Rumanians and their armored forces struggled accordingly. Senior Rumanian officers trained earlier by the French resisted, while younger officers studied in Germany and caught on more quickly. Equipment consisted of a combination of purchased Czech, captured (by the Nazis)

Dutch, loaned French, donated German, interned Polish, and indigenous Rumanian gear – a maintenance disaster.

The Rumanian Third and Fourth Armies – Army Group Antonescu – numbered 325,000 men. German training concentrated on the 5th, 6th, and 13th Infantry Divisions and the German leaders naturally considered these, along with the Frontier and Guards Divisions, the three cavalry and three mountain brigades, the most combat ready. They regarded Rumanian soldiers as resourceful and tough fighters with only modest needs. However, they also felt their allies' officers were corrupt and indifferent to their troops. Nevertheless, a former German general gave the Rumanian military credit for *Barbarossa*'s successes. The German Military Mission headquarters, trainers, and "advisors" became the Eleventh Army in May 1941 and technically took control of all operations as soon as Axis forces crossed the Prut River on July 2.

Slovakia

As part of the former Austrian Empire the Slovak military had some familiarity with German methods and language. The German military did not train Slovak units although some officers and NCOs went to Germany for military schooling. Slovakia contributed c.45,000 men to *Barbarossa*, mostly marching infantry in two divisions under Minister of Defense and Chief of Staff Ferdinand Catlos. One motorized unit, the Slovak Mobile Command under 2nd Division commander Rudolf Pilfousek, numbering 132 tanks and 43 other armored vehicles, managed to keep up with the German forces and came under the control of 17th Army. The marching elements soon fell behind the front lines and were divided into two units: 1) the 1st Fast Division under 1st Division commander Augustin Maler, eventually rejoined the fighting in the First Panzer area; 2) the remainder, the 2nd Security Division, was relegated to rear security missions for Army Group South. German commanders considered Slovak officers indolent and lacking any concept of duty and their soldiers generally poor. Their first encounter with the Red Army at Lipovec resulted in a stinging defeat. By October the German leaders assigned even the better formations to reduced missions only.

Spain

In appreciation for German assistance during the Spanish Civil War, General Francisco Franco sent one 18,000-man formation, the Blue Division (so named because of its blue Falangist uniform shirts), to Germany. One of

Spanish volunteers from the 250th "Blue" Infantry Division, in this case former students from Valencia, photographed on September 18. The Spanish fought bravely in the Army Group North sector until as late as 1944. (NARA)

Franco's trusted Moroccan comrades, General Augustin Munoz Grandes, commanded the outfit. Its "volunteers," consisting mostly of army officers and soldiers but also Falangists and anti-Communist students, fought mainly around Leningrad and Volkhov with uneven results. After three months of combat the Blue Division had sustained 3,000 casualties.

Occupation Policies

With *Barbarossa*, the political lordship over eastern Poland and western Belorussia and Ukraine passed from the NKVD to the SS. The Soviet Union's own brutal 21-month occupation of these areas prior to June 1941 caused many inhabitants to welcome the Wehrmacht; Nazi concepts on the relative value of human life soon put an end to such naive notions. The main outcomes of the Nazis' genocidal racial obsessions were a vengeful populace, a new legitimacy for Stalin and Communism, the tying down of huge and wasteful occupation forces, and, ultimately, shame for the German nation.

Members of the Reichsarbeitsdienst (RAD) "Tomaschek" unit. Numerous paramilitary organizations competed with the military for a share of the German manpower pool. The RAD and "Organization Todt" perhaps contributed most to the military effort. (NARA)

Closely related is the German's inhumane and illegal treatment of Red Army prisoners of war. On the one hand, they treated these Slavic *Untermenschen* in accordance with Nazi racial theories. On the other hand, despite accurately anticipating huge encirclements, they were completely unprepared for the massive numbers of POWs actually captured during *Barbarossa* (exacerbated by fact that the campaign far exceeded its anticipated eight- to ten-week length).

Wehrmacht lawyers urged proper treatment of POWs but Keitel overruled them. Seventy percent of Red Army POWs died in transit to the rear, most others died of gunshots, disease, starvation, and neglect. They were the first victims of Zyklon B poison gas at the new Auschwitz concentration camp. Nearly 3 million POWs died in 1941 alone. On October 31, 1941 Hitler somewhat reversed himself and ordered that Soviet POWs be sent to the Reich to fill some of the 1.5 million vacant industrial worker positions there.

GERMAN ORDER OF BATTLE*:
ARMY GROUP NORTH AREA OF OPERATIONS

NORTHERN THEATER
Army of Norway – GenObst N. von Falkenhorst
Mountain Corps Norway – Gen MtnTr E. Dietl
2nd Mtn Div – GenMaj E. Schlemmer
3rd Mtn Div – GenLt H. Kreysing

Higher Commando XXXVI – Gen Inf H. Feige
169 Inf Div – GenMaj K. Dittmar
SS-Division Nord – SS-Brigadeführer K.-M. Demelhuber
6th Div (Finnish)

Finnish Army – Marshal Mannerheim
14th Div – Col Raapana

Karelian Army – GenLt Heinrichs
1st Div (Res) – Col Paalu
17th Div – Col Snellman
163rd Inf Div (Germ) – GenLt Engelbrecht
Group Oinonen – GenMaj Oinonen
Cavalry Bde – Col Ehrenrooth
2nd Jäger Bde – Col Sundman
1st Jäger Bde (Res) – Col Lagus

VI Corps – MajGen Talvela
5th Div – Col Koskimies
11th Div – Col Heiskanen

VII Corps – MajGen Hagglund
7th Div – Col Svensson
19th Div – Col Hannuksela

II Corps – MajGen Laatikainen
2nd Div – Col Blick
15th Div – Col Hersalo
18th Div – Col Pajari
10th Div (Res) – Col Sihvo

IV Corps – LtGen Oesch
12th Div – Col Vihma
4th Div – Col Viljanen
8th Div – Col Winell

ARMY GROUP NORTH – GFM W. Ritter von Leeb
XXIII Corps – Gen Inf A. Schubert
206th Inf Div – GenLt H. Hoefl
251st Inf Div – GenLt H. Kratzert
254th Inf Div – GenLt W. Behschnitt

CDR Rear Area 101 – GenLt F. Roques
207th Sec Div – GenLt K. von Tiedmann
281st Sec Div – GenLt F. Bayer
285th Sec Div – GenMaj W. Elder *Herr und Freiherr* von Plotho

In transit to the theater:
Polizei Division – SS-Gruppenführer A. Mülverstedt/
SS-Obergruppenführer W. Krüger
86th Inf Div – GenLt J. Witthoeft

18th Army – GenObst G. von Küchler
291st Inf Div – GenLt K. Herzog

I Corps – Gen Inf K.-H. von Both
1st Inf Div – GenLt P. Kleffel
11th Inf Div – GenLt H. von Boeckmann
21st Inf Div – GenLt O. Sponheimer

XXVI Corps – Gen Art A. Wodrig
61st Inf Div – GenLt S. Haenicke
217th Inf Div – GenLt R. Baltzer

XXXVIII Corps – Gen Inf F.-W. von Chappuis
58th Inf Div. – GenLt I. Heunert

4th Panzer Group – GenObst E. Hoepner
SS-Division Totenkopf – SS-Obergruppenführer T. Eicke

XLI Pz Corps – Gen PzTr G.-H. Reinhardt
1st Pz Div – GenLt F. Kirchner
6th Pz Div – GenMaj F. Landgraf
36th Mot Inf Div – GenLt O. Ottenbacher
269th Inf Div – GenMaj E. von Leyser

LVI Pz Corps – Gen Inf E. von Manstein
8th Pz Div – GenMaj E. Brandenburger
3rd Mot Inf Div – GenLt C. Jahn
290th Inf Div – GenLt T. *Freiherr* von Wrede

16th Army – GenObst E. Busch
253rd Inf Div – GenLt O. Schellert

II Corps – Gen Inf W. Graf von Brockdorff-Ahlenfeldt
12th Inf Div – GenMaj W. von Seydlitz-Kurzbach
32nd Inf Div – GenMaj W. Bohnstedt
121st Inf Div – GenMaj O. Lancelle

X Corps – Gen Art C. Hansen
30th Inf Div – GenLt K. von Tippelskirch
126th Inf Div – GenLt P. Laux

XXVII Corps – Gen Inf M. von Wiktorin
122nd Inf Div – GenMaj S. Macholz
123rd Inf Div – GenLt W. Lichel

Naval Command Group North

---

*   No two sources on orders of battle for *Barbarossa* agree. The primary source for the German order of battle is Boog (ed.), *Germany and the Second World War.*

ARMY GROUP CENTER AREA OF OPERATIONS

ARMY GROUP CENTER – GFM F. von Bock
OKH Reserve:
Higher Command XXXV – Gen Kav R. Koch-Erpach
15th Inf Div – GenLt E-E. Hell (from July 3)
52nd Inf Div – GenMaj L. Rendulic (from June 26)
106th Inf Div – GenMaj E. Dehmer (from July 1)
110th Inf Div – GenLt E. Seifert (from June 26)
112th Inf Div – Gen Inf F. Mieth (from July 1)
197th Inf Div – GenLt H. Meyer-Rabingen (from June 26)
Lehr Bde (mot) 900 – Obst W. Krause (from June 22)
Army Group Reserve:
293rd Inf Div – GenLt J. von Obernitz

Third Panzer Group – GenObst H. Hoth
XXXIX Panzer Corps – Gen PzTr R. Schmidt
7th Pz Div – GenMaj H. von Funck
20th Pz Div – GenMaj H. Stumpff
14th Mot Inf Div – GenLt F. Fuerst
20th Mot Inf Div – GenMaj H. Zorn

LVII Panzer Corps – Gen PzTr A. Kuntzen
12th Pz Div – GenMaj J. Harpe
19th Pz Div – GenLt O. von Knoblesdorff
18th Mot Inf Div – GenMaj F. Herrlein

V Army Corps – Gen Inf R. Ruoff
5th Inf Div – GenMaj K. Allmendinger
35th Inf Div – GenLt W. von Weikersthal

VI Army Corps – Gen Pi O-W. Foerster
6th Inf Div – GenLt H. Auleb
26th Inf Div – GenMaj W. Weiss

Ninth Army – GenObst A. Strauss
VIII Army Corps – Gen Art W. Heitz
8th Inf Div – GenMaj G. Hoehne
28th Inf Div – GenLt J. Sinnhuber
161st Inf Div – GenLt H. Wilck

XX Army Corps – Gen Inf W. Materna
162nd Inf Div – GenLt H. Franke
256th Inf Div – GenLt G. Kauffmann

XLII Army Corps – Gen Pi W. Kuntze
87th Inf Div – GenLt B. von Studnitz
102nd Inf Div – GenLt J. Ansat
129th Inf Div – GenMaj S. Rittau

Fourth Army – GFM Günther H. von Kluge
VII Army Corps – Gen Art W. Fahrmbacher
7th Inf Div – GenLt E. von Gablenz
23rd Inf Div – GenMaj H. Hellmich
258th Inf Div – GenMaj W. Henrici
268th Inf Div – GenLt E. Straube

XIII Army Corps – Gen Inf H. Felber
17th Inf Div – GenLt H. Loch
78th Inf Div – GenLt C. Gallenkamp

IX Army Corps – Gen Inf H. Geyer
137th Inf Div – GenLt H. Kamencke
263rd Inf Div – GenLt F. Karl
292nd Inf Div – GenLt M. Dehmel

XLII Army Corps – Gen Inf G. Heinrici
131st Inf Div – GenLt H. Meyer-Buerdorff
134th Inf Div – GenLt C. von Cochenhausen
252th Inf Div – GenLt D. von Boehm-Benzing

Second Panzer Group – GenObst H. Guderian
Reserve:
255th Inf Div – Gen Inf W. Wetzel

XXIV Panzer Corps – Gen PzTr L. Geyr von Schweppenburg
3rd Pz Div – GenLt W. Model
4th Pz Div – GenMaj W. von Langermann
10th Mot Inf Div – GenLt F-W. von Loeper
1st Cav Div – GenLt O. Mengers
267th Inf Div – GenMaj R. Martinek

XLVI Panzer Corps – Gen PzTr H. von Vietinghoff
10th Pz Div – GenLt F. Schaal
Inf Regt "Grossdeutschland" – Obst W-H. von Stockenhausen
SS Reich – SS-Ogruf P. Hausser

XLVII Panzer Corps – Gen PzTr J. Lemelsen
17th Pz Div – GenLt H-J. von Arnim
18th Pz Div – GenMaj W. Nehring
29th Mot Inf Div – GenMaj W. von Boltenstern
167th Inf Div – GenLt H. Schoenhaerl

XII Army Corps – Gen Inf W. Schroth
31st Inf Div – GenMaj G. Berthold
34th Inf Div – GenLt H. Behrendorff
45th Inf Div – GenMaj F. Schlieper

Rear Army Area 102 – GenLt M. von Schenkendorff
221st Security Div – GenLt J. Pflugbeil
286th Security Div – GenLt K. Mueller
403rd Security Div – GenLt W. Ditfurth

ARMY GROUP SOUTH AREA OF OPERATIONS

ARMY GROUP SOUTH – FM G. von Rundstedt
Chief of Staff: Gen G. von Sodenstern
99th Light Inf Div – GenLt K. von der Chevallerie

Higher Commando XXXIV
4th Mtn Div – GenMaj K. Eglseer
113th Inf Div
125th Inf Div – Gen W. Schneckenburger
132th Inf Div

LI Army Corps
79th Inf Div
95th Inf Div

First Panzer Group – Col Gen E. von Kleist
13th Pz Div – GenLt F-W. von Rothkirch
16th Mot Inf Div – GenMaj S. Henrici
25th Mot Inf Div – GenLt H. Cloessner
SS Mot Div LSSAH – Obergruppenführer S. Dietrich

III Motorized Corps (Pz) – Gen Kav E. von Mackensen
14th Pz Div – GenMaj F. Kuehn
44th Inf Div – GenLt F. Siebert
298th Inf Div – GenMaj Graessner

XIV Motorized Corps (Pz) – Gen Inf G. von Wietersheim
9th Pz Div – GenLt Dr. A. *Ritter* von Hubicki
16th Pz Div – GenMaj H. Hube
SS Mot Div Viking – Brigadeführer F. Steiner

XLVIII Motorized Corps (Pz.) – Gen W. Kempff
11th Pz Div – GenMaj L. Cruewell
57th Inf Div – GenLt O. Bluemm
75th Inf Div – GenLt E. Hammer

XXIX Army Corps – Gen Inf H. von Obstfelder
111th Inf Div – GenLt O. Stapf
299th Inf Div – GenMaj W. Moser
II Flak Corps – Gen O. Dessloch

Sixth Army – FM W. von Reichenau
LV Army Corps (Res) – Gen Inf E. Vierow
168th Inf Div – GenLt Dr. Mundt

XVII Army Corps – Gen Inf W. Kienitz
56th Inf Div – GenMaj K. von Oven
62nd Inf Div – GenLt W. Keiner

XLIV Army Corps – Gen Inf F. Koch
9th Inf Div – GenMaj F. von Schleinitz
297th Inf Div – GenLt M. Pfeffer

Eleventh Army – Col Gen E. *Ritter* von Schobert
Rumanian Cavalry Corps (Res) – Gen M. Racovita
22nd Inf Div – GenLt H. *Graf* von Sponek
Rumanian Defense: 72nd Inf Div – GenLt F. Mattenklott

XI Army Corps – Gen Inf J. von Kortzfleisch
76th Inf Div – GenLt M. de Angelis
239th Inf Div – GenLt F. Neuling
8th Rumanian Inf Div
6th Rumanian Cav Bde

XXX Army Corps – Gen Inf H. von Salmuth
198 Inf Div – GenMaj O. Roettig
14th Rumanian Inf Div
5th Rumanian Cav Bde

LIV Army Corps – Gen Cav E. Hansen
50th Inf Div – GenLt K. Hollidt
170th Inf Div – GenMaj W. Wittke

Rumanian Mtn. Corps – Gen G. Arramescu
7th Rumanian Inf Div
1st Rumanian Mtn Div
2nd Rumanian Mtn Div
4th Rumanian Mtn Div
8th Rumanian Cav Bde

Seventeenth Army – Gen Inf C-H. von Stulpnagel
97th Light Inf Div – GenMaj M. Fretter-Pico
100th Light Inf Div – GenMaj W. Sanne

IV Army Corps – Gen Inf V. von Schwedler

24th Inf Div – GenMaj H. von Tettau
71st Inf Div – GenMaj A. von Hartmann
262nd Inf Div – GenLt E. Thiessen
295th Inf Div – GenMaj H. Geitner
296th Inf Div – GenMaj W. Stemmermann

XLIX Mountain Corps – Gen Mtntr L. Kuebler
1st Mtn Div – GenMaj H. Lanz
68th Inf Div – GenMaj G. Braum?
257th Inf Div – GenMaj C. Sachs

LII Army Corps – Gen Inf K. von Briesen
101st Light Inf Div – GenMaj E. Marcks
Slovak Corps
1st Slovak Inf Div
2nd Slovak Inf Div

Rear Army Area 103 – Gen Inf K. von Rocques
213rd Sec (Security) Div – GenLt l'Homme de Coubiere
444th Sec Div – GenLt Russwurm
445th Sec Div – GenLt Krantz

ARMY GROUP ANTONESCU – Gen I. Antonescu
11th Rumanian Inf Div

II Rumanian Corps – Gen N. Macici
9th Rumanian Inf Div
10th Rumanian Inf Div
7th Rumanian Cav Bde

Third Rumanian Army – Gen P. Dumitrescu
IV Rumanian Corps
1 x Cav Bn
6th Rumanian Inf Div

Fourth Rumanian Army – Gen N. Cuiperca
III Rumanian Corps – Gen V. Atanasiu
Rumanian Guards Div
15th Rumanian Inf Div
35th Rumanian Res Inf Div

V Rumanian Corps – Gen L. Gheorghe
Rumanian Frontier Div
21st Rumanian Inf Div

XI Rumanian Corps – Gen I. Aurellian
1st Rumanian Fortress Bde
2nd Rumanian Fortess Bde

Luftflotte 4 – Col Gen A. Lohr
Luftwaffe Mission Rumanian – Gen W. Speidel

Fliegerkorps IV – GenLt K. Pflugbeil
KG 27
JG 77

Fliegerkorps V – GenLt R. *Ritter* von Greim
KG 51
KG 54
KG 55
JG 3

Rumanian Air Combat Group
1st Bomber Wing
2nd Bomber Wing
2nd Fighter-Bomber Wing
1st Fighter Wing

Soviet Forces

At three times the size of the continental United States, the USSR was the world's largest country. While it also had the largest army, internal tensions, including the effects of the purges and doctrinal turbulence, almost negated much of this advantage. Far from being the brittle "colossus of clay" hoped for by the German High Command, it survived despite many failings. However, the Red Army very nearly proved incapable of saving the USSR. In fact during *Barbarossa* numerous Soviet units mutinied or killed their commissars. In the final analysis, despite losing 4.5 million men in first five months of war, it was the Soviet system that held the state together.

National Leadership

The Soviet Union was born in war and was in crisis, at war, or preparing for war for most of its existence. Despite the dictator's supposed leadership experiences gained during the Russian Civil War, Zhukov considered Stalin strictly a military dilettante. During the early stages of the Nazi–Soviet War he constantly interfered in military decisions with disastrous results. Unlike Hitler, however, Stalin learned to trust his professional experts as the war progressed. Quite apart from the manifest failures of the Tsarist army, Soviet theorists blamed Russia's collapse during World War I on three other factors: the incompetence or outright rebellion of the peasantry, the corrupt bureaucracy, and poor railroads. Uncompromising Communist Party leadership rectified these issues and took pains to eliminate earlier "isolated caste relations" so that no alternative to Stalin's state arose during what was referred to as the Great Patriotic War in the USSR.

A Soviet described in the German caption as a divisional political officer ("commissar") is interrogated by his captors, although the red star forearm badge of that status is not visible in this print. If he is a commissar then his life expectancy is now minimal; Hitler issued express orders that such prisoners were to be executed. (Author's collection)

By 1941 the USSR was a garrison state; if it was to survive, internal security had to be the first priority. Stalin's notorious purges lasted from 1937 right up to *Barbarossatag*; among their first and most famous victims was Marshal M.N. Tukhachevsky, who was persecuted on the basis of trumped-up evidence known to have originated with the Gestapo. The psychological damage of the purges was perhaps greater than the material. It is often said that fear stifled the initiative of field commanders; as significant is the fact that the purges caused a widespread lack of trust in the Soviet leadership and a diminished faith in the institutions of the state. Soldiers might wonder why it had taken Stalin so long to uncover the "traitors"; and, if the rank and file could not trust stalwarts such as Tukhachevsky, whom could they trust?

Other forms of turbulence plagued the Soviet military during the interwar period as well. Political commissars in military units had proved their worth during the Russian Civil War, lost favor in the 1920s, and regained influence during the purges, but were again discredited after the Winter War. The Red Army led much of the world in military mechanization through the mid-1930s, but stagnated after the Spanish Civil War only to rebound after watching the blitzkrieg dismember France. By mid-1940 the Red Army re-established general and admiral ranks and toughened discipline. There became no such thing as a criminal order from above; all orders needed to be obeyed accurately, punctually, and without contradiction.

New commanders came to the fore in mid-1940 following the debacle in Finland. Marshals S.K. Timoshenko and B.M. Shaposhnikov took over as Defense Commissar and Deputy/Chief of Staff respectively. They, and Zhukov from January of the next year, tried but failed to reform the Soviet military after decades of chaos bordering on negligence. Entrenched conservatives (as everywhere) challenged the efforts of the reformers, as did the NKVD. Like Germany, the USSR suffered from a

German Generals

Field Marshal Walther von Brauchitsch, 1881–1948, German Army Supreme Commander

Field Marshal von Brauchitsch was German Army Supreme Commander from 1938–1941. He was a page in the court of Wilhelm II. Commissioned as a lieutenant in the guards artillery, he served as a captain and general staff officer throughout World War I. He succeeded General Werner von Fritsch as army commander when the latter succumbed to Nazi intrigues. In 1938, von Brauchitsch divorced his estranged wife of 28 years (with whom he had four children) and remarried with Hitler's financial support. His second wife was an ardent Nazi. The general always seemed to be short of money and compensated for an unhappy family life by "working like an ox" in his office at all hours.

While negotiating with Hitler for the army commander position he agreed to 1) "lead the Army closer toward the state and its philosophy"; 2) choose a more suitable chief of staff to replace Beck; and 3) reorganize the Army High Command structure. He refused to participate in any of the anti-Hitler opposition prevalent in the Army's leadership. Supposedly von Brauchitsch admired Hitler personally yet detested the Nazis: however, in many photographs a Party pin is conspicuous on his uniform.

Von Brauchitsch complained but went along with preparations for the Polish operation. The 1939 campaign was his first and last in a position of real operational authority. When Hitler unilaterally decided to invade the West later that same autumn, von Brauchitsch demurred, citing army ill-discipline and uneven training. The Führer grudgingly went along with the recommendation, one of the last times he paid serious attention to his army commander. Von Brauchitsch showed some understanding of the blitzkrieg and made positive contributions to the Western campaign. However, by then Hitler and Halder had taken increased roles. Nevertheless, on July 19, 1940 he was rewarded by Hitler with a field marshal's baton.

As commander in chief von Brauchitsch was involved in *Barbarossa's* planning, operations, and direction. In many instances he intervened in the petty personality conflicts between senior commanders. But as the campaign went on he became marginalized by stronger-willed men such as Hitler himself, Halder, von Bock, and von Rundstedt. Evidently Hitler did not speak to his generals with the decorum to which they were accustomed; this had a negative effect on the health of von Brauchitsch. On November 10 he suffered a heart attack and deteriorated further. With the failure before Moscow Hitler cast about for scapegoats and settled on von Brauchitsch.

The field marshal retired for medical reasons on December 19 and disappeared into relative obscurity while Hitler took the title of Army Supreme Commander for himself. Never recalled, he was captured by British forces in May 1945. Nearly blind, in October 1948 he died of heart problems awaiting war crimes trials.

Colonel General Franz Halder, 1884–1972, Chief of the German General Staff

Halder was a Bavarian Protestant and artillery officer who during World War I never served below the corps echelon. He earned a reputation as a solid officer with a good mind for staff work. Early in the Third Reich he helped oversee the Wehrmacht's massive expansion and he seems to have had a generally positive view of Hitler's chancellorship. Like many German officers he disliked radical Nazism but approved of

lack of strategic thinking. At a three-week meeting of the Main Military Council held immediately before the famous December–January wargames, most participants concentrated on the tactical lessons of the Spanish Civil War, Khalkin Gol, and the Winter War (these three small wars made up the bulk of the USSR's interwar combat experiences); it seemed that only Timoshenko thought of strategy and a possible war against Hitler.

Hitler's strengthening Germany's position in Europe. After the Nazis engineered the removal of Ludwig Beck as army chief of staff, Halder replaced him in August 1938.

Halder's superiors and peers, including Beck, saw him as a diligent but dull mediocrity, "a very good soldier but hardly a man of great caliber." Telford Taylor described him as "a stuffy, schoolmasterish and unimpressive, a little man who was, like von Brauchitsch, constantly torn between ambition and anxiety."[1] His moral fiber was stronger than the commander-in-chief's, but he was also more opinionated and prideful and not bound by personal obligation to Hitler. Halder, "deeply resented being overruled by Hitler in the sphere of military questions."[2]

Prior to the outbreak of World War II Halder developed a pattern of passive-aggressive resistance to Hitler. His plot against the Führer during the Czechoslovak crisis was stillborn when Britain and France caved in at Munich. He frequently schemed against the dictator but always insisted that others do the heavy lifting. Alan Clark wrote that Halder and the *Generaltät* were "outmanoeuvred politically, forsaking one foothold after another in a downhill retreat from their pinnacle of influence [under von Hindenburg]."[3] Many factors contributed to this phenomenon, none vital in isolation, but in the atmosphere of disillusionment, confused loyalties, self-interest, and escapist devotion to the narrow technicalities of their positions, all combined to create discontent.

Halder assertively intrigued against Hitler well past the Polish campaign. In every case Halder backed down, a sobbing, trembling nervous wreck. His Case Yellow plan against France was an unimaginative rehash of the von Schlieffen plan. When von Manstein presented Hitler with a brilliant alternative Halder did all he could to subvert it. After the fall of France, William Shirer attended Hitler's Reichstag victory speech on July 19, 1940. "Saddest figure in the assembly was General Halder," he wrote. "I watched him — classically intellectual face — seemed to be hiding a weariness, a sadness, as he warmly congratulated the younger generals who were now ... over him as field marshals."

As the present narrative makes clear, Halder strived to make *Barbarossa* work only so long as it suited his selfish purposes. When Hitler deviated from the chief of staff's concept, notably over the importance of Moscow, Halder conspired against him like a petulant adolescent. Unlike von Brauchitsch, the general evaded becoming a casualty when *Barbarossa* smashed against the rocks of Zhukov's Moscow defenses.

After Hitler dismissed von Brauchitsch relations between Hitler and Halder grew steadily worse. Von Manstein saw the two men in August 1942: Hitler taunted Halder with his lack of combat experience while Halder mumbled under his breath about the differences between professional and "untutored" opinion. Finally on September 24, 1942, Hitler released Halder, who according to John Toland, had annoyed him above all others as a prophet of doom.[4] Hitler told Halder, "Half my exhaustion is due to you. It is not worth going on." Halder somehow avoided execution, either after the 1944 *Attentat* or at Nuremberg. After the war he worked for the US Army's Historical Division, where he would foist his self-serving revisionist history on anyone who would listen.

---

1   Taylor, *Sword and Swastika*, p.214.
2   Ibid
3   Clark, *Barbarossa*, p.20.
4   Toland, *Adolf Hitler*, p.719.

Soviet riflemen in action. Infantry bore the brunt of the fighting for both armies. The Red Army proved tenacious in defense, always ready to counterattack and willing to continue fighting past the point where soldiers of other armies would have surrendered. (NARA)

Of course Stalin stood at the top of the Soviet national security hierarchy as the chairman of the State Defense Committee. That war cabinet functioned through the Stavka – the new headquarters of the High Command – created the day after *Barbarossa* began, and directed operations by issuing orders which coordinated their timing, conduct, and objectives. Stavka's main executive organ was the Red Army's General Staff, the chief of which since January 1941 was Zhukov.

Doctrine

Writings in the 1920s had voiced fuzzy theories about a "proletarian" way of war; but, even in 1939, a Field Regulation boasted that the "invincible, all shattering Red Army" would take war to the enemy and "achieve decisive victory with little blood" – an emphasis that carried over to the next year's edition. Soviet doctrine was essentially offensive: after a brief defense along their borderlands, the Red Army would attack into the enemy's home territory. Even after the fall of France, Soviet leaders – ignoring both the lessons of blitzkrieg and their own maneuver doctrine – thought in anachronistic terms of a lengthy border battle followed by breakthrough operations.

Marshal Tukhachevsky and others stressed the attack. Nevertheless, in the winter of 1939–40 Soviet offensives failed against Finland despite a 5:1 superiority. In the aftermath of the fall of France and the Soviet High

Command shakeup of January 1941, Stalin and Zhukov hoped Hitler would not attack until 1942, allowing them time to improve the Red Army's defensive capabilities. The official Soviet history states, evidently without irony, "Our prewar theory had not fully worked out the problems of organizing and conducting the defense."

The assumption that the Red Army would have time to mobilize before launching its counteroffensive stands out as a critical failure of the October 1940 and May 1941 State Defense Plans; however, prior to June 22 the Soviet commanders had actually implemented most of the conditions required of their "special threatening military period." Since the Red Army had given little thought to the defense it had no shield behind which to prepare. They also failed completely to anticipate the nature of a potential German attack. After the war, Zhukov wrote that neither he, Timoshenko, nor Shaposhnikov "calculated that the enemy would concentrate such a mass of armored and motorized forces and hurl them in compact groups on all strategic axes on the first day."

Prewar German assessments rated Marshal S.K. Timoshenko (center left) as the Red Army's best senior general. Events proved to be a harsher judge, and within a year Stalin had relegated his old Civil War crony to marginal jobs. Never far from power, the stooping General G.K. Zhukov stands to the marshal's immediate left. The senior generals in both German and Soviet armies had to subordinate their prerogatives to strong and revolutionary political overlords, to learn new technologies and doctrines, and to adjust to massive expansions of forces. (Elukka)

Time to go! Seemingly in a hurry, Red Army soldiers with Maxim machine gun abandon their fighting position. (From the fonds of the RGAKFD in Krasnogorsk via Stavka)

Force Structure

Stalin's purges certainly weakened the senior Soviet military and administrative leadership; but new scholarship shows that this NKVD *Yezhovshchina*[20] had less impact than earlier thought. Nevertheless, disruptions in most echelons of command were great as nearly 55,000 officers were affected from 1937 to 1941. Slightly more than 8 percent of Red Army officers were purged in 1938 (the worst year) – far short of the 30–50 percent previously quoted. Massive Soviet military expansion, especially following 1938, had far more impact on the decline of the army's quality. The Red Army added 111 rifle divisions, 12 rifle brigades, plus 50 tank and motorized divisions between January 1939 and May 1941, overall personnel strength growing from 1,500,000 to more than 5 million. Therefore in a great number of cases officers were promoted significantly above their competency levels. During that period the proportion of officers attending required schooling plummeted, course length shrank from 36 to 24 months and later to 18 months, and the rank of instructors fell from major or captain to senior lieutenant.

The purges had also caused a decline in respect for all officers. This attitude applied to a purged officer's replacement and even to those officers who were quickly reinstated to service (one-third of the total). Discipline throughout the army was universally poor, with what was called *shapkozkidatel'stvo* (hat tossing) symptomatic of the malaise. The transfer of too many field-grade officers to new higher headquarters contributed to this weakness and one

---

20　The NKVD's (People's Commissariat for Internal Affairs) arbitrary arrests and shootings, named after commissariat chief N.I. Yezhov.

report described the loose relations between company-grade officers and their men as "pseudo democratic." The system then in place had no formalized rewards or punishments. Timoshenko implemented changes in summer 1940, but nearly a year later inspections of units reported frustratingly little progress. *Barbarossa* would expose these weaknesses all too clearly.

Fatefully, the Soviet leaders made a conscious decision to field more partial-strength formations rather than fewer full-strength ones. This sent many field-grade officers and generals to the staffs of additional division and corps headquarters rather than retaining quality leadership at the lower tactical levels. The infantry, which would do most of the fighting in any future war, also gave up many of its junior officers to other branches such as tank troops, the Red Army Air Force, and NKVD security units.

After the shocking wake-up call represented by Hitler's destruction of France, the USSR accelerated its frantic military reforms. These changes negatively affected nearly every aspect of its national security establishment. Also, the closer one got to the frontier region adjacent to Nazi-occupied Poland the worse the situation became. Stalin's old warhorse Timoshenko faced a daunting task.

Red Army infantry firing from a trench while their comrades advance with the ubiquitous fixed bayonets. (Corbis)

Furthermore, on the eve of *Barbarossa* the 170 divisions in the western USSR were short by 1.5 million men. Even if all 800,000 soldiers mobilized in the spring of 1941 had gone to these units they would have made up only half the shortfall; in fact, half of those newly mobilized men went to the Army Air Force, and to units deep in the interior of the USSR. Combined, these factors meant that at the critical point of attack the Red Army was missing essential leadership at the battalion and regiment level in addition to being under-strength everywhere.

Guards Divisions

In a bow to Imperial tradition, the Red Army reintroduced the honorific title of Guards for divisions (and later corps and armies) which excelled on the battlefield. Following the battles of Smolensk, on September 18 it created the first four when the 100th, 127th, 153rd, and 161st Rifle Divisions became the 1st, 2nd, 3rd, and 4th Guards Rifle Divisions (the first-named already had elite status as the Order of Lenin Division, established in 1923). Initially the only benefit of the new title was a boost to morale; however, later in the war Guards organizations received greater numbers of above-average personnel and equipment.

Infantry

The infantry represented the Red Army's backbone. The Wehrmacht acknowledged this before the campaign when it listed tough and brave soldiers plus indirect-fire weapons as Soviet strengths. German soldiers discovered through harsh experience that the Red infantry was also *Panzersicher* (secure against panzers). Prewar infantry divisions technically consisted of 14,483 men although new tables of organization in July reduced this to 10,859 (in reality closer to 6,000). These divisions were also short of weapons, trucks, and equipment in general. Rifle divisions supposedly included a tank battalion, but earlier these had been removed and absorbed into the mechanized corps. Most fronts had an airborne corps of three brigades of four battalions each but these were never used in their intended roles. In fact, most airborne soldiers had made only one or two parachute jumps and many none at all.

The Russian infantryman had a well-earned reputation for toughness, especially in the defense. The German soldiers noted how they "sat in their slit trenches until they were either run down or killed by hand grenade or bayonet." In the forests common in the north any advantages were magnified; the German troops left their artillery behind and the MG34 lost much of its effectiveness. Here close combat was the rule. Soviet soldiers did not have a scabbard for their bayonet; it was always fixed on their rifle.

Despite conventional wisdom that Red Army soldiers possessed natural field craft skills, the Soviet campaigns of 1939–40 revealed a poor grasp of personal camouflage, entrenching, river-crossing, and other basic tasks. Officers could not read maps, and displayed both drunkenness and *naprasnoi smelosti* (futile bravery). All were too prone to panic when confronted with opposition or the unexpected. Excessive secrecy, which pervaded all of Soviet society, meant that leaders and soldiers at all levels were surprised by battlefield situations and conditions and therefore less able to adapt. (One week into *Barbarossa*, rumors ran rampant that Marshal S.M. Budenny had taken Warsaw and Voroshilov was advancing on Berlin!)

Artillery

The Red Army considered artillery its decisive branch. In contrast to that of the Germans, Russian artillery performed poorly in the Great War requiring a complete overhaul between the wars. A rifle division included 12 152mm and 20 122mm howitzers and 16 76mm guns, all excellent pieces. Approximately 37,500 indirect-fire weapons were deployed in the western

Early in *Barbarossa*, a Red Army gun crew training prior to going into action. (Elukka)

border areas. Even so, prior to *Barbarossatag* the artillery branch also suffered from shortages in gun tubes, prime movers, and ammunition. Combat losses almost obliterated divisional artillery by July. Most Red Army artillery operated in the direct-support role at corps and division level where it was easier to control. The Katyusha (codenamed Guards Mortars) fired 36 82mm or 16 132mm rockets per launcher. They were cheap and easy to produce and terrified the German soldiers but suffered from inaccuracy and a slow reload rate plus from being deployed as a new, untried weapons system directly onto the battlefield.

Antitank artillery represented a critical part of the Red Army's defensive doctrine and was a sub-set of Soviet artillery. It represented the Red Army's preferred weapon to destroy enemy tanks. Guns of 45mm and 57mm size and mines were concentrated in antitank brigades. The standard 45mm gun could defeat all contemporary panzer variants. Supposedly motorized, the brigades lost many of their trucks to the new mechanized corps so were essentially un-mobilized like the rest of the artillery branch on *Barbarossatag*. Another part of the artillery branch was antiaircraft artillery, which was also playing a desperate game of catch-up following the blitzkrieg's demonstration in 1940.

The world's most technologically advanced tank squandered in a bog: behind a knocked-out T-26, three T-34s are stuck where incompetent crews drove them. The T-34 was the world's best tank until the arrival of the German PzKpfw V Panther in 1943. (Author's collection)

Armor and Mechanized Forces

The Red Army had the world's largest tank park in 1941 while Soviet industry produced prodigious numbers of excellent tanks during the interwar years. Many were obsolete by *Barbarossatag*, but "older" BT-7 and T-26 tanks were better than Panzer Is or IIs and equal to some marks of Panzer IIIs and IVs. A new generation of tanks, led by the T-34 about which the German military had known since late 1940, was just arriving on the battlefield. The T-34 epitomized the first true main battle tank, combining antitank and infantry-support functions. But even the T-34 had limitations, specifically its weak transmission and two-man turret. The heavy KV-1 mounted the same 76mm gun but its much greater armor weight overtaxed the defective T-34-type transmission. Poor crew skill, maintenance, and supply deprived the Red Army of their potent armored offensive weapon, accounting for fully one-half of all Red Army tank losses during *Barbarossa*.

The Red Army drew many misguided lessons from the Spanish Civil War, notably identifying tanks as primarily infantry-support weapons. In 1939 they attributed the fall of Poland to the rotten regime, not the Wehrmacht's panzers, with the result that a month later they disbanded their mechanized corps, only to recreate them the following summer in the aftermath of France's defeat. David Glantz calls the mechanized corps the armored heart of Red Army. He mentions, however, that there was confusion in the Red Army over the mechanized corps' two missions: the frontier fight and operational counterattacks.

Always thinking bigger is better, the Red Army created huge unwieldy organizations with the mechanized corps, which were further hamstrung by weak leadership and poor training. Usually consisting of two tank and one motorized division, they proved far beyond their commanders' ability to manage and lacked any of the panzer corps' flexibility. The Soviet leadership vainly tried to raise 20 new mechanized corps in the six months preceding *Barbarossatag*. Mechanized corps that the Red Army did manage to field suffered personnel, weapons, and equipment shortages endemic to the entire Red Army.

Cavalry

Partially because of tradition and partly out of common sense, cavalry played a larger role in the Red Army than many other World War II armies. Unfortunately cavalry command cadres were frequently stripped to create mechanized corps headquarters. The branch's four corps and 13 divisions in many cases represented the only "mobile" formations in some areas of the fighting. It managed to avoid the dangerous reorganization that hamstrung other elements of the Red Army on the eve of war.

Soviet cavalry scout returns from patrol. Early in *Barbarossa* cavalry was the perfect weapon for the wide open spaces of the USSR. (Corbis)

NKVD

The political enforcement forces and border guards under the People's Commissariat for Internal Affairs (NKVD) contributed over 170,000 men to Soviet manpower numbers. The NKVD's main mission was internal security, and during the interwar years, mass murder throughout Eastern Europe. NKVD and other security forces included numerous division-, regiment-, and battalion-sized units which guarded important state organizations, railroads, critical defense enterprises, and other sensitive sites. Neither border guards nor NKVD troops were heavily armed and cannot be considered trained combat forces.

The terrible mud of the *rasputitsa* season affected all equally. Here soldiers and civilians (note the woman in a skirt, left) man-handle a Soviet supply truck which has got itself stuck axle deep. (Podzun)

Logistics

Soviet logistics were arguably in an even worse state than the German. All teeth and no tail meant the Red Army had difficulty conducting sustained operations. Much of their logistics base consisted of easily captured or destroyed static dumps. Their mechanized corps, for example, carried only one day's supplies. In the swirling conditions of *Barbarossa* the German forces easily interdicted soft-skinned supply vehicles. Out of fuel and often broken down due to untrained crews and poor maintenance, their tanks became, at best, immobile pillboxes. Further, stories are legion about units of all descriptions beginning the war with no ammunition.

Trucks were at a premium despite the high production values of the Five-Year Plans. Mechanized corps' tanks attacked without motorized infantry because their trucks were hauling supplies in the rear and, critically, many artillery pieces had no prime movers.

Fortifications

An integral part of the shield behind which the Soviet leaders would prepare for their strategic counteroffensives was their fortified regions. Called the Stalin Line by the Germans, these were in no way comparable to the Maginot Line; the main works consisted of bunkers with light artillery and machine guns guarding a specific geographic location or axis of advance. Each fortified region was manned by a regiment with five to ten artillery bunkers, 10–15 machine-gun bunkers, and 15–30 antitank bunkers. One of the two oldest fortified regions was that at Polotsk astride the River Dvina, where the Soviet, Polish, and Lithuanian borders came together. Others, at Minsk, Mozyr, and Slutsk, dated from the 1930s.

Stalin insisted that the defensive lines move west into occupied Poland in 1939. In June 1940, a month after replacing Voroshilov, Timoshenko ordered new construction in these areas, including updating fortress Brest's defenses. On *Barbarossatag* most divisions manning the Soviet–German frontier lacked their engineer battalions which were busy building new bunkers and obstacles, markedly degrading the divisions' combat power. Construction went slowly, partially owing to the same miserable transportation infrastructure that would soon hamstring the Germans' advance.

After March 1941 Kirponos put maximum effort into their construction, employing 43,000 workers per day. Prior to *Barbarossa*, Red Army inspectors found the Minsk defenses "deplorable." The German after-action report claimed that only 193 of the 1,175 forts throughout the Western Front area were equipped and occupied. In the Southwestern Front area the Germans subsequently counted 1,912 completed, combat-ready positions and 192 under construction.

Red Army Air Force

Unlike their brothers on the ground, the air force suffered no inferiority complex after their occupation of Poland or the Winter War. By 1940 the Red Army Air Force received 40 percent of the Soviet military budget. It had fewer than 10,000 aircraft based in the border regions. However, its effectiveness had also peaked in the 1930s and by 1941 it was growing increasingly obsolete. Many veterans of the Spanish Civil War had been framed and arrested during the purges. The dangerous paucity of radios mirrored that of the army. Further, Soviet aviators stubbornly retained the ineffective, three-aircraft "V" formation.

Red Army Air Force crew training and combat experience was far behind that of the Luftwaffe. It also had weak antiaircraft artillery, no protected parking, and limited temporary airfields to which aircraft could disperse when threatened. Only senior leaders carried radios, maps, and target information in their aircraft. The Air Force did have some advantages over the Luftwaffe, however: the benefits in sub-zero temperatures enjoyed by the air-cooled engines of some Soviet fighters over the water-cooled Messerschmitts were obvious. The German military considered the IL-2 Sturmovik "an excellent machine" while the I-16 fighter possessed twice the rate of fire of the Bf 109 and fired a heavier projectile.

The Air Force's mission under the 1936 regulations was limited to CAS; the USSR gave up on strategic bombing in the late 1930s, when it disbanded

Soviet partisans were especially active in the north and particularly effective in the broken, wooded, and swampy terrain that the Germans encountered as they pressed further into Russia. Here some mine a road while their comrades keep watch for German troops. (NARA)

its three strategic air armies and canceled the four-engine TB-7 bomber. Fighter forces grew correspondingly. The air force reorganization impacted more than force development, its basing and infrastructure on June 21 were also in turmoil. Prewar Luftwaffe intelligence identified 38 air divisions (120–240 aircraft each) and suspected the existence of 50 more.

Red Army Air Force losses during the first days and weeks of *Barbarossa* are well known. But it came fighting back, many aircraft flying 10–14 sorties on June 22. In the Soviet leadership vacuum that day (and for many days to follow) regimental commanders improvised by sending their men against any target. They made little effort to evade German fighters or flak. But total German losses that day of 78 aircraft significantly exceeded their worst day during the Battle of Britain (61 aircraft on September 15, 1940).

Soviet Partisans

From *Barbarossa's* first days many Soviet people rose up against the Axis invaders and did not wait for Stalin's famous speech of July 3. Numerous partisan bands sprang up spontaneously. These could include any mix of civilians, Communist cadres, soldiers who had avoided capture, and escaped POWs. The line between legitimate combatants (soldiers) and partisans (civilians, "bandits" to the Germans) became quickly blurred, as if Hitler would have paid much attention to legal subtleties. Throughout *Barbarossa* and indeed all of the Nazi–Soviet War rear area security duties took more and more German strength due to the partisan threat, diluting combat power at the front lines.

Soviet Navy

The Red Banner Baltic Fleet had great potential on June 21. It had a competent leader in Admiral Tributs and two battleships, two light cruisers, 47 destroyers or large torpedo boats, 75 submarines, over 200 smaller craft, and hundreds of aircraft. Outnumbering the Kriegsmarine, it nevertheless relied mainly on mines and submarines.

Unfortunately, the loss of all but one naval base and a passive doctrine meant the Red Banner Fleet did not realize its potential. It did survive, however, and in May 1945 it, not the Kriegsmarine, was the victor. In the Arctic Ocean the Northern Fleet was more active, often with the assistance of the Royal Navy.

The USSR dominated the naval war in the south. Against the small Rumanian Navy and a few German E-boats, the Black Sea Fleet counted one old battleship, five cruisers, 17 destroyers, 43 submarines, numerous smaller craft, and 624 aircraft. The Dnepr Flotilla had four monitors weighing up to 900 tons and mounting guns as large as 150mm, plus many gunboats.

SOVIET ORDER OF BATTLE*: SOUTHWEST FRONT, SOUTHERN FRONT

SOUTHWEST FRONT
LtGen M.P. Kirponos
5th Antitank Brigade

Front units
31st Rifle Corps – MajGen A.I. Lopatin
193th Rifle Division
195th Rifle Division
200th Rifle Division

36th Rifle Corps – MajGen P.V. Sisoev
140th Rifle Division
146th Rifle Division
228th Rifle Division

49th Rifle Corps – MajGen I.A. Kornilov
190th Rifle Division
197th Rifle Division
199th Rifle Division

55th Rifle Corps – MajGen K.A. Koroteev
130th Rifle Division

169th Rifle Division
189th Rifle Division

1st Airborne Corps – MajGen M.A. Usenko
1st Airborne Brigade
204th Airborne Brigade
211th Airborne Brigade

19th Mechanized Corps – MajGen N.V. Feklenko
213th Rifle Division
40th Tank Division
43rd Tank Division

24th Mechanized Corps – MajGen V.I. Christyakov
216th Motorized Division
45th Tank Division
49th Tank Division

5th Army – MajGen M.I. Potapov
1st Antitank Brigade

15th Rifle Corps – Col I.I. Fedyuninsky
45th Rifle Division
62nd Rifle Division

27th Rifle Corps – MajGen P.D. Artemenko
87th Rifle Division
124th Rifle Division
135th Rifle Division

9th Mechanized Corps – MajGen K.K. Rokossovsky
131st Motorized Division
20th Tank Division
35th Tank Division

22nd Mechanized Corps – MajGen S.M. Kondrusev
215th Mechanized Division
19th Tank Division
41st Tank Division

6th Army – LtGen I.N. Muzychenko
3rd Antitank Brigade

6th Rifle Corps – MajGen I.I. Alekseev
41st Rifle Division
97th Rifle Division
159th Rifle Division

37th Rifle Corps – BrigGen S.P. Zibin
80th Rifle Division
139th Rifle Division
141st Rifle Division

5th Cavalry Corps – MajGen F.V. Kamkov
3rd Cavalry Division
14th Cavalry Division

4th Mechanized Corps – MajGen A.A. Vlasov
81st Motorized Division
8th Tank Division
32th Tank Division

15th Mechanized Corps – MajGen I.I. Karpezo
212th Motorized Division
10th Tank Division

37th Tank Division

12th Army – MajGen P.G. Ponedelin
4th Antitank Brigade

13th Rifle Corps – MajGen N.K. Kirillov
44th Rifle Division
58th Rifle Division
192nd Rifle Division

17th Rifle Corps – MajGen I.V. Galanin
60th Mountain Division
69th Mountain Division
164th Rifle Division

16th Mechanized Corps – BrigGen A.D. Sokolov
240th Motorized Division
15th Tank Division
39th Tank Division

26th Army – LtGen F. Ya. Kostenko
2nd Antitank Brigade

8th Corps – MajGen M.G. Snegov
72nd Mountain Division
99th Rifle Division
173rd Rifle Division

8th Mechanized Corps – LtGen D.I. Ryabyshev
7th Motorized Division
12th Tank Division
34th Tank Division

KIEV V.V.S. – A.P. Ionev
19th Bomber Division
62nd Bomber Division
14th Mixed Aviation Division
15th Mixed Aviation Division
16th Mixed Aviation Division
17 Mixed Aviation Division
63rd Mixed Aviation Division
44th Fighter Division
64th Fighter Division

SOUTHERN FRONT
Front units
7th Rifle Corps – MajGen K.L. Dobroserdov
116th Rifle Division
196th Rifle Division
206th Rifle Division

9th Rifle Corps – MajGen V.A. Batov
116th Rifle Division
156th Rifle Division
32nd Cavalry Division

3rd Airborne Corps – MajGen V.A. Glazunov
5th Airborne Brigade
6th Airborne Brigade
212th Airborne Brigade
47th Rifle Division

9th Army – LtGen Ya. T. Cherevichenko
14th Rifle Corps – MajGen D.G. Egorov
25th Rifle Division
51st Rifle Division

35th Rifle Corps – BrigGen I.F. Dashichev
95th Rifle Division
176th Rifle Division

48th Rifle Corps – MajGen R. Ya. Malinovsky
30th Mountain Division

74th Rifle Division
150th Rifle Division

2nd Cavalry Corps – MajGen P.A. Belov
5th Cavalry Division
9th Cavalry Division

2nd Mechanized Corps – LtGen Y.V. Novoselsky
15th Motorized Division
11th Tank Division
16th Tank Division

18th Mechanized Corps – MajGen P.V. Volokh
218th Motorized Division
44th Tank Division
47th Tank Division

ODESSA V.V.S. – Gen F.G. Mishugin
20th Mixed Aviation Division
21st Mixed Aviation Division
45th Mixed Aviation Division

BLACK SEA FLEET V.V.S.
63rd Bomber Brigade
62nd Fighter Brigade

---

*   As with the Axis order of battle, the sources conflict on
the details of Red Army organization. The primary
source for the Soviet order of battle is Glantz, *Barbarossa*.

NORTHERN FRONT, NORTHWEST FRONT

NORTHERN FRONT
LtGen M.M. Popov
177th Rifle Division
191st Rifle Division
8th Rifle Brigade

Northern PVO – MajGen M.M. Protsvetkin
39th Fighter Aviation Division
3rd Fighter Aviation Division (PVO)
54th Fighter Aviation Division (PVO)
2nd Mixed Aviation Division

14th Army – LtGen V.A. Frolov
14th Rifle Division
52nd Rifle Division
1st Tank Division

1st Mixed Aviation Division

42nd Rifle Corps – MajGen R.I. Panin
104th Rifle Division
122nd Rifle Division

7th Independent Army – LtGen F.D. Gorelenko
54th Rifle Division
71st Rifle Division
168th Rifle Division
237th Rifle Division

55th Mixed Aviation Division

23rd Army – MajGen P.S. Pshennikov
19th Rifle Corps – MajGen M.N. Gerasimov
115th Rifle Division
142nd Rifle Division

50th Rifle Corps – MajGen V.I. S'cherbakov
43rd Rifle Division
70th Rifle Division
123rd Rifle Division

10th Mechanized Corps – MajGen I.G. Lazarev
21st Tank Division
24th Tank Division
198th Motorcycle Division
7th Motorcycle Regiment

41st Bomber Aviation Division
5th Mixed Aviation Division

NORTHWEST FRONT – ColGen F.I. Kuznetsov
5th Airborne Corps – MajGen I.S. Berugly
9th Airborne Brigade
10th Airborne Brigade
214th Airborne Brigade

Baltic VVS – MajGen A. Ionov
57th Fighter Aviation Division
4th Mixed Aviation Division
6th Mixed Aviation Division
7th Mixed Aviation Division
8th Mixed Aviation Division

9th Antitank Brigade

8th Army – LtGen P.P. Sobennikov
10th Rifle Corps – MajGen I.F. Nikolaev
10th Rifle Division
48th Rifle Division

50th Rifle Division

11th Rifle Corps – MajGen M.S. Shurnilov
11th Rifle Division
125th Rifle Division

12th Mechanized Corps – MajGen N.M. Shestopalov
23rd Tank Division
202nd Mechanized Division
10th Motorcycle Regiment

11th Army – LtGen V.I. Morozov
23rd Rifle Division
126th Rifle Division
128th Rifle Division

16th Rifle Corps – MajGen F.S. Ivanov
5th Rifle Division
33rd Rifle Division
188th Rifle Division

29th Rifle Corps – MajGen A.G. Samokhin
179th Rifle Division
184th Rifle Division

3rd Mechanized Corps – MajGen A.V. Kurkin
2nd Tank Division
5th Tank Division
84th Mechanized Division

27th Army – MajGen M.E. Berzarin
16th Rifle Division
76th Rifle Division
3rd Rifle Brigade

22nd Rifle Corps – MajGen M.P. Dukhanov
180th Rifle Division
182nd Rifle Division

24th Rifle Corps – MajGen K. Kachalov
181st Rifle Division
183rd Rifle Division

Red Banner Baltic Fleet – Vice Adm V.F. Tributs
Northern Fleet – Rear Adm Gorlovko

WESTERN FRONT

WESTERN FRONT
Colonel General D.G. Pavlov
Front units:
2nd Rifle Corps – MajGen A.N. Ermakov
100th Rifle Division
161st Rifle Division

21st Rifle Corps – MajGen V.B. Borisov
17th Rifle Division
24th Rifle Division
37th Rifle Division

44th Rifle Corps – MajGen V.A. Yushkevich
64th Rifle Division
108th Rifle Division

47th Rifle Corps – MajGen S.I. Povetkin
50th Rifle Division
55th Rifle Division
121st Rifle Division
143rd Rifle Division

4th Airborne Corps – MajGen A.S. Zhandov
7th Airborne Brigade
8th Airborne Brigade
214th Airborne Brigade
8th Antitank Brigade

17th Mechanized Corps – MajGen M.P. Petrov
27th Tank Division
36th Tank Division
209th Motorized Division
22nd Motorcycle Regiment

20th Mechanized Corps – MajGen A.G. Nikitin
26th Tank Division
38th Tank Division
210th Motorized Division
24th Motorcycle Regiment

3rd Army – LtGen V.I. Kuznetsov
4th Rifle Corps
27th Rifle Division
56th Rifle Division
85th Rifle Division

11th Mechanized Corps – MajGen D.K. Mostevenko
29th Tank Division
33rd Tank Division
204th Motorized Division
16th Motorcycle Regiment
7th Antitank Brigade

4th Army – MajGen A.A. Korobkov
28th Rifle Corps – MajGen V.S. Popov
6th Rifle Division
42nd Rifle Division
49th Rifle Division
75th Rifle Division

14th Mechanized Corps – MajGen S.I. Oborin
22nd Tank Division
30th Tank Division
205th Motorized Division
20th Motorcycle Regiment

10th Army – MajGen K.D. Golubev
1st Rifle Corps – MajGen F.D. Rubtsev
2nd Rifle Division
8th Rifle Division

5th Rifle Corps – MajGen A.V. Garnov
13th Rifle Division
86th Rifle Division
113th Rifle Division

6th Cavalry Corps – MajGen I.S. Nikitin
6th Cavalry Division
36th Cavalry Division
6th Antitank Brigade

6th Mechanized Corps – MajGen M.G. Khatskilevich
4th Tank Division
7th Tank Division
29th Motorized Division
4th Motorcycle Regiment

13th Mechanized Corps – MajGen P.N. Akhliustin
25th Tank Division
31st Tank Division
208th Motorized Division
18th Motorcycle Regiment

OPPOSING COMMANDERS

German Commanders

Army Group North

Field Marshal Wilhelm *Ritter* von Leeb, age 64, commanded Army Group North. A Bavarian artillery officer, he served in China in the Boxer Rebellion. During the Great War he earned the Bavarian Max Josef Order and the non-hereditary title of *Ritter* (knight). During the interwar years he authored the book *Defense*, which even the German editor of his diary called "essentially unnoticed then and forgotten today." Von Leeb was a devout Catholic and anti-Nazi. He asked to be relieved of his command on January 16, 1942 and Hitler never recalled him. The Nuremberg tribunal sentenced von Leeb to three years in prison and he died in 1956.

Colonel General Georg von Küchler, 60 years old, another career artillery officer, commanded the Eighteenth Army. During the campaign in the West the Eighteenth captured Dunkirk. Von Küchler succeeded von Leeb but his command of Army Group North was uninspired. After the war he served six years in prison and died in 1969.

The 55-year-old Sixteenth Army commander, Colonel General Ernst Busch, is considered pro-Nazi. After commanding VIII Corps in Poland and the Sixteenth Army for four years, he took over Army Group Center, presiding over that organization's destruction in the summer of 1944. He died of a heart attack in British captivity in July 1945 and was buried in an unmarked grave.

A lifelong cavalry officer, Colonel General Erich Hoepner, age 54, commanded von Leeb's mobile formation, Fourth Panzer Group. In 1938 anti-Hitler army leaders earmarked his 1st Light Division to hold off SS units in Munich if the Czech crisis went badly for Germany. Hoepner commanded the XVI Panzer Corps in Poland and France. For Operation *Typhoon*, his Fourth Panzer Army transferred to Army Group Center and bore the brunt of the fighting for Moscow.

PREVIOUS PAGE:
Von Leeb (right foreground) and von Küchler (facing camera) at a forward observation post. The officer wearing little more than a peaked cap lying on the mound behind them is making himself a good target for enemy snipers. (Topfoto)

Hoepner has an anti-Nazi reputation but nevertheless on May 2, 1941 wrote the obligatory letter to his troops describing the upcoming "Battle for the existence of the German Volk against Jewish Bolshevism." In January 1942 he disobeyed Hitler's "No Retreat" order. The Führer accused him of "disobedience before the enemy," in addition to "endangering my authority as Supreme Commander" and ordered Hoepner "cashiered with all the resulting consequences." Implicated in the conspiracy surrounding the July 1944 attempt to assassinate Hitler, he was hanged by SS men that August.

Colonel General Nikolas von Falkenhorst was 56 years old when he commanded German forces operating from Norway and Central Finland. In 1918 he served in Finland as part of the German forces sent there to ensure the country's independence. In 1940, von Falkenhorst led the joint conquest of Scandinavia. The Nuremberg tribunal condemned him to death but commuted the sentence.

Two corps commanders are especially noteworthy: General of Infantry Erich von Manstein, commander of LVI Panzer Corps, had a superlative reputation well before *Barbarossa* and went on to become one of the most highly regarded German generals of World War II. Bavarian General of Mountain Troops Eduard Dietl joined the pre-Nazi German Workers' Party in 1919, before Hitler did. The "Hero of Narvik" died in an air crash in June 1944.

Among the Luftwaffe generals supporting Army Group North, Luftflotte 1 commander Colonel General Alfred Keller was an "old eagle" (a pre-1914 aviator, born in 1882). He joined the new Luftwaffe in 1935 and rose through various high commands only to retire in 1943. Lieutenant General Helmuth Förster, also a decorated World War I aviator, took command of I Fliegerkorps after the Royal Air Force shot down his predecessor shortly before *Barbarossa*. He left operational command for an Air Ministry staff position in 1942. Luftflotte 5 commander Colonel General Jürgen Stumpff was a World War I staff officer who became Chief of the Luftwaffe General Staff during the interwar years. He commanded in the far north, attacking Arctic convoys such as PQ17 until November 1943, when he was reassigned to command the Reich's air defense. Stumpff represented the Luftwaffe at the May 8, 1945 surrender ceremony. He died in 1974.

Army Group Center

The 64-year-old Field Marshal Fedor von Bock, commanding Army Group Center, has been described as a "difficult man." In April 1918 Major von Bock had earned the *Pour le Mérite* for "reckless bravery." He spoke French

Von Bock gets smiles from passing German soldiers. (Topfoto)

fluently and English and Russian well. He seems to have been neutral about the Nazi seizure of power. Von Bock led Army Group North in 1939 and Army Group B in Holland and Belgium. Usually "the stoic guardsman," he was the only senior leader to question *Barbarossa* when briefed on its plan in January 1941. Hitler relieved him of command of Army Group Center on December 19, 1941, but a month later recalled him to lead Army Group South. Unsatisfactory progress in Operation *Blau* caused Hitler to relieve von Bock for good in July 1942. He was killed along with his wife and stepdaughter when Royal Air Force aircraft strafed road traffic on May 2, 1945.

Colonel General Maximilian *Reichsfreiherr* von Weichs, age 59, commanded Second Army. A Bavarian cavalry captain in World War I, he was the first commander of 1st Panzer Division. Von Weichs commanded XIII Corps during the *Anschluss*, against Czechoslovakia and in Poland, then led the Second Army in France and the Balkan campaigns. He later led the northern wing of Operation *Blau* against Stalingrad, earning promotion to field marshal in February 1943 despite his questionable leadership during the Stalingrad crisis. Thereafter he commanded the German defense of Greece and Yugoslavia through 1944, until sent to Führer Reserve in March 1945. He died of natural causes in 1954.

Field Marshal Günther von Kluge (center) was a solid if unspectacular performer, but troublesome as both a superior and a subordinate. He earned his well-deserved reputation for deliberate and old-fashioned (i.e., non-blitzkrieg) leadership in France and the USSR, to the frustration of more decisive commanders. He still managed to get into the thick of battle, however, and like the more venturesome Guderian he was sometimes forced to draw his personal weapon for self defense. (MHI)

One of two field marshals to command a field army during *Barbarossa*, the 58-year old Günther Hans von Kluge led Fourth Army as he had in Poland and France. An artillery officer since the Great War, he resigned in 1938–39 over Hitler's aggressive policies. Recalled, he took command of Army Group Center upon von Bock's removal and undoubtedly came under the spell of the anti-Hitler conspirators rampant there. He led that organization in Operation *Citadel*, but was severely injured in an automobile crash in October 1943. He came out of hospital the following July just in time to replace Gerd von Rundstedt as Supreme Commander/West. He lasted in that post only until the next month when, suspected by Hitler of negotiating peace with the Western Allies, he swallowed poison.

Colonel General Adolf Strauss, age 61, had commanded Ninth Army under von Bock since the Western campaign. He trained his army to be the first wave of the stillborn Operation *Sealion* against Great Britain, until transferred east for *Barbarossa*. He led the Ninth with ability until January 12, 1942, when he asked to be relieved "for health reasons." Thereafter he sat out the rest of the war. He spent four years in POW camps and died in 1973.

Colonel General Heinz Guderian, 53 years old on *Barbarossatag*, commander of the Second Panzer Group, is one of the war's best-known generals. During the Great War and the Weimar period his experiences in *Jäger* units, his signal and transport duties, service with the Freikorps, and training at Kazan, USSR all prepared him to become one of the world's foremost theorists and practitioners of armored warfare. Perhaps because of this, he could act like a prima donna who refused to subordinate his desire for personal glory to the higher strategic purpose. He commanded XIX Motorized (Panzer) Corps in Poland and France. At von Kluge's urging, Hitler relieved him of command of Second Panzer Group on Christmas Day 1941. Guderian became Inspector General of Panzer Troops in February 1943. The Führer made him Chief of the German General Staff the day following the July 1944 *Attentat*, a position he held until March 1945. He died in 1954 after three years of captivity.

Third Panzer Group commander Colonel General Hermann Hoth, age 56, is one of the Wehrmacht's most underrated generals. He commanded XV Motorized (Panzer) Corps with distinction during the Polish and Western campaigns. In October 1941 he took over Seventeenth Army in the Ukraine. Starting in July 1942, he commanded Fourth Panzer Army, which he led toward Stalingrad, in the subsequent attempted relief of Sixth Army, in Operation *Backhand Blow* and as the Schwerpunkt of Operation *Citadel*'s southern wing in July 1943. Hitler relieved Hoth in December 1943, making him a scapegoat for the loss of Kiev, and did not recall him. He was a POW until 1954 and died in 1971.

Fifty-five-year-old Second Air Fleet commander Field Marshal Albert Kesselring started as a Bavarian artillery officer during the Great War, rising to the rank of army colonel in 1931. He transferred to the Luftwaffe in 1933 and within two years he became its chief of staff. He led Germany's largest aerial formations from Poland throughout *Barbarossa*. In November 1941 he (and many of his units) transferred to Italy, where he became the Axis Supreme Commander/South.

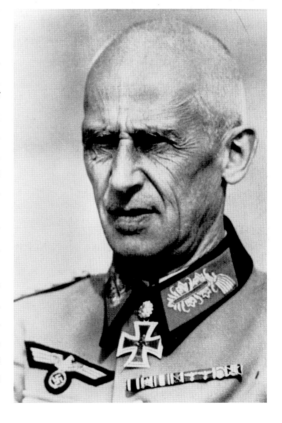

Colonel General Hermann "Papa" Hoth proved himself to be an exceptionally reliable commander from the outbreak of the war until 1943. A team player and a good man in a crisis, the commander of the Third Panzer Group suffered from few of Guderian's prima donna tendencies, and adhered better to *Barbarossa*'s plans and von Bock's orders. (MHI)

Colonel General Wolfram von Richthofen (in the leather coat) and his VIII Fliegerkorps set the standard for CAS by any air force during World War II; he had been specializing in such operations since the Spanish Civil War. A hands-on leader comfortable near the fighting, von Richthofen often landed in his Fieseler Storch liaison aircraft to confer directly with the army commanders he was supporting. (Podzun)

He held this position, very ably, through the North African, Sicilian, and most of the Italian campaigns. His final assignment as Supreme Commander/West came in January 1945 after Hitler relieved von Rundstedt for the last time. The death sentence from his war crimes trial was commuted and he was released from captivity in 1952 and died eight years later.

Colonel General Wolfram *Freiherr* von Richthofen, only 50 years old in 1941, commanded the elite VIII Fliegerkorps. A World War I cavalry officer, he was a civilian engineer during the Weimar years and transferred to the new Luftwaffe in 1933, within two years serving as the Condor Legion's chief of staff. Judging that strategic bombing would not win the war for Franco, he perfected CAS instead, developing and improving its planning, communications, and liaison with ground troops. He led his air corps from Poland through *Barbarossa*, served in the Mediterranean theater, in the Crimea, and during the Stalingrad relief effort, and became a field marshal in February 1943. He was diagnosed with a brain tumor in October 1944, and died in captivity nine months later.

The smaller II Fliegerkorps was commanded by Colonel General Bruno Loerzer, a 44-victory World War I ace and *Pour le Mérite* recipient. A lifelong personal friend of Hermann Göring, he was a leader of average talents, who did show some intelligent interest in ground support operations. His air corps was transferred to the Mediterranean in October 1941.

Army Group South

Army Group South commander Field Marshal Gerd von Rundstedt enjoyed respect from friend and foe throughout World War II. Von Rundstedt was 65 years old in June 1941. During the Great War he had served on divisional and corps staffs. Twice superiors nominated him for the *Pour le Mérite*. He commanded the Wehrmacht's main efforts during the Polish and Western campaigns.

At the end of *Barbarossa* Hitler accepted von Rundstedt's resignation on December 1, 1941. In four months the Führer recalled him to command in northwest France. Frustrated and arguing with Hitler over the conduct of the fighting in Normandy, von Rundstedt again resigned. Two months later Hitler ordered him back to duty to command the Ardennes offensive, only to relieve him one last time in March 1945. Perhaps the worst black mark on his otherwise impressive career followed the July 1944 assassination attempt against Hitler when he presided over the cynically named "Court of Honor," which removed suspected conspirators from the Army to be tried by the People's Court. He was spared a war crimes trial due to age and poor health, served in POW camps until 1949 and died in 1953.

Field Marshal Walter von Reichenau commanded the Sixth Army. He was 57 years old and had commanded this formation (named Tenth Army during the Polish campaign) for two years. Von Reichenau offered army assistance to Nazi Party elements purging the Sturmabteilung (SA) in June 1934, and authored the personal oath to Hitler sworn by all members of the Wehrmacht. Von Reichenau's men occupied Paris on June 14, 1940, and Hitler promoted him to field marshal the following month. After von Rundstedt's departure in December he simultaneously commanded Army Group South. He died of a heart attack in January 1942 while jogging in the Russian winter, becoming the first field marshal to die in World War II.

Eleventh Army commander was the 58-year-old Bavarian Colonel General Eugen *Ritter* von Schobert. He stood firmly in the pro-Hitler camp during the interwar intrigues that dominated the Army. He commanded the VII Corps in Poland and France. He was killed on

Colonel General Von Kleist did an outstanding job leading his First Panzer Group (later First Panzer Army) to Rostov. He wears the Knight's Cross awarded at the beginning of the 1940 campaign. (NARA)

September 12, 1941 when his liaison aircraft landed in a Soviet minefield.

General of Infantry Karl-Heinrich von Stülpnagel, 55 years old, commanded the Seventeenth Army, having led the II Corps in France. Colonel General Hermann Hoth replaced him as Seventeenth Army commander on October 10, 1941. Actively opposed to Hitler since 1938, von Stülpnagel became entangled in the July 1944 assassination plot. He tried committing suicide in the aftermath of the plot's failure, but only managed to blind himself. He was subsequently tried and hanged on August 30, 1944.

Colonel General Ewald von Kleist, age 60, led the First Panzer Group. He had served on the Eastern Front in World War I, fighting in the German victory at Tannenberg in 1914. Another long-time von Rundstedt subordinate, he commanded a panzer corps in Poland and panzer groups in France and the Balkans. In 1942 his First Panzer Army won a victory at Kharkov then raced to the Caucasus as part of Operation *Blau*. He defended first Kuban, then the Crimea, and finally Rumania. He demonstrated expertise in both offense and defense. Von Kleist died in Soviet captivity in 1954, the only field marshal to do so.

A number of Army Group South corps commanders achieved notoriety. Soviet aircraft killed General of Infantry Kurt von Briesen of LII Corps southeast of Kharkov on November 20. The Bavarian General of Mountain Troops Ludwig Kuebler was executed in Yugoslavia for war crimes in 1947. General of Infantry Hans von Salmuth served as Field Marshal Fedor von Bock's chief of staff in Poland and France. After commanding XXX Corps he led the Seventeenth, Fourth, Second, and Fifteenth Armies.

Some of *Barbarossa*'s division commanders also had interesting careers. Austrian Lieutenant General Max de Angelis, 76th Infantry Division, commanded his country's army, the Bundesheer, after the *Anschluss* with Germany in 1938. Major General Ludwig Cruewell gave up command of 11th Panzer Division on September 1, to take command of the Afrika Corps, only to be captured by the British on May 29, 1942. The 16th Panzer Division commander, one-armed Major General Hans Hube, was among the first German soldiers to reach the Volga River north of Stalingrad in 1942. As First Panzer Army commander he died in an airplane crash the day after receiving the Diamonds to his Knight's Cross on Hitler's birthday in 1944. Lieutenant General Hans *Graf* von Sponeck initially led the 22nd Infantry Division. On December 31, 1941 General Erich von Manstein relieved him as XXX Corps commander for making an unauthorized withdrawal in the Crimea. Herman Göring presided over his court martial and the SS shot him on July 23, 1944.

Luftwaffe commanders included Luftflotte 4 chief Colonel General Alexander Lohr, age 56. He served on the Austrian General Staff in World War I and prior to 1938 commanded the Austrian Air Force. He supported von Rundstedt in both Poland and the West and was in charge of all Luftwaffe forces during the 1941 Balkan campaign. After commanding Luftflotte 4 in 1942 in the Crimea and at Stalingrad he became Commander-in-Chief South East. Yugoslavia executed him for war crimes in 1947.

Lohr's principal subordinates from Poland through Operation *Blau* were World War I pilot Lieutenant General Kurt Pflugbeil (IV Fliegerkorps) and Lieutenant General Robert *Ritter* von Greim (V Fliegerkorps). Von Greim succeeded Göring as head of the Luftwaffe on 26 April 1945 and committed suicide less than a month later.

A number of Army Group North commanders earned the *Pour le Merite*: Busch and Keller mentioned above, plus Siegfried Haenicke (61st Infantry Division), Otto Lancelle (121st Infantry Division), and Ferdinand Schörner (6th Mountain Division). In addition to von Bock and Loerzer, Army Group Center commanders Wilhelm von Ditfurth (403rd Security Division) and Hermann Wilck (161st Infantry Division) received the award. No commanders from Army Group South earned it.

Soviet Commanders

Baltic Special and Leningrad Military Districts

Lieutenant General F.I. Kuznetsov commanded the Northwest Front. He was one of Stalin's most senior generals and although a well-regarded theoretician, had no combat experience since participating in the Civil War in 1920. The official Soviet history of the war dryly noted that Kuznetsov suffered from liabilities common to most other Front commanders: he was "unprepared to cope with the exceptionally complicated task" and "lacked the necessary operational and strategic preparation and practice." He commanded the Front only until June 30. He later commanded the Central Front in July, until German forces destroyed it a month later, and led the ill-fated 51st Army defending the Crimea in September. After he failed in that mission, Stalin shifted him to command of the 61st Army until he lost that job because of his alcoholism.

Colonel General F.I. Kuznetsov barely lasted a fortnight before being relieved of command. The Soviets' prewar assumption was that the Germans would largely bypass Kuznetsov's Northwest Front as they drove for Moscow; thus, he was ill-prepared for Army Group North's onslaught. (David Glantz)

Marshal K.E. Voroshilov replaced Kuznetsov as commander of the Northwest Front. He had joined the Communist Party in 1903 and was active in the October Revolution and Russian Civil War. During the latter he served in the 1st Cavalry Army with Stalin at Tsaritsyn (Stalingrad). This association protected Voroshilov from the consequences of his own mistakes and Stalin's paranoia. He held the position of Commissar for Military and Naval Affairs (renamed Commissar for Defense) from 1925–40. Never known for his intelligence, much of the USSR's ill-preparedness is directly attributed to Voroshilov's incompetence.

Voroshilov did bring new spirit to the Northwest Front when he first arrived. As the situation deteriorated and Stalin contemplated relieving him, the Marshal behaved recklessly at the front, seemingly wanting a hero's death. This was not to be and in September Zhukov replaced him. Stalin kept him in various high-visibility, but menial, positions until turning against him after the war. Voroshilov fell further from grace during the Nikita Khrushchev era, but Leonid Brezhnev rehabilitated the old marshal.

Lieutenant General M.M. Popov commanded the Northern Front from the Arctic Ocean to Leningrad's southern approaches. A former Tsarist colonel, he fought for the Red Army in the Crimea during the Russian Civil War. He is generally credited with steady leadership of his front despite Voroshilov's incompetence. Popov commanded in the Voronezh sector during the German 1942 campaign, an overambitious mobile attack group as part of Operation *Saturn*, and led the Bryansk Front during the 1943 Kursk battles. He ended the war commanding the 2nd Baltic Front.

Lieutenant General P.P. Sobennikov led the 8th Army. In August he took over the Northwest Front when Voroshilov was kicked upstairs to a new position coordinating Leningrad's defense. When the Northwest Front dissolved, Sobennikov became commander of the 43rd Army defending the northern Moscow area. He survived the war.

In command of the 11th Army was Lieutenant General V.I. Morozov. The historian Albert Seaton considered him one of the Red Army's most experienced generals. Morozov contributed to the design of the T-34 tank. Although *Barbarossa*'s opening blows almost annihilated the 11th Army, Morozov managed to maintain it in the field and the 11th was counterattacking near Staraya Russa in 1942.

In the far north, Lieutenant General V.A. Frolov commanded the 14th Army (later the Karelian Front) against Dietl's *Gebirgsjäger*. He did such a good job that in 1944 when the time came to take the offensive, Stalin considered Frolov too defensively minded.

Another significant Soviet leader was Vice Admiral V.F. Tributs, commanding the Red Banner Baltic Fleet, the Soviet's largest. In contravention of Stalin's orders he took preparatory measures prior to *Barbarossa* that very likely saved his fleet. As Axis ground forces gobbled up

Lieutenant General V.A. Frolov was one of the few Red Army leaders to survive *Barbarossa*. His command of Soviet forces in the far north benefited from a number of factors: unity of command, superior logistics, a relatively large naval contingent, and good lateral rail lines. (David Glantz)

its forward bases, the Baltic fleet was finally trapped on the island base of Kronshtadt. He planned to scuttle the fleet in September but Army Group North ran out of steam before he gave the orders. Tributs commanded the fleet until the end of the war.

Western Special Military District

Lieutenant General D.G. Pavlov, the luckless commander of WSMD and the 671,165-man Western Front, was cruelly nicknamed "the Soviet Guderian." A World War I cavalry officer, he had served in the Spanish Civil War, but mislearned its lessons: he judged that armored forces were not suited for employment in large formations and that the Red Army's tanks should supplement rifle divisions in battalion strength. He did lead Soviet armor against Vyborg in the closing days of the Winter War in Finland. During the last hours of peace he was enjoying

The cruel realities of *Barbarossa* completely outclassed Lieutenant General D.G. Pavlov who was equivalent to a man who brought a knife to a gun fight. Within a month Stalin had Pavlov, Pavlov's chief of staff, and 4th Army commander Korobkov standing before firing squads. (Corbis)

comedy theater at the Minsk Officers Club, and dismissed (literally) eleventh-hour warnings that night as rumors. He was arrested for "disgraceful cowardice, negligence, breakdown in command and control"; Stalin had Pavlov shot in late July, but Khrushchev posthumously rehabilitated his reputation in 1956.

The 3rd Army commander, Lieutenant General V.I. Kuznetsov, managed to survive *Barbarossa*. He went on to lead the 21st, 58th, 1st Shock, 4th Reserve, 63rd (at Stalingrad), 1st Guards, and 3rd Shock armies. In this final assignment his soldiers captured the Reichstag in May 1945.

The 4th Army commander, Major General A.A. Korobkov, suffered the same fate as his superior Pavlov; Korobkov never had control over his organization, but was executed as a traitor nonetheless.

Major General K.D. Golubev initially commanded 10th Army. Later in *Barbarossa* he took over 43rd Army, remaining in command until severely wounded in action in 1944.

The following corps commanders did not survive Operation *Barbarossa*: Major Generals V.B. Borisov (21st Rifle); M.P. Petrov (17th Mechanized, died of wounds); F.D. Rubtsev (1st Rifle, died in German captivity); A.V. Garnov (5th Rifle); I.S. Nikitin (6th Cavalry, executed in German captivity for "organizing an underground organization"); and M.G. Khatskilevich (6th Mechanized, dead before the end of June).

In the wake of the unmitigated disasters which immediately befell the leaders of the West Front, a second echelon of commanders rose up. These included Red Army luminaries Budenny, Timoshenko, and Zhukov. Unknown in 1941, but also significant later were the following:

Lieutenant General I.V. Boldin, Pavlov's deputy, was enjoying the same comedy play as his commander on June 21, but he managed to escape serving in close proximity to his superior. Boldin had served on the Turkish Front during World War I; he commanded mechanized forces that occupied eastern Poland in 1939, and the 9th Army which invaded Bessarabia a year later. During Operation *Typhoon* he commanded 50th Army, frustrating Guderian's attempts

Lieutenant General I.V. Boldin, Commander of the 50th Army. Boldin escaped from the Minsk pocket in July 1941 and the Vyazma pocket in October 1941. His dogged defense of Tula and persistent counterattacks against Guderian's left flank doomed the German southern pincer against Moscow. (David Glantz)

The pitiless realities of the attempts to halt von Bock's assaults almost cost 19th Army commander Lieutenant General I.S. Konev his job (and perhaps his life) within weeks of his arrival on the Moscow axis. He soon regained his balance, and went on to become one of Stalin's best operational commanders. (Elukka)

to take Tula. His soldiers recaptured Bryansk in 1943. Boldin is considered a mediocre general who used political acumen to keep his job until 1945.

Ukrainian Lieutenant General A.I. Yeremenko arrived at the West Front on June 29 and immediately went to work. Wounded in action in October, he spent nearly a year in hospital, and was then almost captured by German tanks near Stalingrad. After *Barbarossa* he went on to command the Southeast, Stalingrad, Southern, Kalinin, 2nd Baltic, and 4th Ukrainian Fronts. Yeremenko earned promotion to marshal in 1958.

Soviet Generals

G.K. Zhukov, 1896–1974,
Marshal of the Soviet Union

Arguably the most successful general of World War II, the peasant Zhukov began his military career as a cavalry trooper during Word War I. He was twice awarded the Cross of St George. During the Russian Civil War he served in the fabled 1st Cavalry Army, earning the Order of the Red Banner. He climbed through the ranks of Red cavalry and managed to avoid persecution during Stalin's purges.

Commanding Soviet forces in Mongolia in 1938, Zhukov faced off against the rogue Japanese Kwantung Army. He patiently built up his forces to a 3:2 superiority in manpower, a 2:1 ratio in artillery and aircraft, and a 4:1 advantage in armor. He launched his attack supported by mechanized attacks on the Japanese flanks. John Erickson described the battle of Khalkin Gol (Nomonhan to the Japanese) as "a brilliant but costly operation" because of Zhukov's lavish expenditure of manpower.[1] For Zhukhov Khalkin Gol became the blueprint for his future operations. Strategically the battle had immense import. The victory occurred during negotiations of the Molotov–Ribbentrop Pact, but due to the state of communications at the time only the Soviet leadership knew of its outcome. Ultimately Stalin could be fairly sure he would have no more trouble from the Japanese.

Zhukov's victory brought him notoriety, a Hero of the Soviet Union medal and promotion to command of the Kiev Military District. Here he demonstrated high-level administrative skills to match his battlefield abilities. In June 1940 he led the Soviet occupation of Bessarabia. His star continued to rise during the Kremlin wargames seven months later and Stalin named him Chief of Staff, Deputy Defense Minister, and therefore member of the Supreme Soviet in February 1941; he was now also a political leader.

Harrison Salisbury called Zhukov, "… the master of disaster … the general who was sent in when all else failed, whose terrible temper, iron will and savage determination … wore men down (and condemned not a few to the firing squad)."[2] Regarding his October defense of Leningrad Zhukov said, "I have cobbled together a reasonable organization and have virtually stopped the enemy advance; and you know how I propose to go on: I will wear him out and then beat him." On more than one occasion he did exactly that.

It seems Zhukov could get away with conduct others could not. A Red Army colonel who observed Zhukov in November 1941 observed, "I was surprised by Zhukov's behavior. He spoke in a sharp, commanding tone. It looked as if Zhukov were really the superior officer here. And Stalin accepted this as proper. At times a kind of bafflement even crossed his (Stalin's) face."

Even Zhukov was guilty of missteps, most notably his poor performance west of Moscow in a November 1942 offensive meant as a bookend to operations against Stalingrad. He is also criticized for being careless with the lives of his men, but his meticulous operational planning saved many Red Army soldiers. He was personally involved in every major Soviet operation of the war; in addition to those already mentioned, the liberation of the Ukraine in 1943 and Belorussia in 1944 as well as the capture of Berlin in 1945.

Major General I.S. Konev spent *Barbarossa*'s first weeks away from the fighting, until called to command 19th Army. After his initial poor performances there, only Zhukov's personal intervention saved Konev from Stalin's wrath. By Operation *Citadel* he had regained the dictator's confidence, and he too commanded a large number of fronts after *Barbarossa*: West, Steppe, Northwest, 2nd and 1st Ukrainian. He and Zhukov raced for Berlin in 1945. Promoted to marshal in 1956, Konev commanded Soviet forces that crushed the Hungarian Uprising of that year.

Fearing Zhukov's popularity, after the war Stalin banished him to Odessa. The marshal nevertheless venerated Stalin, even after the dictator's disgrace in the late 1950s. To this day the Russian people continue to have immense respects for Zhukov's accomplishments.

Marshal A.M. Vasilevsky, 1895–1977, Chief of Soviet General Staff and Deputy Minister of Defense

As the son of an Orthodox priest, a seminary student and cultured World War I infantry captain and battalion commander, Vasilevsky was an unlikely choice for Stalin's World War II Red Army chief of staff. In 1936 he earned selection to the new General Staff Academy; three-quarters of his class fell afoul of Stalin's purges and did not graduate. While at the academy Vasilevsky caught the attention of then-chief of staff General B.M. Shaposhnikov (himself a Tsarist colonel) who became the junior officer's mentor. After graduating he headed the general staff section responsible for operational training of senior officers; this position put him into close contact with the Red Army leaders who would eventually defeat Hitler.

On August 1, 1941 Vasilevsky became the head of the general staff operations section so therefore accompanied Shaposhnikov to daily meetings with Stalin. The two generals tried unsuccessfully to convince the dictator to evacuate Kiev and save Kirponos' command. When most of the general staff evacuated Moscow on October 16–17, Vasilevsky became Stalin's closest military confidant, earning promotion to lieutenant general by the end of the month. He worked closely with Zhukov on the defense of Moscow. In May 1942 he was Stavka representative at the Northwestern Front when Stalin recalled him to Moscow. Despite his protests, on June 26 he took Shaposhnikov's chief of staff position in place of the ailing marshal.

Vasilevsky's baptism of fire in his new job came two days later when Hitler launched Operation *Blau* toward Stalingrad and the Caucasus oil region. During this campaign he began to work more closely with Zhukov. Later that summer, along with Stalin the two conceived the subsequent Soviet counteroffensive and the following year the defensive operation at Kursk. Vasilevsky was promoted to marshal in February 1943. Harrison E. Salisbury noted that Zhukov's "closest and most important collaborator was his brilliant general staff colleague, General Vasilevsky."[3]

Stalin leaned heavily on the chief of staff and his "intellectual acuteness." But Vasilevsky also did double duty as Stavka representative on far-flung theaters and Stalin sorely missed him when he was absent from Moscow. On February 17, 1945 Vasilevsky gave up his chief of staff job to command the Soviet Manchurian offensive against the Japanese. After the war he served as Defense Minister from 1949–53, when, upon Stalin's death, Vasilevsky's closeness to the dictator became a political liability.

1   Erickson, *Road to Stalingrad*.
2   Salisbury's introduction to *Marshal Zhukov's Greatest Battles*, p.12.
3   Salisbury (ed.), *Marshal Zhukov's Greatest Battles*, p.111.

Kiev Special and Odessa Military Districts

Lieutenant General M.P. Kirponos ably led the Southwest Front through the battle of Kiev. He served in World War I, the Russian Civil War, and at Khalkin Gol in 1939. He rose to prominence when his 70th Rifle Division captured the Vyborg fortress in the closing days of the Winter War. Shortly afterwards Stalin rewarded him with command of the Leningrad Military District. As part of the Red Army command shakeup following the January 1941 wargames, Kirponos took over the Kiev Special Military District. He died trying to escape the Kiev pocket.

Marshal S.M. Budenny, aged 58, gained prominence as a crony of Stalin while commanding the 1st Cavalry Army during the Russian Civil War (guaranteeing his safety during the purges). After commanding the doomed South West Direction destroyed at Kiev he led the North Caucasus Front until relieved in September 1942. The following year Stalin appointed him to the largely ceremonial position of Commander of Red Army Cavalry.

Marshal S.K. Timoshenko was born in 1895. An NCO in World War I and another 1st Cavalry Army veteran, he oversaw the occupation of eastern Poland in 1939 and the climax of the war against Finland in 1939–40. Stalin thereupon appointed him Defense Commissar. Timoshenko initiated Red Army reforms in view of the early blitzkrieg victories and had the unenviable job of preparing for *Barbarossa*. Considered the most competent prewar Soviet marshal, he commanded numerous fronts throughout the war and occupied Vienna in 1945.

Lieutenant General I.V. Tyulenev commanded the Southern Front until wounded in September 1941. He was a cavalry officer in World War I and commanded a brigade in the 1st Cavalry Army. He presented a paper on defensive operations during the January 1941 wargames and subsequently commanded the prestigious Moscow District. On June 22 Stalin sent him and his staff to the Odessa Military District that two days later became the Southern Front.

In his postwar memoirs Zhukov singled out army commanders Kostenko, Muzychenko, and Potapov for special praise. In 1938 the 5th Army leader, Major General M.I. Potapov, graduated from the Military Academy of Mechanization and Motorization. His skillful defense on the Southwest Front's northern wing created the salient in the Soviet lines that became the Kiev pocket. He later commanded the 61st Army in its defense of Moscow.

The 6th Army commander, Major General I.N. Muzychenko, had previously commanded the 15th Corps in the Winter War against Finland in

1939–40. Captured at Uman, he survived and returned home in 1945. Major General F.Y. Kostenko of the 26th Army went on to command a rebuilt Southwest Front in January 1942. He died in action near Kharkov four months later. Lieutenant General Y.T. Cherevicenko eventually succeeded Tyulenev and subsequently led the Bryansk Front near Moscow in early 1942 and the Coastal Group against Operation *Blau*. Major General A.K. Smirnov served as interwar Inspector General of Infantry and spoke on rifle division defense as part of the January wargames. He died in action when von Manstein crushed his 18th Army against the Sea of Azov in October 1941.

Two naval leaders excelled in land combat during *Barbarossa*. Vice Admiral F.S. Oktyabrsky, Black Sea Fleet commander, was in charge of the besieged city of Sevastopol. Rear Admiral G.V. Zhukov (no relation of the Red Army chief of staff) ably defended Odessa against the Rumanians. Both survived to command beyond 1942. Red Army Air Force commanders during *Barbarossa* were Lieutenant General F. Astakov (Southwest Front) and Major General M.V. Zakharov (Southern).

Some mechanized corps commanders deserve mention: Major General A.A. Vlasov (4th Mechanized Corps), a Russian Civil War veteran, went on to lead the 38th Army in Moscow's defense and near Leningrad. Captured near Volkov in July 1942, he created the three-division-strong Russian Liberation Army, a force of former Red Army POWs fighting for Germany. Vlasov was captured, tried for treason and hanged in 1946. The 9th Mechanized Corps commander, Major General K.K. Rokossovsky, was a World War I NCO and Civil War cavalryman who had been jailed during the purges. Interestingly, he was Zhukov's superior during the 1930s while commanding 7th Samara Cavalry Division. Later in the war he commanded the 16th Army, the Don, Central, and 1st and 2nd Byelorussian Fronts. After the war he served as Poland's Defense Minister. Within six months of *Barbarossatag* 16th Mechanized Corps leader Brigadier General A.D. Sokolov was promoted to Lieutenant General and commanded 2nd Shock Army near Moscow. Major General N.V. Feklenko of the 19th Mechanized Corps had served under Zhukov at Khalkin Gol.

THE FRONTIER BATTLES

A key to the blitzkrieg was sending the enemy into "systems overload" from the very first shot. From the youngest soldier holding the frontlines to opposing political leadership in the national capital, no defender would be given the opportunity to get his bearings or a take moment's pause. As Zhukov observed, the German forces attacked northeast, east, and southeast in seemingly equal strength all along the 1939 Molotov–Ribbentrop demarcation line. Panzer spearheads and fast reconnaissance units showed up dozens of miles behind the front, where defenders expected friendly reinforcements to be. Headquarters of Soviet tactical and operational commands were overrun, captured, or otherwise rendered ineffective. Communications were cut, interdicted, or delayed to the point where instructions reached units that were already destroyed, in headlong flight, or in some other fashion completely unable to comply.

From Memel to L'vov the Wehrmacht command system, German units in contact with the enemy, and Luftwaffe CAS overwhelmed the defenders. Everywhere they operated within the Boyd Loop of the Red Army.[21] Coherent defenses occasionally sprang up under competent commanders almost despite the actions of higher headquarters. Soviet defenders fought to the death, surrendered in droves, melted into the countryside to later become partisan bands, or retreated – sometimes in good order and other times in panic. No one would confuse Poland or France with the Soviet Union, but Germany had basically defeated the first two nations by the time the 1939 and 1940 campaigns were a fortnight old. Military experts around the globe assumed the outcome would be the same for the USSR, even if the country's size doubled or tripled the required timeframe.

The deadly dance began on that Sunday morning and would not end for nearly four years. In many places the initial breakthroughs were as easy, the river crossings as quick, and the exploitation sprints as deep as initially expected. But

---

21   USAF Colonel John Boyd developed the OODA loop to evaluate decision-making, initially for fighter pilots. Since then it has been used to evaluate leadership, especially in stressful situations like those found in war. The key components are Orientation, Observation, Decision, and Action. The side that cycles through this loop faster will usually be successful.

the defenders were tougher, the roads alternately dustier or muddier, and the distances longer than previously assumed. Yet within mere days the German forces breached the Dvina River line, a key to the entire Soviet plan, and began to form the Minsk pocket on the critical Moscow axis. In the Ukraine, mechanized corps threw themselves piecemeal against the panzer thrust. Soon no coherent opposition stood in the panzers' way and the first pockets began to close.

The encirclements were not so watertight, however, and executing them cost more in losses and time than the German commanders would have liked. Ammunition and petroleum usage far exceeded prewar logistics estimates but the count of vaporized Soviet formations mounted. Leningrad, Smolensk, and Kiev all seemed within the German forces' grasp. Meanwhile between the Gulf of Finland and the Arctic Circle Axis and Soviet forces fought bitterly in their short campaign season. Hitler, Stalin, and their staffs understood the strategic importance of the USSR's northern lifeline to the outside world.

The Lithuanian Frontier

On April 22 von Leeb's headquarters moved from Dresden to Waldfrieden, barely 50 miles from Hitler's *Wolfsschanze* (Wolf's Lair). However, this proximity did not engender conceptual closeness between the two men. On May 30, regimental commanders received their attack orders. Officers in troop units still spoke of "bluff" and "demonstration" against the USSR and an invasion of Great Britain instead. Reality intruded at 1300hrs on June 21 when Army Group North received the codeword "Düsseldorf," indicating *Barbarossa* would start the next morning, and passed down its own codeword, "Dortmund."

Surprise attacks, without declarations of war, were central to Soviet military theory. Yet one hour before the Germans' artillery preparation, Red Army High Command signaled its armies: "No provocations will be made which could lead to complications… Meet a German surprise attack with all forces available." Stalin might have been worried about "victory-drunk German generals" but seemed more concerned about not provoking a war than preparing for one.

Panzer Thrust to the Dvina River

Von Leeb's units moved into jumping-off positions in the crowded Memelland on June 18. Leaders reconnoitered the front dressed as East Prussian farmers. At around 0345hrs on June 22 their artillery preparation began, lasting between 45 minutes and three hours. Irregular Soviet artillery defensive fire began within an hour, followed by Red Army Air Force attacks a further hour later, both indicating at least a degree of preparedness. Thick fog confused the situation until about 0500hrs and advancing Landsers immediately encountered the swamps and marshes that characterized the campaign in the north. Although Kuznetsov defended with only one regiment per division forward, already on the first day older German officers noted they faced stiff defenses and "a different enemy than in 1914."

Long days and short nights meant hard marching and fighting, and little rest for either side. On June 22 the 291st Infantry Division advanced 40 miles, while the 8th Panzer Division covered nearly 50 miles to capture a crossing of the Dubysa River's deep ravine at Ariogala. In some locations Soviet defenders fought bitterly, elsewhere the Germans reported "the enemy is not to be seen." It took 18 days for Stavka to receive a situation report from the Northwest Front. Stalin's High Command ordered Königsberg and Memel bombed, and the 3rd and 12th Mechanized Corps to occupy attack positions. Kuznetsov was relatively lucky that he faced only one panzer group. However, his advancing 2nd Tank Division (which included 55 T-34 and KV tanks out of a total of 200, but was separated from the remainder of the 3rd Mechanized Corps) missed the 8th Panzer Division like two ships passing in the night.

German intelligence misinterpreted the enemy's tactical retreats as a general withdrawal. The Soviet High Command had different, aggressive plans. On the morning of June 23 Sobennikov ordered the 3rd Mechanized Corps to attack northwest and the 12th Mechanized Corps to advance southeast by noon. Their objective: blunt XLI Panzer's thrust. To get to their assembly areas the 3rd and 12th Mechanized marched 60 and 50 miles respectively while both corps had less than one and a half hours to prepare. Therefore Soviet counterattacks against General of Panzer Troops Georg-Hans Reinhardt began slowly on the 23rd, but intensified over the next two days.

Generals Hoepner, seen here on a field telephone, and Reinhardt led the main panzer drive toward Leningrad. Reinhardt's XI Panzer Corps bore the brunt of the fighting for the city while von Manstein struggled on a more easterly bearing. (Scharnhorst Verlag)

Sobennikov's target was spread out. The 1st Panzer Division had fought its way through Taurage, where the Soviet forces had turned every building into a small fort. By the evening of June 23, with the assistance of the Brandenburger's *Wachkompanie*, 1st Panzer captured a critical 300-yard-long railroad bridge at Tytuvenai. To the southeast the 6th Panzer Division outran its logistical support on the first day and desperately needed ammunition. The division failed to achieve its initial mission, another Dubysa crossing, and now assumed an *Igel* (hedgehog or all-round defensive position) defense near Raseiniai as over 100 Red Army tanks struck. Its motorcycle infantry battalion survived barely 20 minutes. General Reinhardt sensed danger, and ordered the 1st Panzer to halt and turn east in support. Panzers and KV-1s engaged at ranges of 30–60 yards. Sunlight illuminated the slaughter for 18 hours a day.

The XLI Panzer Corps battled to save its spearhead. With its PzKpfw 35(t)s the 6th Panzer Division appeared isolated and overwhelmed. The 2nd Tank Division smashed its 114th Motorized Infantry Regiment, crushing vehicles and mutilating German wounded. For the first time in the accompanying infantry divisions, the cry went out "*Panzerjäger* to the front!"

Briefing armored car crewmen of the 12th Mechanized Corps during the battles against the XLI Panzer Corps at Raseiniai. Parked in the tree line are BA-6 or BA-10 scout cars. (HITM)

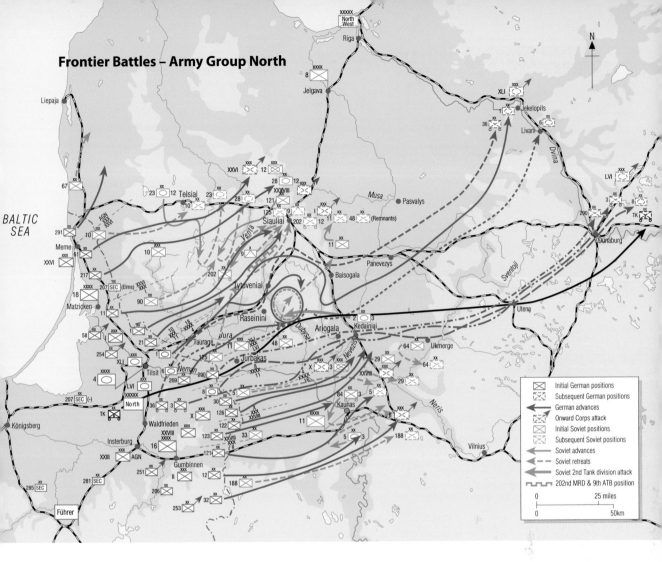

Frontier Battles – Army Group North

The 25th was the critical day of the armor battle. Soviet tanks and infantry ambushed the 1st Panzer Division's command post, where General Kirchner and his staff defended themselves with their individual weapons. However Kuznetsov forfeited mass and concentration by ordering his mechanized formations to "operate in small columns to avoid enemy aircraft." The 1st Panzer made slow progress through the sand and moorland, but soon arrived to help the beleaguered 6th. Together these two units averted the crisis and actually trapped much of the 3rd Mechanized Corps; the 12th Mechanized Corps was destroyed soon after.

The 12th Mechanized had mustered 690 tanks on June 22. A week later it counted 50 operational tanks. Tanks that ran out of fuel became pillboxes, which German sappers had to take out in difficult and time-consuming individual actions. I Fliegerkorps alone claimed over 200 tanks destroyed on the Raseiniai battlefield. David Glantz considers the Soviet 28th Tank Division's losses of 198 out of 220 tanks to be typical. Now free to advance, and with a contingent of Brandenburger commandos, the 1st Panzer Division gained its own Dvina bridgehead at Jekolopils to bring it up alongside with the LVI Panzer Corps. For Reinhardt's men *Barbarossa* had had a very rocky beginning.

To their southeast, Army Group North achieved greater success with von Manstein's rush to the critical Dvina crossing at Dünaburg. After seizing the bridge at Ariogala, his three divisions stretched along the single suitable road like an "armored centipede." In 100 hours they covered 200 miles, the same distance as from the western German border to Dunkirk. Luftwaffe reconnaissance could see no enemy forces to their front. The LVI Panzer Corps had exploited an 80-mile gap created in the Soviet defenses when the Sixteenth Army and Hermann Hoth's Third Panzer Group pushed the 11th Army east, instead of north along with the remainder of Kuznetsov's Front.

Hoepner's panzer group had not been associated with an infantry army as the others had on *Barbarossatag*, primarily so it could race for Dünaburg unencumbered. But with Reinhardt struggling around Raseiniai, Hoepner shifted his Schwerpunkt to the more successful von Manstein. For his part Kuznetsov ordered the 27th Army, augmented by the 21st Mechanized Corps, to make for the fortified city but von Manstein got there first. A flying column, led by Brandenburgers riding in captured Soviet trucks followed by pioneers and the 29th Motorized Infantry Regiment, streaked across the countryside in the early morning of June 26, watched passively by awakening Red Army soldiers. By 0800hrs, first the Brandenburgers then the other German elements arrived at Dünaburg in 15–20-minute intervals capturing one vehicle and one railroad bridge. The Soviet forces attempted to torch the latter, but were thwarted by German pioneers.

To his credit Kuznetsov initiated counterattacks in the evening of June 27. Though Landsers marched quickly to close the 75-mile gap to von Manstein's position, for three days the isolated LVI Panzer Corps' only outside assistance came from Luftwaffe CAS. The Red Army Air Force flew 2,100 sorties against von Manstein's men, and the Luftwaffe Bf-109s of Jagdgeschwader 54 went on a killing spree. Zerstörergeschwader 26 alone destroyed over 200 tanks.

On June 25 Timoshenko ordered Kuznetsov to hold the Dvina but he failed to do so. To compound the error of allowing the 11th Army to slip eastward from the border battles toward Opochka (above), Kuznetsov now

ordered the remnants of the 27th Army to do the same. The 8th Army made matters worse by slipping north toward Riga, leaving von Leeb's men an almost open field. If giving the German forces a clear run to Dünaburg was not bad enough, Kuznetsov had now opened the Ostrov–Pskov road to Leningrad. On June 29, Stavka instructed him to defend the Stalin Line, another mission in which he would soon fail. Stalin relieved Kuznetsov and his political officer the next day for having "failed to organize a stable front." Sobennikov was promoted to command of the hapless front, and General F.S. Ivanov in turn took command of the 8th Army. A beneficial side effect of these changes was that the Northwest Front received a new and energetic chief of staff tasked to master the situation "at all cost" and halt the Germans, Lieutenant General N.F. Vatutin.

A medic attends to a wounded soldier fighting in the Dünaburg bridgehead in late June. The capture of the bridge after just four days represented a major coup for von Manstein although his men then had to fight hard to hold it. (HITM)

Infantry Armies on the Flanks

As Eighteenth Army advanced through the Baltic States, on *Barbarossa's* second day elements of its 291st Infantry Division neared Liepaja on the coast, ably defended by the 67th Rifle Division. Inland the 11th Infantry Division fought past trenches and fortifications dating from 1915–17. Siauliai fell on June 26. Ventspils in Courland was soon flying a white flag and the 61st Infantry Division, destined to play crucial roles in the story of

ABOVE Soviet 8th Army attempts to break out, Dünaburg bridgehead, June 28, 1941: the Germans considered the Dvina–Dnepr River line the Red Army's last, best hope at halting *Barbarossa* early. If their panzers could rush the rivers and establish bridgeheads on the far bank they believed they could unhinge the Soviets' defenses and prevent a withdrawal. (**1**) Dünaburg, the massive 17th-century brick fortress faced the invaders; (**2**) German heavy weapons from the fortress fired down in support; (**3**) Soviets picked their way forward, in this case with a Maxim 1911 machine gun; (**4**) a Panzer Mark II has been destroyed by a shot to the turret; (**5**) the battlefield is littered with death and destruction and the sky is criss-crossed with the smoke of falling Soviet aircraft. (© Osprey Publising, Peter Dennis)

this campaign, crossed the Dvina on June 30 to capture Riga against minimal resistance a day later. Von Küchler's men covered over 150 miles in ten days. To avoid marching in the worst of the heat, the general often limited movement to 0300–0800hrs and 1800–2200hrs.

Southeast of Riga and by now surrounded on three sides by Fourth Panzer Group and the Eighteenth Army, the Soviet 8th Army was threatened with destruction. Both I and XXVI Infantry Corps amalgamated all their trucks with their assault guns to create fast detachments in an attempt to encircle the 8th Army. Von Küchler led from the front but after three days he feared his small mobile groups would be crushed by the mass of Soviet troops and so slowed the chase; the Soviet forces escaped the parallel pursuit.

The Sixteenth Army simultaneously tried to stay close behind Hoepner, cover von Leeb's eastern flank and maintain contact with Army Group Center. Within two days its 121st Infantry Division reached the fortress city of Kaunas, the interwar Lithuanian capital, and 11th Army headquarters. Red Army defenders had destroyed the Neman and Neris River bridges but X Corps engineers rebuilt them by June 25. The Soviet forces launched fierce counterattacks on the 26th but General Busch's men used every infantry weapon at their disposal plus assault guns and Lithuanian "activists" to hold their bridgehead.

On the army group right the Sixteenth Army then maintained the pursuit through two weeks of heat and dust interrupted by an occasional day of rain. Marching was tough but morale remained high. Brandenburgers captured 24 intact bridges throughout the army's area. By the night of July 3/4 the 30th Infantry Division captured Busch's first crossing of the Dvina near Livani. The II Corps fell in behind Hoepner's panzers. The Sixteenth Army relied on aerial resupply and captured Soviet stocks as late as mid-July due to the interdiction of German convoys by Red Army groups still operating behind their lines.

However, a growing major concern of Army Group North (and Halder) was its boundary with von Bock. Busch dedicated an entire corps to maintaining contact with the latter's Ninth Army. This became more difficult when the Ninth veered south to the Bialystok Kessel. As the two army groups subsequently diverged toward individual objectives the gap would widen and became even more dangerous. By July 4 Halder noted threatening Soviet movement to Velikie Luki, "between Hoth and Hoepner."

Two German M-class minesweepers tied up under the medieval spire of Riga's Lutheran cathedral on September 10. With Luftwaffe assistance the small Kriegsmarine detachment in the Baltic kept the larger Red Banner Fleet bottled up at Kronshtadt. (Corbis)

The Twin Battles of Bialystok and Minsk

The last few weeks of peace in the east passed quickly for the German forces. The code words alerting them of an imminent Soviet invasion, "*Achtung Berta*," never came. By May 30, German units in occupied Poland learned of their change of mission: they were no longer on the defensive, but were preparing to invade the USSR. Among the German troops rumors circulated that Red border guards would give them free passage to the Persian Gulf oilfields. Headquarters of all echelons completed preparations; new units arrived constantly from the Reich, France, and the Balkans, some rolling off rail cars to their final assembly areas even after June 22. Besides practicing long marches, conducting marksmanship training, and checking equipment, some soldiers marked their final days of occupation duty with soccer games and unit equestrian competitions. The Ostheer waited for the unusually high, fast-flowing rivers of that spring to subside. During the night of June 20–21, von Bock's men moved their heavy weapons forward. The next night was dark with only a faint crescent of the waning moon. Austrians of the 137th Infantry Division watched their Soviet counterparts across the border working to improve their positions under illumination provided by their vehicle headlights. In Minsk, General Pavlov returned from the theater, but was kept from his bed by reports of increased German activity. Sunrise came at 0410hrs on that Sunday of June 22, but by that time *Barbarossa* was already an hour old.

A good idea of the complexity of bridge-building in order to cross Russia's many and often wide rivers can be gained from this collection of combat vehicles, trucks and trailers, timber, and watercraft photographed by the Bug River in June 1941. (HITM)

Breakthrough

Sunday, June 22, 1941 was one of those incredibly eventful days common in history. After numerous requests, Timoshenko finally allowed Pavlov to alert his troops at 0300hrs, but this was generally a futile gesture. The Ninth Army and Third Panzer Group attacked at 0305hrs in coordination with Army Group North, while Fourth Army and Second Panzer Group moved out at 0315hrs, as did von Rundstedt to their south. As the mission and enemy situation dictated, certain units enjoyed massive artillery preparatory fire while others did without. A member of the 87th Infantry Division called the bombardment "a macabre salute to death and destruction."

In some places along the River Bug, Guderian's men captured bridges intact by ruse; elsewhere they used assault boats covered by StuG fire to force their way across. In the 18th Panzer Division sector, 80 specially modified submarine tanks of I/Panzer Regiment 18 crossed under water. Hoth's men faced a dry front, but would encounter three rivers within a little over 40 miles of the frontier. In the former Soviet zone many Polish peasants naively greeted the German troops with salt and bread, their traditional gifts to travelers.

Pavlov's men offered little or no resistance for hours. Since mid-June he had been asking in vain for permission to occupy forward positions. Timoshenko telephoned for a fourth time on *Barbarossatag* to tell Pavlov's deputy Boldin, "No action is to be taken against the Germans without our knowledge… Tell Pavlov that Comrade Stalin has forbidden artillery fire

Colonel General Heinz Guderian and subordinates at an impromptu commanders' conference. Usually leading from the front, the headstrong Guderian had to defend himself with his personal weapon to avoid capture on several occasions, including June 24. On the same day the future Field Marshal Walter Model, commanding 3rd Panzer Division, narrowly survived the destruction by gunfire of his armored vehicle. (HITM)

Frontier Battles – Army Group Center

Legend:

German Infantry Division	Soviet Rifle Division
German Motorized Infantry Division	Soviet Motorized Division
Panzer Division	Soviet Tank Division
German Cavalry Division	Soviet Cavalry Division
German Security Division	Soviet Antitank Brigade
SS Division	
German Motorized Infantry Regiment	
German attack	Soviet attack
Luftwaffe attacks, 24 June 1941	Soviet retreat
	Boldin counteroffensive
	Sub-pocket

0 — 50 miles
0 — 50km

against the Germans." The front commander requested permission to employ his infantry, artillery, and armor to which the marshal replied, "Nyet." Pavlov meekly concluded in true Soviet-speak that "some kind of devilry" by German "provocationists" must be going on.

At 0200hrs on June 22, West Front air commander Colonel I.I. Kopets reported to Pavlov that his forces were "at full readiness." By nightfall he had lost 738 aircraft – 40 percent of his strength; he would commit suicide shortly afterward. His pilots essentially did the same, flying hopeless counterattacks with their SB and DB-3 medium bombers.

German radio intercepts overheard Soviet transmissions asking, "The Germans are attacking, what should I do?" The Third Panzer Group captured all three essential bridges on their assault axis, the final one when they arrived at Altyus ahead of the 1900hrs demolition time when the Soviet engineer officer had been instructed to detonate the demolition charges. Two thousand vehicles of VIII Fliegerkorps intermingled with Hoth's armor on the few decent roads in their sector. Traffic jams were his biggest headache until 7th Panzer Division encountered 5th Tank Division's hull-down T-34s guarding the east bank of the 150-yard-wide Neman River. A day later the 5th numbered only 15 functioning tanks and XXXIX Panzer Corps marched on. Operationally Hoth pulled off a major coup by splitting asunder the boundary between the Northwest and West Fronts. He would cause Stavka continued headaches.

By 1500hrs on that first day Guderian's 3rd Panzer Division, followed by the 4th Panzer, had worked their way around the fortress of Brest, on to the *Panzerstrasse* (so called because its use was dedicated to mobile units only) and into the open country near Kobrin. But no sooner did the German forces cross the border than they hit sandy terrain that multiplied their fuel consumption. They also learned quickly that the Soviet soldiers fought better in the woods than they did.

Pavlov had no idea of conditions at the front but nevertheless went about issuing attack orders to imaginary shock groups. Although his 3rd and 4th Armies began to fall back on their own initiative, the 10th remained close to the border. German ground and air attacks had scattered the headquarters of both 3rd and 4th Armies; Kuznetsov at the 3rd managed to send one signal that entire day, "We are through." Meanwhile Pavlov sent his deputy Boldin to the command post of the 10th Army to assess the situation. In fact, its commander Golubev had already ordered his 13th Mechanized Corps to counterattack.

Soviet T-26 tanks move out as dug-in infantry look on. Not considered to be the USSR's likely main defensive effort, the West Front had to make do with second-rate equipment and weaker numbers – a fact that spelled doom for many of Pavlov's counterattacks. Later in the campaign the T-26 was often still the only tank type available. (Elukka)

Zhukov and the High Command knew less about the front than Pavlov and what they did know paled in comparison to the reality. In many cases Moscow depended on local Party officials to confirm army information. Conflicting stories describe Stalin as suffering a nervous breakdown and disappearing from the Kremlin for the remainder of June. He is famously quoted as having said at the time, "Lenin created our state and we have fucked it up." However, historian David Murphy has written that at 1300hrs that terrible Sunday did Stalin "begin to act as a commander."[22] He dispatched Chief of Staff Shaposhnikov to the West Front headquarters, a useless gesture given the chaos and misinformation that reigned there.

In the north of the army group sector, within 24 hours Hoth had broken through the main defensive belt and von Bock rewarded his achieving operational freedom by releasing Third Panzer Group from Ninth Army control. Hoth's advance widened the gap between 3rd Army (Western Front) and 11th Army (Northwestern Front) to nearly 100 miles. All did not go well on the 23rd, however. The 20th Panzer Division, which had been competing with 7th Panzer for the same road, had to delay its 0900hrs attack on Vilnius because of continuing a lack of fuel. This trend did not bode well for *Barbarossa*. Also that day, the Red Army Air Force made a feeble ten-aircraft bombing raid on Königsberg in accordance with the USSR's Red Folder prewar offensive plans.

---

22   Murphy, *What Stalin Knew*, p.220.

Von Bock's reported advance looked incredible from Rastenburg and by the second day of *Barbarossa* German plans were already beginning to fray. First, Hitler wanted to halt the armor in order to eliminate the developing Bialystok Kessel. Halder resolutely fought this idea and ordered von Bock to create successive inner infantry and outer armored encirclements all the way to Minsk. Von Bock protested this interference, but ultimately obeyed orders. To soften the blow, von Brauchitsch intervened and allowed von Bock to send Hoth's "strong security forces" ("reconnaissance in force" in military parlance) toward Vitebsk and Polotsk while Guderian made for Slutsk, Bobruisk, and Rogatchev.

A heavily laden group of infantry occupy the burning village of Lutky, near Vitebsk, on July 15. The spare barrels, ammunition boxes, and sustained-fire tripod for the MG34 squad machine gun are recognizable among their burdens. (MHI)

Hoth's arrival in Vitebsk and Polotsk unhinged the Soviet defense; having a panzer group running loose deep in the defender's rear area was one of von Bock's operational goals and a blitzkrieg staple. However, less than 48 hours into the campaign, the dispersal of the army group's panzer forces began, tactically prudent but operationally fatal. A lack of consensus between the supreme warlord, the army commander-in-chief, his chief of staff, and the field generals was already developing.

Meanwhile Pavlov too tried to launch counterattacks as demanded by naive plans. The Soviet High Command instructed him on the 23rd to "use all measures to defend Grodno." But Strauss' 8th Infantry Division continued to pound that town with 29 batteries of artillery. Pavlov still had virtually no communications with his field armies and therefore had little command and control over them. In any event they were sorely pressed on all sides and in no position to launch the called-for counteroffensives. Pavlov therefore sent Boldin to assemble an attack force and move on Grodno, theoretically to threaten Hoth's southern flank and restore the situation.

Grodno

As would be the case throughout *Barbarossa* this comic opera at the strategic level did not equate to inactivity farther down the chain of command. Hoth's tanks were advancing at a tremendous rate and already threatened Minsk from the north. The Soviet forces were not idle, however; following Pavlov's orders Boldin's shock group, basically the 6th (with over 1,000 tanks) and 11th Mechanized and the 6th Cavalry Corps, advanced toward Grodno in a counterclockwise arc with an ultimate objective of Augustovo. Luftwaffe reconnaissance had been looking deep in the Soviet rear and missed this build-up, so Boldin initially surprised Strauss. But he completely missed Hoth, his primary target, who was already far to the east.

In common with Soviet attacks all along the front during those early days, Boldin's suffered from poor command and control, no effective air support, weak combined-arms tactics, and insufficient logistics. Approximately half of the 6th Mechanized Corps' tanks were modern T-34s and KVs, but these had only been received a month earlier, so the crews were unfamiliar with them. Likewise a Luftwaffe attack savaged the 6th Cavalry Corps, destroying 70 percent of its 36th Cavalry Division in 24 hours. Boldin's assault created a small tactical crisis among the German 256th Infantry Division around Grodno, but could not distract Third Panzer Group. Since these early battles were principally meeting engagements they all heavily favored the more experienced German units.

ABOVE Soviet 6th Rifle Division defend Brest Fortress, June 22–30, 1941. In this scene, Soviet infantrymen, led by Lieutenant Kizhevatov of the NKVD Frontier Guards (**1**), take up firing positions in a fort archway after overrunning an emplacement formerly occupied by a German MG34 crew (**2**); their weapons include a Maxim M1910 machine gun (**3**). The combination of bunker-busting German heavy howitzers and mortars, flamethrowers, and the sheer exhaustion of relentless close-quarter fighting took their toll by June 29 and 30. The final blow fell on the 29th, when seven Junkers Ju 88 bombers of Kampfgeschwader 3 dropped 2-ton bombs on the last pockets still holding out. (© Osprey Publishing, Peter Dennis)

Pavlov's counterattacks had shot their bolt by June 25, one mile shy of Grodno's center, low on fuel and ammunition and with little to show for their efforts. The 11th Mechanized Corps lost all but 30 of its 305 tanks and melted away from 32,000 men to 600 in four days. Caught behind enemy lines near the western edge of the front, Boldin and about 2,000 of his men began a 45-day exodus that would eventually lead them to freedom east of Smolensk.

Conflict raged over the battlefield as well. More than 200 of von Richthofen's aircraft had a field day destroying Boldin's stranded, often out-of-fuel tanks. The Bf-110, which could make 340mph and take heavy punishment but was outclassed in air-to-air combat over Great Britain, began to enjoy a new lease of life as a ground-attack aircraft in the east. As soon as the panzer troops captured Soviet airfields the Luftwaffe fighter squadrons, led by battle-proven veterans of Spain, Poland, France, and the Battle of Britain, began operating from them against their comparatively inexperienced opponents. Nevertheless, within three days of the invasion the first of the formidable Il-2 Sturmovik ground-attack aircraft, fresh from the Voronezh factory, appeared in the Army Group Center sector.

On the southern side of the bulge Guderian's tanks neared Baranovichi, site of Grand Duke Nicholas' Stavka headquarters in 1914. The 22nd Tank Division attempted to bar the way of the 3rd and 18th Panzer Divisions; its commanding general became one of the battle casualties on the war's second day. Equally futile, the 14th Mechanized Corps next tried to halt the panzer general; it counted 478 operational tanks on June 22, but against Guderian's veterans that number shrank to 250 two days later and to only 30 on the 26th.

By the 25th Timoshenko bowed to the inevitable and instructed the West Front to withdraw to the Lida–Slonim–Pinsk line. Pavlov tried to establish an additional defensive position slightly to the north near Radun, with 21st Rifle Corps supported by 8th Antitank Brigade. These maneuvers had already been overcome by events and besides, Pavlov could not disengage quickly enough to make them effective.

A German soldier with his plunder following the surrender of fortress Brest: a banner – possibly Red Army unit colors – with an image of Lenin. (Topfoto)

Completing the Minsk Encirclements

On the Molotov–Ribbentrop line fortress Brest still held out despite the pounding of 12 210mm howitzers, two 600mm "Karl" siege guns, and 2,880 *Nebelwerfer* rockets. Elsewhere, both High Commands hummed with activity. The Bialystok salient had been custom-made for a huge Kessel, a weakness Hitler and the Wehrmacht wanted to exploit as quickly as possible. Von Bock was already thinking past that, past even Minsk and the Vitebsk–Orsha land bridge and on to Moscow. True to *Barbarossa*'s objectives, higher headquarters still thought in terms of exterminating Red Army units before reaching the Dnepr, so Army Group Center slowly began to squeeze the life out of Pavlov's trapped West Front as ordered.

In Moscow, on June 25 the newly-formed Stavka was also considering the next move and ordered a 1st Cavalry Army crony of Stalin's, Marshal S.M. Budenny, to create the Reserve Front using 19th, 20th, 21st, and 22nd Armies, on exactly the same Vitebsk–Orsha line for which von Bock aimed. Luftwaffe reconnaissance noticed this development beginning to take shape on July 1. In Stalin's personal study a day later, Zhukov drew two arcs on a map where 24th and 28th Armies (13 rifle, six tank, and three motorized divisions) would establish a second defensive line centered on Yelnia and a third stretching from Viazma to Kaluga. All these towns would play critical roles in the days to come. The Red Army would soon begin to occupy row after row of defensive fortifications between Smolensk and Moscow; the German forces would have to fight for every step along the way to the USSR's capital.

Главнокомандующий войск Юго-Западного направления Маршал Советского Союза С. М. БУДЕННЫЙ

On June 27, Zhukov ordered the embattled Pavlov to: 1) achieve positive control over front units; 2) not abandon tanks and artillery; 3) evacuate Minsk and Bobruisk; 4) counterattack to separate the German armor from the slower infantry; and 5) detach cavalry into the Rokitno Marshes to initiate partisan warfare there. He did not clarify the apparently contradictory nature of items 3 and 4, and, anyway, West Front forces were still too decisively engaged to withdraw and too overwhelmed to follow Stavka's instructions.

Also on the 27th Voroshilov arrived at Pavlov's headquarters to prop up the West Front commander; "the main thing is to overcome the panzer phobia," he advised. On that same day Shaposhnikov received captured German maps indicating that their Schwerpunkt lay in the direction of Moscow and not the Ukraine as the Soviet leaders had previously assumed. A blind man could see what was about to happen to the West Front's entire first echelon but the chief of staff demurred at recommending the full-scale withdrawal that could have saved some of Pavlov's command – after all, Stalin was still thinking offensively. However, it seems that the Western Front was indeed a sacrificial speed bump.

On June 25, von Kluge, still unable to close the trap on Pavlov, took the 29th Motorized Division away from a protesting Guderian in order to establish a blocking position at Volkovysk. The division's position divided two

Marshal S.M. Budenny had few qualifications for high-level command except for personal friendship with Stalin. His mediocre performance commanding the Reserve Front and subsequent disaster at Kiev quickly relegated him to secondary and ceremonial posts, as a new generation of combat-tested generals took over to defeat the Wehrmacht. His long survival was probably due to his stupidity – he could never be considered as a rival even during Stalin's worst fits of paranoia. (David Glantz)

The Minsk Encirclement

After the initial border battles the Second and Third Panzer Groups raced east past Minsk and on 27 June slammed the door shut on Army Group Center's first Kessel. Actually a number of smaller encirclements, the Minsk pocket meant the Western Front's initial defense lasted only two weeks.

Note: Gridlines are shown at intervals of 50km/31miles

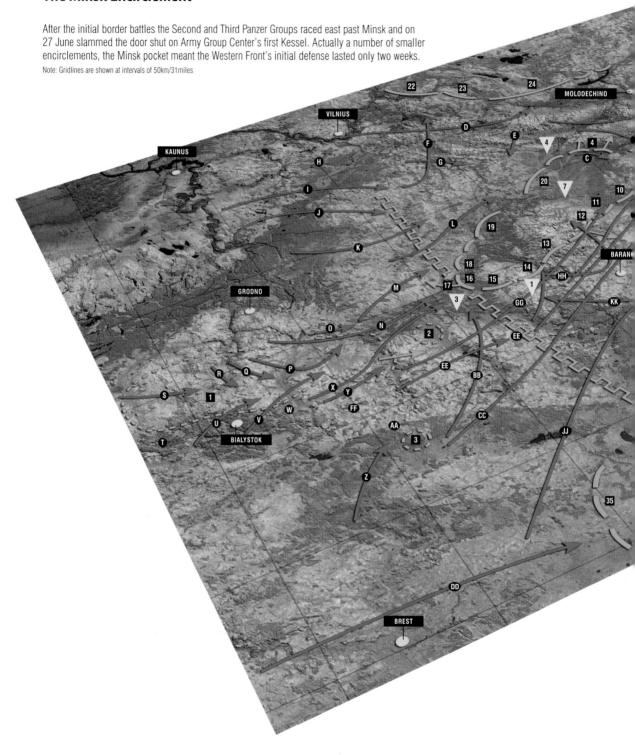

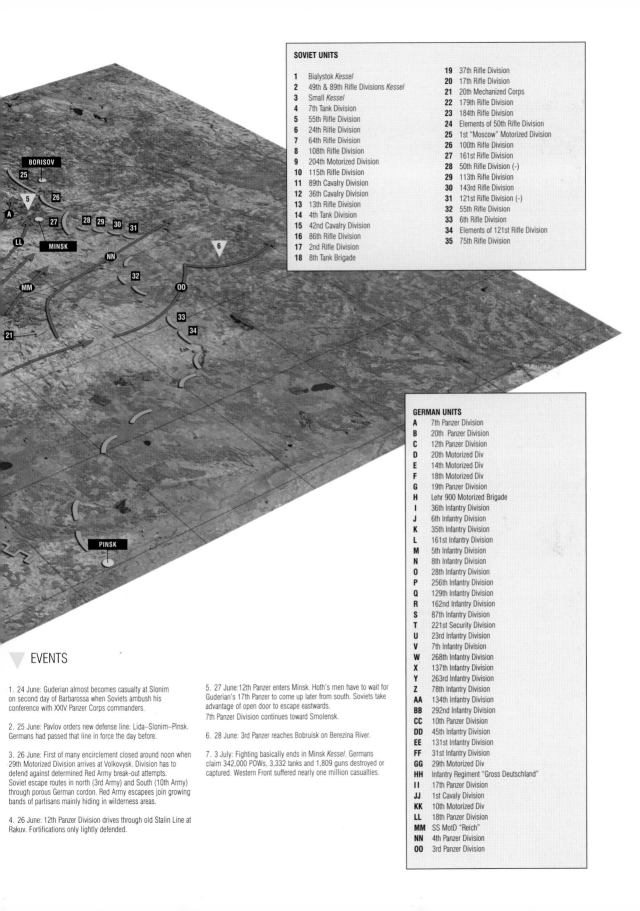

SOVIET UNITS

1	Bialystok *Kessel*
2	49th & 89th Rifle Divisions *Kessel*
3	Small *Kessel*
4	7th Tank Division
5	55th Rifle Division
6	24th Rifle Division
7	64th Rifle Division
8	108th Rifle Division
9	204th Motorized Division
10	115th Rifle Division
11	89th Cavalry Division
12	36th Cavalry Division
13	13th Rifle Division
14	4th Tank Division
15	42nd Cavalry Division
16	86th Rifle Division
17	2nd Rifle Division
18	8th Tank Brigade
19	37th Rifle Division
20	17th Rifle Division
21	20th Mechanized Corps
22	179th Rifle Division
23	184th Rifle Division
24	Elements of 50th Rifle Division
25	1st "Moscow" Motorized Division
26	100th Rifle Division
27	161st Rifle Division
28	50th Rifle Division (-)
29	113th Rifle Division
30	143rd Rifle Division
31	121st Rifle Division (-)
32	55th Rifle Division
33	6th Rifle Division
34	Elements of 121st Rifle Division
35	75th Rifle Division

GERMAN UNITS

A	7th Panzer Division
B	20th Panzer Division
C	12th Panzer Division
D	20th Motorized Div
E	14th Motorized Div
F	18th Motorized Div
G	19th Panzer Division
H	Lehr 900 Motorized Brigade
I	36th Infantry Division
J	6th Infantry Division
K	35th Infantry Division
L	161st Infantry Division
M	5th Infantry Division
N	8th Infantry Division
O	28th Infantry Division
P	256th Infantry Division
Q	129th Infantry Division
R	162nd Infantry Division
S	87th Infantry Division
T	221st Security Division
U	23rd Infantry Division
V	7th Infantry Division
W	268th Infantry Division
X	137th Infantry Division
Y	263rd Infantry Division
Z	78th Infantry Division
AA	134th Infantry Division
BB	292nd Infantry Division
CC	10th Panzer Division
DD	45th Infantry Division
EE	131st Infantry Division
FF	31st Infantry Division
GG	29th Motorized Div
HH	Infantry Regiment "Gross Deutschland"
II	17th Panzer Division
JJ	1st Cavaly Division
KK	10th Motorized Div
LL	18th Panzer Division
MM	SS MotD "Reich"
NN	4th Panzer Division
OO	3rd Panzer Division

▼ EVENTS

1. 24 June: Guderian almost becomes casualty at Slonim on second day of Barbarossa when Soviets ambush his conference with XXIV Panzer Corps commanders.

2. 25 June: Pavlov orders new defense line: Lida–Slonim–Pinsk. Germans had passed that line in force the day before.

3. 26 June: First of many encirclement closed around noon when 29th Motorized Division arrives at Volkovysk. Division has to defend against determined Red Army break-out attempts. Soviet escape routes in north (3rd Army) and South (10th Army) through porous German cordon. Red Army escapees join growing bands of partisans mainly hiding in wilderness areas.

4. 26 June: 12th Panzer Division drives through old Stalin Line at Rakuv. Fortifications only lightly defended.

5. 27 June: 12th Panzer enters Minsk. Hoth's men have to wait for Guderian's 17th Panzer to come up later from south. Soviets take advantage of open door to escape eastwards. 7th Panzer Division continues toward Smolensk.

6. 28 June: 3rd Panzer reaches Bobruisk on Berezina River.

7. 3 July: Fighting basically ends in Minsk *Kessel*. Germans claim 342,000 POWs, 3,332 tanks and 1,809 guns destroyed or captured. Western Front suffered nearly one million casualties.

of the three Minsk pockets – Bialystok to the west and Novogrudek to the east. The 29th held until June 29 against numerous Soviet breakout attempts by cavalry, tanks, and human-wave assaults four men deep. However, on the northern edge of the pocket Ninth Army and Third Panzer Group's hammer struck before Fourth Army or Second Panzer Group's anvil was in place to the south, thereby allowing many Soviets to escape to the southeast.

Climate and terrain assisted the Soviet defenders further. Extreme heat dried up various watercourses. While this made fording easier for the advancing Germans, thirst caused hardships on men and horses. Flies and mosquitoes tormented everyone regardless of uniform. With their armies no longer effective fighting forces Red Army soldiers melted away into "ancient" forests that were so thick they seriously degraded German lines of sight and fields of fire. The sandy soil slowed the Germans further; moving an artillery piece often required 12–16 horses (of which a standard

A temporary transfer of power in Belorussia: on July 10, German troops pass the Minsk "House of Soviets" with its statue of Lenin. The Soviet emblem would soon be replaced with SS runes. (NARA)

infantry division had about 6,000). Commandeered Russian panje pony-wagons and captured Soviet farm tractors used as artillery prime movers added to the shabby, gypsy-caravan aspect of their columns. Three days after *Barbarossa* began many trailing units of the lead corps had yet to cross the frontier, daily widening the gap between them and the slashing panzer divisions far to the front.

Guderian raced east, seemingly oblivious to the German goal of closing encirclements with which to destroy the Red Army, the prime directive of *Barbarossa*. Neither was "Fast Heinz" overly concerned with his personal safety; some of Korobkov's troops almost captured him on June 24. The same day the 3rd Panzer commander and future field marshal Walter Model escaped death when his armored car was "shot out from under him" by Red Artillery. The 17th Panzer Division took Slonim from the 4th Army, uncovering the southern route to Minsk, but was in turn surrounded and had to be saved by its sister division 18th Panzer.

On June 25, thee days into *Barbarossa*, Hitler worried that the impending Minsk pocket was too large. On that same day 19th Panzer's motorcycle battalion led Hoth's panzer group to Minsk with its commanding general Otto von Knoblesdorff at the point. Naturally this small formation received considerable attention from the Soviet defenders. Guderian's advanced units closed on the flaming town of Slutsk, which two days later Pavlov would futilely order the 20th Mechanized and 4th Airborne Corps to recapture. The Second Panzer Group had now left Belorussia and entered into Russia. By the 28th, von Kluge considered that Guderian had also achieved operational freedom and cut him loose from Fourth Army control.

In the north Hoth continued to exploit the gaping hatchet wound in the Soviet defenses represented by growing separation between the Northwest and West Fronts. He too would rather have headed due east than have to worry about closing encirclements, but Hoth was less blatant in his obstinacy than Guderian. His LVII Panzer Corps took Vilnius, "Jerusalem of the North," on the 24th, while XXXIX Panzer Corps drove on Minsk itself. That same day Pavlov ordered 13th Army, "a mishmash of troops," to attack the latter city. However, a day later the 13th evacuated Molodechno opening the way to Minsk for the ever-opportunistic 7th Panzer Division. General Filatov, the harried commander of the 13th Army, wanted to give up Minsk: after all the Communist Party fled the city on June 25. Reflecting the continuing confusion resulting from Zhukov's instructions that day, Pavlov ordered Filatov of 13th Army to stand fast instead. Meanwhile, Hoth received Lehr Brigade 900 to reinforce his over-extended panzer group.

Early July: a *Nebelwerfer* battery with 7th Panzer Division preparing to fire. Projectiles can be seen protruding from the rear of the launcher's lower tubes. Note that the crewmen are wearing protective overalls. (NARA)

Beyond Minsk

Third Panzer Group broke through the Stalin Line on June 26–27; XXXIX Panzer Corps radioed, "7th Panzer Division, Halt!" to which Rommel's old outfit irreverently replied, "Say again?" and kept plunging forward. By 1600hrs on the 28th, 12th Panzer Division entered Minsk, but the Kessel remained only half closed, since the willful Guderian headed east for Moscow rather than northeast toward Minsk and a rendezvous with Hoth. Soviet units trickled out southeastward for another two days. To the west, while his infantry marched in the heat and dust on poor roads unwanted by the panzers, von Kluge dallied by methodically lining up his corps for the final assault on Minsk. Actual occupation of the city would have to wait until fires begun by Luftwaffe bombs on June 24 had died down.

The advancing Guderian soon discovered what Korobkov had learned the hard way when earlier ordered to occupy and defend the Stalin Line: in many places it existed in name only. This was a good thing, too, since during *Barbarossa*'s first week his personnel losses had been double those of Hoth. Guderian's 18th Panzer Division finally closed the Minsk Kessel on the afternoon of June 29. The entire trap consisted of three main pockets, including those at Bialystok and Novogrudek. In places Red Army soldiers escaped through Guderian's weak southeastern cordon, while others fought to the last bullet or attacked in suicidal waves (especially at night), forcing many German units to form defensive *Igel*. Hunting down and capturing Soviets in dark forests, occupying and securing rear areas, and inventorying booty took until July 23.

With the *Sturmgeschütz* armored assault gun the Germans realized the Napoleonic dream of having artillery able to accompany infantry in the attack. Here a group of pioneers hitch a ride on a StuG III near Minsk on July 17. (NARA)

By June 29, Stalin realized that Belorussia was lost; Lieutenant General V.I. Kuznetsov's failure against Army Group North had contributed mightily to this disaster. The next day Lieutenant General Yeremenko finally arrived at West Front headquarters with orders relieving Pavlov from command. Stalin made an example by executing the hapless Pavlov, so that all commanders "know defeatist behavior will be punished mercilessly." Yeremenko knew the terrain well, having led 6th Cavalry Corps into Poland in 1939 and to Kaunas in 1940, but he would hold command for only three days before becoming Marshal Timoshenko's deputy. On the other side of the lines, also on the 30th, Guderian flew to the Third Panzer Group command post to coordinate with Hoth on future operations (but also to conspire with him to defy von Kluge by their selective disobedience). While Hoth welcomed the gesture, a more sincere visit a couple of days earlier would have made a better encirclement of Minsk.

The German leadership had long anticipated that capturing Minsk would mark a watershed. At that point Hitler and OKH were to decide if von Bock's panzers would turn north toward Leningrad, continue east, or execute some other course of action. With Rastenburg growing indecisive, Hoth and Guderian awaited instructions. While visiting Hoth, Guderian gave lip service to their cooperation in completing the Minsk Kessel but Luftwaffe reconnaissance had earlier noticed that the road to Bobruisk was unprotected and it was there that Guderian next directed his attention. Ever aggressive, these two generals would not wait long before going back into action.

By early July both panzer groups were approaching the River Berezina ("River of Birches" and site of Napoleonic drama in 1812) whose defenders proved only a minor hindrance. Swampy headwaters in Hoth's area and along much of its east bank plus the numerous, long, wooden bridges proved to be worse obstacles. It was here that Yeremenko vainly sought to make his first stand. Trying simultaneously to contain the Minsk pocket and also stretch toward Smolensk robbed the panzer groups of any coherent formation. This was especially true for Guderian's Second Panzer Group, which sprawled back over 150 miles, aiming for Yelnia. Hoth's Third meanwhile had to contend with terrible weather and terrain. Worst of all, his panzer group was also becoming spread out with units sacrificing mutual support and other benefits of concentration.

Once again free to maneuver, 3rd Panzer Division made straight for Bobruisk. General Model escaped serious injury yet again as the Soviet forces fought hard to hold the Bobruisk citadel and river crossing site. Between

A tank unit with mixed Czech and German vehicles – thus probably from 6th, 7th, or 12th Panzer Division – is towing its own fuel trailers as it drives through Minsk. German logistics often failed even with such a basic requirement as getting fuel forward to keep the panzers rolling; Hoth was halted by such a shortage on October 4 during the Viazma/Bryansk battles. (HITM)

June 30 and July 1, 18th Panzer Division made a 60-mile raid to Borisov (originally Hoth's objective). 17th Panzer followed in support, both violating specific orders from von Kluge but securing yet another breach in the Soviet wall. The willful attitudes of Guderian and Hoth prompted von Kluge to threaten both with courts martial. After a harrowing journey, the newly arrived 1st Moscow Motorized Division, with 1,000 tanks (including T-34s and KVs) and 500 guns, reached Borisov the next day and launched immediate counterattacks; these all failed versus Hoth's spearhead.

Stavka tried to adjust to these new developments. Budenny's and Yeremenko's commands barely lasted a few days; Timoshenko took over leadership of the West and Reserve Fronts with Yeremenko as his deputy while Stalin sent Budenny to Kiev. The Soviet leaders had blundered through one crisis at Minsk and were about to face another, more severe one at Smolensk. For their part, the German commanders reorganized their armored forces effective midnight July 2/3, when OKH created Fourth Panzer Army, formally subordinating Hoth and Guderian under von Kluge (and soothing Hitler's nerves). It simultaneously assigned the latter's infantry to von Weichs thereby essentially creating the Second Army. Von Bock now had *de facto* command of two separate armies, one fast and mechanized, the other slow and marching, each with very different missions and often little contact between them.

Back where Army Group Center's war began, at Brest, the Soviet defenders held out until the end of June. The garrison commander and commissar committed suicide but 400 POWs marched into captivity. The conquering 45th Infantry Division buried 414 of its dead at a ceremony on July 1 and then moved out to catch up with the rest of von Bock's command, nearly 150 miles east. While the tankers received much of the glory, German infantry did yeoman service as the massive shaft behind the blitzkrieg's armored spearhead.

A welcoming arch greets a German column early during *Barbarossa*. Galicia had been part of Austria since the partitions of Poland and had many settlements with a German heritage. Stalin had deported many, but not all, *Volksdeutsche* from Soviet border regions. (Nik Cornish at www.Stavka.org.uk)

The Galacian and Volhynian Frontiers

At 0300hrs on June 22 the last train out of the USSR crossed the San River at Przemysl into Greater Germany. From his new command post at Ternopol, Kirponos ordered units forward under the cover of darkness. Significantly these included the 37th Rifle Corps "training" in and around Przemysl. NKVD border troops moved from their barracks to their advanced positions. In Germany the Führer told his men "German soldiers! You're entering a hard struggle, heavy with responsibility. The success of Europe, the future of the German Reich, the existence of our people lies in your hands alone."

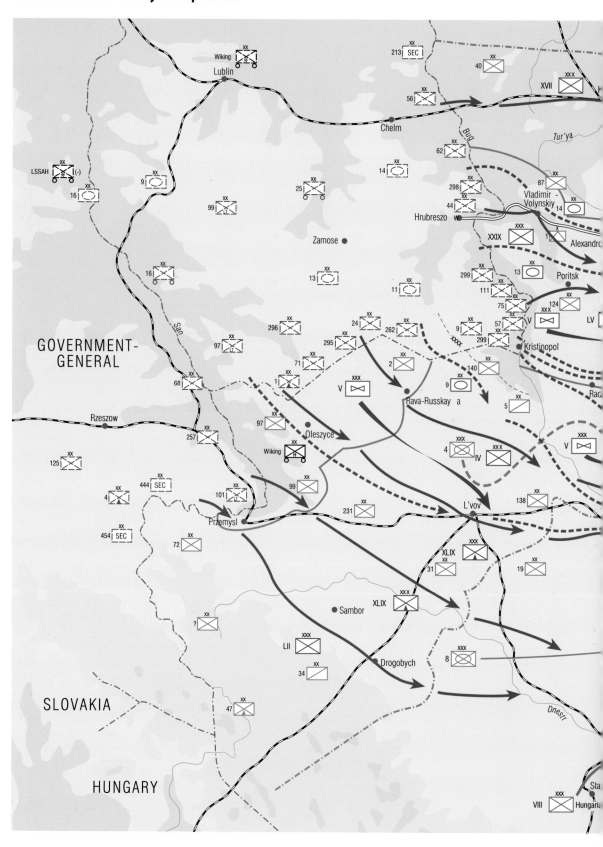

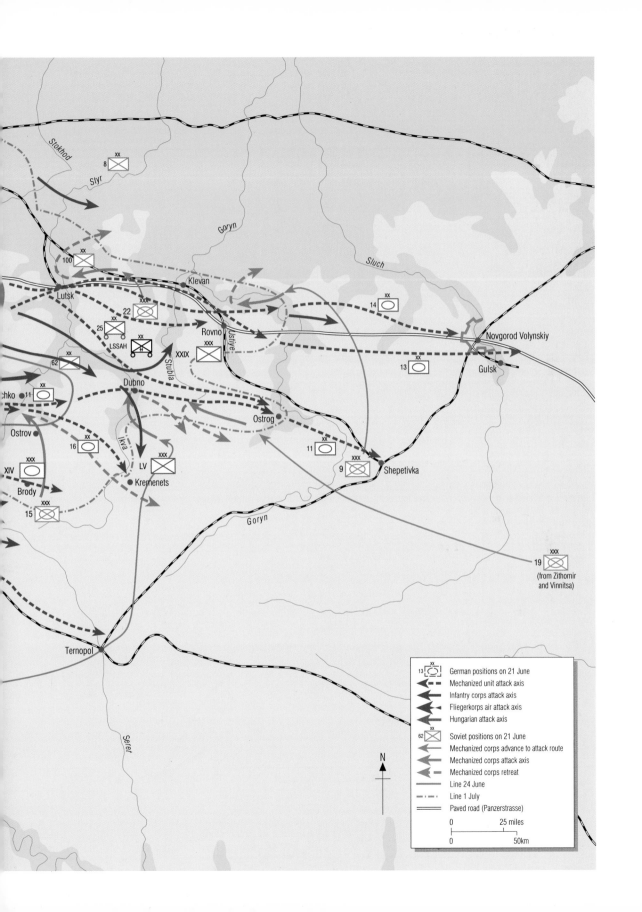

Stokhod

Styr

8 ⊠ xx

Goryn

Sluch

100 ⊠ xx

Lutsk

Klevan

14 ◯ xx

Novgorod Volynskiy

22 ⊠ xxx

25 ⊠ xx

LSSAH

Rovno

Ustiye

13 ◯ xx

Gulsk

62 ⊠ xx

XXIX ⊠ xxx

Slubla

chko ●11 ◯ xx

Dubno

Ostrog

11 ◯ xx

Ostrov ●

16 ◯ xx

Ikva

LV ⊠ xxx

9 ⊠ xxx

Shepetivka

XIV ◯ xxx

Brody

Kremenets

15 ⊠ xxx

Goryn

19 ⊠ xxx
(from Zithomir
and Vinnitsa)

Ternopol

Seret

N

13 [⊡] xx	German positions on 21 June
	Mechanized unit attack axis
	Infantry corps attack axis
	Fliegerkorps air attack axis
	Hungarian attack axis
62 ⊠ xx	Soviet positions on 21 June
	Mechanized corps advance to attack route
	Mechanized corps attack axis
	Mechanized corps retreat
	Line 24 June
	Line 1 July
	Paved road (Panzerstrasse)

0   25 miles

0   50km

Rubber rafts of Infantry Regiment 222 crossing the Bug River on *Barbarossatag*. Many eastern European rivers were at high flood late into spring 1941, mitigating the significance of the delay caused by the Balkan campaign. (NARA)

Main Axis

Reconnaissance troops of the 101st Light Infantry Division and commandos from Infantry Regiment 800 – Brandenburgers – rushed the Przemysl bridge over the San that morning. They failed in the face of alerted Soviet defenses but regular infantry secured the crossing later in the day. Opposite L'vov assault guns supported the 1st Mountain Division's attack against the 97th Rifle Division. Further north the III Panzer Corps opened the invasion with a barrage by 300 artillery pieces.

Kirponos reacted immediately by ordering the 15th and 8th Mechanized Corps against the XLVIII Panzer Corps. Their reaction was piecemeal; 8th Corps units were garrisoned up to 300 miles from the fighting. The Southwest Front put the 22nd Mechanized in motion while the commander of the 9th Mechanized, Rokossovsky, moved on his own initiative. Kirponos' best hope on *Barbarossatag* was pairings such as the 87th Rifle Division and 1st Antitank Brigade at Vladimir-Volynskiy.

At 1300hrs on June 22 Stalin dispatched Zhukov to Ternopol. Luftwaffe air superiority that day meant he had to drive much of the way and did not arrive until late in the night. Fortuitously Zhukov gave Kirponos on-the-spot approval to the latter's counterattack plan to blunt the German assault. Army Group South's relative slowness would allow him and Kirponos time to fine tune their defenses.

During the second day, on von Kleist's critical left the 44th and 298th Infantry Divisions smashed a hole for the III Panzer Corps in the north along the Lutsk–Rovno axis while the 57th and 75th Infantry Divisions opened the way for the XLVIII Panzer Corps on the Dubno–Ostrog road to the south. However, between Vladimir-Volynskiy and Lutsk the 14th Panzer hit the 1st Antitank Brigade and stalled. Only after the Landsers outflanked the antitank gunners did the Soviet troops conduct a fighting withdrawal closely pursued by the 14th Panzer.

On June 24, 4th Mechanized Corps assaulted the "Lucky" 71st Infantry Division's antitank battalion. Quickly reinforced by bicycle infantry the Germans waited. The first wave of 20 Soviet tanks got stuck in the marketplace of Niemerov, northwest of L'vov, where they could not fight well, maneuver effectively, or retreat. Disaster awaited successive groups of ten or a dozen tanks until 50 sat destroyed or abandoned. Overall slow progress near L'vov caused some at army group headquarters to advocate sending the XIV Panzer Corps to support Seventeenth Army. Cooler heads prevailed and a dangerous precedent, breaking up panzer groups at every minor crisis, was avoided.

On Lieutenant General Eberhard von Mackensen's right, arriving piecemeal, the 15th Mechanized lost ground against the XLVIII Panzer Corps. In all during in their first major armor battle von Mackensen's men destroyed 267 enemy tanks. The following day the III Panzer Corps forced the 27th Rifle Corps out of Lutsk and threw a bridgehead across the Styr River. Greim's V Fliegerkorps flew 1,600 sorties, attacked 72 airfields, destroyed 774 Soviet aircraft, and interdicted untold convoys in three days. The 15th and 22nd Mechanized had been fighting since June 23 and 24 respectively and were either decisively engaged or mired in swamps. Seemingly just in time, following march and countermarch covering over

A Soviet mechanized corps, consisting here mainly of T-26 tanks, heads for the front on *Barbarossatag*. These organizations proved to be too inexperienced, untrained, and unwieldy to confront the blitzkrieg head on. (Corbis)

100 miles, the 8th, 9th, and 19th Mechanized Corps arrived near the front, albeit at greatly reduced strengths mainly due to mechanical breakdown.

To simplify command and control of the northern pincer Southwest Front placed the 9th and 19th Mechanized Corps under the 5th Army. Their mission was to assault von Mackensen's left at Rovno. Although ordered by Stavka, the attacks lacked synchronization and the 13th Panzer defeated each portion in detail. The 1st Antitank Brigade halted the 14th Panzer again, this time near Klevan.

The corresponding Soviet attack on the south flank near Dubno began poorly when the Luftwaffe bombed the 15th Mechanized headquarters, wounding Karpezo. Soon it and the 8th Mechanized were holding their own against the 11th and 16th Panzer Divisions. The 8th, "reduced [by losses] to a manageable size" according to Rokossovsky, even worked its way behind the two panzer formations. Northern and southern pincers stood barely 6 miles apart with the 16th Panzer holding a division-sized *Igel* in-between. But initial gains abruptly fell afoul of poor Soviet communications and mutual support. The 75th Infantry and 16th Panzer Divisions soon restored the German situation with Luftwaffe help. Kirponos heard only the bad news from the northern sector so called off his offensive. Stavka, trying to manage the counterattacks from Moscow, had even less visibility on the situation. Together they missed a golden opportunity to give von Rundstedt a stinging reverse.

Kirponos ordered his remnants to make one last attack on June 30, but lacked sufficient strength. Political Commissar N.N. Vashugin, overruling the commander, personally led the 8th Mechanized Corps' tank division

Destroyed Soviet T-26 tanks at Ostrov, part of the counterattacks Kirponos ordered in accordance with the Red Army strategy. A mere 6 miles separated his pincers but poor communications meant he knew nothing of his successes. (NARA)

Starting the spiral of genocide by both sides. Ten days into *Barbarossa* Germans discovered *Volksdeutsche* murdered by Soviet state police in L'vov. SS Division Viking initiated a vengeful rampage. Pogroms by the Germans at Kiev and the Rumanians at Odessa followed. (NARA)

directly into a swamp, losing all its tanks. Vashugin promptly committed suicide. Zhukov, present on the scene, called the swirling battle around Dubno the toughest fighting in the Ukraine. Soon First Panzer Group prepared to exploit the hard-won gap between the 5th and 6th Armies. Potapov fell back northward toward the Rokitno Marshes, unfamiliar and uncomfortable territory for the German forces.

One situation mastered, von Rundstedt now worried that the Seventeenth Army lagged behind the panzers. Until Axis forces in Rumania moved out, Army Group South labored with an exposed right face. The LII Corps had the overall mission of protecting von Stülpnagel's southern flank. It was here that *Barbarossa's* author, Erich Marcks, now commanding the 101st Light Infantry Division, suffered severe wounds near Prezmysl resulting in an amputated leg just four days into the campaign.

The 6th Army held a dangerously extended line, however. German signals-deception units in the Carpathians tied down many Soviet units needlessly along the Hungarian frontier. Musychenko resolved to hold L'vov. Although it initially did not face any panzers, this sector's defense possessed the 2nd, 3rd, 4th, and 5th Antitank Brigades. At one point the German leadership considered pivoting First Panzer Group formations south to attack L'vov from the rear. Von Rundstedt would not hear of splitting his main offensive force. He feared a huge enemy logjam in L'vov that would defy either speedy maneuver or encirclement. However, just then the newly committed 9th Panzer Division achieved a breakthrough and threatened the city from behind.

Kirponos decided on June 26 that his border fight was over and began to withdraw on the 27th. Two days later the 1st Mountain Division occupied L'vov without a fight. To cover the retreat Vlasov's 4th Mechanized Corps counterattacked to regain the city the next day. At times German and Red Army troops were only paces apart. In the cemetery 71st Infantry Division Landsers fought from headstone to headstone. German troops eventually took the city for good, after which *Einsatzgruppen* went on a violent ten-day pogrom.

On July 1 SS Division Viking took up the pursuit but the Soviet withdrawal went smoothly. The Hungarian VIII Corps took the field on the 2nd, soon crossing the Dniestr near Stanislav. The Seventeenth Army had ripped a 20-mile hole between the 6th and 26th Armies. Soon these German and Hungarian units met at Ternopol. Von Rundstedt pushed his men to occupy the Stalin Line before the Red Army could. In turn Kirponos instructed his men to occupy the Stalin Line by July 9.

Back in the northern portion of the sector von Kleist's tankers spread out with the 11th Panzer in the lead. First Panzer Group had destroyed 1,200 Soviet tanks in about ten days. Southwest Front's initial armored vehicle superiority dwindled; Red Army battlefield tank losses were permanent while the German troops, in possession of the battlefields, recovered and repaired damaged panzers. During the same period Red Army Air Force elements supporting Kirponos admitted to losing a similar number of aircraft. Their commander, Major General Ptukhin, a Spanish Civil War veteran, was relieved on July 1 and executed.

A German inspects a KV-2 helplessly mired in a swamp south of Ostrov in early July. Kirponos' counterattacks during *Barbarossa's* first weeks came to naught mainly due to incompetence and poor maintenance. (NARA)

Gebirgsjäger on outpost duty near the Arctic Circle. What the Lapland theater lacked in mountainous altitude it made up in northern latitude. Dietl, in common with von Leeb, also fought a "poor man's war" in the far north. (HITM)

The Arctic

German strategic overstretch during *Barbarossa* is perhaps best seen in the far north. Hitler had excellent reasons for wanting Murmansk and for cutting its rail connections to the heart of the Soviet Union. It was the one Soviet connection to the rest of the world that he could reasonably interdict: both overland routes to Persia and Vladivostok were clearly beyond his grasp. As much elsewhere during the campaign his commanders would have to fight a war on the cheap and depend primarily on such intangibles as will and luck. But inadequate resources, underdeveloped infrastructure and unsure allies conspired against German success.

Operation *Platinfuchs*

On *Barbarossatag* von Falkenhorst ordered the Mountain Corps Norway to attack in one week. Dietl had 27,500 men in two divisions plus an engineer and signal battalion, half a Flak battalion, a panzer company, and a *Nebelwerfer* battery. Preparatory to the general assault the 2nd Mountain Division moved from Kirkenes to Petsamo and the 3rd Mountain marched from Narvik to Loustari. Colonel Andreas Nielsen, who had been present at Hitler's 1923 Beer Hall Putsch in Munich, led Luftwaffe forces consisting of 36 Stukas, 11 Ju-52s, ten bombers, and ten fighters. Dietl's mission was to attack to Motovka on the Litsa River and then press on to Murmansk. He placed the 2nd Mountain Division, which was to constitute the Schwerpunkt,

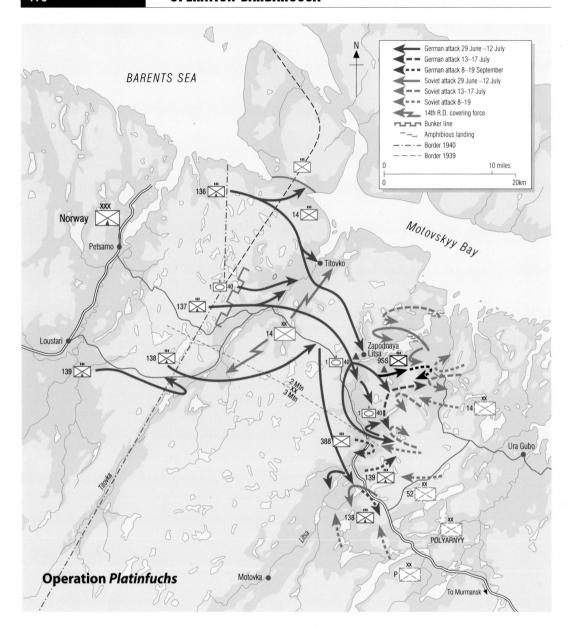

Operation *Platinfuchs*

on the left, and 3rd on the right. His armored reserve, 1/Panzer Battalion 40, waited at Petsamo. The Soviet forces defended with their 14th Rifle Division forward while the 52nd Rifle moved up from near Murmansk.

The assault began as planned on the 29th, and with panzer support a *Kampfgruppe* ("Battle Group," in this case an *ad hoc* formation) of the 3rd Mountain reached the Titovka River the next day. At that point roads shown

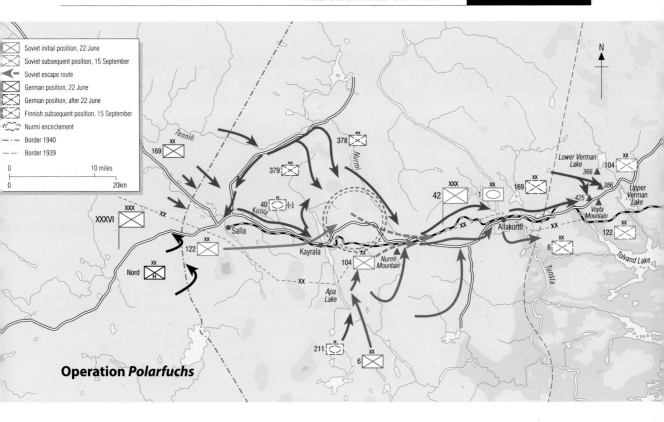

Operation _Polarfuchs_

on German maps ceased to exist. Dietl therefore pulled the 3rd out of the line and placed it behind the 2nd. Events had derailed his plans in less than 24 hours and within a week Northern Fleet warships landed Red Army soldiers behind German lines. Between July 7 and 8, Dietl's men crossed the Litsa River but Soviet counterattacks pushed them back.

Dietl developed a less ambitious plan that took account of terrain and logistics difficulties. He attacked the 205th Rifle Regiment on July 12 and had seven battalions across the Litsa the next day but the Soviet Navy landed 1,350 soldiers behind his lines again on July 14. Up to that point the small _Jäger_ divisions had used one regiment to fight and the other to run supplies forward on mule trains. Increasingly, however, combat forces accumulated in the bridgeheads and logistics ground to a halt.

A week later von Falkenhorst and Dietl met and attempted, unsuccessfully, to persuade Hitler to release three regiments of the Norwegian garrison. On July 24 they decided it would be futile to continue the offensive unless they received reinforcements within one month. At the end of July Hitler relented, promising Schörner's 6th Mountain Division by the second half of

A Red Army patrol in the Murmansk region. Stalin allocated just enough resources to the far-north theater to deny Hitler any success there. (Corbis)

September. Prompted by Royal Navy attacks against Kirkenes and Petsamo, on August 12 the Führer also agreed to transfer the 9th SS and 388th Infantry Regiments from Norway.

With Allied ships outnumbering its five destroyers, two U-boats, and various smaller vessels around the North Cape, the Kriegsmarine was losing the battle at sea. Rear Admiral A.G. Golovko's Northern Fleet mustered a cruiser, eight destroyers, three large and eight small torpedo boats, 27 submarines, and 45 other craft. Just as Dietl prepared to resume his attack Soviet submarines sank two German merchantmen full of reinforcements. On September 8 the Royal Navy chased other cargo ships into Norwegian fjords. British naval pressure delayed the 6th Mountain Division's arrival for weeks.

The German forces suffered from a similar disadvantage in the air. Major General A. Kuznetsov commanded combined Red Army Air Force and naval air elements in the north. His 49 bombers, 139 fighters, and 44 floatplanes more than held their own against Nielsen's tiny force.

After constant delays, Jodl visited Mountain Corps headquarters to investigate difficulties there. On September 5 Dietl told him Murmansk was out of the question even with the 6th Mountain's help. Both agreed Schörner's men would only further stress the logistics chain. In addition, the Soviet forces had by now reinforced their lines; the 14th and 52nd Rifle Divisions stood north and south of the Ura Gubo road and the Polyarnyy (Polar) Militia Division held the left flank.

Nevertheless Dietl attacked on September 8 and made good initial progress. In the 2nd Mountain's southern sector, the inexperienced 388th Infantry Regiment bypassed part of the 14th Rifle Division, which promptly counterattacked into the Landsers' rear; the same happened further north shortly thereafter to the untried 9th SS Regiment. Dietl suspended operations for 24 hours to stabilize the situation and bring up supplies. The 3rd Mountain struggled forward until September 16. On September 21 Dietl cancelled the assault and ordered his men to occupy good defensive positions.

The 6th Mountain arrived from Greece to relieve the 2nd and 3rd by mid-October. In two and a half months Dietl advanced 22 miles at a cost of 10,000 casualties with over 30 miles left to go. Terrain favored the defenders and Red Army supplies only had to travel 40–50 miles from Murmansk. For the Mountain Corps *Barbarossa*'s road to Murmansk had been anything but "laughable" as Hitler had stated dismissively before the campaign.[23]

Operation *Polarfuchs*

General Feige commanded the scaled-down attack toward Kandalaksha and the Soviet rail line. His XXXVI Corps

German soldiers on the march behind the frontline near the Polar Sea in World War II. The aurora borealis scene was probably photographed in the area of Murmansk in 1941. (Topfoto)

consisted of the 169th Infantry Division, 6th Nord (minus the 9th Regiment sent to Dietl), two panzer, two motorized artillery, and two engineer battalions, half a Flak battalion, and a *Nebelwerfer* battery, totaling over 40,000 men. Its mission was to attack along the road from Rovaniemi to Kandalaksha, and later turn north to link up with Dietl. The Finnish III Corps, basically their 6th Division, added a supporting attack to Allakurtti. The Luftwaffe contributed 30 Stukas and ten bombers, ten fighters, and ten reconnaissance aircraft. German intelligence identified the Soviet defenders as the 122nd Rifle Division supported by approximately 50 tanks.

---

23   Mann and Jogensen, *Hitler's Arctic War*, p.70.

The Axis plan called for the 169th Infantry to encircle Salla with two-thirds of its strength while the remaining regiment made a frontal assault on the Red Army defenses. The two regiments of Nord would also attack south of Salla. With nearly 24 hours of daylight, the German troops attacked at "night" on July 1 with the sun to their backs.

Division Nord encountered stubborn resistance and very heavy defensive fire. On July 2 the attack was called off. Nord spent two days preparing to resume the attack but early on July 4 the Soviet forces launched a counterattack of their own. Although the attack was beaten back by army and Finnish units, SS troops streamed to the rear with tales of a breakthrough by Soviet tanks, demanding all bridges blown up behind them. Nord had been organized for police duty in Norway but nevertheless their poor conduct infuriated Hitler, who ordered the division back to the front. Luckily for the German forces the Red Army was unable to exploit its failings.

Two days later Feige reorganized and attacked again. Armored support consisted of Panzer Battalion 40 (less the company with Dietl) and Panzer Battalion 211 (equipped with captured French Hotchkiss and Somua tanks). Armor was restricted to traveling on main roads (minor roads were too poor) so those panzers actually in combat seldom amounted to more than two companies. With artillery support and CAS, five battalions of the 169th and the panzers advanced and attacked the town. The 122nd Rifle evacuated Salla, leaving behind 50 tanks. The next day Nord, the only motorized unit in the Army of Norway, took up the pursuit. The 122nd fell back through the 104th Rifle Division to refit.

General Feige sought to create a Kessel east of Apa Lakes with the XXXVI Corps, reinforced by Infantry Regiment 324, advancing around from the north and the Finnish 6th Division and Panzer Battalion 211 from the south. Major General H. Siilasvou's Finnish III Corps made good progress using *motti* tactics (quick, small encirclements rather than the larger ones favored by the German commanders). At this point, August 22, the 169th Infantry and remainder of Nord broke free northeast of Salla, trapping the 104th and 122nd Rifle Divisions, who eventually fell back. The cordon in the German sector was especially porous and weather prevented a Luftwaffe vertical envelopment, with the result that the Red Army troops managed to escape the trap, albeit without their heavy equipment. The 6th Finnish and 169th Infantry Divisions pursued to Allakurtti without the panzers, which were too heavy for the soggy terrain and flimsy bridges in the area. The town was taken from the north on

September 1. Remnants of the 104th and 122nd Rifle Divisions deployed along the Voytayoki River line, and eventually fell back along the Vermanyoki River. The front stabilized.

At the southern edge of the German area, slow German preparations gave the Soviet forces time to reinforce, angering von Falkenhorst. From July 16–23 he badgered Feige at the latter's headquarters until the XXXVI Corps committed to attack down the Kasten'ga axis on July 26. The terrain rendered the panzers practically useless and with the Luftwaffe elements commanded from distant Oslo, their CAS was ineffective. As the Schwerpunkt shifted north and south the panzers marched and countermarched, engineers cutting new roads each time. Meanwhile, the Finns continued their advance augmented by elements of Nord, most of Panzer Battalion 40, and Stuka CAS, arriving at Kasten'ga on August 7. The Soviet commanders raced their 88th Rifle over from Belomorsk to halt them. By mid-month Group "J" (six battalions) and three battalions of Nord were exhausted. The Finns switched their main effort to Group "F," which attacked in the rain on August 19 completely surprising the defenders.

Führer Directive 36 of September 22 ordered resumption of the Kandalaksha offensive. Delays hampered Feige until Führer Directive 37 (October 10) cancelled further attacks, stating that the Soviet position along the main front appeared to be on the point of imminent collapse. Hitler halted the assault just when the situation began to look bright and the Soviet forces were at the end of their endurance. Group "F" advanced until November 15. Five days later, still about 40 miles from the railroad, both sides halted and sought good defensive terrain. *Barbarossa* in central Finland was over as well.

Granted, as the defender the Soviet High Command arguably had an easier mission than that of the attacking Germans, but it is clear that Stalin resourced his Arctic forces for success while Hitler did not. Dietl always seemed to be one battalion or regiment short. Like the fighting at the other extreme of the Führer's empire, North Africa, that in the far north was a slave to boring and unglamorous logistical masters such as port capacity and long lines of communications. It seemed that the Narvik shield on Dietl's uniform bought him no special advantage and snatching victory at Murmansk eluded him.

Summary

Panzer troops interrogate a Soviet POW. The officer with his back to the camera wears a black panzer jacket while the German tank crewman center wears the mouse-gray "Trikot" shirt. The odds that the Red Army prisoner survived German captivity are very slim. (NARA)

Overall the German leaders had every reason to be satisfied with *Barbarossa*'s first two weeks. On July 3 Halder famously boasted in his diary, "It is very likely not saying too much when I observe that the campaign against the Soviet Union has been won in less than fourteen days."

Much earlier, on June 24 von Leeb enthusiastically wrote in his diary that von Manstein's Dünaburg bridgehead represented "A stake into the heart of the enemy." Hoepner's appropriate motto was "Surprise, then forward, forward, forward." Yet Reinhardt wondered when the unified panzers would hit the Soviet divisions. However, Hoepner's superiors seldom allowed the panzer group to fight as more than two separate corps. From the start, LVI Panzer Corps raced for Dünaburg while the XLI Panzer Corps fought for its life against the bulk of two mechanized corps. This disastrous trend continued beyond the Dvina River. Along the Baltic Sea coast the Eighteenth Army was too weak and too thinly spread to spring a trap on the Soviet 8th Army. Inland Sixteenth Army was unable to maintain a solid link with Army Group Center.

Overhead, in the first three days of the war I Fliegerkorps flew 1,600 sorties, bombed 77 airfields, shot down 400 aircraft, and destroyed a further 1,100 on the ground. By June 25 there were no more Red Army Air Force bases to attack and evidently few aircraft left to destroy. Therefore the Luftwaffe had little choice but to change missions from air superiority to

The United Kingdom's Dominions and *Barbarossa*

Ironically the invasion Hitler meant to irretrievably separate the United Kingdom from its Soviet continental base of support brought the two nations closer together. On *Barbarossatag* Churchill broadcast a speech to his fellow Britons and members of the Dominions, saying although, "no one has been a more consistent opponent of Communism than I… Any man or state who fights against Nazism will have our aid… It follows, therefore, that we shall give whatever help we can to Russia and to the Russian people. We shall appeal to all our friends and Allies in every part of the world to take the same course and pursue it as we shall, faithfully and steadfastly to the end." *Barbarossa* was a Godsend to the United Kingdom; it distracted Hitler while simultaneously earning him a huge and implacable enemy.

It had not always been that way; in the summer of 1939 the British and French clearly wanted an agreement more than Stalin did. Prior to Hitler's invasion Stalin long distrusted British moves in the eastern Mediterranean and Near East areas. As the quotation above indicates, Churchill was under no illusions concerning Stalin and the USSR. He was a realist and helping the USSR was a key aspect of that realism. Another part was to see that Stalin at that point in time represented more of a Russian nationalist than a Communist ideologue. The dictator's interests were largely traditional Russian interests which Churchill understood and respected, not doctrinal Communist interests which the prime minister hated.

Other moral support for the USSR followed quickly. A Soviet military mission arrived in London on July 9; the two nations concluded an agreement on future operations three days later and British representatives reported to Moscow on the 27th. Churchill received the same strongly positive opinion of Stalin and the USSR from Harry Hopkins, Roosevelt's unofficial emissary to the prime minister, as the president did. A major objective of the Atlantic Conference between Churchill and Roosevelt in early August 1941 was aid for the USSR. A month later Stalin sent Churchill a letter stating that, "the Soviet Union is in a position of mortal peril." Within days Churchill sent his Minister for Aircraft Production, the Canadian Lord Beaverbrook, to Moscow with Roosevelt's envoy Averell Harriman.

British–Soviet military plans soon bore fruit when on August 25 both nations invaded Iran and marched into Teheran on September 16 (the same day Army Group South closed the Kiev pocket). The Dominion contingent consisted of six brigades, five of them Indian. This operation opened the Persian Corridor, in particular the Trans-Iranian Railroad; eventually one-quarter of the Lend-Lease aid to the USSR came via this route. Above the Arctic Circle, at the other great entrepot of Lend-Lease support on the White Sea, the first convoy from the UK, "Dervish," arrived at Archangel on August 31. It carried 40 Hawker Hurricanes (two squadrons) with crews and support staff. Number 151 Wing was operational over the critical northern ports by September 11 and claimed its first victory the following day. Throughout 1941 six more of the famous PQ convoys would arrive there or Murmansk. During that time they delivered, among a great many other things, 487 British and 182 American tanks.

Stalin requested that Churchill open a second front in Western Europe as soon as possible, but this could not be done; aerial bombardment of Germany from Great Britain was the best he could do. Once the US entered the war, the issue of a second front would be one of the most contentious between the three allies. Stalin also requested that 25–30 Dominion divisions join the fighting in Russia, 30,000 tons of aluminum plus other material aid that Churchill could never hope to provide. Throughout *Barbarossa* Stalin pressed the UK to declare war on Finland, Hungary, and Rumania, which His Majesty's Government finally did on the last day of the campaign, 5 December. Most ironically, however, Britain's greatest contribution to *Barbarossa* probably came three months prior to *Barbarossatag*: in early March the Royal Navy plus commandos raided the Norwegian coast in Operation *Claymore*. Hitler's exaggerated and irrational decision to keep more than a third of a million Wehrmacht men stationed in Norway in response to this raid severely hamstrung *Barbarossa*.

CAS. Nevertheless, on the ground Landsers griped of aggressive and ubiquitous re-equipped Soviet flyers, while Luftwaffe generals complained about being nothing more than aerial artillery.

During the border battles, Kuznetsov lost 1,444 tanks and armored vehicles, nearly 4,000 guns, 90,000 men killed, but "only" 35,000 captured. He failed to defend his sector and lost his job. Hitler pushed for Hoepner to concentrate at Dünaburg and push northeast but von Brauchitsch and von Leeb dawdled until the Sixteenth Army arrived. This six-day pause to allow Busch to catch up with Hoepner killed Army Group North's momentum and would allow the Northwest Front to avoid total destruction. On June 29 Hitler told his OKW Chief, Field Marshal Wilhelm Keitel, to "concentrate Hoepner's panzers at Dünaburg … and drive through Ostrov." Both von Brauchitsch and von Leeb disagreed and did all they could to delay the panzers. Their willfulness and caution put "a stake into the heart" of their own chances of victory.

Von Bock's early accomplishments were only slightly less spectacular than those in Lithuania. Although fortress Brest held out longer than desired, his two panzer groups lunged forward relentlessly. The well-resourced Guderian advanced recklessly on the right. But it was Hoth on the left who split two major Soviet command echelons on the more direct tack to Moscow that caused Stavka most concern. Demonstrating that he was not a completely inept commander, Pavlov managed to have his deputy Boldin launch a substantial counterattack against Grodno.

Between Grodno and Minsk the struggle did not slacken. Panzers headed east without looking back while Landsers trudged on to keep pace. Soviet mechanized corps and infantry armies initiated numerous counterattacks wherever and whenever possible. But the undeniable realities of *Barbarossa*'s opening weeks and the confluence of the vulnerable Bialystok salient and Army Group Center's strengths lent an air of inevitability to the fighting. Besides the two prongs represented by the panzer groups, fighting centered on the struggles over the various pockets that made up the greater Minsk phenomenon.

At Minsk the Germans claimed to have taken 341,000 POWs and captured or destroyed 4,799 tanks, 9,427 guns, and 1,777 aircraft. By inflicting these losses, plus an estimated similar number of wounded and missing, in about ten days, Army Group Center had arguably achieved its goals as set out in the numerous orders for *Barbarossa*. By July 2, Stavka realized that the "disorganized and much weakened forces of the first echelon of the Red Army cannot halt the advance of the enemy." However, German intelligence was already picking up indications of second- and third-echelon forces occupying successive defensive lines on the road to Moscow. As Hitler wrote Mussolini on June 30, "The might and resources of the Red Army are far in excess of what we knew or even considered possible." These words are quite different from Halder's of just three days hence. Even so, few observers envisaged any end to *Barbarossa* other than an overwhelming German victory.

Despite near-ideal tank country in his sector, von Rundstedt's men endured slow going in the face of the Kirponos–Zhukov team and their steady defenses. The Soviet armor advantage in numbers and quality almost cancelled the twin disadvantages of overwhelmed tactical leadership and poor crew skills. In the south the German forces withstood fairly constant counterattacks like their comrades in the north and center theaters, only more concentrated and sustained. Army Group South had to fight earnestly for every yard; there were no gifts of geography, incompetence, or negligence here. However, von Kleist on the main Kiev axis and von Stülpnagel at L'vov strove hard at working their way around the initial Red Army defensive positions and would soon be rewarded by breaking into the open country.

But to achieve this they first had to overcome Kirponos' resistance in the confined border area. Soviet countermoves were more successful than anyone in the Soviet hierarchy realized. Unfortunately for them the then common handicaps of questionable commanders, no air support, and inadequate support plus excessive distance between attacking units condemned their actions. On the other side of the frontlines German reactions were uniformly effective. However, breakout success for Army Group South would have to wait.

Soviet soldiers defend the village of Kamenka northwest of Moscow. Taken in early November before the snow built up, this photograph shows a mix of weapons. (Corbis)

THREE STEPS FORWARD, ONE STEP BACK

A central feature of *Auftragstaktik* was that in the absence of explicit orders a subordinate would act in accordance with the higher commander's intent. It was within this framework that in early July, in violation of Hitler's instructions that the Minsk pockets be eliminated first, and largely on their own initiative, both Hoth and Guderian moved their panzer groups toward Smolensk from positions north and south of Minsk. As the slower marching infantry arrived at each of the smaller pockets they freed the armor to continue eastward. Every German leader knew that *Barbarossa*'s success depended upon not allowing the Red Army a moment's respite in which to re-establish a credible defense.

Only in hindsight do we know that *Barbarossa*'s first few weeks did not represent the knockout blow that the German leadership needed. The same can also be said of its next stage. It should come as little surprise that Army Group Center scored the first major victory of *Barbarossa* at Minsk. Its status as the campaign's Schwerpunkt, its two armored groups, two Fliegerkorps (including the elite VIII), plus Pavlov's extremely vulnerable position made this practically inevitable. Von Leeb would never achieve a giant Kessel in the north, while down at Kiev von Rundstedt would require another two months to reach von Bock's body count. With success at Minsk fresh in the German leaders' minds, on June 30 OKH instructed von Bock's headquarters to prepare to continue "operations in the direction of Smolensk."

To the north, results looked similarly decisive for von Leeb. On the middle Luga, Hoepner replicated his earlier success at Dünaburg, but this opportunity was likewise squandered when the panzer bridgehead first languished for weeks and then came under serious Soviet attack. However, the German forces eventually fought their way tantalizingly close to Leningrad but the question remained, would they attempt to take the city or allow it to starve under the

A Soviet locomotive destroyed near Tarnopol, probably by the Luftwaffe. Within weeks shortages of rolling stock and usable roadbed made themselves sorely felt. The availability of Soviet rolling stock such as this would have been invaluable at this point. (NARA)

PREVIOUS PAGE:
More Flak used in the direct-fire mode. Here a 20mm Flak 30 on a SdKfz 10/4 supports infantry with MG34 near Smolensk on July 13. (Topfoto)

Nazis' Hunger Plan? More importantly, were their strategic objectives better served by making a close siege of Leningrad or by earnestly joining hands with the Finns on the Svir River?

Army Group South also started off slowly, but then managed to skirt the edge of the Rotkino Marshes and threaten Kiev, bag over two armies at Uman and approach the Dnepr in numerous places, all this against the heart of the Red Army's defenses. But perhaps Kirponos had done too well too early; German staffs noticed weakness along the Soviet line that seemed ripe for exploitation. Meanwhile, early in July, fighting began along the Rumanian front, adding hundreds of miles to the Red Army's defensive woes. Finally, the Finns in Karelia made impressive advances and far exceeded the 1939 frontier except where it mattered most, in Leningrad's hinterland.

Beyond the Dvina and into Russia

Von Leeb violated a central tenet of the blitzkrieg when he halted Hoepner for six days on the Dvina. Furthermore, he breached another by preventing the already too small panzer group from concentrating. Neither Führer Directive 18 nor the *Aufmarschanweisung* firmly stated whether von Leeb should aim directly for Leningrad or veer northeast so he could attack either Leningrad or Moscow – Halder's pet project. Even if von Leeb had been of a mind to fight an aggressive blitzkrieg campaign, OKH maintained tighter control over Fourth Panzer Group than its contemporaries because of the imagined "danger of being encircled and destroyed in the vast forests in front of Leningrad unless it has the support of closely-following infantry divisions."

On the Soviet side, the average strength of a Northwest Front rifle division shrank to about 2,000 men. As their tanks melted away in uneven combat the Red Army could create nothing larger than tank brigades. By the end of June the Soviets had lost their first echelon formations. In response, they did add 30 small (3,447 troopers) but mobile cavalry divisions. Following *Barbarossatag*, the Soviet High Command managed to mobilize nine new armies in June, 13 in July, and 15 in August. Aware Kuznetsov had made a mess of his Front's defense, on July 2, Stavka instructed the Northern Front to re-orient Leningrad's defensive efforts on the Luga River, facing toward the south. The burden of the defense would fall on the newly created Luga Operational Group (LOG), holding the river line between Narva and Lake Il'men.

Having decided to defend Leningrad along the Luga, Northern Front commander Popov sent his deputy General K.P. Piadyshev to survey a possible defense line there. On July 9, Piadyshev took command of the LOG, consisting at first of two rifle and three militia divisions (the latter divisions 1, 2, and

Stavka threw General K.P. Piadyshev into command of the Luga Operational Group in order to prepare to defend Leningrad against a threat from an entirely unexpected direction in less than three weeks with many sub-standard units. Although he slowed the Germans considerably, Stalin had him arrested for dereliction of duty. (David Glantz)

3, created by the Leningrad Military Soviet five days earlier) and a mountain brigade. He later received four more rifle divisions and the 21st and 24th Tank Divisions. Behind this line stood two more defensive positions reaching back to Leningrad's suburbs. The scene was set for the battle for the USSR's second city.

At Führer Headquarters near swampy Lake Mauer, Hitler came down with dysentery and stomach pains and suffered through much of July and half of August. While his personal physician, Dr Theo Morell, pumped the dictator full of medications, a crisis of command paralyzed the Ostheer's decision making. Von Brauchitsch, Halder, and others took full advantage of this leadership vacuum to push their own agendas and hamstring *Barbarossa*.

The Stalin Line

With his army group temporarily consolidated until the panzers would again outpace the infantry, von Leeb instructed his men to resume the advance in early July. Reinhardt on the left again served as the panzer group's Schwerpunkt. Leading the XLI Panzer Corps, the 1st Panzer Division advanced 70 miles on July 2 against weak Soviet resistance to a point only 30 miles from Ostrov and its Velikaya River crossings. Red Army defensive efforts seemed to be directed against the sister LVI Panzer Corps coming up from Rezekne. Reinforcing success, Hoepner would not allow dilution of Reinhardt's advance in order to help von Manstein further upstream.

Arriving just hours ahead of the 27th Army, the 1st Panzer Division took Ostrov on July 4, clearing its railroad bridge by 1730hrs. The 27th Army immediately counterattacked and soon the entire town was in flames. Under Red Army Air Force CAS and with KV tanks the Soviet forces renewed their assaults on July 8. By noon that day the German situation became desperate and they fell back into the relative safety of the burning town. When Reinhardt's men finally stabilized the situation, 100 burning enemy tanks illuminated the night. New, well-coordinated Soviet attacks against the German bridgehead began at 0300hrs on July 11. However, by this point the Red Army units were spent and the panzers renewed their advance the next day. The Luftwaffe flew 1,200 sorties and claimed 140 tanks and 112 aircraft destroyed during the Velikaya River battles. By July 10 Red Army Air Force elements counted only 102 aircraft from an original 1,142. The old bunkers along the former Latvian–Russian border behind them, with difficulty Hoepner's men had turned the Stalin Line. The weakened 27th Army retreated east through the swamps toward Opochka with von Manstein in pursuit. Reinhardt's relative success

caused Hoepner to take 3rd Motorized Division from von Manstein and transfer it north. With the Soviet 8th and 27th Armies split apart once again, the situation looked bright for the German forces.

Von Küchler had previously isolated remnants of the 8th Army but the latter now manned the Parnu–Tartu line. The 61st Infantry Division briefly captured Tartu, but did not have sufficient ammunition to maintain its position. By July 13 the 61st occupied an *Igel* south of Poltsamaa against the 10th Rifle Corps. Further inland to the southeast Busch's Landsers finally caught up to the fight after weeks of marching 20–30 miles day after day. To the southeast, the Sixteenth Army fought the fresh 22nd Army near Polozk. With the Soviet forces mounting a serious defense there, combat in the unusual terrain required new tactics. Communications between neighboring German units was difficult and large gaps existed between formations.

Now in Russia proper, the wilderness and the impoverished conditions of the people there stunned the German troops. By July 6 von Manstein was stuck in the Velikaya swamps near Opochka. Confusion reigned within army group headquarters as von Leeb, Hoepner, and von Manstein argued over

A camouflaged bunker on the original Stalin Line west of Pskov captured in mid-July. Much of the line's weaponry had been stripped a year earlier as the Red Army redeployed west after the seizure of eastern Poland, Bessarabia, and the Baltic States, rendering many of the defenses of doubtful value. (NARA)

the direction LVI Panzer Corps should take next: reinforce Reinhardt or strike out on its own toward Staraya Russa? On the 10th von Leeb remarked in his diary "the Russians defend every step." In fact, it took von Manstein's men until the night of July 10/11 to capture Opochka, only to be subjected to immediate Soviet counterattacks. Hoepner wanted to swing north to trap Red Army forces facing the Eighteenth Army west of Lake Peipus. This course of action, the third offered up in von Leeb's languid command atmosphere, had even less operational logic that the previous two. Miserable terrain plus Red Army defenders employing minefields, abatis, and other obstacles slowed the operation. East of the big lake the XLI Panzer Corps, using the primitive roads, reached the Plyussa River on July 12. But Luftwaffe air attacks failed to halt the Soviet's continued withdrawal.

Soviet 45mm M1937 antitank gunners come under fire near Pskov in early July. These 11th Army soldiers had been conducting a fighting withdrawal without effective command from above, falling back in front of von Leeb's men rather than halting them. (HITM)

As early as June 30 Hitler toyed with the idea of sending two panzer groups (Hoth in addition to Hoepner) first to Leningrad and then to Moscow. This plan might have worked if the German leaders had not delayed pulling the trigger, but by July 4 he still had not made the decision. After squandering nine irreplaceable days and thinking the Soviet forces were beaten, on July 8 Hitler and Halder agreed that Third Panzer Group would not participate against Leningrad (this proved to be a temporary, four-day decision). On July 9, von Brauchitsch, von Leeb, and Hoepner met at army group headquarters and hammered out a compromise with regard to Fourth Panzer Group's actual method of attack. Both of Hoepner's panzer corps would make for the massive city, XLI via Pskov and the lower Luga, LVI through Novgorod. On a map this looks like a concentrated panzer group attack, but in actuality intervening terrain and vegetation meant the two panzer corps operated in isolation. The Sixteenth Army would cover Hoepner's exposed right while the Eighteenth would continue to clear the Baltic States and then follow Reinhardt. This plan also lasted only four days; by July 13 the issue was not whether Hoth would support von Leeb, but whether his panzer group would go all the way to Leningrad or only so far as Velikie Luki and whether all or some of Hoth's units would come north.

Around this time Stalin made some leadership changes of his own. The USSR created a new echelon of command, the Strategic Direction. Directions came from the World War I tradition and were not independent staffs but extensions of Stavka under the command of a marshal. Accordingly, on July 10 Marshal K.E. Voroshilov arrived to coordinate the efforts of the Northern and Northwest Fronts as well as the Northern and Red Banner Fleets. Voroshilov may have been a trusted crony of Stalin's but he could not lead; his Northwest Direction would be the first to go on August 30. On July 15 the Red Army temporarily disbanded rifle corps as a superfluous command echelon. In any event it no longer had sufficient staffs or qualified staff officers to man those rifle corps that remained.

Army Group North into Russia

The area between Lakes Peipus and Il'men and south of Petersburg is the historical Ingermannland. It marked the boundary between the Russians and first the Teutonic Knights, then the Swedes and later the Baltic States. Sixteenth Army and Fourth Panzer Group fought here until the end of August. Logistics, sanguinely sidestepped during most of *Barbarossa*'s planning, now dominated operations. It is appropriate to quote Martin van Creveld at length:

> In the second half of July the supply service was incapable of supporting even the most limited offensive because it was fully occupied moving its base forward from Dünaburg to the area around Luga, and in this period the start of the attack was postponed no fewer than seven times... The offensive was resumed on 8 August but by that time the defense of Leningrad was ready.[24]

---

24   Creveld, *Supplying War*, p.162.

269th Infantry Division destroy Soviet T-34 tanks using captured antitank guns. The ZiS-3 76mm antitank gun (**1**) was a modification of a standard field gun of the same size. As another field-expedient method of destroying Soviet armor, the Germans became adept at turning these fine weapons against their former owners within minutes of capturing them. Members of the 269th Infantry Division are shown here attempting to keep up with Reinhardt's XLI Panzer Corps as it advances across the marshy terrain between the Velikaya and Luga Rivers. The Landsers occupy temporary defensive positions but as soon as they dig out a spadeful of dirt the hole fills with brackish water (**2**). The German antitank gun crew prepares to put the captured piece into operation (**3**) while a couple of infantry squads provide security to the flanks (**4**). Across the marshy meadow the T-34 comes out of the tree line on a forest trail (**5**), which they then aim for. (© Osprey Publishing, Peter Dennis)

Fortuitously for the defenders, less than 24 hours into the German invasion, Popov in Leningrad began looking south at the axis of attack along the Pskov highway as the city's main threat. His commissar, A.A. Zhandov, soon had 200,000 civilians digging hundreds of miles of antitank ditches and trenches, creating 15,000 fighting positions and 22 miles of barricades in front of Leningrad. Fearing the worst, authorities evacuated two-thirds of a million civilians from the city by August.

Reinhardt advanced on the left as planned along the highway toward Luga with the XXXVIII Army Corps behind. Hoepner's second coup de main of *Barbarossa* in capturing a critical bridgehead came in early July near

Kingisepp. The 1st and 6th Panzer Divisions raced north on roughly parallel courses east of Lake Peipus. A *Kampfgruppe* under Colonel Erhard Raus, including Brandenburger commandos, worked its way through forest and marsh to a bridge at Ivanovskoye early on July 14. His men discovered the bridge unguarded plus another bridge not shown on their maps. Farther south at Sabsk, the 1st Panzer Division likewise secured a bridgehead. The Soviet leaders rushed reinforcements directly to the threatened area on trains from Leningrad. Many of them were militia units that achieved little. Until August 19 Reinhardt's isolated men relied exclusively on Luftwaffe resupply.

The XLI Panzer Corps had fought across 650 miles in less than one month and Leningrad was fewer than 100 miles away from its bridgeheads. However, although they had having crossed the last major river barrier blocking their advance to the city, Leningrad itself would prove beyond XLI Panzer Corps' reach. While the Red Army dug a network of obstacles, trenches, and bunkers to their front, Reinhardt's men settled into a relatively costly defensive battle. His panzer raid that gained two bridgeheads in the shadow of Leningrad reaped none of the operational benefits that von Manstein's had just weeks earlier at Dünaburg or as Model would later at Novgorod-Severskiy as part of the Kiev encirclement (pages 274 – 6). On July 27, an exasperated Reinhardt tried in vain to resign his post, saying, "This [wait] is dreadful ... the decisive opportunity [to rush Leningrad] has passed."

To his southeast the LVI Panzer Corps hacked its way through the massive wilderness region between Opochka and Novgorod. Limited to one major road von Manstein's troops stretched out in a long isolated and vulnerable line, 60 miles from Reinhardt and over 50 miles ahead of the trailing marching infantry. The situation was even worse for Kuznetsov, however. On July 10 Stavka told him of its "absolute dissatisfaction with the work of the Northwest Front," saying commanders at every echelon "have not fulfilled our orders and like criminals have abandoned their defensive positions." By mid-month Piadyshev had been arrested, perhaps unjustly. The headquarters subsequently divided the 250-mile long Luga defenses into three parts, each commanded by a major general: Kingisepp under V.V. Semashko, Luga (town) under A.N. Astanin, and Eastern under F.N. Starikov.

Von Manstein's thrust aimed initially for Novgorod with a subsequent objective of cutting the Moscow–Leningrad rail line at Chudovo. Taking advantage of the German forces' exposed positions, and perhaps spurred by Stavka's criticism, the 11th Army struck the LVI Panzer Corps near Soltsy. With the supporting German I Army Corps far to the rear, Vatutin's forces fought a

A 20mm Flak 30 aboard an SdKfz 10/4 halftrack during *Barbarossa's* opening days. Even at this early stage, however, the Red Army Air Force was capable of making life miserable for ground troops without such accompanying antiaircraft support. (NARA)

desperate battle against von Manstein's spearhead from July 14–18. The northern arm of the attack consisted mainly of the 10th Mechanized Corps, and the southern of the 16th and 22nd Rifle Corps. They cut off 8th Panzer Division, von Manstein's vanguard, from the rest of LVI Panzer Corps which, surrounded in marshy terrain, could not maneuver off of the narrow corduroy roads.

Over a two-day period 3rd Motorized and SS Totenkopf fought their way forward to rescue the 8th Panzer. By the time von Manstein stabilized the situation 8th Panzer Division had lost 70 of its 150 operational panzers. Von Manstein required four days to save General Brandenburger's division while Hoepner diverted valuable resources from the XLI Panzer Corps' successful operations to assist. The attack left the 8th Panzer Division severely shaken.

The ever-cautious von Leeb again insisted that his forces halt and clean the untidy situation before continuing. He therefore detached von Manstein's most powerful formation, the recently rescued 8th Panzer, in order to reinforce Reinhardt. Meanwhile over half of Busch's army struggled to secure the boundary with Army Group Center and was therefore unavailable for action around Leningrad. Most of his supplies still had to be flown in due to Red Army stragglers and partisan bands active in the Sixteenth Army's rear area.

Another crisis mastered, von Manstein continued to the Luga River with the 3rd Motorized, Totenkopf and 269th Infantry Divisions. On July 22 von Brauchitsch visited Hitler as the latter leveled criticism at von Leeb. Hitler, and indeed the OKH, insisted von Manstein's thrust be Hoepner's Schwerpunkt. They agreed on the need to send Hoepner's right-hand corps on a great counterclockwise arc to cut off Leningrad from Moscow and effect a junction with the Finns at the Svir. In hindsight this wider encirclement of Leningrad was probably the wiser choice. With the issue still unresolved, beginning on July 24, and with *Nebelwerfer* support, the LVI Panzer Corps fought slowly forward against determined defenders. The Soviet forces inflicted numerous losses and more than once von Manstein pulled his men back to their starting positions, but by August 2 they were once again ready to assault the town of Luga.

In the Sixteenth Army area, in front of the 30th Infantry Division near Staraya Russa, Luftwaffe reconnaissance noted a defensive system of trenches, mines, and barbed wire many miles deep. Weather delayed D-Day three times in four days. South of Lake Il'men Landsers of the 30th Infantry Division resorted to flamethrowers, bayonets, and hand-to-hand combat to inch forward in the face of the Soviet forces' tenacious defense. To their left the 121st Infantry Division prepared to attack near Utogorsh. Von Richthofen's VIII Fliegerkorps (four Stuka and three fighter Gruppen) arrived to help. German artillery could not destroy Soviet bunkers buried beneath six feet of soil and after two days 121st Infantry Division battle casualties exceeded a third of those suffered during *Barbarossa*'s first five weeks. Division headquarters issued its General Instructions #4 which concluded that the enemy's talents "can be a remarkable example to us."

The Fall of Tallinn

Far to the west, the weak Eighteenth Army with just six divisions struggled up the strategic Baltic Sea littoral against an even weaker 8th Army. In central Estonia the 16th Rifle Division ably defended Tartu while the 11th Rifle held Viljandi with effective Red Army Air Force CAS. Frustrated at the delay, on July 12 army group headquarters ordered the Eighteenth Army to attack with the XXVI Army Corps the next day. At 0300hrs, exactly one month after *Barbarossa*'s start, the 61st Infantry Division and StuG Abteilung 185 assaulted Poltsamaa. A day later the 217th Infantry attacked at Turi and by the evening of July 25 these two units had trapped most of the 48th and 125th Rifle Divisions against Lake Peipus, capturing over 9,000 POWs. The XXVI Corps kept up the pressure and by August 8 its 245th Infantry Division reached the Gulf of Finland at Kunda, half way between Tallinn and Narva.

Intent on depriving the Red Banner Fleet of its last base outside Kronshtadt (itself full of revolutionary Bolshevik significance), the German leaders planned to reduce Tallinn. Under overall command of Admiral

German infantry cross a pontoon bridge over the Narva River in September. The fortress dominating the photograph is the Russian Ivangorod while that in the far left is the Estonian Hermannsfeste. (Corbis)

Tributs, but tactically led by the 10th Corps (two rifle and two mechanized divisions under Major General I.F. Nikolaev), 20,000 soldiers and 25,000 civilians prepared the defense. From west to east Nikolaev stationed the 22nd Motorized, 16th Rifle, and 10th Motorized Divisions backed up by marines. The Soviet commanders expected the main attack to come from the south, but the German Schwerpunkt was to the east.

The XLII Infantry Corps attacked at 0330hrs on August 20 with the 217th, 61st, and 254th Infantry Divisions (west to east) supported by 210mm mortars and assault guns. Estonian Self Defense Forces kept the German rear areas safe from partisans. Red Army defenders put up tough resistance but by August 27 the German troops reached Tallinn's outskirts. The 61st entered the city a day later, marching single file over miles of railroad embankments. Tributs had evacuated most of the garrison except for an 11,000-man rearguard on the night of August 27. Nearly 190 vessels of all descriptions participated in the disastrous operation. Under German pressure, cargo loading was haphazard and discipline almost nonexistent. Luftflotte 1 bombers preyed on the 15-mile-long convoy, sinking 18 ships. A further 13 transports and 18 warships fell victim to mines while Finnish torpedo boats accounted for even more. Ultimately only one transport reached Kronshtadt 200 miles away and the German soldiers pulled 12,000 Soviet soldiers out of the sea while a further 10,000 perished.

Smolensk

Guderian, and to a lesser extent Hoth, did not conceal their belief that Moscow should be the Ostheer's main goal. In his June 22 order of the day the former went so far as to say, "The objective is Moscow, every man must know this!" This opinion agreed with neither the various *Barbarossa* directives, nor Hitler's oft-stated belief that Moscow "is not very important." However, neither Stalin, Timoshenko, nor Zhukov had any knowledge of this, another failure of the otherwise very effective Soviet spy network. For the remainder of the summer the Soviet commanders threw every possible obstacle in von Bock's way, to the detriment of their defenses along other fronts.

At Minsk, von Bock had supposedly crushed everything the Soviet forces had with which to defend Moscow. Thus the exposed tips of both panzer spearheads received a nasty surprise when, on July 4, Stavka ordered Timoshenko to "organize a reliable defense, concentrate reserves ... deliver counterstrokes along the Lepel, Borisov, and Bobruisk axes" (basically the Berezina River line). Timoshenko arranged his defenses north to south thus: 20th Army plus 5th and 7th Mechanized Corps guarded the middle Berezina due west of the River Gate versus Hoth's right. Lieutenant-General P.A. Kurochkin's 128th, 153rd, 229th, 233rd, 73rd, 18th, and 137th Rifle Divisions blunted the drive of Guderian's northernmost XLVII Panzer Corps.

Panzer IIIs of 11th Panzer Division pass a brewed-up BT-7 tank. The division's unofficial ghost tactical symbol can be seen on the equipment box mounted on the panzer's rear deck. (Topfoto)

Guderian's central corps, XLVI Panzer, had it easier and his southern thrust by XXIV Panzer Corps had it easiest of all near Rogatchev, despite the opposition of 36 artillery batteries and the 117th Rifle Division on the east bank. He would overcome the Berezina obstacle here against the 117th Rifle Division.

Meanwhile to the north, Hoth was dangerously spread out, with a 100-mile gap between his XXXIX Panzer Corps near Vitebsk and LVII Panzer at Polotsk and Disna. The likelihood for mutual support did not exist. Following orders to "destroy the Lepel enemy concentration," the Soviet 5th and 7th Mechanized Corps now turned their attention on XXXIX Panzer Corps, just slightly north of Guderian's XLVII Panzer; if executed properly, the Red Army attack would split the seam between the two panzer groups. This meeting engagement, centered on Senno – northwest of Orsha – initially pushed 7th Panzer Division back 20 miles and eventually involved 12th, 17th, and 18th Panzer as well. Of the 2,000 mostly obsolete tanks available to the two Soviet mechanized corps, only 70 percent even made it to the battlefield and after five days the German forces had destroyed 832 of these. Beaten, the remnants of 5th and 7th Mechanized withdrew toward Smolensk.

In order to give Timoshenko no opportunity to establish his second echelon, XXXIX Panzer Corps took up the pursuit. Its 7th Panzer Division, followed by 20th, lay strung out along the one usable road from Lepel to Vitebsk. Rain slowed their advance and bought the Soviet forces time to stiffen their defenses. With their 22nd Army holding a 175-mile front with six weak divisions, they desperately needed such a pause. Elsewhere in the panzer group sector, Hoth's men had to cross nearly 100 wooden bridges on the 50-mile long road from Borisov to Lepel, most of which collapsed under the weight of modern equipment.

Stavka noticed the vulnerable flanks of the panzer groups from the start, but lacked the wherewithal to defeat them. Soon the bulk of the marshal's defenders were streaming east; with the Berezina line abruptly abandoned, the next stop were the Dvina and Dnepr rivers.

Toward Smolensk

Stalin had sent the Reserve Front forward on July 1, too soon and not massed, thereby creating a counteroffensive in name only. Fortunately for Stalin and the Red Army, the German forces had significant troubles of their own. Strategically, since *Barbarossa's* inception, Minsk marked the point when Hitler would decide what to do during the second phase of the campaign. With forces in place and ready to continue the advance, he nevertheless deferred that decision. German strategic intelligence, wildly inaccurate before *Barbarossa* began, continued to flounder. At an July 8 conference at Rastenburg they put Timoshenko's strength at 11 divisions; in reality Army Group Center faced 66 (24 in first echelon with 37 actually in position). Three days later Halder wrote that the Soviets had no reserves behind the fighting front; in fact, Stavka had created reserves that OKW could only envy.

The German leaders' final problem was von Kluge, who now suffered a crisis of confidence in his new role as a panzer army commander. On July 5 he complained to OKW that he could not control Hoth and Guderian. Von Brauchitsch reminded him that his duty was to coordinate, not to micromanage his panzer commanders and advised him to give these capable subordinates free rein, creating his Schwerpunkt with the one who first gained freedom of action. A day later a frustrated von Bock admonished von Kluge to "Make a [panzer] fist, somewhere." The army group commander correctly believed that a field marshal should be able to handle the two subordinate panzer group commanders. Von Bock soon concluded that von Kluge's leadership was "useless" and henceforth frequently bypassed this superfluous command echelon altogether and sent liaison officers directly to Guderian and Hoth. An essential prerequisite for creating a pocket at Smolensk was for Hoth and Guderian to rupture the Dvina–Dnepr line at Vitebsk and Mogilev. This is where von Bock turned his attention next.

Hoth had already moved out, ordered by army group headquarters to continue towards Vitebsk and Polotsk, thunderstorms and rising rivers hampering his every step. Five or six new Red Army divisions established defensive positions at Polotsk astride both banks of the Dvina. With VIII Fliegerkorps flying overhead and after racing 120 miles in 24 hours, 19th Panzer Division seized a bridge intact at Disna on July 4. The 18th and 14th Motorized Divisions provided flank protection while engineers built a second bridge. On the same day 7th Panzer Division ran into Konev's 19th Army defenses at Vitebsk and halted to wait for Strauss's infantry to lend support.

At Disna, Red Army counterattacks were ably supported by aircraft and artillery. On July 5, heavily armored Sturmoviki attacked 7th Panzer without suffering a loss, despite some aircraft taking 200 hits. New pressure at Disna came from an unexpected source, the 27th Army, being shoved southeastward by Army Group North. Nevertheless, Hoth's vanguards continued to expand their bridgeheads.

Smolensk Encirclement

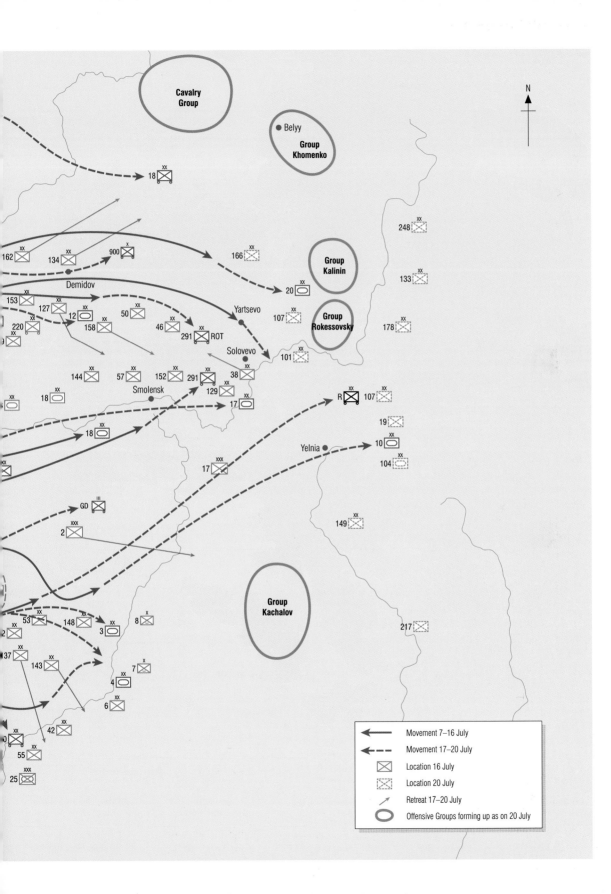

Cavalry
Group

● Belyy

Group
Khomenko

18

248

162   134   900

Demidov

166

Group
Kalinin

20

133

153   127   12   50

220   158   46

Yartsevo

291   ROT

Solovevo

107

Group
Rokessovsky

178

101

144   57   152   291

38

Smolensk

129

17

18

18

R   107

19

10

104

Yelnia ●

17

GD

2

149

Group
Kachalov

53   148

3   8

217

37   143

7

4

6

42

55

25

	Movement 7–16 July
	Movement 17–20 July
	Location 16 July
	Location 20 July
	Retreat 17–20 July
	Offensive Groups forming up as on 20 July

When Hoth's troops arrived at Ulla they discovered the bridge over the western Dvina destroyed (left); engineers constructed the new bridge to the right. (MHI)

With 7th Panzer stalled before Vitebsk, Hoth opted for the indirect approach to spring them free. Between July 5 and 7, 20th Panzer, slowed by rains but supported by the 20th Motorized Division, encountered 62nd Rifle Corps defenses upriver at Ulla. But with support from von Richthofen's flying artillery they sent across two waves of assault boats, and finally overcame the numerous bunkers late on July 8. With the Dnepr behind them and now in the open country, the 20th Panzer's Kampfgruppe von Bismarck circled around clockwise from Ulla and assaulted burning Vitebsk from the rear the next morning. Red Army units counterattacked desperately against the bridgeheads and the smoldering city in an attempt to throw them back, but ultimately Hoth's men made a deadly crack in the northern portion of Timoshenko's Dvina–Dnepr line.

Unfortunately for them, approximately ten weak divisions of Erashkov's 22nd Army plus some 27th Army stragglers sat astride the boundary between Army Groups North and Center near Nevel. Against von Bock's wishes – he called helping von Leeb a "useless venture," higher headquarters ordered his LVII Panzer Corps to liquidate this force. Spread too thin to close the trap at

Having just broken through the Stalin Line, Landsers hitch a ride aboard an assault gun. The defensive fortifications were of uneven quality, offering little resistance at one point or delaying the Germans for days elsewhere. (NARA)

Nevel, this diversion accomplished little. Amid confusion and poor communication, 19th Panzer Division continued 30 miles to Velikie Luki and captured the town on the 20th, only to give it back to the Red Army days later when the division was redirected yet again; the same troops would have to retake it at a higher cost a month later. This Nevel detour reduced Hoth to only one panzer corps on his main axis, severely curtailing his ability to influence events at this critical time.

Also on July 4, Guderian's 4th Panzer Division reached Bychov on the Dnepr, a well-defended town complete with a stout antitank ditch – one of the few places where the Stalin Line challenged the German units. They managed to cross the river, only to have the Soviet forces chase them back to the west bank and demolish the bridge. To the south, Model's 3rd Panzer Division crossed the Dnepr at Rogatchev aided by its wading tanks, despite the fact that the 800-yard-wide river was in flood. By 0445hrs on July 5, 4th Panzer Division engineers had thrown a new bridge across and continued the assault with the support of 210mm howitzers; the bridge collapsed at 0730hrs, but would be rebuilt by 1100hrs.

For Second Panzer Group, the Stalin Line did not appear to be a hollow shell. The operational rate for tanks of 3rd and 18th Panzer Divisions stood at only 35 percent and 58 percent respectively. With the German rail and logistics system severely disrupted back at Brest, 4th Panzer Division sent a staff major all the way to Germany to scrounge for spare parts. On July 11, 87th Infantry Division received its first reinforcements since June 22, 350 men, which they promptly had to hand over to Guderian. Initially rejected on the left, Guderian shifted his Schwerpunkt first to the right and then to his center. The fight along the Dnepr raged during July 7–16, and as the Soviet troops retreated they managed to destroy many bridges over the wide river. Guderian's new attack axis would send him straight for the fortress town of Mogilev.

Despite supply difficulties and stiff resistance, the German troops had turned the Dvina–Dnepr line into a shambles. From his bridgehead at Ulla, Hoth wrecked Timoshenko's right, separating 27th, 22nd, and 20th Armies so they could be defeated in detail. Reinforcing success, he took the 12th Panzer and 18th Motorized Divisions from Kuntzen's LVII Panzer Corps and gave them to Lieutenant General Rudolf Schmidt's XXXIX Panzer Corps. Three infantry corps of the Ninth Army soon arrived at Vitebsk, freeing Hoth's armor to continue advancing. Strauss now dealt directly with Konev's 19th Army while air reconnaissance detected a general Soviet exodus toward Smolensk. The entire Dvina–Dnepr defensive line had become unhinged.

Guderian's success on the Dnepr had been less spectacular than Hoth's. Despite rougher terrain and poorer roads in its sector, the Third Panzer Group enjoyed a much straighter route to Moscow, placing Hoth in a better strategic position. Therefore von Bock recommended to von Kluge that Fourth Panzer Army immediately reinforce Hoth, making him the Schwerpunkt of Army Group Center. Consistent with von Kluge's leadership style, he hesitated.

Events bore him out as Guderian broke free. On July 10 and 11, Second Panzer Group's attack with 450 operational tanks achieved bridgeheads over the Dnepr on either side of Mogilev at Shklov (XLVI Panzer Corps) and Kopys (XLVII Panzer Corps), and for a second time at Bychov (XXIV Panzer Corps). At Kopys the 29th Motorized Division required numerous attempts plus the support of StuG *Abteilung* 203, a heavy Flak battery, corps engineer assets and other units just to get a foothold across the river. The division fended off numerous counterattacks so that dead Red Army soldiers piled up "corpses upon corpses." By the 14th, von Bock ordered the Second Panzer Army to continue its advance to the line Belyy–Yartsevo–Yelnia.

In Guderian's center, an interesting drama played out at Mogilev, encircled on July 17 where units of 61st Rifle and 20th Mechanized Corps established a fortress-like defense of the city. These forces under Major General M.T. Romanov, especially 172nd Rifle Division, held out against repeated attacks by Guderian's men until July 27 with the help of air dropped supplies. The defenders' efforts against 23rd, 15th, 7th, and 78th Infantry Divisions earned the accolades "Gallant Mogilev" and "Russian Madrid" (the Spanish Civil War was still a fresh memory). Eventually more than 35,000 *frontoviki* (frontline soldiers) marched into captivity. Romanov escaped the trap, only to be captured by the German forces later and executed as a partisan. XXIV Panzer Corps crossed the Dnepr south of the town, and made for Krichev.

Bicycle infantry still made up a significant part of the strength of German infantry division reconnaissance units. These soldiers, with their comrades on horses, motorcycles, and in light armored and field cars, were often far ahead of the foot-sloggers, and carried much of the burden of fighting on first contact. (HITM)

Meanwhile the hard-marching German infantry struggled to keep up with their panzers, reduce the encircled Kessels and fight off partisan attacks that were growing in boldness and intensity. Soviet units or semi-organized groups could attack at any moment, screaming the well-known "Urrah!" The 35th Infantry Division spent the first three months of *Barbarossa* marching 500 miles, an average of 20 miles per day. Men from 137th Infantry Division tore Russian houses apart and used the planks to cross swamps. Whatever rest days the infantry enjoyed were often more for the benefit of their thousands of draft horses than for the Landsers. The Heer had an entire veterinary system to care for its horses, with reserve horses at the division and army level plus a rotation plan to take horses out of the front line and even return them to Germany.

Back at his *Wolfsschanze* Hitler continued to fret over the ability of Army Groups North and South to accomplish their missions without reinforcement by von Bock's panzers. On July 13 the German forces captured documents ordering Timoshenko to hold the already abandoned Dvina–Dnepr line and to counterattack. The previous day Stavka (via Zhukov) had instructed him to:

> Immediately organize a powerful and coordinated counterstroke by all available forces from Smolensk, Orsha, Polotsk and Nevel regions to liquidate the enemy penetration at Vitebsk [Hoth] … [and to] conduct active operations along the Gomel and Bobruisk axes to exert pressure on the rear of the enemy's Bobruisk grouping [Guderian].

This was good news for Hitler and Halder since it indicated that the Soviet forces had no intention of withdrawing into the interior – the dreaded 1812 gambit. However, it was their first inkling of what Guderian would later call the Timoshenko Offensive and hinted at threats to von Bock's southern flank on his boundary with Army Group South. By July 5, Hitler had already been pondering the second phase of the invasion for a week. A few days later OKH began toying with the idea of sending Guderian to Army Group South and Kiev. Stavka's intercepted instructions to Timoshenko and their implied threats could only serve to solidify the idea in Hitler's mind of swinging south.

Closing the Trap

Now across the Dvina–Dnepr line, Army Group Center set itself to close the Smolensk Kessel and continue eastward. After the war Yeremenko wrote that "There were no troops ... to prevent the enemy from crossing the Dnepr and then advancing in any direction he pleased." Von Bock's Schwerpunkt now clearly lay on his southern flank; Guderian had three times as much armor as Hoth, while Second Army fielded the unusually high number of seven corps (VII, IX, XII, XIII, LXVIII, LIII, and XXXV).

On July 11, XLVI Panzer Corps broke out of the Shklov bridgehead and made for Yelnia, XLVII Panzer Corps went from Kopys toward Orsha under von Richthofen's CAS experts, while to the south XXIV Panzer Corps covered Guderian's right. A day later his men split 13th and 20th Armies, outflanking Orsha and advancing almost to Mogilev. Air activity was intense: II Fliegerkorps flew 885 sorties on July 14 against 21st Army and 615 sorties two days later. Such responses as the Soviet forces could muster were ineffectual. The 13th Army's new commander, Remizov, was wounded, and replaced by Lieutenant General V.F. Gerasimenko. Just to show that he was not ignoring Smolensk as he had Minsk, Guderian sent 29th Motorized Division (a "splendid unit" he called it) in that direction.

More importantly, finally clear of Vitebsk, Hoth's 7th Panzer Division closed in on Smolensk from the north and by July 13 only 25 miles separated it from Guderian's 29th Motorized. Two days later the 7th "Rommeled" into Yartsevo, cutting the main road and rail line into Smolensk and sealing the fate of the city and most of its defenders. However, as mentioned previously, both Hoth and Strauss had been stripped of valuable assets and were ordered to maintain contact with Army Group North in addition to continuing their push east; therefore many of their units were too far north to participate in the Smolensk battles in a timely fashion.

By the evening of July 15 the 29th Motorized Division arrived at the southwest end of the city, a ghost town which paid mute tribute to Stalin's scorched-earth policy. The old section, south of the Dnepr, was occupied by Guderian's men within 24 hours. The Soviet defenders launched repeated counterattacks, especially when the German troops tried to cross over to the north bank and 29th Motorized had to fight these off until July 22.

Inside the Kessel

Before the trap closed, trains with reinforcements were pulling out of Bryansk for Smolensk every ten minutes. Many of these forces manned the far western reaches of the pocket although the defense of the city itself left much to be desired. What had been intended to be a bastion city constructed by 300,000 workers under Communist Party control was in fact a feeble crust, held by a couple of General Lukin's weak divisions plus militia battalions, totaling 18,000 men; many of the 16th Army units had been bled off to fight Hoth near Demidov. Stalin nevertheless enforced "stand until the last man" orders upon Stavka which were passed down to local commanders.

Demolition of the city's bridges slowed the German advance and allowed 129th Rifle Division to augment the defense of the north bank. Tactically,

MiG-3 fighters in formation over Moscow: the Kremlin, St Basil's Cathedral, and Red Square can be seen below. Most Soviet cities boasted formidable air defenses. The MiG-3 was available in large numbers during *Barbarossa* but was considered inferior to the German Bf-109 and the RAAF's own Yak-3. (Courtesy of the Central Museum of the Armed Forces, Moscow via Stavka)

7th Panzer and 29th Motorized Infantry Divisions link up, closing the Smolensk Kessel, July 16, 1941. As reconnaissance elements of the 29th Division pushed east they linked up with troops of 7th Panzer; this scene reconstructs such a meeting. (**1**) Crewmen from a PzKw 38(t) of the 7th Panzer Division's reinforced Panzer Regiment 25 stretch their legs while awaiting orders; the tank bears the division's yellow runic symbol, and the white temporary marking of Third Panzer Group – a stylized "Hh" for Hoth; (**2**) farther off is an SdKfz 232(Fu) radio-equipped armored car of 29th Motorized Infantry's divisional Aufklärungs Abteilung, marked with the white "G" of Guderian's Second Panzer Group; (**3**) A group of senior officers speculate about the next objective – assumed at this stage by many German soldiers to be Moscow; (**4**) meanwhile infantrymen deploy to provide local security, and guard a few of the 300,000-plus Soviet prisoners (**5**) who were rounded up in the Smolensk Kessel. (© Osprey Publishing, Peter Dennis)

Red Army units acquitted themselves well, especially in house-to-house fighting as combat around Smolensk dragged on for nearly five days. Inside the pocket the NKVD rounded up nearly 104,000 Red Army stragglers and returned them to the fighting. Although the German forces held the city proper in the face of Soviet counterattacks, they had not yet completely sealed off the pocket.

The air war over the pocket raged with savage intensity. The Luftwaffe interdicted rail lines leading into the city. Between July 10 and the end of the month the German air force launched 12,653 sorties and the Soviet air force approximately 5,200. When VIII Fliegerkorps departed north on August 3 for the hoped-for climactic battle of Leningrad, the Soviet air effort increased dramatically. Luftwaffe strength was further dissipated by bombing raids on Moscow beginning on the night of July 21. These were mainly symbolic and they had little material effect; in over three-quarters of the 76 raids conducted over the next month, fewer than ten bombers participated. All told, these nuisance raids killed only 736 Muscovites and wounded 3,513 more.

The German leaders considered the Smolensk trap officially closed on July 26, but von Bock had already complained in his diary that "it has a hole," the 10-mile gap near Yartsevo and Solovevo through which, between July 31 and August 4, substantial portions of 16th and 20th Armies escaped the Kessel. Unfortunately for the German forces, many of their infantry divisions had been marching for the previous month and had done little or no fighting. The baptism of fire for these units came at least four weeks into the campaign; many formations and men were not prepared and therefore acquitted themselves poorly at Smolensk.

Von Bock ordered Hoth and Strauss to edge further to the south to compensate for Guderian's eastward movement. The 7th Panzer Division again bore the brunt of the fighting, fending off Rokossovsky's infantry attacks which came supported by 80 to 100 tanks. Of the division's 284 Panzers, only 118 were operational and of its 166 damaged tanks, 70 were beyond repair. A rumored German airborne operation near Yartsevo was little more than aerial resupply of the hard-pressed 7th Panzer.

On August 5, von Bock announced the conclusion of the battle of Smolensk and the capture of 302,000 POWs, 3,205 tanks, 3,120 guns, and 1,098 aircraft. The previous day Hitler had flown to Army Group Center headquarters to offer his congratulations in person. The Führer reaffirmed his decision to divert Second and Third Panzer Groups towards Kiev and Leningrad. But he also authorized limited offensives from the vicinity of Yelnia. Von Bock, Hoth, and Guderian all approved, since they believed that the Soviet forces had only the barest means left for a defense of Moscow. They had no way of knowing that only five days earlier Stalin had ordered Zhukov to eliminate the threat to his capital represented by the Yelnia salient. At the August 4 meeting Hitler ordered Yelnia be held at all costs, devoting ten divisions to the effort. With von Richthofen transferred to Leningrad, only portions of II Fliegerkorps remained to provide CAS. Defending the salient, advancing on Moscow, and assisting its two neighboring army groups would have been a tough enough mission for von Bock, even if OKH had had a clear idea of where *Barbarossa* was going next.

The Western Ukraine

The Stalin Line

Thus far the Southwest Front's performance far surpassed the bulk of the Red Army. Kirponos avoided allowing a penetration of his lines and, though outclassed, kept the enemy squarely to his front. On June 30 Stavka authorized Kirponos to withdraw to the fortified regions. But as his defenses fell back its frontage increased from just over 500 miles on *Barbarossatag* to nearly 850 miles at the end of June. However, by occupying the old Polish–Soviet border, Kirponos reduced his front by 200 miles. The permanent defenses that awaited Kirponos' men there were described by von Stülpnagel to his troops as "like the Westwall," which was falsely flattering to both lines. By July 4, however, the Soviet defense had lost all cohesion and the German troops stood in the midst of the fortified region near Novgorod-Volynskiy.

Von Rundstedt issued his Order No.2 on June 28, initiating the race for the Stalin Line. In the lead, von Mackensen's panzer divisions oriented southwards and boldly planned to penetrate the obstacle. In places 210mm mortars were required to break the line. Soviet artillery, antitank, and antiaircraft guns cooperated to good effect. One company of the 16th Panzer Division lost three successive company commanders in two hours of tough fighting. While the 13th Panzer had an easier time of it near Gulsk, the 14th Panzer struggled near Novgorod-Volynskiy. The 25th Motorized maintained tenuous contact between the two. The V Fliegerkorps provided CAS, its fighters keeping the skies free of Red Army Air Force interference. The 13th Panzer reached Berdichev by July 7 while the 14th Panzer took Zithomir and its stout bunker line two days later. Von Kleist finally had freedom to maneuver. He sent the III Panzer Corps "to occupy Kiev as a deep bridgehead east of the Dnepr," the XIV Panzer Corps through Fastov to Balaya Zerkov, and the XLVIII Panzer Corps toward Kasatin.

The Soviet commanders reacted quickly. On July 7 Zhukov ordered Southwest Front to attack Berdichev while on the 9th Kirponos dispatched 5th Army to Broniki and Chenitsa. As usual, internal conflict now distracted the German High Command. On July 9 Hitler advocated splitting the First Panzer Group into its separate corps. He wanted it to both head for Kiev and seek an encirclement inside the Dnepr bend. OKH and army group leaders opposed the move, wanting to leave the city to the Sixth Army's infantrymen. The Führer remained focused on destroying enemy forces and issued orders

to trap the Soviet troops near Vinnitsa. With that in mind, von Brauchitsch arrived at von Rundstedt's headquarters on the 10th to work out details for a Belaya Tserkov encirclement to accomplish this. Two events rendered the argument moot and made the Belaya Tserkov operation impossible. First, the 13th Panzer reached and then crossed the Irpen River; 20 miles from Kiev, they stood among the city's first line of defense. Secondly, Stavka created a new echelon of command, the Strategic Direction, and appointed Marshal Budenny to oversee the efforts of the Southwest and Southern Fronts plus the Black Sea Fleet. The offensive-minded marshal and his Political Commissar, N.S. Khrushchev, ordered vigorous counterattacks against the German spearheads.

A regimental command post at an abandoned Stalin Line bunker near Kiev. A lieutenant colonel points at his map as signalmen wait by their Pack Wireless Type d2 to transmit either by voice or by Morse Code. The communications net of the German forces was vastly more extensive and robust than that of the Red Army. (NARA)

The 13th Panzer stood at Kiev nearly 70 miles in front of the bulk of von Mackensen's corps still back near Zithomir. The III Panzer Corps maneuver had bisected Kirponos' command; henceforth the 5th Army held north of Kiev while the 6th and 12th Armies slipped to the south. To rectify this

A destroyed bridge over the Bug River at Vinnitsa. Von Rundstedt's first encirclement opportunity slipped away at Vinnitsa when the Seventeenth Army's marching infantry could not close the trap alone in the face of Soviet resistance and demolitions. (NARA)

situation Budenny ordered forward the remainder of the mechanized forces with the 16th, 18th, 19th, and 62nd Air Divisions flying overhead. The 9th (down to 64 tanks), 19th, and 22nd (only 30 remaining tanks each) Mechanized Corps continued attacking von Reichenau in the north while the 4th, 15th, and 16th struck near Berdichev. Keeping the isolated 13th Panzer supplied became problematic as heavy fighting raged to the panzer group's rear between July 13 and 18. The 14th Panzer Division defended Makarov as the 25th Motorized, battling nine rifle divisions, held near Zithomir with the recently assigned LSSAH.

Kirponos' 5th and 6th Armies maintained pressure against this Zithomir corridor. Von Rundstedt threw in reinforcements and Stukas. Red Army artillery halted numerous attacks but its rifle regiment strength sank to 300 men. Budenny's counterattacks foundered due to material weakness not lack of enthusiasm. For example, at Berdichev his men made human-wave assaults without the benefit of heavy weapons. The 11th Panzer Division suffered 2,000 casualties in these battles alone. With the help of Sixth Army's infantry a route to the 13th Panzer opened on the 19th, though Soviet resistance had caused a critical expenditure of time and material.

It made no sense for the First Panzer Group to turn back southwest to Vinnitsa so it would drive directly south to Uman. This maneuver had the twin tasks of driving toward the Black Sea and creating Army Group South's first encirclement. As for Kirponos, his defense in the southern theater henceforth would have to rely on the broad Dnepr and surviving Red artillery.

North of Kiev von Reichenau kept the pressure on the 5th Army, which nevertheless retired in good order. As ordered, von Kleist turned south toward the intended encirclement at Uman. But this move also created a gap generally south of Kiev. To fill the void von Rundstedt created an ad hoc army of six – later nine – infantry divisions called Group Schwedler (named after the IV Corps commander). Further south Seventeenth Army pushed southeast but faltered mainly due to the weather and mud. Kirponos sensed the growing threat, recognized that the German forces were about to outmaneuver him and ordered a general withdrawal from the Vinnitsa area.

Von Stülpnagel finally punched through the Stalin Line in mid-July. On the 18th, the 1st Mountain Division with StuG support took a Bug River bridge close to Vinnitsa. After coming up empty handed at L'vov Hitler saw an opportunity to trap over 50,000 Soviets. Along with the 4th Mountain and 24th Infantry Divisions, the 1st Mountain tried to close the pocket at Vinnitsa. But with von Kleist's Panzers still far off to the north and east and the Eleventh Army slowed to the south the cordon was too thin; Red Army forces escaped as Kirponos had ordered. Had Hungarian forces been available, it is likely that the Soviet troops would have been completely cut off; therefore it appears that Hitler paid dearly for his spiteful decision to not include Hungary in *Barbarossa*'s initial planning. Destruction of the Soviet forces was postponed not avoided, however, as the 6th and 12th Armies slipped away southeastwards. The day before they retreated over the Bug River Hitler ordered another, even larger encirclement near Uman.

Kiev Threatened

Hitler had high expectations now that Army Group South advanced beyond the Stalin Line. Operations were disjointed as usual while the German High Command solved problems remaining from the initial ambiguities of Führer Directive 21. While Hitler wanted to split up First Panzer Group for a number of objectives, von Rundstedt argued for its continued concentration. Hitler sought a quick capture of Kiev (i.e. by von Kleist) while the field marshal wanted to leave the fortified city to the Sixth Army. Halder simply craved progress on the flank army groups that would dissuade the dictator from weakening the Moscow axis.

A Panzerbefehlswagen Ausf. E or H of 36th Panzer Regiment staff proves too heavy for a wooden bridge in rural Ukraine during battle for Kiev. German engineers repaired the bridge the same day so the regiment could continue its advance. (NARA)

Ultimately von Rundstedt's men achieved two breakthroughs, First Panzer Group slicing toward Kiev and Seventeenth Army aiming south past Vinnitsa. Stavka encountered difficulty discerning *Barbarossa*'s geographic objectives because there weren't any; Army Group South's goal was the destruction of Red Army units, a moving target. Kirponos maintained an intact defense but positive control of the Southwest Front began to slip from his grasp. His 6th and 12th Armies fell southward into the Southern Front's area of operations. Meanwhile the 5th Army slid further north into the Rokitno Marshes.

Identified from *Barbarossa*'s inception but downplayed by German planners, this massive terrain feature now demanded a solution. The marshes are often mislabeled a swamp. It is a primeval forest, primarily deciduous trees. On either side of this low area are bogs while the high ground is covered with pine trees. The Soviet commanders wanted to capitalize on the marshes' defensive benefits as much as their German counterparts hoped the problem would simply go away.

A month into *Barbarossa*, von Reichenau found his Sixth Army in a very awkward position. When von Kleist sliced through to Kiev creating his own front, he split the Sixth Army. The southern portion was task-organized as Group Schwedler while the northern units remained under von Reichenau. The field marshal was not up to the task; in one of the Wehrmacht's best-kept secrets, von Reichenau had suffered a "light stroke" the winter before and he suffered a fatal heart attack the winter after.

Potopov's 5th Army, separated from the bulk of Kirponos' forces, avoided decisive engagement and sniped at the Sixth Army from the relative safety of the marshes. German intelligence failures contributed to the Sixth Army's discomfort by inflating the enemy, never larger than 12 divisions, to nearly 20. The Soviet 5th Army launched disrupting attacks as the Red Army Air Force lavished attention on exposed German units. Together they succeeded in keeping von Reichenau distracted from his main objective, Kiev.

However, even with his lines of communication through the Zithomir corridor cut, von Kleist focused on the Ukrainian capital. By July 10 the 13th Panzer Division soldiers could see the Kremlin spires. The 14th Panzer pulled alongside the next day. Soon the 25th Motorized Division joined them, making a solid line on the Irpen River, barely 10 miles from the city. Knowing infantry and artillery support necessary for the traditional assault was 100 miles to the rear, the decision of whether or not to take the city by coup de main rested with von Mackensen.

The Irpen is a small river with more than half a mile of swamp on either bank, representing quite an obstacle to the panzers. Initially Khrushchev commanded the Kiev garrison, a collection of regular infantry equal to three rifle divisions, an airborne brigade, a tank regiment, NKVD motorized forces, the 1st Kiev Artillery school, two antitank battalions, and approximately 29,000 militia. At a July 11 meeting Kirponos concluded that First Panzer Group had the mission of taking Kiev. Almost simultaneously

An assault gun of Sturmgewehr Abteilung 191 at Malin is resupplied by a half-track one month into *Barbarossa*. Assault guns were intended to help infantry reduce fortifications and force river crossings, but were also employed fighting enemy tanks. Sturmgewehr Abteilung 191 was nicknamed the Buffalo battalion after its unit emblem. It was established following the campaign in France and fought in the Balkans prior to *Barbarossa*. It remained deployed on the Eastern Front, ending the war as StuG Brigade 191 in Hungary. (NARA)

Hitler halted von Kleist and prohibited a direct assault on the increasingly heavily defended city. At army group headquarters von Brauchitsch added his belief that the panzers could not both take the city and execute the Uman Kessel mission. Von Rundstedt concurred while von Reichenau compared the proposed city fight to Verdun.

The marching infantry of the Sixth Army finally broke through the Stalin Line and by late July approached Kiev. They relieved III Panzer Corps on siege duty, work made difficult by heavy Soviet artillery fire. Von Reichenau could expect little assistance from the army group and any help from Army Group Center, fighting for Smolensk, was unlikely. The Uman encirclement now required the attention of von Mackensen's men.

Army Group South's ground-air team. Field Marshal Von Rundstedt and Colonel General Lohr await Hitler's Fw-200 aircraft at Uman on August 28. Hitler visited army group headquarters one more time: in December to replace von Rundstedt. (NARA)

Uman

When the panzers pulled out of the Kiev line Kirponos thought he had succeeded in blunting the German assault. He did not realize von Kleist had swung south toward Uman. The German commanders had decided on this less ambitious but more practical pocket instead of following the great bend in the Dnepr.

Splitting the Soviet 5th and 6th Armies even further apart, First Panzer Group pivoted on Belaya Zerkov. Kirponos ordered all of his air assets in this direction. Although it took nearly a week, Stavka finally saw the threat to Uman. It therefore created the 26th Army out of the 4th Rifle and the 5th Cavalry Corps and placed them east of the Dnepr, opposite Kanev. The 26th Army was to cross the river on July 15 and get into the rear areas of the First Panzer Group, thereby disrupting von Rundstedt's plan for Uman. However, the German commanders learned of these intentions when a Soviet liaison aircraft landed behind their lines. Alerted, Group Schwedler set a trap. Nevertheless, the force of the Red Army's blow near Kanev, launched finally on the 18th, surprised the Germans and von Kleist was forced to face the XIV Panzer Corps eastwards to assist Group Schwedler. This left only XLVIII Panzer heading for Uman. The German forces contained the emergency but failed to completely eliminate the threat at Kanev.

With III and XIV Panzer Corps thus diverted, XLVIII Panzer continued southward alone. By July 21 it reached Monastyrishche, Budenny's headquarters only 24 hours earlier. Here elements of the trapped 6th Army attacked the XLVIII Panzer's inner flank. The 11th and 16th Panzer and 16th Motorized Divisions, later augmented by the LSSAH, stabilized the situation by the 25th. The Soviet counterattack collapsed two days later. With the situations at Kiev and Kanev under control, the XIV Panzer rejoined the advance while the III Panzer covered the eastern flank; finally the panzer group was fighting united again. Meanwhile, the 1st Mountain Division and the Hungarians led the Seventeenth Army across the upper Bug River. Soviet defenders and poor weather slowed their right pincer. Losses among their horses forced the Landsers to leave heavy weapons behind while many had worn through their boots so marched barefoot. Nevertheless, by the 27th von Stülpnagel broke into the open country.

Major General I.N. Muzychenko was among the 103,000 Soviets captured at Uman. Responsibility for treatment of POWs, including their murder and neglect, lay with the Heer, not any Nazi organization. In 1941 200,000 died in one POW camp near L'vov alone. (NARA)

Tyulenev's frustration increased in direct proportion. He sent the 18th Army to buttress the Uman defenses but it too only became part of the half encircled Soviet forces. He then ordered the 4th Mechanized Corps to create an escape route. The attack severely tested the German troops but with few tanks and no surprise 4th Mechanized ultimately failed. Budenny reported to Stavka, "All efforts to withdraw the 6th and 12th Armies to the east and northeast are fruitless." The V Fliegerkorps contributed with a vertical envelopment. First Panzer and Seventeenth Army units finally linked up on August 3 after the 16th Panzer Division captured the 100-yard-long Bug River bridge at Pervomaysk.

Tyulenev ordered Musychenko and Ponedelin to break out. But the Southern Front commander complained they remained trapped "on account of a completely incomprehensible slowness." By the 5th the pocket had been reduced to an area 14 miles square. In just four days German artillery fired more ordnance into the Kessel than had been expended during the entire Western campaign. Fighting raged inside the Kessel until August 8. The German forces captured 103,000 prisoners from 25 divisions and captured or destroyed 317 tanks, 858 artillery pieces, and 242 antitank and antiaircraft guns.

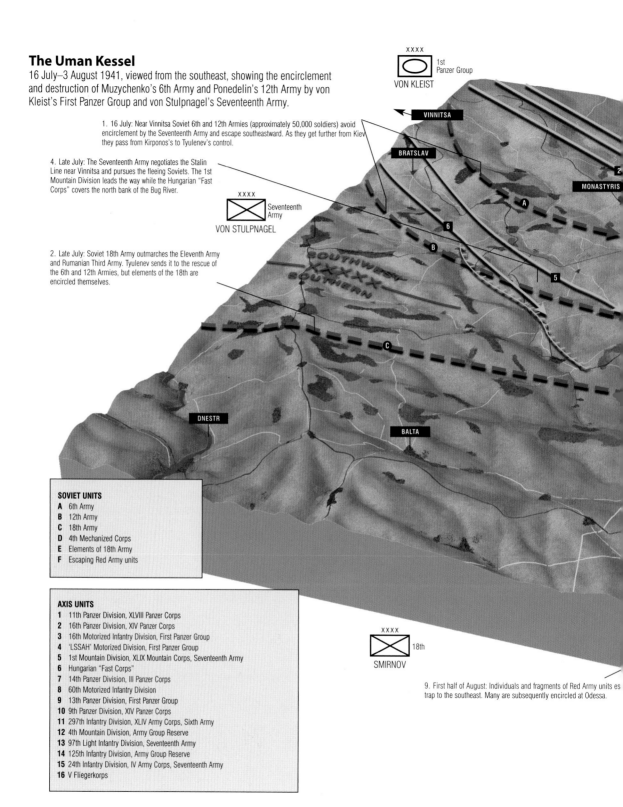

The Uman Kessel

16 July–3 August 1941, viewed from the southeast, showing the encirclement and destruction of Muzychenko's 6th Army and Ponedelin's 12th Army by von Kleist's First Panzer Group and von Stulpnagel's Seventeenth Army.

1. 16 July: Near Vinnitsa Soviet 6th and 12th Armies (approximately 50,000 soldiers) avoid encirclement by the Seventeenth Army and escape southeastward. As they get further from Kiev they pass from Kirponos's to Tyulenev's control.

4. Late July: The Seventeenth Army negotiates the Stalin Line near Vinnitsa and pursues the fleeing Soviets. The 1st Mountain Division leads the way while the Hungarian "Fast Corps" covers the north bank of the Bug River.

2. Late July: Soviet 18th Army outmarches the Eleventh Army and Rumanian Third Army. Tyulenev sends it to the rescue of the 6th and 12th Armies, but elements of the 18th are encircled themselves.

xxxx
1st Panzer Group
VON KLEIST

VINNITSA

BRATSLAV

MONASTYRIS

xxxx
Seventeenth Army
VON STULPNAGEL

A

6

B

5

C

DNESTR

BALTA

xxxx
18th
SMIRNOV

9. First half of August: Individuals and fragments of Red Army units es trap to the southeast. Many are subsequently encircled at Odessa.

SOVIET UNITS
A 6th Army
B 12th Army
C 18th Army
D 4th Mechanized Corps
E Elements of 18th Army
F Escaping Red Army units

AXIS UNITS
1   11th Panzer Division, XLVIII Panzer Corps
2   16th Panzer Division, XIV Panzer Corps
3   16th Motorized Infantry Division, First Panzer Group
4   'LSSAH' Motorized Division, First Panzer Group
5   1st Mountain Division, XLIX Mountain Corps, Seventeenth Army
6   Hungarian "Fast Corps"
7   14th Panzer Division, III Panzer Corps
8   60th Motorized Infantry Division
9   13th Panzer Division, First Panzer Group
10 9th Panzer Division, XIV Panzer Corps
11 297th Infantry Division, XLIV Army Corps, Sixth Army
12 4th Mountain Division, Army Group Reserve
13 97th Light Infantry Division, Seventeenth Army
14 125th Infantry Division, Army Group Reserve
15 24th Infantry Division, IV Army Corps, Seventeenth Army
16 V Fliegerkorps

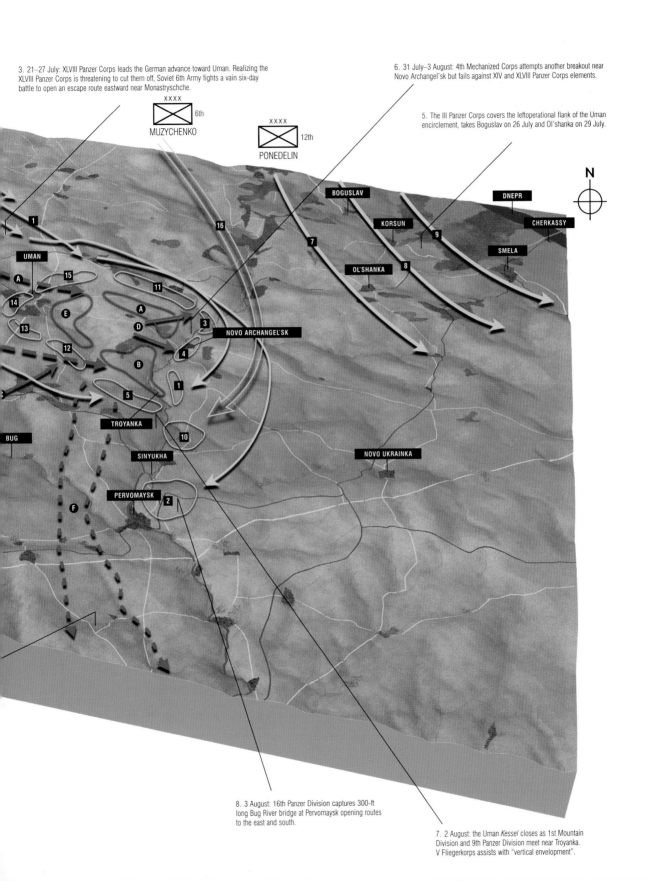

3. 21–27 July: XLVIII Panzer Corps leads the German advance toward Uman. Realizing the XLVIII Panzer Corps is threatening to cut them off, Soviet 6th Army fights a vain six-day battle to open an escape route eastward near Monastryschche.

6. 31 July–3 August: 4th Mechanized Corps attempts another breakout near Novo Archangel'sk but fails against XIV and XLVIII Panzer Corps elements.

5. The III Panzer Corps covers the leftoperational flank of the Uman encirclement, takes Boguslav on 26 July and Ol'shanka on 29 July.

xxxx 6th
MUZYCHENKO

xxxx 12th
PONEDELIN

N

BOGUSLAV

DNEPR

KORSUN

CHERKASSY

1

16

7

9

SMELA

UMAN

A

15

11

OL'SHANKA

8

14

E

A

13

D

3

NOVO ARCHANGEL'SK

12

4

B

1

5

TROYANKA

10

SINYUKHA

NOVO UKRAINKA

BUG

PERVOMAYSK

2

F

8. 3 August: 16th Panzer Division captures 300-ft long Bug River bridge at Pervomaysk opening routes to the east and south.

7. 2 August: the Uman *Kessel* closes as 1st Mountain Division and 9th Panzer Division meet near Troyanka. V Fliegerkorps assists with "vertical envelopment".

A briefing at Army Group headquarters in Uman following the Kessel battle there. From left at the map table are General Messe, Mussolini, Hitler, von Rundstedt, and Lohr. Cap devices in the audience indicate representatives from many Nazi and Fascist Party organizations. (NARA)

Back near Kanev the reinforced 26th Army attacked again on August 7. The V Fliegerkorps hastily redirected Stukageschwader 77 and Kampfgeschwader 51, 54, and 55 against the bridgehead. They destroyed 94 tanks in three days. Stavka decided to abandon the Dnepr on August 10 and concentrate its stay-behind forces at Odessa but much fighting continued near Kanev. Two days later von Brauchitsch issued a directive for von Kleist to continue the exploitation south and southeast. By the 13th the Soviet forces were in full flight. Group Schwedler manned most of the broad river by August 21. First Panzer Group would soon do the same along the middle course of the Dnepr. Red Army units held on for another ten days in small groups, finally evacuating the west bank on the last day of the month. The Soviet counterattack had cost little in the way of resources but likewise failed to halt von Rundstedt's Uman operation.

Von Rundstedt's panzers broke through the Stalin Line at Novgorod-Volynskiy on July 7. German indecision over Kiev, however, meant the Uman Kessel would not be closed for nearly another month. Even so, when von Kleist did turn south operational surprise was complete. Ultimately, however, Uman represented a compromise within the German High Command between those, like Hitler himself, who wanted a smaller, more certain pocket at Uman and those, like Halder, who considered a potentially larger one near Kirovograd. Von Rundstedt expertly maneuvered his meager forces against widely separated objectives, always keeping his center strong. Nevertheless, Kirponos avoided the destruction of the Southwest Front and kept Army Group South behind schedule thereby allowing Stavka to shift forces to the critical Smolensk theater.

A PzKpfw III of XIV Panzer Corps (with uninterested Soviet POWs on board) while clearing the Dnepr bend following the battle of Uman. Army Group South lost valuable time by not immediately establishing bridgeheads over this large river. (NARA)

The Rumanian Front

In April the 170th Infantry Division made a 17-day train trip to Rumania to join other German forces to guard the Ploesti oil fields. They reconnoitered the Soviet border in civilian clothes and trained Rumanian units. After *Barbarossatag* the Red Army Air Force launched hundreds of attacks against the Ploesti oil facilities without success. Hitler finally felt the chances of a Soviet ground attack were low enough that his far right flank could move out under Operation *Munich*.

All Axis forces in Rumania nominally fell under the command of dictator Ion Antonescu. But von Schobert's staff conducted most planning while *de facto* controlling the Rumanian Third Army. The IV Fliegerkorps provided CAS. To the south the Rumanian Fourth Army initially guarded the Black Sea coast and lower Prut. As for the Soviet commanders, Tyulenev left Moscow on June 22 and arrived at Southern Front headquarters at Vinnitsa two days later. He found no phones, telegraphs, or radios. At least he had one week longer than the rest of the Red Army to prepare.

Prior to Operation *Munich*, Army Group South was constricted between Army Group Center and Hungary, thus restricting the area that the Soviet forces needed to defend. However, when von Schobert got under way this area suddenly tripled. To avoid detection, prior to attacking German soldiers bivouacked by day and marched toward the border only by night. On the evening of June 30, 46 men of Infantry Regiment 399 stormed a 300-foot bridge over the Prut and took it without a shot. The Soviet forces counterattacked and by the next morning half the German troops were dead but their bridgehead remained.

Von Schobert's main offensive began on July 2 from these bridgeheads on either side of Iassy while assault boats crossed the Prut at 0315hrs. Eleventh Army struck the boundary between the 9th and 18th Armies where the Soviet troops were not fully prepared. Fighting centered on Beltsa where the XXX Corps tangled with the 48th Rifle Corps and at Kishinev, soon taken by the Fourth Army. Farthest north, where the distance between the Prut and Dniestr rivers was smallest, the XI Corps and Rumanian Cavalry and Mountain Corps closed in on the latter watercourse at Mogilev-Podol'skiy. Attempts to gain a bridgehead by coup de main failed when XI Corps could not negotiate the 45-mile gap and relieve the company of Brandenburgers. These commandos managed to hang on only for a few hours before being overwhelmed. Southern Front's Dniestr River defensive line remained intact, a fact that had long-term negative effects on German operations until Uman.

Operation *Munich*. Rumanian cavalry crossing the Prut River to reoccupy Moldavia. Employed in brigade-sized divisions, cavalry units were among Rumania's best troops. (NARA)

Simultaneously Tyulenev took two defensive measures: he created a counterattack force of 2nd Cavalry, 2nd Mechanized, and 48th Rifle Corps to reconquer Kishinev and he created the Coastal Group of three rifle divisions to cover the lower Prut. The Kishinev offensive struck the boundary of Eleventh and Rumanian Fourth Armies. Originally *Barbarossa's* plan called for the assignment of the XIV Panzer Corps to Eleventh Army. But Hitler reversed this decision, leaving von Schobert without panzers and vulnerable to Red armor. However, the Soviet assault soon foundered but not before scattering the Rumanians which forced von Schobert to dispatch the LVI Corps to shore them up.

Meanwhile German pressure on the Moscow axis had a negative effect on defensive operations in the south. As part of the northward migration of Red Army units Stavka ordered Tyulenev to transfer the 7th Rifle Corps (116th, 196th, and 227th Rifle Divisions) north to the Southwest Front while Kirponos lost the 16th and 19th Armies to the Western Front. On July 16 Budenny ordered Tyulenev to evacuate the Dniestr and on the next day instructed him to mass near Uman. This played directly into von Rundstedt's hands. The Eleventh Army now planned its own encirclement between the Dniestr and Bug rivers. Von Schobert ordered his left, the XI Corps, Rumanian Third Army, and the newly arriving Italians, to swing clockwise along the west bank of the Bug and behind Tyulenev.

The XI Corps began a deliberate crossing of the Dniestr on July 17. The steep slopes and thick woods reminded the German soldiers of their own Mosel valley. Stukas provided CAS, assault guns fired from the near bank, while 88mm Flak guns destroyed Soviet bunkers across the river. They succeeded this time against limited resistance and the XI, XXX Corps and Rumanian Cavalry and Mountain Corps crossed over by the 21st. Further south the LIV Corps, having just fought its way through Kishinev, lagged behind.

Poor weather and Soviet scorched-earth policies slowed the Axis forces, allowing the Southern Front to escape. Arriving on the Ostfront to great fanfare, the Italian Expeditionary Corps experienced its baptism of fire. Its commander, General Messe, consolidated his transport for the Pasubio Division. This unit bore the brunt of the fighting while the now un-motorized "Torino" marched far to the rear. Pasubio earned von Schobert's praise during the battles between the Dniestr and Bug rivers. Tyulenev's 18th Army had a difficult time fighting its way rearward; the Luftwaffe destroyed bridges over the numerous waterways, Soviet pioneers rebuilt them for their retreating comrades, then attempted to demolish them again to deny their use to the advancing Axis troops. Tyulenev's men eventually escaped eastward denying the Eleventh Army its own Kessel.

Karelia

Finland's war was not Germany's war. Finnish strategy was mainly to secure easily defended lines across Karelia and along the Svir River. As good "brothers in arms," the Finns would neutralize the Soviet base at Hanko and assist Army Group North by threatening Leningrad. Significantly, Mannerheim had few illusions about leaving behind the relative security of the Finnish forests and venturing too far into the more open Russian terrain.

Finnish forces in Karelia accounted for over half her military manpower, 230,000 men compared to the USSR's 150,000 men. Karelia was defended by Major General M.N. Gerasimov's 23rd Army with four rifle divisions and Meretskov's 7th Independent Army with five rifle divisions. At Hanko the Finnish 17th Division faced two rifle brigades and 23,000 Soviets. Two Finnish divisions and the German 163rd Infantry Division (less the 388th Regiment) represented Mannerheim's reserve.

The Finns began their Continuation War after the requisite provocation following *Barbarossatag*: Soviet air raids and a tank attack. General Axel Heinrich's Army of Karelia north of Lake Ladoga moved out on July 10. Attacking north of Lake Yanis on the Finnish left, VI Corps and Group "O" created a breakthrough at Kopisel'kaya. The 71st Rifle Division gave way and the *Jäger* occupied Muanto on July 14, followed by Koirinoye on Ladoga's north coast on the 16th. The Finns had covered 65 miles in ten days and trapped much of the 7th Army between the frontier and Lake Ladoga. VI and VII Corps applied frontal pressure, reaching the Yanis River on July 17 against ineffective Soviet resistance. Finnish 1st and German 163rd Infantry Divisions covered the far left flank.

VI Corps took Salmi on July 21, following a three-day battle. On the 24th, Red Army counterattacks forced the Finns to assume a defensive posture. The understrength 163rd Infantry Division, now alone in the north, became bogged down. A VI Corps' attack toward Suvilakhti failed to rectify the situation. VII Corps exerted pressure on the 168th Rifle Division barely hanging on in Sortavala by the end of July. The Finns, now under command of I Corps, continued to push forward. However, weak Luftwaffe and Finnish Air Force elements precluded an effective vertical envelopment and these Soviets showed no more willingness to surrender than those encircled elsewhere during *Barbarossa*. Late in August the Ladoga Flotilla evacuated the bulk of the 142nd, 168th, and 198th Rifle Divisions across the lake.

A group of casual-looking Finnish soldiers. The Finns bested the Red Army every time the two clashed, but Finland's limited objectives minimized its contributions to Hitler's crusade in the East. (HITM)

On August 31, II Corps began its assault south of Lake Ladoga. By August 5, Mannerheim, in direct control of the northern elements, moved up his reserve 10th Division. Keksgol'm fell the same day and in combination these maneuvers cut off two more Red Army divisions.

On July 13 Mannerheim ordered II Corps south toward Pakkola on the Vuosalmi River. The 18th Division won a bridgehead there on the 18th. This move threatened the Vyborg fortress from the east. IV Corps began the

Finland's Karelian Offensive

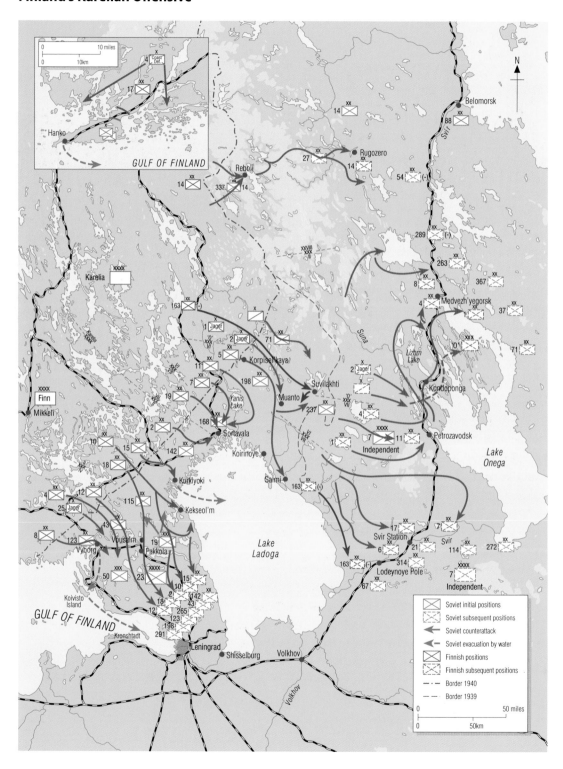

Legend:
- Soviet initial positions
- Soviet subsequent positions
- Soviet counterattack
- Soviet evacuation by water
- Finnish positions
- Finnish subsequent positions
- Border 1940
- Border 1939

T-34 tanks negotiate a ravine in Karelia. A stillborn attack 2 miles into Finland by elements of the 21st Tank Division on July 2 provided the "provocation" Finland needed to attack the USSR. (HITM)

frontal assault on August 22. Three days later the 8th Division crossed the bay, cut the rail line to Primorsk and completed the encirclement of Vyborg, trapping three rifle divisions. A Soviet counterattack opened a hole long enough for the 43rd and 123rd Rifle Divisions to escape. IV Corps troops entered the fortress on the 29th. Leaving their equipment and vehicles behind, a third rifle division retreated first to Koivisto Island then, in late November, to Leningrad. With IV Corps pressing on the right and I Corps (again reassigned a new sector) on the left, the Soviet 23rd Army withdrew behind the 1939 border by the end of August. Outside Leningrad the front stabilized barely 5 miles south of the old frontier for the next three years. By leaving Leningrad with such a large hinterland northwest of the German siege lines the Finns helped ensure the city's survival.

Unresolved issues began to bedevil Fenno-German strategy. A binding strategic agreement never existed between the two nations. Two months into *Barbarossa*, Keitel wrote a letter to Mannerheim asking the Finns to attack past the Svir in order to link up with von Leeb. The marshal showed the letter to President Risto Ryti; both men agreed advancing beyond the Svir was not in Finland's interests and that "under no circumstances" would they attack Leningrad, clearly "a German task." The Finns feared that Army Group North would get no further than Volkhov and that Finland would have to push further forward to effect a juncture.

On September 4 Jodl arrived at Mannerheim's Mikkeli headquarters with Iron and Knight's Cross decorations for the marshal. Following their largest artillery preparation of the war the Finns began a general offensive that same day. VI Corps shoved aside the 3rd Rifle Division and reached the Svir in three days. Elements of the 17th Division captured the Svir Station the next day, cutting the Murmansk railroad. Until reinforcements arrived, the Siberian 114th Rifle Division held the river line against all threats. VII Corps made slower progress toward Lake Onega, finally capturing Petrozavodsk on October 1 after a two-week fight. At this point many Finns considered "their" war won, so morale and discipline began to wane.

Finally, north of Lake Onega, after regrouping, II Corps and Group "O" attacked north toward the upper Svir and the Stalin Canal on October 19. Passing west and east of Lake Lizhm, the two pincers joined on November 5. One month later the Finns reached Edvezh'yegorsk, destroyed two rifle divisions, cut the Murmansk rail connection again, and went onto the defensive on December 6. Three days earlier the Soviet forces had evacuated Hanko under virtually no Finnish pressure.

Axis operations in the far north failed for a number of reasons, primarily few common interests and disjointed command and control. The German forces were neither equipped, trained, nor inclined to fight effectively in the theater. They consistently underestimated the Red Army's strength in terrain that particularly favored the defender. The Soviet leadership also had the flexibility to transfer forces laterally along the Murmansk railroad. Likewise Luftwaffe air support lacked its usual effectiveness: it was too weak for the massive frontage; it shifted Schwerpunkt constantly with changing objectives and weather often grounded its missions.

The importance of Archangel and Murmansk as supply conduits was obvious from the Great War. Nevertheless the far north represented *Barbarossa*'s poor relation. The Finns cut the Karelia rail line twice, but an eastern line ran uninterrupted. The Luftwaffe breached this eastern rail line over 100 times in 1941 alone but the Soviet troops quickly repaired the roadbed. Ju-88 pilots claimed that due to antiaircraft fire they would "rather fly over London three times than once over Murmansk." Although potentially of great importance, the theater became a backwater of *Barbarossa*.

Summary

After considerable success during *Barbarossa's* first two weeks when it advanced 270 miles, Army Group North required an entire month to advance the next 75 miles. Hitler complained openly to Halder about von Leeb's failures, while the army group's success carried it into inhospitable countryside and stiffening enemy resistance.

Inability to concentrate Fourth Panzer Group and difficult terrain deprived it of much of its punch. The talents of General Reinhardt, "one of the best Panzer leaders" according to von Lossberg, were poorly utilized. As the gap between Army Group North's right and Army Group Center's left increased, so did the danger to the flanks of both. Although David Glantz considers the Soltsy counterattack a failure, in reality it prompted a costly German overreaction. But contemplate the possibilities and the changed strategic situation if in early August von Leeb and Hoepner had made von Manstein's drive toward Chudovo and Volkhov Army Group North's Schwerpunkt so that in September Germans and Finns arrived on the Svir River together.

At the highest levels German command suffered a meltdown. The normally persuasive Hitler wanted to keep pressure on Leningrad but could not impose his will on senior generals beguiled by Moscow. Logistics hamstrung Army Group North as well; fuel consumption was three times the pre-*Barbarossa* estimates. By mid-summer von Leeb had ten of the Ostheer's "stricken" divisions while Luftwaffe maintenance officers went in search of wrecked aircraft to scavenge for repair parts.

Finnish soldiers charge into smoke and dust in a typically thick forest found in their theater of operations. (Nik Cornish at www.Stavka.org.uk)

Lieutenant General M.M. Popov was a highly regarded general commanding the prestigious Leningrad Military District. He served as operational commander at Leningrad under the figurehead Voroshilov until Zhukov's arrival. (David Glantz)

On the Soviet side, Kuznetsov had failed to manage a coherent defense anywhere. Therefore the German forces threatened Leningrad from unexpected directions, south and southeast. Three days into *Barbarossa*, General Popov noted the advantages of defending his city along the Luga River. Increasingly Soviet defensive efforts centered on improvised ad hoc formations such as the LOG. Their countermoves at the Velikaya River, Soltsy, Staraya Russa, Luga, and central Estonia all contributed to the Soviet leaders' death-by-a-thousand-cuts defensive strategy.

Army Group Center continued to enjoy good fortune into *Barbarossa*'s second phase. In the Minsk battles it had destroyed the Soviet forces' first echelon defenses trying to implement DP 41 and then at Smolensk did the same to the second echelon. In between these two battles Second and Third Panzer Groups overcame the Dvina–Dnepr River line. Guderian managed to keep his group massed, something Hoth could not do. The ad hoc Fourth Panzer Army failed due to an unsuitable commander and vague purpose. Also, by mid-summer von Bock's men, in exposed salients and at the end of their logistical umbilical cords, were suffering badly under the flurry of Soviet wrath.

Although the unrealistic prewar plans to launch an immediate counteroffensive into Germany were quickly forgotten, the Soviet desire to counterattack, somewhere, remained. Red Army countermeasures had mixed results. Objectively they cost tremendous numbers of Soviet men and equipment and ultimately did not seem to halt the blitzkrieg or even slow it appreciably. Subjectively, however, they caused the German considerable losses plus, critically, used up the one commodity that the Ostheer never had enough of, time. German delays in reducing the Kessels, getting supplies forward and even making decisions took a toll on the entire campaign.

Von Rundstedt's panzers broke through the Stalin Line at Novgorod-Volynskiy on July 7. German indecision over Kiev, however, meant that the Uman Kessel would not be closed for another month. When von Kleist eventually turned south, Soviet operational surprise was complete. Ultimately the southern Kessel represented a victory within the German High Command of those like Hitler who wanted a smaller, more certain pocket at Uman over those, like

Hungarian–Rumanian Conflict

The borderlands in southeastern Europe had been unsettled for many centuries preceding World War II. Most notably, during the early modern period, it saw the frequently changing frontier between the Habsburg and Ottoman Empires. With the decline of the Turks and the rise of nationalism the region truly became a fracture zone. In an almost colonial fashion boundaries had been drawn along rivers, ridgelines, or the limits of advance of armies with little regard for ethnic or linguistic considerations.

Following World War I, the Treaty of Trianon signed in 1920 between the Allies and Hungary split the multi-ethnic country, formerly part of the Austro-Hungarian Empire, into several nations. Over 7 million people, 31 percent of them ethnic Hungarians, and 72 percent of Hungary's territory (some of it resource rich) were transferred to Czechoslovakia, Rumania, and Yugoslavia.

The Hungarians considered the treaty a national humiliation and its provisions dominated their public life and political culture during the interwar years. After Admiral Horthy, Hungary's regent, established close relations with Hitler, he was able to regain a part of southern Czechoslovakia with the First Vienna Award in November 1938 and Carpathian Ruthenia from Rumania in 1939. This was not enough. More important was Trianon's assignment of Transylvania to Rumania.

The 1939 Molotov–Ribbentrop Pact only complicated the problem. In June 1940 the Soviet Union took back Bessarabia and Northern Bukovina, two areas incorporated into Rumania after World War I. Rumania was already in a dramatically weakened position following the defeat of its principal patron, France. These two factors exposed Rumania's vulnerabilities and prompted Hungary to seek a resolution to the Transylvania question. The Hungarian government began direct negotiations with Rumania on August 16, 1940 without

success. Rumania therefore asked Italy and Germany, both of which wanted stability in the region, to arbitrate the dispute.

Hitler did not see Rumania as an ally at this point and the Fascist take over of that country was still weeks in the future. By supporting the concept of Greater Hungary Hitler hoped to win it over as a future ally. Foreign Ministers von Ribbentrop of Germany and Ciano of Italy met, and in what became known as the Second Vienna Award, on August 30 returned to Hungary 16,600 square miles of northern Transylvania. Historian Keith Hitchins noted, "Far from settling matters, the Second Vienna Award exacerbated relations between Hungary and Romania. It did not solve the nationality problem by separating all Magyars from all Romanians."[1]

After the award, Rumania was given only 14 days to evacuate the territories. The Rumanian government committed atrocities on the Hungarian population, while Hungary retaliated after annexing the new territory. Rumania's shame was complete on September 6 when it lost Dobrudja to Bulgaria in a separate treaty. On the following day King Carol II abdicated, ushering in the Fascist National Legionary State. Rumania and Hungary kept large security forces on their mutual border and almost came to blows right in the middle of World War II! Indeed, it has been said that the Hungarians and Rumanians would have preferred to kill each other rather than their common Soviet enemies. The German leadership had to take care to keep armies of their two allies separated by their own units or those of the Italians. The Allies nullified the Second Vienna Award in September 1944 and in 1947 the Treaty of Paris confirmed the Hungary and Rumania borders set by Treaty of Trianon.

1　Hitchins, *Rumania*, p.486.

Halder, who wanted a potentially larger one near Kirovograd. Von Rundstedt expertly maneuvered his meager forces against widely separated objectives, always keeping his center strong. Nevertheless, Kirponos avoided the total destruction of the Southwest Front and kept Army Group South behind schedule thereby allowing Stavka to shift forces to the critical Smolensk theater.

General Hoth credits Kirponos' resistance in the border region for denying von Rundstedt the same initial breakthroughs enjoyed by Army Groups North and Center. The battles around Rovno and Dubno held up von Rundstedt at least one week. This hard-won delay represented a double-edged sword, however: once the frontier battles concluded, little organized opposition stood in the way of Army Group South. In addition, Soviet prewar offensive doctrine had succeeded in fixing Red Army forces too far forward, leaving untrained armor at the mercy of the panzers and making an effective withdrawal difficult. Formations defending along the Kiev axis proved inadequate to hold von Kleist while elements further south counterattacked into Rumania in accordance with prewar "Red Folder" plans. The unexpected severity of Luftwaffe interdiction of Ukrainian industry upset Zhukov's plans for coordinated operational-level counteroffensives. With minor interruptions Axis forces advanced east. But even then the Red Army possessed considerable powers of resistance.

It is unsurprising that in a campaign as vast and complex as *Barbarossa*, the combatants had to make numerous alterations to their plans, organization, operations, and in many other areas. The German leaders moved from a mood of celebration to the hard work of deciding what to do next. But despite this obvious need, after Smolensk neither Hitler, OKW, OKH, nor commanders in the field could agree on the next logical move. From before mid-July to beyond mid-August a colossal power struggle hamstrung the Wehrmacht senior leadership, until the Führer imposed his will on the generals in late August. Meanwhile, major developments occurred to the north and south, while both armies prepared for the ultimate battle for Moscow.

Barely a month into *Barbarossa* most of the prewar Red Army had ceased to exist. However, while the Red Army foundered, the Soviet state reacted decisively. It immediately mobilized new forces, and evacuated significant portions of its economy and industry beyond the Nazis' reach, while Stalin reorganized the national leadership for a war of attrition.

OPPOSITE PAGE:
Many Soviet reinforcements from all across the USSR arrived on trains and often went directly to the fighting, occasionally very close by. The quality of their training and leadership was uneven, but these reinforcements were essential for plugging holes in the Soviet lines. (Elukka)

BARBAROSSA IN THE BALANCE

Concerning *Barbarossa*'s main points, in the months leading up to June 22 Hitler had done his part but the German military had not done its. The Führer and his Directive 21 had specified the ends, for example capturing or neutralizing Leningrad, but the German Army general staff system had not worked out the means. One month after the invasion the German High Command hit the "what next" point and required a further month to develop and execute a plan that should have been decided upon six months earlier. In view of the strategic impasse at the very pinnacle of German leadership, how could the Wehrmacht destroy "the bulk of the Russian army in western Russia … in a rapid campaign" as called for the previous December? Decision making therefore devolved on operational leaders, a suboptimal solution. Since Hitler, the OKW, and OKH seemed unable to mold the Ostheer's significant individual, operational victories such as closing in on Leningrad and executing the Smolensk and Kiev pockets into a coherent, strategic whole, their cumulative strategic effect was lessened.

In the north Reinhardt's one panzer corps stood alone fewer than 100 miles from Leningrad; but it had no significant logistical or aerial support. Certainly even the arrogant and overconfident German High Command did not believe that 50,000 of their own troops could carry the huge metropolis of nearly 3 million. Therefore von Leeb had to wait, not only for von Manstein, marching Landsers from his two infantry armies plus all of his heavy siege equipment, but also for panzers and Stukas from Army Group Center.

Stalin sent Marshal Kuznetsov to light a fire under the defenders, but by temperament and training he was completely unqualified. That job fell on Vatutin, part of the new generation of Red Army generals, on the far-eastern extremity of the northern theater. His attacks in the wilds on either side of Lake Il'men distracted the German chain of command all the way up to Hitler.

Army Group Center had just come off a very successful month and two massive encirclement battles. However, Timoshenko would allow it no rest while German logisticians behind the front labored to bring forward much needed support. With panzer spearheads at Velikie Luki and Yelnia, von Bock also had to wait for his High Command to decide, "What next?" Along with the answer to that question came the loss of Guderian and Hoth's panzer groups (although Hoth remained). As forewarned eight months earlier, the drive on Moscow would have to await satisfactory developments to the north and south. German infantry, often only now showing up to their first combat of the campaign, would bear the brunt of the Soviet troops' revenge at places like Yelnia and along the boundary between Army Groups North and Center.

Until Uman dramatic victories eluded von Rundstedt and his men. Their one breakthrough only placed von Mackensen's panzer corps at the gates of Kiev, which did about as much good as having Reinhardt's in front of Leningrad. But Kirponos' delay of Army Group South, effective in terms of time and space, was disastrous in terms of men and units, especially the now extinct mechanized corps. With the "armored heart" of their doctrine gone, tanks operated in brigade and division-sized formations only, so results were limited to the tactical level. In the south Red Army fortunes would hang on the Dnepr, which they hoped would prove a more of a significant barrier than the Dvina.

Closing in on Leningrad

Von Leeb's panzers diverged like fingers on an open hand. To compound matters the results of the Finns' attack across Karelia were the opposite of what the German leaders had anticipated. The High Command had too much hope on taking Leningrad by direct assault. They despaired of linking up on the Svir River and therefore did not place the justified emphasis on von Manstein's right hook. Lacking mass, each panzer corps fought in near isolation over terrain that favored the defenders while the infantry armies were likewise dangerously dispersed.

Other factors impacted von Leeb's plans. In the army group's center, supply problems delayed the Sixteenth Army's attack along the Luga five times between July 22 and August 6. Weather repeatedly grounded Luftwaffe air support, further postponing planned attacks across the front from Tallinn to Lake Il'men. On August 7, von Leeb's meteorological staff told him the weather next day would be good.

Finally at 0900hrs on August 8 the general offensive began along the Luga River. Advances were limited to 2–3 miles that day. Hoepner reinforced XLI Panzer Corps with the 8th Panzer and 36th Motorized Divisions and slowly Reinhardt avulsed the defenders out of positions under construction for six weeks. The panzers struggled to accomplish a breakthrough and it was only after Busch's Landsers weighed in that the offensive began to go the German forces' way. Von Manstein finally attacked at Luga town on the 10th, also making halting progress against the 41st Rifle Corps. Hoepner changed his Schwerpunkt back and forth between his two panzer corps in order to gain some advantage. In four days XLI Panzer suffered 1,600 casualties and LVI Panzer 900.

An engine for a panzer is unloaded from a Ju-52. Difficult terrain and weather, poor roads, and increasing partisan activity made aerial resupply essential for Hoepner's panzer spearheads throughout *Barbarossa*. (NARA)

Reinhardt finally achieved a hard-won breakthrough on August 12–13. The next day 8th Panzer swung south in order to meet von Manstein's men coming up from the town of Luga. But first, near Lake Il'men, Vatutin launched a counterattack to relieve pressure on Leningrad's defenders. This attack and the German reaction had a significant impact on the final assault.

A Panzer 38(t) of the 8th Panzer Division near Leningrad. Of a total of 223 panzers, 118 were these near-obsolete Czech models, yet the 8th Panzer represented von Manstein's main striking force. (HITM)

German Command Problems

With *Barbarossa* one month old, on July 21 Hitler, Keitel, two staff officers, some SS bodyguards, and propaganda photographers arrived by air at Army Group North headquarters. Hitler appeared "pale and nervous," perhaps symptoms of his summer illnesses. His only visit to von Leeb during *Barbarossa* accomplished nothing substantial. None of the participants knew it then, but the German High Command was in the middle of its debilitating five-week debate over strategic decisions on the campaign's future during the prime summer campaigning season.

Not satisfied with his own visit, Hitler next sent Paulus, considered an expert in mechanized warfare, to Army Group North headquarters on July 24 and 26. Instead of convincing Hoepner to continue attacking between Lakes Peipus and Il'men he returned to the *Wolfsschanze* reporting that the area was completely unsuited for panzers. Hitler sent Keitel back north on July 30 with the promises of assistance of VIII Fliegerkorps. Von Leeb told him the army group needed 35 divisions but had only 26, and that the Sixteenth Army could not adequately defend its 200-mile-plus front dangling loosely in the direction of Army Group Center.

As happened elsewhere along *Barbarossa*'s front during the German High Command's tomfoolery, operational commanders took matters into their own hands. Intrigue at the strategic level did not equate to inactivity at the operational or tactical levels. With the LVI Panzer Corps bogged down on the road to Novgorod, on July 15 Hoepner decided Reinhardt would attack alone from his bridgeheads towards Leningrad. Von Leeb visited the panzer group command post the next day, approved this decision and returned I Army Corps to Hoepner to serve as his right flank protection. However by late July LXI Panzer still waited for von Manstein who spent weeks trying to negotiate the Luga Line. On July 30 a frustrated Reinhardt again wrote in his diary, "More delays. It's terrible. The chance we opened up [to Leningrad] has been lost for good…" Defending the Sabsk bridgeheads cost many more casualties than capturing it.

Meanwhile the Kremlin was having its own command and control problems. Relying on leadership by fear, commissars "advised" with threats though most commanders did everything possible under the circumstances. The situation

A Stuka flies over the bombed-out ruins of Novgorod the day after a massive VIII Fliegerkorps attack. The walled Kremlin and Volkhov River (lower left) are clearly visible. (NARA)

improved slightly under Voroshilov, but as the German forces approached Leningrad the old marshal's principal response was to create the Military Soviet for the Defense of Leningrad, probably to spread the blame for anticipated failures. During the second half of August, Stalin dispatched a deputation from his own headquarters to rectify the situation. His men broke up the ad hoc Soviet and dismissed the entire leadership of the Northwest Front (Voroshilov received a temporary face-saving position as Leningrad Commander) until Zhukov arrived on September 9.

Artillerymen of the 212th
Infantry Division ride on a
caisson as they approach
Utorgosh west of Lake Il'men.
For them the war of movement
would soon be over as they now
had to fight through successive
defensive lines guarding
Leningrad. (NARA)

Sixteenth Army: Staraya Russa and Demyansk

Vatutin had been husbanding remnants of the 11th and 27th Armies plus the
new 34th and 48th Armies to attack Army Group North's extended eastern
flank. He originally developed overoptimistic plans of striking Busch on both
sides of Lake Il'men and advancing 10 miles per day. Stavka told him this was
"clearly beyond the capacity" of the front and instructed him to settle on a
more "limited mission." Vatutin therefore decided to attack only south of the
lake on August 3 or 4 and try for 2–3 miles per day. In the center of his assault,
supported by the 11th Army, the robust new 34th Army represented the main
effort, driving into the 30-mile gap between the Sixteenth Army's X and II
Corps. On the flanks, the 48th Army aimed for Novgorod while the 27th
moved on Kholm. The attack was delayed until August 12, first by the writing
of new orders and poor weather and then by the Germans' Luga offensive.

German intelligence failed to spot Soviet preparations. To the south, the
27th Army did not make much progress against Kholm but closer to Lake
Il'men the 34th advanced 24 miles in two days to cut the Dno–Staraya Russa
railroad. Hansen's three divisions fell back under the blows of Major General
K.M. Kachalov's 12. Soon the same miserable terrain with which Army
Group North had to contend, plus poor command and control, conspired to
slow the Soviet offensive. The town of Dno represented Busch's headquarters
and a logistics hub supporting much of the Leningrad offensive. The gap

between the X and II Corps grew to almost 50 miles as Vatutin added four divisions to his order of battle. The German 30th Infantry Division abandoned Staraya Russa on August 16. A 30-mile retreat, following their earlier strenuous advance and difficult defensive battle, further exhausted the Landsers. Von Leeb, and to a lesser degree Hitler, overestimated the impact of the Red Army attack. Halder dismissively called them "irrelevant pinpricks." Unsurprisingly, Hoepner did not want the Staraya Russa attacks to detract from his own assault and advocated keeping pressure on the lower Luga Line and even pulled LVI Panzer Corps out of the middle of Luga to reinforce Reinhardt for a final push on Leningrad.

Landsers (trans. "those of the land") belonging to the 11th Infantry Division fighting near Dno in August. The steel helmet of the soldier to the left still bears the black-white-red national badge, in theory phased out before *Barbarossa*. (HITM)

However von Leeb refused to accept the risk of a threatened right, and transferred the 3rd Motorized and SS Totenkopf (plus I Fliegerkorps and VIII Fliegerkorps air support) from the Luga Line to Dno to prepare for a German counterattack. Under cover of the night von Manstein's divisions made a 150-mile march to reinforce a situation that was already stabilizing. On August 19, first Totenkopf at 0300hrs and then 3rd Motorized Division struck the 34th Army unexpectedly like a hammer. Rain and Soviet resistance made the going rough, but by 23 August the German forces restored the Lovat River line, taking 18,000 POWs, 300 guns, 200 tanks, and the first Katyusha rocket launchers to fall into their hands. The bulk of four rifle divisions and one cavalry division were crushed.

Soviet Attacks around Staraya Russa

Soviet attacks south of Staraya Russa and German counterattack, 12–23 August 1941. Viewed from the southeast shows General Vatutin's attack to distract Army Group North and take pressure off Red Army defenders in front of Leningrad.

Note: Gridlines are shown at intervals of 10 km

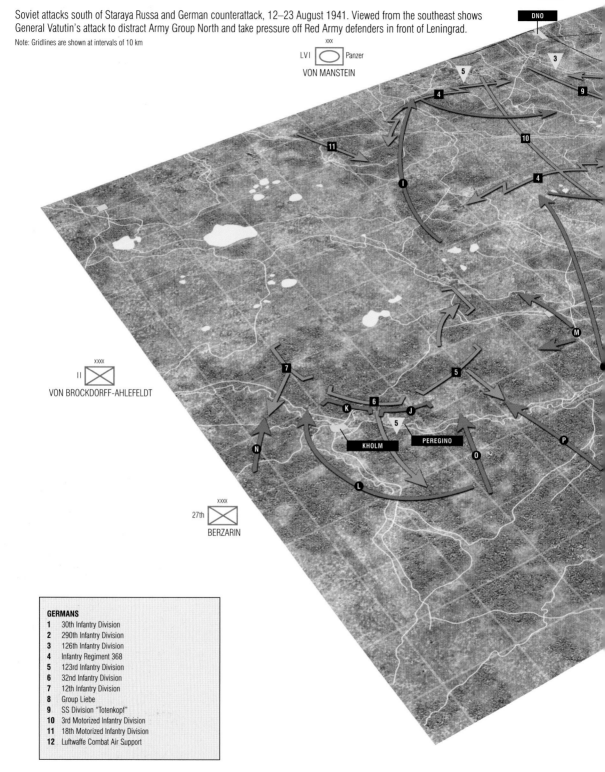

16th BUSCH

DNO

LVI Panzer
VON MANSTEIN

II VON BROCKDORFF-AHLEFELDT

27th BERZARIN

KHOLM

PEREGINO

GERMANS

1	30th Infantry Division
2	290th Infantry Division
3	126th Infantry Division
4	Infantry Regiment 368
5	123rd Infantry Division
6	32nd Infantry Division
7	12th Infantry Division
8	Group Liebe
9	SS Division "Totenkopf"
10	3rd Motorized Infantry Division
11	18th Motorized Infantry Division
12	Luftwaffe Combat Air Support

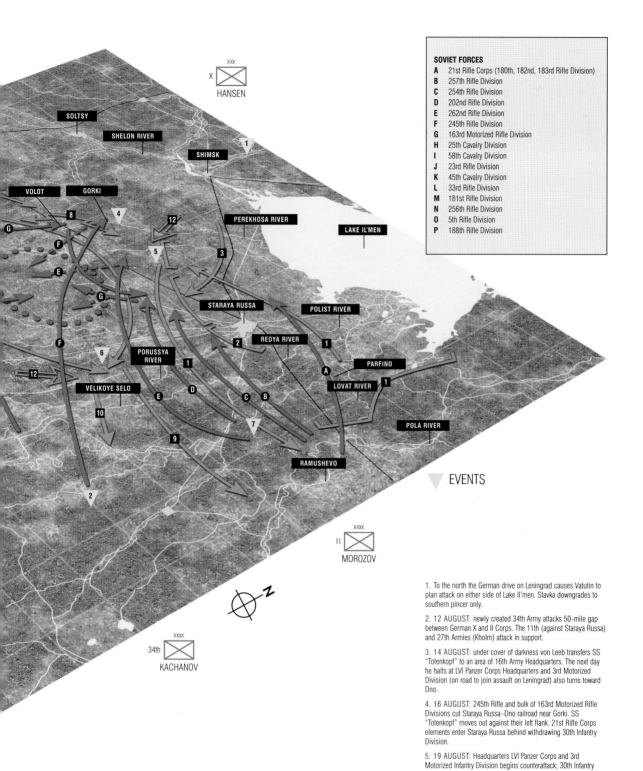

SOVIET FORCES

A 21st Rifle Corps (180th, 182nd, 183rd Rifle Division)
B 257th Rifle Division
C 254th Rifle Division
D 202nd Rifle Division
E 262nd Rifle Division
F 245th Rifle Division
G 163rd Motorized Rifle Division
H 25th Cavalry Division
I 58th Cavalry Division
J 23rd Rifle Division
K 45th Cavalry Division
L 33rd Rifle Division
M 181st Rifle Division
N 256th Rifle Division
O 5th Rifle Division
P 188th Rifle Division

HANSEN

SOLTSY
SHELON RIVER
SHIMSK
VOLOT GORKI
PEREKHOSA RIVER
LAKE IL'MEN
STARAYA RUSSA
POLIST RIVER
REDYA RIVER
PORUSSYA RIVER
PARFINO
VELIKOYE SELO
LOVAT RIVER
POLA RIVER
RAMUSHEVO

EVENTS

MOROZOV

34th
KACHANOV

1. To the north the German drive on Leningrad causes Vatutin to plan attack on either side of Lake Il'men. Stavka downgrades to southern pincer only.

2. 12 AUGUST: newly created 34th Army attacks 50-mile gap between German X and II Corps. The 11th (against Staraya Russa) and 27th Armies (Kholm) attack in support.

3. 14 AUGUST: under cover of darkness von Leeb transfers SS "Totenkopf" to an area of 16th Army Headquarters. The next day he halts at LVI Panzer Corps Headquarters and 3rd Motorized Division (on road to join assault on Leningrad) also turns toward Dno.

4. 16 AUGUST: 245th Rifle and bulk of 163rd Motorized Rifle Divisions cut Staraya Russa–Dno railroad near Gorki. SS "Totenkopf" moves out against their left flank. 21st Rifle Corps elements enter Staraya Russa behind withdrawing 30th Infantry Division.

5. 19 AUGUST: Headquarters LVI Panzer Corps and 3rd Motorized Infantry Division begins counterattack; 30th Infantry Division transitions from defense to offense. II Corps attacks at Kholm.

6. 20 AUGUST: despite terrible weather, but with Luftwaffe close air support, SS "Totenkopf" and 3rd Motorized Divisions meet near Velikaya Selo and close trap on bulk of 163rd, 202nd, 245th, 262nd Rifle, and 25th Cavalry Divisions.

7. 23 AUGUST: the 16th Army restores Lovat River Line but drive on Leningrad has had to continue minus valuable armored and Luftwaffe elements.

Landsers of the 290th Infantry Division fighting in Staraya Russa during the second half of August; the town changed hands three times that month. (HITM)

Ironically, about the same time as LVI Panzer Corps regained the line of the Lovat, General of Panzer Troops Adolf Kuntzen's LVII Panzer Corps set out from Hoth's panzer group; this was the long-anticipated but long-delayed support from Army Group Center to the Leningrad efforts. Soviet resistance around the Smolensk pocket took longer than expected to reduce, delaying their departure. To reach von Leeb, LVII Panzer began an attack at 0330hrs on August 23 toward Velikie Luki, following a bombardment by artillery, *Nebelwerfer* and Stukas. The nature of the terrain meant that the corps' two panzer divisions operated almost independently. The battle for Velikie Luki ended on the 26th with another Kessel of 30,000 POWs. Although German losses were significant, Soviet dead lay in heaps. The bulk of the 22nd Army, 126th, 110th, 124th, 179th, 186th, 14th Rifle Divisions plus the 48th Tank Division, was destroyed. Kuntzen's men struggled northward while Red Army defenders made effective use of mines, antitank ditches, and fortified houses. After its two-week trek the LVII Panzer Corps arrived at Kholm and linked up with Army Group North on September 9.

Soviet pioneers belonging to the 34th Army emplacing mines amongst antitank obstacles in August. At this point they were engaged in a seesaw battle against the Sixteenth Army south of Lake Il'men. (HITM)

Reunited after Staraya Russa the II and X Army Corps, plus the LVI and LVII Panzer Corps, headed east for Demyansk and the Valdai Hills beginning on September 12. The flat, swampy ground, mud 18 inches deep and undergrowth-clogged wilderness slowed the German troops. Moving at night for better concealment attracted partisans and cavalry. They reached Demyansk four days later in piecemeal fashion, but halted due to the desperate logistics situation. Ju-52 transport aircraft provided emergency resupply. By September 18, however, most of the mobile formations were loading onto trains for the Moscow front. It seems their exertions would have been more worthwhile if they had been spent reaching out toward the Finns on the Svir River. But with the panzers departing, the Sixteenth Army Landsers would henceforth be on their own.

Busch's men closed another small Kessel near the Valdai Heights, encircling 35,000 more Soviet troops, 334 guns, and 117 tanks. Finally the Sixteenth eliminated the elusive 11th and 27th Armies and the newer 34th Army. The 12th Infantry Division reached the source of the Volga near Lake Ostashkov in the Valdai Heights, essentially marking the end of Sixteenth Army's progress in *Barbarossa*. The entire Valdai sideshow had only won a tactical victory for the Germans.

A column of Stoewer light cross-country vehicles negotiate muddy roads and thick forests near Demyansk in September. As the German advance pressed further from the Soviet border, so the transport infrastructure became increasingly primitive. (HITM)

Combined losses for the 11th, 27th, and 34th Armies from August 10–31 were 128,550 men (30 percent) and 481 tanks (89 percent), but von Leeb forfeited operational success on the Leningrad axis or an even more fecund linkup with the Finns, all for tactical victories on a secondary front. Granted he secured the seam between the two army groups, but at a cost to the German forces in lost time and expended efforts that crippled drives on Leningrad or the Svir River. Halder stubbornly and willfully resisted reinforcing von Leeb with Hoth's panzers for nearly a month only to relent by dispatching the XXXIX and LVII Panzer Corps northward when it was arguably too late for them to achieve more than limited success.

The Eighteenth Army and the Baltic Islands

Lacking a third panzer corps with which to build a Schwerpunkt, Hoepner had again to wait for infantry to march forward to fulfill that role. These forces came in the form of von Küchler's XXVI and XXXVIII Army Corps, which finally arrived on the Neva River in the second half of August. They had three missions: 1) shield the panzer group's left; 2) push the 8th Army north; and 3) destroy the 8th before it could add its strength to the defenses of Leningrad. But these operations, plus any final assault on the massive city, would have to wait until the dramas around Staraya Russa and Demyansk played themselves out. Relegated to secondary front status, the Eighteenth Army's attention turned to the islands off the Estonian coast.

In October 1917, Imperial Germany had conducted Operation *Albion*, amphibious landings on the Baltic Islands. The Nordkorps landed on the seaward side, bagging 20,000 Russian POWs before moving on to Reval (later named Tallinn). A generation later von Leeb's men began planning Operation *Beowulf* on April 29, originating instead on the Estonian mainland. Heavy fighting in the Eighteenth Army area, especially at Tallinn, plus the Kriegsmarine's difficulty in assembling the required amphibious craft, repeatedly delayed *Beowulf*. Soviet nuisance air raids launched from Saaremaa against Berlin between August 7 and September 4 (possible responses to Luftwaffe raids on Moscow?) gave launching the assault added urgency.

The 6,700 ton, 6in gun cruiser Leipzig participated in the German operations against the Baltic Islands. Diagonal stripes are often misidentified as "camouflage" but were in reality air-recognition markings for Kriegsmarine ships operating in the Baltic early in the war. (Podzun Verlag)

Saaremaa and Hiiumaa were the largest of the numerous islands at approximately 1,000 and 500 square miles each. Smaller Muhu was connected to Saaremaa by a 2¼-mile-long causeway. All the islands were flat, sandy, and rocky, covered with heather and generally inhabited only by poor farmers and fishermen. Major General A.B. Elisseyev commanded 24,000 defenders (German intelligence estimated 15,000) who had used the preceding ten weeks poorly and were ill-prepared. Initially two battalions of the 79th Rifle Regiment guarded Muhu while the 3rd Independent Rifle Brigade held Saaremaa. One Soviet advantage was their ten coastal and 16 mobile artillery batteries stationed throughout the islands.

Pionier-Sturmboot 39 of the 61st Infantry Division crosses the sound between Estonia and Muhu Island on September 14. German amphibious capabilities were severely tested during this one-division operation. (NARA)

Red Army defenders of the Baltic Islands employing a 50mm M1940/1941 mortar. General Elisseyev and his men did not use the time between *Barbarossatag* and the German landings effectively and were essentially isolated from the remainder of the USSR. (HITM)

The German leaders wanted Elisseyev to think they were repeating their 1917 attack from the sea and thus on the night of September 13 the cruisers *Leipzig*, *Köln*, and *Emden* plus mine sweepers, sub-chasers, and torpedo boats conducted a feint to the west of the islands in Operation *Südwind*. In Operation *Nordwind*, the Finns did the same off the north shore of Hiiumaa with two monitors, two armed icebreakers and various smaller vessels. Unfortunately for them, their flagship, the 10-inch gun monitor *Ilmarinen*, struck two mines and sank within seven minutes with a loss of 271 sailors. However, these naval ruses worked as the Soviet forces rushed to defend the islands' western coastline and therefore were not ready when the real assault came from the Estonian mainland.

Beowulf's plan called for the 61st Infantry Division under General Siegfried Haenicke to assault on September 14, only 17 days after conquering Tallinn. The 151st, 162nd, and 176th Infantry Regiments would cross the 6-mile sound to Muhu in turn, starting at 0400hrs. Brandenburger commandos parachuted in against coastal guns at Kuebassare (seaborne elements failed to arrive) and the Luftwaffe planned robust air support. The first wave in four–six-man boats missed their intended beach by 1 mile as a result of strong winds and currents, as well as inexperienced crews. The second wave got so disoriented that it circled back to Estonia. Aufklärungs Abteilung (Reconnaissance Battalion) 161 landed on the north end of Muhu later in the day. By the first evening five infantry and one light mountain artillery battalions occupied a 4-mile wide beachhead.

151st Infantry Regiment crossed the causeway to Saaremaa against disorganized Soviet resistance on September 15; the defenders had not yet

61st Infantry Division soldiers in a rubber raft on Hiiumaa Island in October. Leading the group is an *Unteroffizier* (foreground) and a *Leutnant* behind him. Although the Baltic Islands were not large they had extensive areas of marshland. (HITM)

recovered from the deception plan. 151st and 162nd Infantry Regiments advanced down the southern side of Saaremaa while Aufklärungs Abteilung 161 and the 176th Regiment moved along the north coast. Resupply came in the form of huge Bf-321 Gigant transport gliders. The capital Kuresaare fell on the 21st.

Soviet remnants numbering 15,000 retreated to the Sorve Peninsula for a final stand. Beginning on September 23, first the 162nd Infantry Regiment then the 151st assaulted the 1½-mile wide isthmus. Fighting ended there on October 5. Haenicke's men captured 5,000 POWs while many escaped to Hiiumaa. Throughout the operation I/KG77 and II/ZG26 provided invaluable air support, coordinated by the air-control ship *Karl Meyer* steaming in the Baltic.

Preceded by another naval feint and supported by gunfire from *Köln* and other ships, the 176th Infantry Regiment landed on the east side of Hiiumaa at 0500hrs on October 12 in Operation *Siegfried*. Somehow surprise was complete once again against the poorly led Soviets. Aufklärungs Abteilung 161 and the 151st Regiment followed on the west and central axes. Severe terrain limited the effectiveness of motorized Kampfgruppe Sierigk. The battle for Hiiumaa lasted nine days against often stubborn resistance by 3,000–5,000 Soviet soldiers.

General Haenicke commanded another exemplary operation after receiving the Knight's Cross for his 61st Infantry Division's role in taking Tallinn just weeks earlier. Aided by naval units and Bf 110s as flying artillery, his men eliminated the threat of artillery interdiction of Riga Bay. At a cost of 2,850 casualties they captured 15,000 POWs and over 200 guns. Poor Red Army leadership, specifically weak command and control plus ineffective use of reserves, handed the Germans a satisfying tactical victory.

German Joint Assaults on Baltic Islands

Operation Beowulf II German joint assault on the Baltic Islands, 13 September–22 October 1941. Viewed from the southeast shows German Army, Kriegsmarine, Luftwaffe elements, and Brandenburg commandos attacking islands off the coast of Estonia to secure Baltic lines of communication.

Note: Gridlines are shown at intervals of 10 km

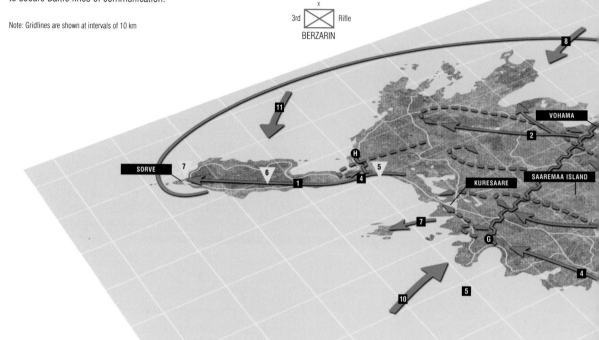

GERMAN FORCES
Army

1	Infantry Regiment 151
2	*Aüflarungs Abteilung* 161
3	Infantry Regiment 176
4	Infantry Regiment 162
5	Motorized Group Sierigk
6	217th Infantry Division elements
7	Capture of Abro Island

Naval

8	Demonstration Westwind
9	Demonstration Nordwind
10	Demonstration Südwind
11	Operation West Storm
12	Operation East Prussia

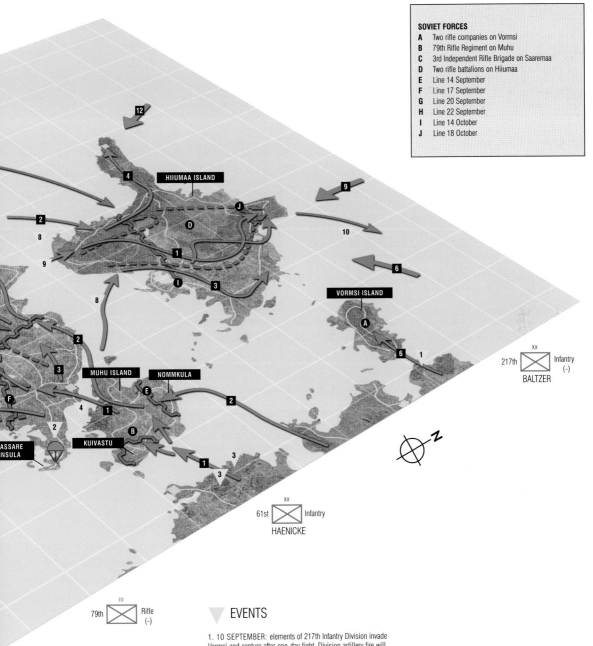

12

4 HIIUMAA ISLAND

J

9

2

8

D

9

I

1

3

10

6

8

VORMSI ISLAND

A

2

6 1

xx
217th Infantry
(-)
BALTZER

3

MUHU ISLAND   NOMMKULA

E

2

F

4   **1**

2

B

BASSARE
IINSULA

KUIVASTU

1

3

3

xx
61st Infantry
HAENICKE

⊕⟋z

III
79th Rifle
(-)

▽ EVENTS

1. 10 SEPTEMBER: elements of 217th Infantry Division invade Vormsi and capture after one-day fight. Division artillery fire will close sound between Hiiumaa.

2. 14 SEPTEMBER: Brandenburg Special Command "Benesch" lands by glider near Soviet coastal battery in fort on Kuebassare Peninsula. Shipborne elements turned back by heavy seas.

3. 14 SEPTEMBER: Infantry Regiment 151 (in 180 boats) and *Aüflarungs Abteilung* 161 (90 boats) cross from mainland to Muhu and manage to hold against uncoordinated Soviet counter-attacks.

4. MORNING OF 16 SEPTEMBER: first elements of Infantry Regiment 151 then *Aüflarungs Abteilung* 161 fight across two and a half mile-long causeway to Saaremaa against disorganized defense. Bridgehead secure by 1100 hours.

5. 22 SEPTEMBER: after easily overrunning most of Saaremaa Red Army remnants make last defense at one and a quarter mile-wide isthmus to Sorve Peninsula. Infantry Regiment 162 attacks on 23–27 September through heavily fortified defense.

6. EVENING OF 27 SEPTEMBER: Infantry Regiment 151, with the help of Luftwaffe close air support and naval gunfire, breeches Soviet defensive lines and captures Sorve Peninsula.

7. 5 OCTOBER: Soviets evacuate Sorve by sea; 1,500 soldiers escape to Hiiumaa.

8. MORNING OF 12 OCTOBER: Infantry Regiment 151 follows to Hiiumaa.

9. AFTERNOON OF 12 OCTOBER: IR 176 and AA161 conduct amphibious landing against south shore of Hiiumaa.

10. 21–22 OCTOBER: Soviets abandon Baltic Islands; 570 men manage to escape.

Resuming the Offensive Against Leningrad

Hitler saw St Petersburg, the seat of the Tsars, as a symbol of Russia's status as a great power, its dominance of Europe, and its naval superiority in the Baltic Sea. His hatred of the renamed city of Leningrad as the cradle of Bolshevism was based on ideology and racism rather than strategy or geopolitics. Vatutin's inconclusive Staraya Russa attack and the arrival of the XXXIX Panzer Corps from the Third Panzer Group sealed Leningrad's fate; If not captured outright the city would at the very least be a hostage of the German forces.

It should come as no surprise that the closer von Leeb got to Leningrad the farther behind he left the blitzkrieg. Early in *Barbarossa*, as a morale-boosting measure the men of 3rd Motorized Division were told they could grow beards until Leningrad fell. By late August commanders bowed to the inevitable and ordered their men to shave again. Panzer thrusts, measured in hundreds of miles per month in June and July, now slowed to a crawl. German losses mounted; the 30th Infantry Division suffered 1,359 casualties during *Barbarossa*'s first month, but 2,947 during the second. The Northwest Front suffered a bloodletting as well with 25 of its 30 divisions whittled down to between 10 and 30 percent of assigned strength in July.

Von Leeb's repeated immobilization of Hoepner's panzers gave the Red Army time to strengthen its lines, even if only slightly. David Glantz has condemned the German leaders' self-imposed surrender of the strategic initiative as Reinhardt stood practically unopposed on the Neva at Kingisepp. Von Leeb compounded this folly by his continued inaction while the Sixteenth Army eliminated a tactical threat at Lake Il'men far from Leningrad.

General Halder initially vigorously resisted reinforcing Army Group North with Hoth's panzers. Only when it was too late, and then in a piecemeal manner, did the chief of staff relent. However, success was now less likely than weeks earlier. Even then the two army groups would not cooperate to liquidate a threat to their mutual flanks. By the time von Leeb had sufficient strength either to slaughter the Northwest Front or to link up with Mannerheim both opportunities had passed. One can only guess whether another Kiev-style Kessel in the north or a rendezvous on the Svir might have been possible if the German forces had committed themselves decisively and fully in that sector.

Von Leeb was optimistic about his army group's chances against the Red Army forces facing them, but Hitler was not. Reinhardt's panzer corps had been stalled within 100 miles of Leningrad since the first half of July. Now, nearly two months later, the Germans finally anticipated the penultimate

Traffic jam at a Luga River bridge in late August. The river is neither wide, with steep banks, nor fast flowing yet was obviously an obstacle. German pioneers have constructed a new bridge to the left. (HITM)

assault on the city. On September 4 von Brauchitsch and Halder arrived at army group headquarters in Pskov. Keitel was already there and the three of them told von Leeb of his new mission, merely to surround Leningrad, not conquer it. The next day Hitler issued instructions giving von Leeb two missions, to encircle Leningrad by attacking toward Shlisselburg and also to drive on Volkhov in order to link up with the Finns on the Svir. On September 6 Hitler issued Führer Directive 35 dealing with the final attack on Moscow (Operation *Typhoon*). This established September 15 as the date when VIII Fliegerkorps and Hoepner's remaining panzers would transfer to Army Group Center for the offensive two weeks later. In return von Leeb received the 7th Airborne Division flown in from Crete, the 250th Spanish Blue Division, plus the 212th and 227th Infantry Divisions arriving from France.

Von Leeb's lack of focus on any single obtainable target would cost him his primary objective. All the while Mannerheim watched critically from Finland for any signs that Army Group North might falter as the United States and Soviet Union applied diplomatic pressure on his tiny nation to remain close to its 1939 borders.

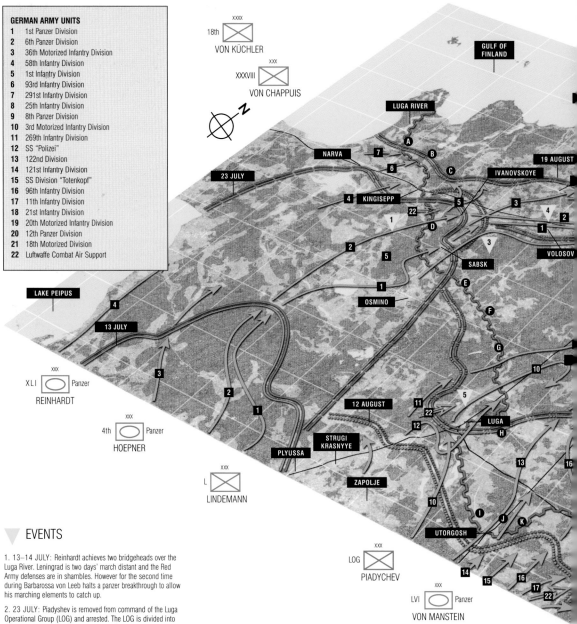

GERMAN ARMY UNITS

1. 1st Panzer Division
2. 6th Panzer Division
3. 36th Motorized Infantry Division
4. 58th Infantry Division
5. 1st Infantry Division
6. 93rd Infantry Division
7. 291st Infantry Division
8. 25th Infantry Division
9. 8th Panzer Division
10. 3rd Motorized Infantry Division
11. 269th Infantry Division
12. SS "Polizei"
13. 122nd Division
14. 121st Infantry Division
15. SS Division "Totenkopf"
16. 96th Infantry Division
17. 11th Infantry Division
18. 21st Infantry Division
19. 20th Motorized Infantry Division
20. 12th Panzer Division
21. 18th Motorized Division
22. Luftwaffe Combat Air Support

18th
VON KÜCHLER

XXXVIII
VON CHAPPUIS

GULF OF FINLAND

LUGA RIVER

NARVA

23 JULY

KINGISEPP

IVANOVSKOYE

19 AUGUST

VOLOSOV

SABSK

OSMINO

LAKE PEIPUS

13 JULY

XLI Panzer
REINHARDT

4th Panzer
HOEPNER

L
LINDEMANN

PLYUSSA

STRUGI KRASNYYE

12 AUGUST

LUGA

ZAPOLJE

UTORGOSH

LOG
PIADYCHEV

LVI Panzer
VON MANSTEIN

▼ EVENTS

1. 13–14 JULY: Reinhardt achieves two bridgeheads over the Luga River. Leningrad is two days' march distant and the Red Army defenses are in shambles. However for the second time during Barbarossa von Leeb halts a panzer breakthrough to allow his marching elements to catch up.

2. 23 JULY: Piadyshev is removed from command of the Luga Operational Group (LOG) and arrested. The LOG is divided into Kingisepp, Luga, and Eastern sectors.

3. 8 AUGUST: 111th and 125th Rifle divisions attack the XLI Panzer Corps' bridgehead from the west.

4. 9–16 AUGUST: after three weeks in a costly defense, 1st and 6th Panzer Divisions attack to expand their bridgeheads in preparation for final assault on Leningrad.

5. 10–26 AUGUST: after numerous delays due to weather hampering *Fliegerkorps* VIII close air support, L Army Corps attacks against southern portion of Luga Line.

6. 15 AUGUST: XXXIX Panzer Corps transferred to Army Group North from Army Group Center. Its first action is attack on Lyuban on the 25th.

7. 16 AUGUST: reinforced 12th Infantry Division captures Novgorod Kremlin from 48th Army elements.

8. 19 AUGUST: the 8th Panzer Division veers southward from XLI Panzer attack to link up with L Army Corps coming north from Luga. Result is Army Group's largest *Kessel*, capturing nearly 20,000 Soviets from 41st Rifle Corps; closes on 30 August.

9. 21 AUGUST: L Army Corps captures Kranogvardiesk from 42nd Army.

10. 8 SEPTEMBER: 20th Motorized Infantry Division and other units capture Shlisselburg, isolating Leningrad from overland communications with remainder of the USSR. Beginning of 900-day siege.

11. 11 SEPTEMBER: final German assault on Leningrad begins. Dudergof Heights captured two days later. Essentially furthest advance toward Leningrad achieved by 24th.

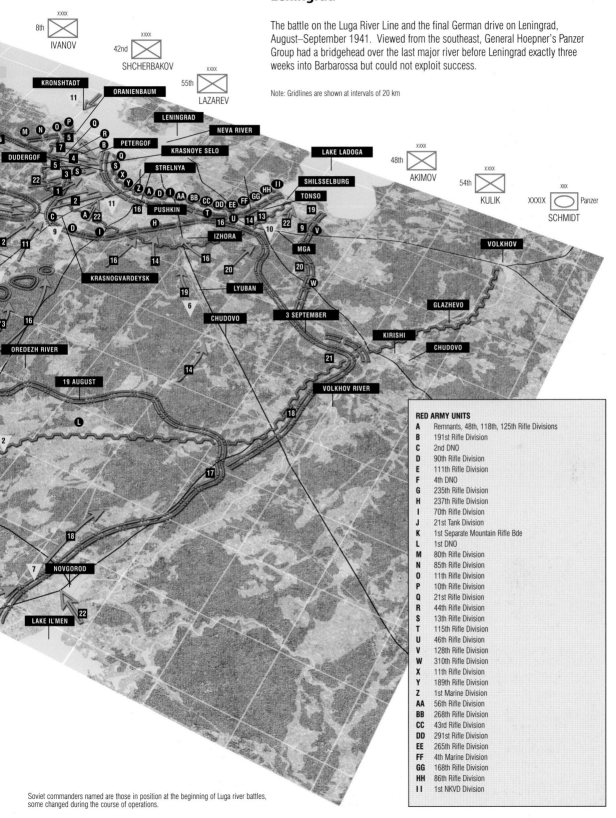

Battle on the Luga River Line and Approaches to Leningrad

The battle on the Luga River Line and the final German drive on Leningrad, August–September 1941. Viewed from the southeast, General Hoepner's Panzer Group had a bridgehead over the last major river before Leningrad exactly three weeks into Barbarossa but could not exploit success.

Note: Gridlines are shown at intervals of 20 km

8th — XXXX — IVANOV

42nd — XXXX — SHCHERBAKOV

55th — XXXX — LAZAREV

48th — XXXX — AKIMOV

54th — XXXX — KULIK

XXXIX — Panzer — SCHMIDT

KRONSHTADT
ORANIENBAUM
LENINGRAD
NEVA RIVER
PETERGOF
KRASNOYE SELO
STRELNYA
DUDERGOF
PUSHKIN
IZHORA
SHILSSELBURG
TONSO
MGA
KRASNOGVARDEYSK
LYUBAN
LAKE LADOGA
VOLKHOV
GLAZHEVO
3 SEPTEMBER
KIRISHI
CHUDOVO
CHUDOVO
OREDEZH RIVER
19 AUGUST
VOLKHOV RIVER
NOVGOROD
LAKE IL'MEN

RED ARMY UNITS

A	Remnants, 48th, 118th, 125th Rifle Divisions
B	191st Rifle Division
C	2nd DNO
D	90th Rifle Division
E	111th Rifle Division
F	4th DNO
G	235th Rifle Division
H	237th Rifle Division
I	70th Rifle Division
J	21st Tank Division
K	1st Separate Mountain Rifle Bde
L	1st DNO
M	80th Rifle Division
N	85th Rifle Division
O	11th Rifle Division
P	10th Rifle Division
Q	21st Rifle Division
R	44th Rifle Division
S	13th Rifle Division
T	115th Rifle Division
U	46th Rifle Division
V	128th Rifle Division
W	310th Rifle Division
X	11th Rifle Division
Y	189th Rifle Division
Z	1st Marine Division
AA	56th Rifle Division
BB	268th Rifle Division
CC	43rd Rifle Division
DD	291st Rifle Division
EE	265th Rifle Division
FF	4th Marine Division
GG	168th Rifle Division
HH	86th Rifle Division
II	1st NKVD Division

Soviet commanders named are those in position at the beginning of Luga river battles, some changed during the course of operations.

Generals Busch, von Richthofen, and Wiktorin (XXVIII Army Corps) plan an assault on the Luga River defenses. The entire nature of *Barbarossa*'s northern theater changed at this point, when the Soviet forces' cobbled-together defenses, terrain, and weather conspired to halt the German troops only a few days' march from Leningrad. (Podzun Verlag)

For a moment during mid-August as the LVI Panzer moved north from Luga and XLI Panzer swung counterclockwise to meet it, Hoepner came close to building a two-panzer corps Schwerpunkt for the first time during *Barbarossa*, but his superiors' overreaction to the Staraya Russa counterattack shattered that vision.

However, Reinhardt had not been completely idle during the Staraya Russa battles of the second half of August and kept up the pressure. The rain fell hard and the Red Army had turned most villages into fortresses. Soviet antitank mines reduced the ratio of destroyed panzers to Soviet tanks to 1:2, a disastrous trend for the German forces. The panzer crews halted their advance periodically and assumed defensive *Igel*. So it continued for another week as 1st and 6th Panzer Divisions inched forward toward Krasnogvardeysk. On August 24, XLI Panzer Corps reached the end of its endurance still short of the town, switching to a defensive posture for another two weeks.

As von Leeb issued orders on September 6, forces for the final assault of Leningrad lined up as follows. The Schwerpunkt under Hoepner consisted of the XLI Panzer and XXXVIII and L Army Corps with the missions of attacking Krasnogvardeysk and cutting off the 8th Army from Leningrad.

Soviet 122mm M1931 guns in action along the Luga line. The Germans took a massive toll on the now-immobile artillery branch, early in the campaign when many prime movers were transferred to the newly raised mechanized corps. (HITM)

Hoepner also commanded the XXVIII Army Corps and elements of the 12th Panzer Division on the Izhora River, with Slutsk and Kolpino as their objectives. To the east stood Schmidt's newly arrived XXXIX Panzer Corps (18th and 29th Motorized Divisions from Army Group Center), which was to chase away any Soviet relief efforts from the direction of Leningrad. Elements of the Sixteenth Army would secure the Lake Il'men and Lake Ladoga shoulder to the east. On the Soviet Leningrad Front were the 8th Army to the west, the 42nd Army (Lieutenant General F.S. Ivanov) near Krasnogvardeysk, and the 55th Army (Major General I.G. Lazarev) around Slutsk and Kolpino. The defenders numbered 452,000 men. Included in that number were 80,000 naval infantry in seven brigades. Popov believed that he had the flexibility to transfer forces from the 23rd Army in Karelia to more threatened sectors if necessary.

Army Group North's last effort to take Leningrad began on the eastern flank. Schmidt's Panzer Corps battled the 55th Army on its right and the 54th on its left as it made straight for Lake Ladoga via Chudovo, which fell on August 25. The noose closed around Leningrad when Shlisselburg fell on September 8. The hero of the moment was Lieutenant Colonel Harry

Army Group North cut overland communications with Leningrad by taking Shlisselburg on Lake Ladoga, shown here on September 8. However, the 5-mile wide toe-hold was inadequate for completely isolating the city. (Topfoto)

Hoppe, the same man who had captured Novgorod's Kremlin the month before. Voroshilov was afraid to tell Stalin of the disaster so the latter learned the bad news via German radio.

As temperatures dropped Reinhardt felt strong enough to attack at 0930hrs on September 9. The 36th Motorized and 1st Panzer Divisions led the way through Krasnogvardeysk and the old Tsarist barracks at Dudergof, which fell on the 11th. But Hoepner had no reserve to exploit the success. A day later the 1st and 6th Panzer Divisions entered Leningrad's inner defensive ring near Krasnoye Selo. Under orders from Stalin not to surrender, Red Army soldiers blew themselves up with hand grenades rather than show the white flag. In the close fighting Stukas from von Richthofen's VIII Fliegerkorps dropped bombs 200–300 yards in front of the German troops. Meanwhile the XXVIII Corps and 55th Army fought to a draw near Slutsk.

Smelling another trap Hoepner released his new reserves, the 8th Panzer, to pass Reinhardt's right and then to swing south. It would rendezvous with the new L Army Corps (269th Infantry and Polizei Divisions) coming up from the town of Luga, which had just fallen with the loss of another 16,000

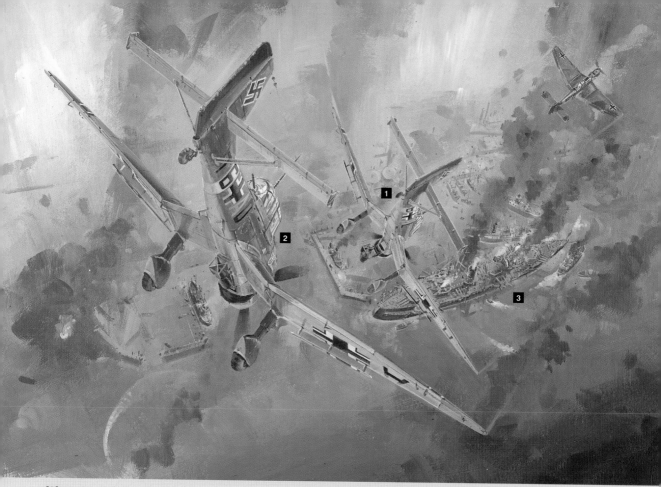

ABOVE Hans Ulrich Rudel sinks the battleship *Marat* at Kronshtadt, September 21, 1941. Flak explodes while the Stukas are still 10 miles out. Starting at 9,000 feet altitude the dive bombers tip over for the final run. They carry 2,000-pound bombs especially made for large warships (**1**). Pilots plunge at about 80° without using dive brakes in order to get through the bursting artillery. Lieutenant Hans Ulrich Rudel (T6+AD) (**2**) keeps his sights on the *Marat* (**3**). He pushes the bomb release then pulls back on the stick. He momentarily blacks out from the G-force until his radioman/gunner tells him "She is blowing up, sir!" However, Rudel and his comrades won an incomplete victory; the crippled *Marat* settled into the shallow water of the bay, but her stern guns continued to bombard German soldiers on the mainland preparing their final assaults on Leningrad. (© Osprey Publishing, Howard Gerrard)

Soviets. Together they encircled nine divisions of the LOG and 41st Rifle Corps near Vyritsa, capturing 25,000 Soviets. By mid-September the Luga defense line had ceased to exist, while the 48th Army could field only 6,235 men and 31 guns. Further German advances looked doubtful, however; the LOG had accomplished its mission.

Hoepner and von Leeb labored under imminent High Command threats to pull Fourth Panzer Group out of the Leningrad fight and send it to Moscow. The field marshal suffered from a fatal resignation, stating "I'm fighting a poor-man's war," while the panzer commander wanted one last push. Command and control arrangements were far from satisfactory for Hoepner. He had

Soviet POWs await their fate near the lower Luga River sector. With a smaller panzer group, Army Group North failed to achieve the massive encirclements that characterized the battles in the Army Group Center and Army Group South sectors. (NARA)

limited authority over the XXXVIII Corps on the left (under the Eighteenth Army) and none over the XXXIX Panzer Corps on the far right. Throughout von Leeb appears to have exercised little decisive leadership. Accordingly German attacks were slow in getting started and poorly coordinated.

On September 9, Zhukov arrived in embattled, encircled Leningrad and gave Voroshilov the following note from Stalin: "Hand over command of the Front to Zhukov and fly back to Moscow immediately…" Zhukov promptly countermanded his predecessor's orders to make preparations to demolish the city and to scuttle the Red Banner Fleet. He issued his own "not one step back" instructions and provided the defense with shape by creating his own main effort near Uritsk, sending reinforcements there and ordering counterattacks.

On September 13, with the battle on a knife edge, Reinhardt committed the 1st Panzer, 36th Motorized, and 1st and 58th Infantry Divisions at Uritsk. A day later he ordered the 6th Panzer (by now down to 9,000 men) to Pushkin and sent 8th Panzer east to assist Schmidt. As often happened, these assaults preempted a countermove planned by Zhukov. Close to the center of the line, the 121st Infantry Division, with many elements at one-third strength, battled in the "haunted" forests. They could see the golden cupolas and towers of Leningrad a mere dozen miles away. Toward the end of the month both sides settled down to an active defense and began a propaganda war using loudspeakers.

Hoepner's men wondered if this was indeed the final assault. Their high-water mark came on September 18 as the XXVIII Corps took Slutsk while the 1st Panzer and Polizei Divisions took Pushkin, with 1st Panzer engaging new Soviet tanks fresh from the factory at Kolpino. That same day, however, the 6th Panzer received orders to pull out and make for Moscow, to be followed on the 20th by the remainder of XLI Panzer Corps.

To the west, on September 16 Reinhardt reached the Gulf of Finland at Strelnya, isolating Major General Cherbakov's 8th Army from Leningrad. To the east, 54th Army counterattacks at Mga failed to dislodge the XXXIX Panzer Corps. The main defense in Leningrad's suburbs began to gel around this time. The 1st Panzer halted at the high-water mark of White Russian forces during the Civil War and by September 25 the front lines had solidified.

With that, 900 days of darkness descended over Leningrad while the moon circled like a vulture; 1 million citizens starved in that first winter alone. Leningrad had been a frontline city during the Winter War but this would be different. The supplement to Führer Directive 33 advocated terror "to discourage any flicker of resistance" within the city. On September 16 Hitler stated "The venomous nest Petersburg out of which Asiatic poison so long gushed into the Baltic Sea would disappear from the face of the earth." A directive of September 22, exactly three months after *Barbarossatag*, made his bombast official but no closer to realization. Many Landsers regretted they would not have the opportunity to capture Leningrad.[25]

Marshal K.E. Voroshilov's political closeness to Stalin did not equate to military skill. First Kuznetsov then Voroshilov made such a hash of defending Leningrad's southern approaches as to almost guarantee German success. (David Glantz)

Surrounding and starving Leningrad was only one option considered by Hitler; a half-hearted alternative had been to allow the still-neutral United States to either supply or evacuate the population. Toward the end of World War I General Erich Ludendorff wrote a study on the difficulties of taking Petrograd, but likely he considered the implications of feeding its 2 million people. Hitler felt unconstrained by similar humanitarian issues. On September 10 von Leeb asked what would be expected if women and children sought to escape starvation by trying to come through the German cordon. The Führer said, "They'd be shot." Von Leeb replied, "That might happen once, but no more. German soldiers don't shoot women and children … that would cause a severe crisis in discipline." The field marshal was obviously naive about what German soldiers would or would not do during

---

25   They needed only to wait one year for Stalingrad to see what they were missing.

Barbarossa was hard on the Luftwaffe. Here the captured crewmen of a bomber are paraded through Leningrad, over which their aircraft was shot down. The *Hauptfeldwebel* in the leather jacket, probably the pilot, looks especially banged up. They await an uncertain fate. (Courtesy of the Central Museum of the Armed Forces, Moscow via Stavka)

the Nazi–Soviet war. However his point was doubtless lost on Hitler. Even more naively some in the German High Command believed that Stalin would forfeit Leningrad.

In any event these issues never arose. For his part, on September 21 Stalin also issued draconian orders concerning Leningrad. The USSR would resupply the city and the population would manage as best it could. Because Hitler halted his forces so early and Finland refused to be drawn into a fight for the huge metropolis, Leningrad maintained a substantial hinterland of over 1,100 square miles. That space provided ample room for troop concentrations, airfields, depots, farms, and factories, all of which dissipated the siege's effectiveness. In fact, industry continued to produce ammunition, weapons, and vehicles, and repaired much of the same, out of the range of German artillery. Finally, due to the city's stout air defenses, the Luftwaffe's September bombardment lasted barely two weeks. Throughout the theater by the end of September all four of the Luftwaffe's top fighter aces were either dead, in the hospital, or removed from active flying duty for political reasons. Worst of all, the Luftwaffe was completely incapable of making up its losses, personnel or equipment.

The Soviet Counteroffensives

While the jaws of von Bock's Panzer groups closed on the Smolensk pocket, Stavka struggled to regain the initiative. The German leaders already had a copy of the July 13 order instructing Timoshenko to attack. Three days later the marshal complained to Moscow that he had "insufficient strength to cover Yartsevo, Viazma, and Moscow. The main thing is no tanks." Stavka (through Zhukov) reiterated its orders on the 20th, essentially telling the West Front to use four armies to encircle the German troops then attempting to surround Smolensk, and save the 16th, 19th, and 20th Armies inside the pocket. The same order demanded "operations by larger groups" than Timoshenko's previous Berezina River attacks by just two or three divisions. Stavka instructed him to create five attack groups, each loosely based on a field army and named after its commander: 29th Army (Lieutenant General I.I. Maslinnikov), 30th Army (Major General V.A. Khomenko), 24th Army (Major General S.A. Kalinin), 28th Army (Lieutenant General V.I. Kachalov), all four NKVD generals, plus an ad hoc group under Major General K.K. Rokossovsky. Initially these forces were all supposed to attack on July 21.

Group Kachalov moved out first, on the 23rd. It was soon creating problems for Guderian, and by July 27 it looked as if the 10th Panzer Division and Grossdeutschland might become cut off. Guderian responded with a counterattack towards the important communications node at Roslavl. By July 31, XXIV Panzer Corps (3rd and 4th Panzer Divisions) and VII Army Corps (197th, 23rd, and 78th Infantry Divisions) were attacking eastward from Krichev into Kachalov's rear. A day later IX Army Corps (263rd and 292nd Infantry Divisions) assaulted southward, sealing Group Kachalov's fate. The fight against these apparently most serious threats to Army Group Center was over by August 7. Even though General Kachalov had died in battle in a Soviet tank, Commissar Lev Mekhlis had him branded as a traitor (only to be rehabilitated after the war).

Groups Kalinin and Khomenko attacked on July 24. VIII Fliegerkorps had not yet departed for Army Group North, so Bf-109s mauled the Soviet close support effort. Kalinin's mission was to exploit Kachalov's "success": an eventuality that never presented itself. Both of these attacks achieved little and were soon turned back. The same day Colonel General O.I. Gorodovikov's Cavalry Group (32nd, 43rd, and 47th Cavalry Divisions supported by 232nd Rifle Division) began causing trouble across Guderian's and von Weich's lines of communication southwest of Bobruisk. Group Maslinnikov

Terrain in the Third Panzer Group's area was more thickly forested than farther south in the Second Panzer Group sector. These vehicles bear the "Hh" of Hoth's formation, plus the yellow Y-rune of the famous 7th Panzer Division – one of several whose tank regiment was still equipped with the Czechoslovak-made PzKpfw 35(t) or 38(t). (Podzun)

(off the "Timoshenko Counteroffensive" map to the north) attacked on July 29, but also achieved little.

Arguably the weakest group had the greatest impact. Rokossovsky had the mission of halting Hoth's direct advance on Viazma and Moscow, but started with a force of only two rifle and four artillery regiments. He soon collected stragglers of 38th Rifle Division plus about 90 tanks. His assault first blunted then actually drove back the advance of 7th Panzer and 20th Motorized Divisions. Von Bock reinforced his hard-pressed units with 17th Panzer, yet still could neither displace Rokossovsky's men nor close the Solovevo gap through which many Red Army soldiers were escaping from Smolensk.

Kachalov's attacks, Rokossovsky's stubbornness, the fact that von Kluge's personal aircraft had been forced down and the field marshal was feared lost, and other factors conspired to cause the German commanders momentary consternation. All combined, the attacks hurt Hoth's panzer group worse than the rest of Army Group Center. But von Bock, having foreknowledge of the Timoshenko offensive, dispatched the Luftwaffe to attack Soviet assembly areas and generally halted the uncoordinated and piecemeal operations. When the Smolensk Kessel slammed shut on about July 27–28, Stavka changed Timoshenko's mission from relieving the trapped defenders

The Timoshenko Counteroffensive

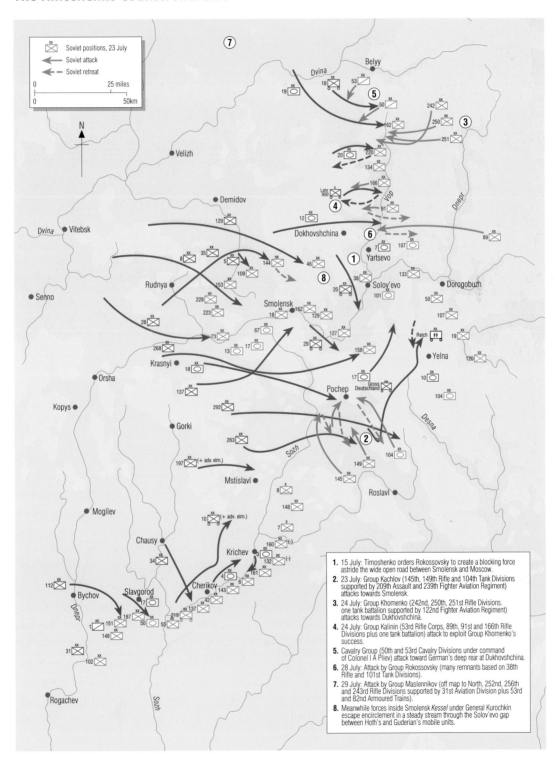

Soviet positions, 23 July
Soviet attack
Soviet retreat

0   25 miles
0   50km

N

Belyy
Dvina
Velizh
Demidov
Dvina Vitebsk
Dokhovshchina
Yartsevo
Rudnya
Senno
Soloy'evo
Smolensk
Dorogobuzh
Krasnyi
Orsha
Yelna
Kopys
Pochep
Gross Deutschland
Gorki
Reich
Mstislavl
Roslavl
Mogilev
Chausy
Krichev
Cherikov
Bychov
Slavgorod
Rogachev
Sozh
Desna
Dnepr
Vop
Sozh

1. **15 July:** Timoshenko orders Rokossovsky to create a blocking force astride the wide open road between Smolensk and Moscow.
2. **23 July:** Group Kachlov (145th, 149th Rifle and 104th Tank Divisions supported by 209th Assault and 239th Fighter Aviation Regiment) attacks towards Smolensk.
3. **24 July:** Group Khomenko (242nd, 250th, 251st Rifle Divisions. one tank battalion supported by 122nd Fighter Aviation Regiment) attacks towards Dukhovshchina.
4. **24 July:** Group Kalinin (53rd Rifle Corps, 89th, 91st and 166th Rifle Divisions plus one tank battalion) attack to exploit Group Khomenko's success.
5. **Cavalry Group** (50th and 53rd Cavalry Divisions under command of Colonel I A Pliev) attack toward German's deep rear at Dukhovshchina.
6. **28 July:** Attack by Group Rokossovsky (many remnants based on 38th Rifle and 101st Tank Divisions).
7. **29 July:** Attack by Group Maslennikov (off map to North, 252nd, 256th and 243rd Rifle Divisions supported by 31st Aviation Division plus 53rd and 82nd Armoured Trains).
8. Meanwhile forces inside Smolensk *Kessel* under General Kurochkin escape encirclement in a steady stream through the Solov'evo gap between Hoth's and Guderian's mobile units.

A Ju 87B Stuka pulls out of a dive after attacking a group of 80 Soviet tanks on August 1. Air–ground co-operation was essential for the success of blitzkrieg, and von Bock would miss von Richthofen's VIII Fliegerkorps after August 3, when it was taken away from Army Group Center and shifted to the Leningrad Front. (NARA)

in the pocket to escaping encirclement himself. In the marshal's after-action report to Stalin he wrote that he "gave all the reinforcements that I could to Khomenko and Kalinin. But you know I had no guns, no aircraft, and very few personnel."

By the end of July personnel losses hurt both sides. As Hitler pointed out, Soviet casualties to that point equaled Russian losses in World War I. But Stalin was not Nicholas II and the USSR was not Imperial Russia. Germans killed and wounded by the same date were 42,000 for Army Group North, 74,500 for Center, and 63,000 in the South. Respectively, replacements amounted to only 14,000, 23,000, and 10,000.

Yelnia

Guderian's XLVI Panzer Corps seized the Yelnia bridgehead over the Desna River on July 20. It was seen as a temporary halt. The town sat on the high ground over the river and housed a stop on the major east–west rail line. Most commanders there assumed that they would resume the advance on Moscow as soon as the infantry had tidied up the Smolensk and neighboring pockets. Yelnia would serve as the ideal jumping-off point for *Barbarossa*'s last big push. However, the second half of July coincided with the crisis of command at Rastenburg. German units at Yelnia had only had an early taste of what would turn out to be a ten-week defensive struggle. In view of its "temporary" nature, the salient had been chosen neither for its defensive qualities nor for its suitability for reinforcement and resupply.

While defensive doctrine did not receive the same emphasis as offensive in the interwar German Army it was not neglected. The Poles never severely tested German defenses and the Western Allies did so only once, at Arras on May 21, 1940. On the other hand Red Army Forces constantly badgered the invaders with their frequent counterattacks and constant attempts to break out of and in to the various Kessels. Less than two months into the *Barbarossa* campaign, and with the mass of von Bock's armor fighting to the north and south, Zhukov now sought to make Yelnia a lightning rod for a series of deadly assaults. The end result was Germany's first operational withdrawal in World War II.

Elements of 10th Panzer Division and SS Reich initially occupied Yelnia. It took Timoshenko only three days to assemble his initial attack forces and they began hitting the German positions for the next two weeks. Their larger (and unrealistic) mission was to relieve their trapped comrades inside the Smolensk encirclement by September 8. Guderian's men often had to fend off a dozen attacks per day, while ammunition and reserves ran dangerously low. Close proximity to Smolensk became a German asset as that Kessel was reduced, freeing up infantry and the Luftwaffe's I Flak Corps for duty around Yelnia.

With Lukin's surrender at Smolensk the immediate need for the Soviet forces to carry the attack forward so vigorously diminished. By the middle of August most of von Bock's panzers began to depart in the directions of Leningrad and Kiev, so the Fourth and Ninth Armies took over the sector's defense. The bulk of Kesselring's two Fliegerkorps also flew north and south. Simultaneously, while the German forces had advanced beyond the reach of their logistical tether the Soviet units retreated back along their lines of supply.

As Army Group Center abdicated the battlefield initiative during the logistics "pause," Timoshenko seized it. Emboldened by strength, logistical, and morale factors by August 11 the Soviet divisions were assaulting all along von Bock's front. Timoshenko's subordinate 19th Army (reinforced by 101st Tank Division and 43rd Mixed Aviation Division) achieved a 6-mile penetration across the River Vop. As Timoshenko pounded German positions north of the salient, Zhukov, now commanding the Reserve Front, lavished his attention on Yelnia itself. His main asset would be Major General K.I. Rakutin's 24th Army. Simultaneously, Major General L.M. Dovator led the 50th and 53rd Cavalry Divisions on a raid deep into the German rear which required three divisions to counter.

This *Obergefreiter* (left) and a private have dug in beside a destroyed T-34. Amongst the clutter of their fighting position can be seen Kar 98 carbines, an MG34, a bayonet, cooking equipment, and an M1938 gas mask canister. (NARA)

To the German soldier on the ground there seemed to be no shortage of Soviet infantry, Katyushas, or CAS. Assaults in battalion strength, parachute drops behind their lines, and night attacks became common. Here the unsuitability of the terrain surrounding the Yelnia defense positions became fatal for many a Landser; the wounded had to wait until dark for medical evacuation away from their exposed locations. They could not even count on help in the form of counterattacks by armor and motorized troops, since Guderian's mobile forces were fighting back the Bryansk Front attacks, reducing the Roslavl threat and making preparations for the upcoming operation against Kiev.

The beginning of the end of the Yelnia salient came on August 30 when, following a three-hour artillery preparation, the Soviet forces stove in 23rd Infantry Division to a depth of 6 miles. On September 2, von Brauchitsch, Halder, and von Bock all agreed to abandon Yelnia and the order went out the next evening. The German commanders tried to put lipstick on a pig by calling the retreat a withdrawal. In the end Yelnia demonstrated the German leaders' somewhat unjustified obsession with rivers and river crossings and represented a waste of scare resources. IX and XX Army Corps left Yelnia on the 5th, and the Soviet 100th, 103rd, 309th, and 120th Rifle Divisions reoccupied the town from the following day.

The German Crisis of Command

Hitler was deathly superstitious about following Napoleon's ill-fated footsteps to Moscow. As early as the end of June he was considering the second phase for *Barbarossa*, but was clear that this did not include Moscow. Hitler never fell under the spell of Stalin's capital and his plan since the previous December had been to send Hoth and Guderian north and south after Smolensk. In diary entries of June 30 and July 8, Halder initially agreed with this thinking and halfheartedly conceded that infantry might be enough to take Moscow. Halder deviously worked to dissuade the Führer; enlisting von Brauchitsch, von Bock, and Jodl's help behind the scenes while falsifying Red Army strength estimates to suit his arguments. However, there was no unanimity among the German leadership.

By the second half of July, initial German euphoria had cooled and Hitler could not sleep. He commented, "One cannot conquer Russia" (so one might ask, what was he doing there?). Soviet powers of resistance were hard to fathom. In view of the prodigious territory lost, estimated Soviet casualties of 3 million dead and wounded and another million captured, it was incomprehensible to Hitler that the enemy could sustain a credible defense much longer. On July 17 Hitler decided to send Hoth north and Guderian south. Two days later, with minimal staff assistance, he issued Führer Directive 33 followed by a supplement days later.[26] Succinctly, these

One reason that the *Sturmgeschütz* was so important to the Germans: their mainly horse-drawn artillery often lagged far to the rear of the fighting, making displacing to new positions a slow process. The standard German infantry division still included some 6,000 horses, for its artillery, supply train, and part of its reconnaissance element. (HITM)

---

26   *Ergänzung* can also be translated as "completion."

documents confirmed the southern strategy, united the First and Second Panzer Groups in a single operation against Kiev and, to Halder's chagrin, left Moscow to von Bock's infantry. By this time Halder had changed his mind again and he tried again to persuade Hitler to continue committing the armor to the central axis. He increased estimates of Soviet forces defending Moscow hoping Hitler would decide in favor of a massive encirclement victory there.

On July 20 Halder flew to von Rundstedt's command post vainly hoping to hear that Army Group South could pull off the Kiev battle alone. Three days later he and von Brauchitsch went to Hitler's headquarters to argue in person for the Moscow option. The Führer continued to insist that his main objective was the destruction of the enemy's forces. Halder correctly presented Moscow as a place where much of the Red Army could be fixed and defeated, but the general's arguments backfired when he told Hitler that owing to logistics problems Second and Ninth Armies could not advance on Moscow until August 10. The Führer replied that in that case neither could the panzers so he would send the tanks north and south as planned. On July 30 Hitler further postponed any decision on future operations until current ones, including closing the Uman pocket and creating Dnepr bridgeheads, were complete.

As regards the northern thrust, Directive 33 and its supplement essentially ordered Third Panzer Group north from the Moscow axis toward Leningrad. The supplement subordinated Third Panzer Group to von Leeb. It correctly implied that two panzer groups would give the final push on a Leningrad greater chance of success. Clearly Army Group North was not strong enough to accomplish its assigned missions alone. Hoth's six divisions would assist Hoepner to encircle Red Army forces in the north and prevent Soviet reinforcement and resupply of the Leningrad area. In his directives Hitler reestablished capturing Leningrad as a prerequisite for turning on Moscow as discussed at his conference on December 5 the year before. However, this went against Halder's fixation on Moscow.

Besides, *Barbarossa* had reached its long-anticipated logistical pause. For example, in the south only two rail lines served von Rundstedt's entire army group when German doctrine called for a minimum of one per army. The Reichsbahn's goal of 24 trains per day in September was achieved on only 12 days and many of those trains were only partially loaded. Therefore OKH ordered Army Group Center to transfer 5,000 tons of *Grosstransportraum* capacity to its southern neighbor.

General staff maneuverings came too late as Hitler issued Führer Directive 34 on July 30 (this was at least written with Jodl's help). A Supplement on August 12 read: "the most important aim ... is not the capture of Moscow but, rather, occupation of the Crimea, the industrial and coal-mining area of the Donets Basin, the cutting of Russian supply lines from the Caucasus oil fields..." Hitler recognized the importance of the Ukraine's resources and knew that before Army Group Center could move on Moscow, Army Group South would have to advance and clear von Bock's right flank.

In the north Hitler reasserted the primacy of Leningrad, specifically pushing von Leeb to swing wide right and link up with the Finns, but Directive 34 further delayed any assistance from Army Group Center and sent Hoth's men only so far as the Valdai Heights. Hitler stressed encircling Leningrad by linking up with the Finnish Army but then denied von Leeb the necessary resources. The supplement spoke of the need to "relieve Army Group North of anxiety about its right flank." Most significantly it stated that before attacking Moscow "operations against Leningrad must be concluded." The Führer acceded to Army Group Center's desire to retain most of Hoth's Panzer Group; with disastrous effects on von Leeb's subsequent fortunes.

These Führer Directives, especially No. 33, confused more than clarified *Barbarossa*'s objectives and its future. At each step the German leaders had to retool their thinking up and down the entire chain of command. Hitler departed on a tour of army group headquarters to speak directly to field commanders, especially those of the panzer groups. On August 4 the Führer, Halder, Keitel, Jodl, and OKW and OKH staff officers met leaders of Army Group Center (including future assassination conspirator Henning von Treschkow) at von Bock's headquarters in Borisov. Under Halder's stern gaze, the generals present toed the chief of staff's line. In the end they could not discourage their Führer, however, now enthused about von Rundstedt's chances following Uman. Hitler's priorities remained, in order, Leningrad, the Ukraine, and then Moscow.

On August 7 Jodl and Halder met to discuss Moscow, as General Warlimont[27] later wrote, for the "first time that anyone can remember." On the 8th Jodl tried to sell Hitler on the idea that massive Red Army forces assembling in front of Moscow represented a valid target for another offensive. Two days later Halder's and Jodl's OKH and OKW headquarters issued a joint situation report recommending the Moscow option.

---

27 A day earlier Warlimont wrote a memorandum doubting the German forces' ability to reach the Archangel–Astrakhan line.

Unfortunately for them the Soviet assault on Staraya Russa in the north which began on the 12th redirected everyone's attention to potential dangers on Moscow's flanks. The following week, on the 18th, OKH submitted a *Denkschrift* (study), supposedly only for von Brauchitsch's eyes (but widely disseminated), claiming that the Ostheer had enough resources and, most importantly, time for one objective in what was left of 1941: Moscow. In reality Halder and Jodl decided not to decide between Moscow or Kiev but instead told Hitler the Wehrmacht could take both!

However, German military leadership could not present a united front to dissuade the Führer from the two flanking operations. A telling exchange occurred when Colonel Adolf Heusinger of the OKH told Jodl that if Germany wanted to destroy Communism it had to attack Moscow. Jodl replied that, "The Führer has a sixth sense…You must admit that the Führer's reasons are well thought out." Other generals were powerless to dissuade Hitler. They could not even successfully exploit Hitler's illness: he was battling dysentery or had suffered a nervous breakdown around this time. By mid-August even Göring, as Director of Economy and Four-Year Plans and, since June 29, Economic Director of Occupied Eastern Territories, waded into the discussion in favor of the Ukraine option.

Too late Halder played his last ace by sending Guderian to the *Wolfsschanze* on August 23. The panzer general belonged to the Moscow "camp" (and was not yet disgraced) but knew nothing of the Halder–Jodl compromise. At one point Guderian told von Bock and Halder that he could not turn south and away from Moscow because of his troops' exhaustion. Yet just one day later, when confronted by Hitler, he selfishly agreed with anything the Führer wanted so long as his Second Panzer Group maintained cohesion, thereby unwittingly torpedoing Halder's scheme. When given the option of digging in or advancing south Guderian's choice was obvious.

Hitler broke the intellectual logjam days earlier on August 21 with his own *Denkschrift*. He stated that sending the panzer groups north and south and not toward Moscow was

> not a new proposition, but a fact that I have clearly and unequivocally stated since the beginning of the operation… The principal object that must yet be achieved before the onset of winter is not the capture of Moscow, but rather, in the south the occupation of the Crimea and the industrial and coal region of the Donets.

The document went on to accuse von Brauchitsch of caving in to the army group commanders. Ultimately, Hitler also authorized both the flank and Moscow options, but at least he had resolved the matter of sequencing; he would stick with German military thinking since Frederick as manifested in *Barbarossa*'s original plan and first destroy Red Army forces in the field. Accordingly OKH issued orders on August 30 for Army Groups Center and South to cooperate in the upcoming operation against Kirponos. Two days later von Rundstedt said "The *Vernichtungsschlact* (battle of annihilation) in the Ukraine is of decisive importance for the outcome of the entire Eastern campaign."

Throughout most of this critical period Soviet reactions had a decisive effect on German thinking. The inability of Army Groups North and South to encircle and eliminate large numbers of Red Army troops had left both of von Bock's flanks vulnerable. Von Leeb and von Rundstedt each had only one panzer group, so double envelopments were difficult, if not impossible. Soviet moves on the flanks often made German plans obsolete before they could be executed. The constant Red Army counterattacks also shook Hitler's confidence; he no longer "walked with the assurance of a sleepwalker."

Barbarossa's strain shows on this soldier's face. Men like him bore the burden when the internal dissention beset the German High Command barely one month into the campaign. (NARA)

Needless to say, Halder was disgusted with all four directives and supplements but by the end of August he held the losing hand and Hitler demanded that operations on the flanks begin as soon as possible. Von Manstein later wrote that "the open tug-of-war between Hitler and OKH over further operational goals [Moscow–Kiev–Leningrad] prevailed" over the need to cooperate in order to insure *Barbarossa*'s strategic success. Halder used Hitler's illness, von Brauchitsch, Jodl, and even Guderian in his attempts to thwart the dictator. For his part, the army commander was too tired either to support Halder or fight Hitler. Von Lossberg commented that after the summer leadership crisis, "it was only a matter of time until von Brauchitsch was relieved."

Kiev

A month into *Barbarossa* similar strategic dilemmas and problems with senior generals bedeviled Stalin as they did Hitler. Like most German soldiers, many Soviets assumed Moscow to be the Wehrmacht's Schwerpunkt. Zhukov, however, believed Army Group Center's losses sustained fighting for Smolensk instead indicated an attack toward Kiev, and he told his boss as much on July 29. The dictator remained unimpressed with the general's arguments, calling them "nonsense." Within a week Stalin replaced the marshal for again pointing out the Ukraine's vulnerability. He was wary of "fighting withdrawals" since retreating from Berdichev and Vinnitsa had only resulted in the encirclement at Uman.

Three days later Kirponos confidently told Stalin that he could hold Kiev. German intelligence inaccurately credited the Southwest Front with considerable forces: 73 rifle, 16 tank, and five cavalry divisions (in reality respectively 30, six and two at full strength). By the second half of August the Red Army Air Force enjoyed a 2.2:1 superiority in fighters and a 1.5:1 advantage in bombers (by the end of the month the Luftwaffe had only 1,045 serviceable aircraft in all of the USSR). Zhukov, now a front commander but still a member of the Supreme Command Staff, sent a telegram on August 18 to reiterate his previous warnings.

Stavka further complicated command arrangements by naming Marshal Budenny to lead the Southwest Direction, supposedly coordinating the efforts of the Southwest and Southern Fronts. Soon after arriving Budenny thought he had convinced Stalin to give up the Dnepr's west bank. A few days later, however, the dictator changed his mind and decided to hold Kiev. While German and Soviet High Commands were thus occupied, in accordance with outdated plans trains from Kharkov poured reinforcements into the trap and near-certain destruction. Most often they went straight into the city rather than on the salient's flanks where they possibly could have halted von Kleist and Guderian.

Between the Marshes and Kiev

Kiev's prewar population exceeded 850,000. The III Panzer Corps under von Mackensen presented the first direct threat to Kiev when it rushed the city on July 10. A surprise assault never materialized and soon Hitler redirected his valuable panzers away from the potentially bloody fight. With Khrushchev as commissar 160,000 civilians dug nearly 40 miles of defensive works, 20 miles of antitank ditches and 750 bunkers. The 1st, 2nd, 28th, 161st, and 193rd Militia Brigades supplemented the 147th, 175th, 206th, and 284th Rifle Divisions of Lieutenant General Kostenko's 26th Army.

When the Sixth Army arrived at Kiev the mission of taking this fortress behind the Irpen River fell to the XXIX Corps. The first assault came on July 30 but the defenders threw the attackers back. Leading from the front, Lieutenant General Kurt von der Chevallerie of the 99th Light Infantry Division was wounded in this action and soon received the Knight's Cross. The German forces regrouped and tried again to no avail. The next onslaught began on August 8 supported by assault guns, *Nebelwerfer* and Stukas. The fighting reminded World War I veterans of the worst combat in Flanders. Stretcher-bearers went forward only at night and battalion doctors worked around the clock. In one day one artillery regiment lost 26 horses to exhaustion and another drowned in a mud hole. By the 12th the XXIX Corps had not broken through. Under the 26th Army's intense artillery fire and counterattacks and to save German lives, XXIX Corps withdrew to its August 7 lines. The Soviet Union's third city could not be taken frontally.

A *Gefreiter* holding two MP38s and another soldier stand watch over the Dnepr, the last major obstacle to *Barbarossa*. This photo gives a good idea of the river's width.

The 5th Army's skillful defense to the north against von Reichenau was the other reason for the existence of the Kiev salient. Von Rundstedt concluded he could not accomplish his main mission, taking Kiev, until the Sixth Army front stabilized. He therefore reinforced von Reichenau with the LI and XVII Corps from OKH Reserve, the LV Corps from Army Group South Reserve and ultimately the 11th Panzer Division as well. The Sixth would have to do without Luftwaffe support, currently dedicated to the fighting at Uman.

At various times in mid- and late August Budenny, Kirponos, and Khrushchev appealed to Stavka for permission to withdraw Potapov to shorter lines and keep pace with the retreating Bryansk Front. The High Command consented on August 19 and the 5th Army crossed the Dnepr four days later.

An 88mm heavy Flak gun in operation supporting an SS unit against Soviet tanks. This photograph gives a good idea of the gun's large crew. (Topfoto)

They failed to destroy the wooden bridge at Garnostoipal behind them, however. In Operation *Biber* (Beaver) the LI Corps and the 11th Panzer Division stormed the only bridge standing between Kiev and the marshes. Within 24 hours German assault parties reached the Desna River.

Kirponos ordered all Red Army Air Force assets against the bridge and two Il-2 Sturmoviks managed to burn the bridge with incendiary bombs. This cut off the German forces in the sand dunes between the rivers. The Soviet troops attacked them from all directions, while German artillery and Dnepr Flotilla monitors dueled for control of the rivers. German engineers finally repaired the bridge on September 2, ending ten days of isolation. On the army's right the XXXIV Corps closed on Kiev from the north on August 25. The next day the XVII Corps took Chernobyl. With its communications now secure Sixth Army units forced the Desna in numerous places. In view of the dangerous situation, on September 7 Kirponos demanded permission to retreat over the Desna. This Stalin granted two days later. Too late; on the 10th von Reichenau linked up with Second Army finally hemming in the 5th Army.

Guderian from the North

The Ostheer reorganized again on July 27, when von Kluge was removed from command of Fourth Panzer Army. The experiment had been a failure; at a high cost it paid no dividends. Either von Brauchitsch or von Bock had to continually prod von Kluge who proved to be equally poor both as a superior and as a subordinate, showing little aptitude for the blitzkrieg. Von Bock and his two panzer group leaders felt a sense of relief, but Hoth's joy was short-lived: he had lost most of his armor to Army Group North and, as of August 5, he also commanded the Ninth Army in place of the ailing Strauss.

Guderian, however, raced on with his newly minted Army Group Guderian, and did not allow details such as reducing the Smolensk pocket or fighting a defensive battle at Yelnia to stop him. He moved south supported by KGs 3 and 53, ZG 210 and JG 51. His abrupt 90° turn south caused confusion in Stavka and Budenny immediately alerted Stalin to the danger in the 5th Army's rear. The dictator did not take the threat seriously, however, since he considered Guderian's move south merely a tactical adjustment prior to resuming the attack on Moscow to the northeast. Within a day the XXIV Panzer Corps broke Major General K.D. Golubev's 13th Army and cut the Bryansk–Gomel rail line, endangering Bryansk Front's rearward communications. Two days later Stavka created the 40th Army under Major General K.P. Podlas, specifically to block Guderian.

When attempts to capture the tactically prudent bridges at Orsha, Mogilev, and Rogatchev failed, Guderian crossed the Dnepr elsewhere, making those towns irrelevant. In typical blitzkrieg fashion he left Mogilev to the Second Army infantry and accepted the risk that the Soviet forces there were too weak and disorganized to present a threat. He ordered IX Army Corps to continue toward Roslavl all night on August 2–3 and marched at the head of the column to ensure his orders were carried out. On the 3rd, IX Corps linked up with General of Panzer Troops Leo Geyr von Schweppenburg's XXIV Panzer Corps, thereby encircling more than 38,000 defenders and capturing 250 tanks and 713 guns.

Krichev was next on Guderian's list. Here on August 14, 16,000 POWs of the resuscitated 13th Army were taken by XXIV Panzer plus VII and XIII Army Corps troops. Von Weichs, moving south on a parallel course between Guderian and the marshes, had the mission of taking Gomel, but by August 12 had not yet attacked owing to mud and shortage of ammunition. By the time his Second Army moved out, XXIV Panzer Corps had slipped behind the defenders and cut off any escape. On August 17 Loerzer's II Fliegerkorps, operating from newly won bases as far south as Rogatchev, flew 180 Stukas and 40 Bf-110s in support of Guderian's 17th Panzer Division. Remnants of the 21st Army evacuated the city on that same day and the German troops occupied it two days later, rounding up another 50,000 POWs.

Guderian continued to Starodub on August 18. Red Army soldiers there mistook the panzer forces as paratroopers and in any event they could not establish a new defense. After occupying the town the Germans sent bogus transmissions to Timoshenko's headquarters saying, "Russians are holding Starodub. Do not bomb us!"

On August 20, Stalin ordered Yeremenko to destroy Guderian. Yeremenko employed the 13th (once again) and 50th Armies plus elements of the badly beaten 3rd and 21st, but failed to halt the panzers. His attacks had some effect against Lemelson's XLVII Panzer Corps, but this was not decisive. The dictator told Yeremenko "Stavka is much displeased with your work. I await your report on the destruction of Guderian's group." but except for three divisions facing XXXV Army Corps in the Rokitno Marshes, the Central Front had ceased to exist. During the same time von Brauchitsch also voiced his frustration. At a conference of army chiefs of staff on August 25 he criticized von Bock for his failure to maintain mass, the misuse of his panzers and the inability to maintain a Schwerpunkt. Army Group Center chief of staff, Major General Hans von Greiffenburg, shot back, how could it do these things when higher headquarters was sending it north, east, and south?

In a daring action Model's 3rd Panzer Division captured the Desna River bridge at Novgorod-Severskiy on August 24. Both sides threw forces into the fight. Stavka ordered the 21st Army to attack into the rear of Gyer von Schweppenburg's XXIV Panzer, but this came to naught. Red Army Air Force reconnaissance saw the entire situation develop but the Soviet forces lacked combat power on the ground to counter it. The 21st Army pulled back without telling its neighbor to the east, 40th Army. Now completely unsupported, any assault into Guderian's flank by Podlas was out of the question.

To make matters worse remnants of the 13th Army disobeyed Stalin's orders and retreated away from the fight just as Model cut the Moscow–Kiev rail line at Shostka. Simultaneously the Second Army burst into action to the west of Guderian and smashed into the 21st Army, which drifted toward Kiev and eventual destruction.

The German forces' road to the south now lay wide open. The Second Army continued down the Gomel–Chernigov highway in late August. XIII, XLIII, and XXXV Army Corps assaulted Chernigov on the lower Desna

with air support; Red Army troops withdrew on the night of September 6–7 but not before putting the city to the torch.

Led by XXIV Panzer Corps, Guderian pushed southward. From September 2 Yeremenko's Bryansk Front, a collection of decimated units with a near-impossible mission, attempted to slow them by counterattacking the 120-mile-long exposed east flank. On September 6 Kirponos in Kiev ordered the 21st Army (formally assigned to the Southwest Front that day) to drive into the rear of the 3rd and 4th Panzer Divisions – Geyr von Schweppenburg's vanguard. Yeremenko's efforts failed to slow the panzers, which crossed the Seim River the next day. A 20-mile gap now existed between the Bryansk and Southwest Fronts.

The 21st Army finally launched its assault against Guderian's exposed left on September 9. Lacking coordination with the Bryansk Front it accomplished little. Later that day Stavka ordered the 5th and elements of the 37th Armies (a new headquarters controlling reinforcements arriving near Kiev) to turn east away from the Sixth Army and toward Second Panzer Group. This move was also too late. The Soviet leaders sensed a trap but could not react to the threat.

Near Kiev a formation of Stukas flies over German lines toward the east and another bombing mission. (Topfoto)

By September 10 the gap between Kirponos in Kiev and Yeremenko outside grew to over 40 miles. When Model's 3rd Panzer Division occupied Romny that day Stalin ordered the Southwest Front to direct 90 percent of all its air missions against Model (including many by the new Sturmoviks). With the 40th Army ingloriously pushed aside and the 27th Army's three rifle divisions guarding 100 miles of front the Soviet forces' north shoulder collapsed.

The Southwest Front's line exceeded 500 miles. Budenny saw the danger represented by the First and Second Panzer Groups and requested permission to withdraw from the Dnepr to the Psel River – a move of approximately 150 miles east that Stalin was unlikely to approve. On September 11 he argued with Chief of General Staff Shaposhnikov over this course of action. Finally Stalin stepped in and settled the matter; he fired Budenny and instructed Kirponos to hold out. As Zhukov had recommended three days earlier, the dictator named Marshal Timoshenko to command the soon-to-be-wrecked Southwest Direction.

Von Kleist from the South

After Uman von Kleist's panzers closed in on the wide Dnepr. The 9th Panzer Division managed to get across at Zaporozhe on August 19 but could not hold its position against determined Soviet counterattacks. Further upstream the Seventeenth Army secured a major bridgehead the next day at Kremenchug. Then the motorized infantry of the 13th Panzer Division captured a 1,000-yard bridge at Dnepropetrovsk on August 25. The 60th Motorized Division joined in the next day and within a week the 198th Infantry Division and SS Viking solidified the bridgehead. Intense Red Army attacks pounded the German forces from three sides but were defeated with the help of the Luftwaffe (and the first appearance of the Italian 22nd Fighter Group). At Kremenchug 80 tanks attacked the LV Corps sector in one day, of which 60 were destroyed. Von Rundstedt created a decoy bridgehead at Cherkassy to help take pressure off those at Dnepropetrovsk and Kremenchug. Budenny took the bait and indeed launched counterattacks against Cherkassy.

At Kremenchug, in the panzers' way, stood the new 38th Army. Stavka created this formation from headquarters, 8th Mechanized Corps, and five rifle and four cavalry divisions, mostly new arrivals to the front. Its 40,000 men defended a 120-mile front around the bridgehead. The main German blow hit the 297th Rifle Division, but most Soviet reserves were to the north resisting Guderian. Dogfighting aircraft swarmed in the skies above. The

Infantry with 37mm Pak 36 and assault gun support making the final attack on Kiev. After the losses sustained at Kiev Hitler forbade any more attacks on large Soviet cities. Losses to mechanized formations over the next year prevented Stalingrad being encircled and necessitated an assault on the city itself, with disastrous consequences. (NARA)

A weary Italian foot column with pack mules from the 3rd Cavalry Division, Duca d'Aosta. Soldiers on the near side of the road seem to be regular infantry. Those on the far side are the division's *Bersaglieri* (light infantry) with distinctive black cockerel feathers on their helmets. (Library of Congress)

38th Army's counterattack planned for September 8 never materialized; with no armor and low ammunition it was "impossible to move in the open terrain due to aerial attacks."

On September 4 von Rundstedt ordered Seventeenth Army north toward Lubny and Mirgorod and a rendezvous with Guderian while First Panzer would exploit due east toward the open country around the iconic historic Russian battlefield of Poltava. However, von Brauchitsch, Halder, and von Rundstedt plus their chiefs of staff and operations officers met at the Army Group South command post on the 8th. Among other things they discussed pulling Group Mackensen (III Panzer Corps and the CSIR) out of the heavily contested Dnepropetrovsk bridgehead. They ultimately decided against von Rundstedt's offensive and reversed the earlier arrangement by sending von Kleist north and von Stülpnagel east. They further agreed to begin the southern leg of the Kiev offensive on the 11th. A day before the attack was to begin von Kleist sent XLVIII Panzer Corps into Seventeenth Army's lodgment at Kremenchug. His group fielded only 331 Panzers, 53 percent of its June 22 strength. Heavy rains delayed the offensive 24 hours and the two armies attacked on September 12. V Fliegerkorps flew air support from its new bases at Kirovograd and Uman while the II Flak Corps provided air defense and antitank fire for the advancing panzers.

An MG34 crew provides the infantry anvil to the panzer hammer on the western edge of the Kiev pocket. The three-man section includes a section leader, a *Feldwebel* (left), who wears the Infantry Assault badge, and an *Obergrefreiter* first gunner (center) and assistant gunner. (NARA)

Hube's 16th Panzer Division led the way with the 9th Panzer Division alongside pulling the corps behind them. Supported by *Nebelwerfer* (*Stukas zu Fuss*), the XLVIII surprised the Soviet forces and covered 43 miles in 12 hours. The II/2 Panzer Regiment overran the 38th Army headquarters building and the commander, now Major General Feklenko, evaded capture by jumping out of a window. With von Stülpnagel, pushing toward Poltava, covering its eastern flank First Panzer Group made for a rendezvous with Guderian.

Closing the Trap

Most Red Army units now had farther to go to escape eastward than the German forces did to close the trap. Sensing their impending doom, the defense stiffened on each tip of the closing jaws. Model's men required two days to fight their way through Romny. On September 13 his 3rd Panzer Division raced the final 30 miles to the outskirts of Lokhvitsa, the planned link-up point with Army Group South.[28] Coming up from Kremenchug, the 16th Panzer Division collided with fanatic NKVD defenders in Lubny. Hube personally led the fighting through the town. V Fliegerkorps contributed by isolating the pocket, keeping the skies free of Red Army Air

---

28   Due to von Kleist's delay moving out the OKH moved the rendezvous point 30 miles south to Lokhvitsa.

The Kiev Pocket

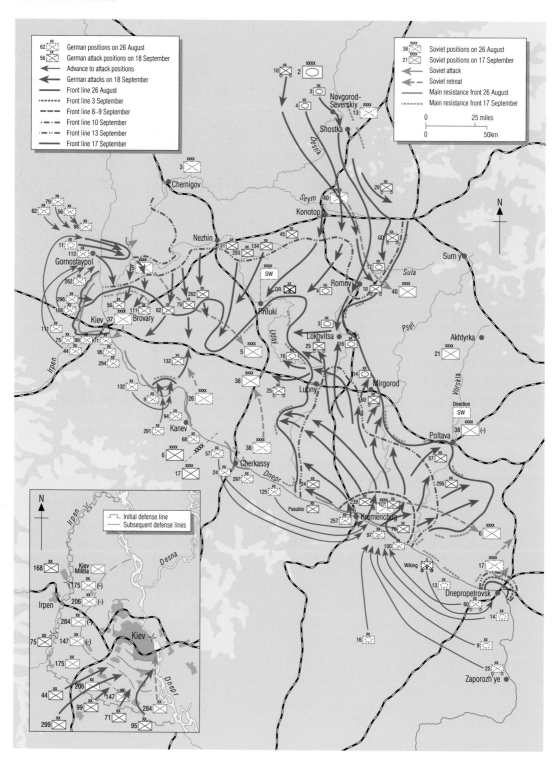

Legend (German):
- 62 — German positions on 26 August
- 56 — German attack positions on 18 September
- Advance to attack positions
- German attacks on 18 September
- Front line 26 August
- Front line 3 September
- Front line 8–9 September
- Front line 10 September
- Front line 13 September
- Front line 17 September

Legend (Soviet):
- 38 — Soviet positions on 26 August
- 21 — Soviet positions on 17 September
- Soviet attack
- Soviet retreat
- Main resistance front 26 August
- Main resistance front 17 September

0 — 25 miles
0 — 50km

Inset legend:
- Initial defense line
- Subsequent defense lines

Place names: Chernigov, Novgorod-Severskiy, Shostka, Konotop, Nezhin, Sum'y, Gornostaypol, Kiev, Brovary, Priluki, Romny, Lokhvitsa, Akhtyrka, Kanev, Lubny, Mirgorod, Poltava, Cherkassy, Kremenchug, Wiking, Dnepropetrovsk, Zaporozh'ye

Rivers: Irpen, Desna, Seym, Sula, Psel, Uday, Vorskla, Dnepr

Inset: Kiev, Irpen, Kiev Militia

Scorched earth: a supply dump burns on the horizon as the Red Army abandons Kiev on September 20. The Dnepr River is in the foreground. (NARA)

Force aircraft and by preventing enemy escape. Hube crossed the remaining 25 miles to Lokhvitsa and Guderian's men, officially sealing the Kessel at 1820hrs on September 14.

That same day Marshal Shaposhnikov reminded Southwest Front "you must fulfill comrade Stalin's order of September 11" to stand and fight. The dictator and Kirponos literally debated the issue over the tickertape as the trap closed. Even after Minsk, Smolensk, and Uman Stalin was still disrespectful or ignorant of the blitzkrieg's speed. Around Lokhvitsa the panzer men at once turned and stood back-to-back anticipating both immediate breakout and relief attempts.

The Soviet Union's senior leadership continued its now moot debate over abandoning Kiev. Just days into his command of the Southwest Direction Timoshenko began to show signs of the strain. He sent his chief of staff, General I.Kh. Bagramian, into the pocket to tempt Kirponos to initiate a mass escape. Knowing the realities of Stalinism, Kirponos demanded "documentary" proof from Stavka. That finally arrived from Shaposhnikov on September 17 at 2340hrs: "Supreme commander [Stalin] authorizes withdrawal from Kiev." But it made no mention of actually escaping the trap nor where the Southwest Front was supposed to go.

Early the next morning Kirponos authorized his command to break out. He made the 37th Army his rearguard but Vlasov's troops never made it out of Kiev. Eventually over 15,000 men avoided the Kessel. Kirponos was not among them. He attempted to evade capture with 1,000 men of his staff and the 289th Rifle Division. German soldiers ambushed the column and killed the general near Shumeikovo on September 20.

Booby-traps started fires throughout Kiev soon after the Soviets abandoned the city. This event drastically affected Hitler's later thinking on taking Soviet cities. Here a German administrative building (note the swastika banner) goes up in flames. (Topfoto)

By that point the encirclement resembled a triangle with each side 30 miles long. Wehrmacht forces divided the battlefield into smaller pieces for easier digestion. The fight for the city proper began with the XXIX Corps' assault on September 16. The 71st and 296th Infantry Divisions led the way over the same heavily defended terrain as before. They soon saw the churches and citadel of Kiev's distinctive skyline. The 95th Infantry and III/StuG Regiment 77 contributed to the reduction of numerous bunkers and dug-in tanks. On the Soviet side, loudspeakers blared Stalin's speeches in order to properly motivate the defenders.

Fighting died away by September 24. That day explosions set off by remote control started fires that raged through Kiev for five days, killed many Germans, and served as a lesson to Hitler about the dangers of combat in large cities. Rear security duty fell to Group von Roques, consisting of three German and one Slovak security divisions plus five Hungarian brigades. They herded two-thirds of a million Soviet POWs who survived three months of war only to succumb to beatings, execution, starvation, disease, and the elements. For civilians the cruelty of the Nazi–Soviet War entered a new phase; with Axis troops shooting from the rim of the Babi Yar ravine 33,771 Jewish dead lay in pools of maroon below.

After three months of seemingly only pushing the Southwest Front back von Rundstedt achieved a major encirclement. The OKW War Diary gave the following account of Soviet prisoners and material losses. This does not include Red Army killed and wounded:

KIEV LOSSES

	POWs	Tanks	Artillery and Antitank Guns
Army Group South			
Pocket (Sept 11–26)	440,074	166	1,727
Kremenchug (Aug 31–Sept 11)	41,805	279	106
Gornostaypol (Sept 4–10)	11,006	6	89
Army Group Centre			
Since Gomel (Aug 20–Sept 10)	132,985	301	1,241
Pocket (Sept 11–26)	39,342	72	273
Total	**665,212**	**824**	**3,436**

A 50mm Pak 38 in action at the Berislav bridgehead on September 9. Its tungsten-core projectile could penetrate a T-34's armor and caused a redesign in the Soviet tank before the year was out. (NARA)

German He-111 bomber flies over the Soviet Black Sea port of Nikolaev. (Topfoto)

Black Sea Coast

Tyulenev's defenses held firm opposite the Eleventh Army and Rumanian forces, but after Uman the Soviet evacuation of Bessarabia and the western Ukraine began in earnest. Von Schobert crossed the Dniestr on a wide front, taking Balta in early August. Tyulenev received permission to evacuate the Trans-Dniestr and leave a garrison in Odessa. Marshal Antonescu (King Michael I of Rumania promoted him on August 23) volunteered his military to clear the Black Sea coast and capture Odessa.

Von Rundstedt issued Order No.5 on August 10, which listed three goals: 1) destroy Soviet forces escaping from Uman; 2) occupy the Dnepr's west bank; and 3) secure the Sixth Army's north flank. Hitler directed that von Kleist take the resource-rich Dnepr bend by direct route, sparing Tyulenev another encirclement. Although reinforced by Hungarians and Italians (both far to the rear and short on supply), First Panzer was too weak, too spread out and too low on supplies to mount an effective pursuit of Tyulenev's men. Von Kleist's diverse post-Uman objectives were Kremenchug

(III Panzer Corps), Krivoi Rog (XIV Panzer) and Nikolaev (XLVIII Panzer). Nikolaev fell on August 16. The LSSAH captured Kherson from Soviet marines on August 19 while the 22nd Infantry Division secured the 700-yard-long Dnepr bridge at Berislav for the Eleventh Army. While the battle for Kiev was going on Eleventh Army broke out of the Berislav bridgehead. Progress was slow at first but by September 17 German forces had cut off the Crimea from overland communications when they reached the Black Sea and Sea of Azov coasts.

Horse-drawn artillery and limber at the XXX Corps' bridgehead at Berislav. The 105mm M18 field howitzer was the standard German divisional gun. (NARA)

Rumanian General Headquarters issued Order No.31 for the assault on Odessa on August 8. The Fourth Army passed this mission primarily on to its 1st and 3rd Corps, with the 4th and 5th Corps initially supporting. Behind an impressive line of prepared defenses stood two rifle divisions and a cavalry brigade backed up by 249 guns under General G.P. Safronov. Support was also provided by 27 warships of the Black Sea Fleet. Rear Admiral G. V. Zhukov was in overall command of the garrison. The Rumanians outnumbered their Soviet counterparts 6:1 in infantry and 5:1 in artillery. Antonescu

SS wearing camouflage tops in village fighting, August 1941. (Nick Cornish at www.Stavka. org.uk)

pushed his men hard and between August 16 and 24 the first defensive belt had been penetrated with heavy losses to each side. Each army counterattacked violently as advance and loss were measured in hundreds of yards. By September 4 General N. Ciuperca admitted to Antonescu that his infantry was decimated. The German leaders sent specialist battalion reinforcements but five days later Ciuperca was relieved. Subsequent Axis assaults under General I. Jacobici generally weakened until finally coming to a halt on September 22. So far the Rumanians had sustained 31,552 casualties.

Renewed attacks began on October 2. By October 8 Rumanian units broke into the main defensive line. Rumanian losses were often two to three times those of the Red Army, another 39,301 men dead. The new offensive lasted ten days. While the Rumanians planned their final attack the Soviet forces abandoned the port. On September 29 Admiral Oktyabrsky suggested to Stalin that the Odessa's defenders might be of more use reinforcing the defenses in the Crimea rather than merely dying in place. Surprisingly, given

Pioneers of the XXVIII Army Corps assault Red Army fortifications near Slutsk on September 15 with a combination of flame throwers and explosives (note the pouches worn by three of the four men at left). This effectively marked the high-water mark of Army Group North's campaign. (HITM)

his frequent "no retreat" orders, the dictator agreed. For fear of being labeled "defeatist" no evacuation plans existed. But the Soviet leaders' careful arrangements avoided a repetition of the earlier disastrous water evacuation of Tallinn on the Baltic.

The new Coastal Army commander, General I.Y. Petrov (Safronov had suffered a heart attack), decided to abandon the port early, during the night of October 15/16. Approximately 86,000 men had been shipped out previously but on that last night 35,000 men, 1,000 trucks, and 400 guns left on 192 sailings. Only rearguards remained by 0200hrs. Engineers demolished port facilities and the last vessel cast off at 0510hrs. The Rumanians did not even realize the Soviet soldiers had escaped. During the siege the Rumanians suffered 96,000 casualties, almost equal to the Soviets' 102,000 and more than the 89,000 total German losses thus far in the entire Eastern campaign. The cream of the prewar Rumanian Army had perished. The survivors took out their revenge on the city's Jews, butchering 20,000 of them.

Summary

A generation earlier Ludendorff's staff had anticipated the near-impossible task of conquering Petrograd. Somehow Reinhardt thought he could rush into Leningrad and take the city by coup de main, similar to a matching bookend of von Manstein's earlier triumph against the smaller Dünaburg. By the time von Leeb was somewhat prepared for a serious attack, his staff could come up with nothing more imaginative than a frontal assault over the well-prepared Luga River defensive positions and the outlying towns to Leningrad's

A *Gefreiter* chalks up another "kill" on the radio sponson of an early model Sturmgeschütz III. The assault gun commander, an *Oberleutnant* wearing the field-gray panzer jacket of the Sturmartillerie, leans out of his hatch. (NARA)

southwest. Due to the delays, the German leaders were overcommitted to that option so could have hardly switched to the less dangerous, indirect approach represented by joining up with the Finns on the Svir River.

Meanwhile the region around and south of Lake Il'men was a constant distraction to the German leadership, bleeding off time and units plus the attention of commanders and staffs – all needed elsewhere. The key to the

The United States and *Barbarossa*

Prince Otto von Bismarck allegedly said that Americans speaking English was the supreme geopolitical fact of the modern era. Between *Barbarossatag* and Pearl Harbor President Franklin D. Roosevelt managed a significant redirection of US security policy, all the while being sensitive to the opinions of the American people and their elected officials in Congress plus outwardly trying to work within US neutrality laws. Early in his presidency Roosevelt was alert to the dangers of Imperial Japan and the Third Reich. Barely six months after taking office he opened back-channel negotiations with the USSR and the two proto-superpowers exchanged ambassadors before the end of 1933.

When *Barbarossa* was launched American diplomats in Moscow, military leaders, and rabidly anti-Communist career State Department officials at home gave the Soviet Union no chance to win. However, on June 23 Under Secretary of State Sumner Wells laid out two main pillars of American policy: common cause with any enemy of Hitler, and its "Europe first" strategy. A day later the president confirmed this view. Of course not all Americans supported this judgment, many believing that two murderous dictatorships slaughtering each other was in everyone's best interests. But as German armies racked up their first victories public opinion in the US softened.

In late July Roosevelt sent personal envoy Harry Hopkins to Moscow (via London) to take the pulse of the USSR. Stalin's honest but ultimately optimistic picture convinced the president's confidante of the wisdom of supporting the Soviet government. On the heels of the Moscow visit Roosevelt and Churchill met aboard warships in Argentia Bay, Newfoundland. Allied promises of support were a bit short on specifics for Stalin's taste but concrete aid to the USSR soon followed. Roosevelt had to first overcome

bureaucratic inertia in Washington before Lend-Lease aid, the main conduit for US support, began to flow eastward. With this in mind Roosevelt sent another New Deal associate, W. Averell Harriman, to Moscow between the twin disasters of the Kiev and Viazma-Bryansk battles. Basically American, British, and Soviet parties signed "no strings attached" protocols concerning support. Fortunately the USSR had plenty of gold bullion and critical natural resources with which to buy US aid.

The United States had less success trying to influence Germany's allies. Misjudging strength of the dysfunctional Pact of Steel, Roosevelt tried to keep Japan from attacking the Soviet Union's far east. He need not have worried; it had already decided to move south into the Pacific. Regarding Finland, many Americans supported Finland's attempts to recapture land lost during the Winter War. However, President Risto Ryti said his nation's goals were "…the defeat of the Soviet Army and complete crushing of Bolshevism…" Strategically and operationally Finland knew better than to venture too far into the Soviet Union, but it ignored American admonitions about going too far. Britain declared war on Finland, the US never did. The Americans also sympathized with Rumanian desires to recapture Bessarabia, yet Antonescu continued well past both the Prut River and Odessa.

The second half of 1941 marked Roosevelt's "undeclared, executive naval war against the Germans" that scared Hitler. This was the beginning of the Roosevelt–Churchill divide when the US decided to aid the Soviet Union directly and not through the British middle-man. It highlighted the shift of American strategy from continental/hemispheric security to global activism and leadership (the Washington–Berlin air distance was less than that of Washington–Rio de Janeiro).

investment of Lenin's city was the 5-mile wide toe-hold on the shores of Lake Ozero at Schlisselburg. By mid-August better-late-than-never reinforcements finally arrived from von Bock but were simply thrown into the meat grinder against Leningrad's defenses, which dated back to late June when Potapov first consulted a map. Exhaustion, losses, overstretch, and reality all conspired to bring a halt to this obvious but unprofitable course of action. With panzers and Stukas streaming back to the Moscow front in mid-September, what mobile formations von Leeb had left considered a race to the east to make Leningrad's entrapment less permeable.

After Smolensk maps of the Moscow axis usually reflect little change until *Typhoon*. This usually suggests the logistics pause which utterly failed to accomplish its intended purposes: losses were not made good, little maintenance was done. Any arrows on maps mainly show Soviet counterattacks, growing in number and boldness. Comparisons of German losses during periods of movement and combat consistently demonstrate the advantages of forward motion. It should come as no surprise therefore that the remnants of panzer spearheads at Yartseveo and Yelnia were magnets for Red Army assaults and very unhealthy for the Landsers holding them. Second Army and Second Panzer Group soldiers probably felt fortunate by comparison to be part of the Kiev operation.

In Hitler's mind the plunges southward by von Weichs and Guderian were logical steppingstones toward Kiev. At the end of July, as Smolensk and its ancillary battles were being cleaned up, von Bock had tempting targets 200 miles east (Moscow) and 200 miles south (the Southwest Front), but the German senior command indulged in a time-wasting contest of wills, particularly between Hitler and Halder. German strategic thinking could not keep pace with the fast-moving panzer formations on the battlefield. But German High Command moves confirmed Soviet leadership thinking that proved to be just as mistaken. Second and Third Panzer Group drives north and south appeared to them as evidence of von Bock's natural desire to firm up his flanks prior to the final frontal assault on their capital. To that end they made Yelnia a symbol at the door to Moscow.

While the German High Command's dysfunction definitely hamstrung *Barbarossa*, of greater significance for the generals was Hitler's deepening involvement in military decisions, the abrogation of traditional Prussian prerogatives over civilian authority, and their inability to pull together to achieve a common goal when threatened from the outside. The German leadership's self-inflicted command paralysis of late July and much of August is arguably the most critical nonoperational factor in *Barbarossa*'s failure. Following a month of stunning initial victories Germany's highest leadership figuratively shut down while Hitler worked through personal illness to impose his will on fractious and obstinate generals.

Von Rundstedt used the third period of the campaign to achieve a number of tasks essential for further prosecuting *Barbarossa*: 1) with the Second Army's help von Reichenau isolated the pesky 5th Army; 2) his men closed on the lower Dnepr along most of its length and crossed it in many places; and 3) farthest south they cut off overland communications to the Crimea. Even with all that success, the capstone of the army group's summer, if not all of *Barbarossa*, was the Kiev encirclement. Finally OKH coordinated the operations of two army groups into one massive battle. The Wehrmacht's effort was immense. In just one example, between September 12 and 21 V Fliegerkorps alone flew 1,422 sorties and dropped 625 tons of bombs. Of course the German forces were aided immeasurably by Stalin's intransigence. Their victory at Kiev attained many prerequisites for the Ostheer's continued advance. The massive amounts of material captured at Kiev permitted the German units increased mobility, although mopping up took until October 4. It is hard to imagine *Typhoon* or any other autumn maneuver being nearly as successful with the Southwestern Front intact in the Ukraine.

For a fleeting moment the Ostheer outnumbered the Red Army in the field but 1.5 million new recruits joined the defenders' ranks in October and November. Stalin put Timoshenko in charge too late to change the course of the battle. Regardless, his continual interference and imposition of so many controls from above contributed to the difficulties that plagued the Red Army. The dictator sacrificed Kiev in order to buy time to prepare Moscow's defenses, to him a more valuable locale. Another relative Soviet bright spot to arise from the Kiev fiasco was that once Stavka realized what was happening to Kirponos it allowed Tyulenev to withdraw the latter's Southern Front to the lower Dniepr, which it did in good order. Although historians will long debate the German leaders' Kiev/Moscow decision one thing is clear; the generals may have won history's greatest encirclement battle but they lost the battle for influence in Hitler's headquarters.

END GAME

September had been an eventful month for *Barbarossa*. The Kiev battle crowned the summer and would motivate the Ostheer through the autumn. Hitler could take comfort in the fact that in the Ukraine "his" operation had paid such handsome dividends. Now Halder and the generals who had been looking longingly at Moscow could execute "their" operation.

Army Group North had Leningrad cut off and in its sights, the Finns did not seem that far away to the northeast while to the southeast the boundary with von Bock finally looked solid after weeks of uncertainty. Von Leeb massed as many troops in the siege lines as he could muster while heavy weaponry moved into position to support them. He also prepared a separate force to attack through the Tikhvin and Volkhov resource areas and on to the Svir River. Few believed that Leningrad's large civilian population, much less its modern military garrison, could hold out long if denied overland contact.

After Kiev, in the south von Rundstedt's men saw only more open vistas before them. How could the Red Army possibly replace two-thirds of a million men and still create a viable defense of the eastern Ukraine? Many in Army Group South must have believed that fuel availability was their only limiting factor. But units detached for the Moscow attack and the weeks necessary to reduce and secure the Kessel were their first reality checks. When the army group moved out for the Crimea, the Don River and points beyond they discovered that their own logistics situation had grown only more tenuous east of the Dnepr and that Stavka had somehow managed to scratch together a force with which to defend the eastern Ukraine.

Von Bock now commanded the force he had always wanted and the mission other German generals had always hoped for. He had to cover the last 200 miles to Moscow in a campaign where others had gobbled up 200 miles in only a few days or a couple of weeks. The subordinate generals and the men under his command had proven themselves over and over during the past three months. In contrast, the prewar Red Army had ceased to exist after *Barbarossa*'s first weeks. Partially trained reserve forces supposed to back them up had perhaps survived another month at most. By the time they launched *Typhoon*, the German High Command reckoned that Soviet defenders now before Moscow would soon be outclassed, leaving the road open to their capital city.

However, three months into *Barbarossa* strategic overstretch was taking its toll on German operations; the Ostheer was on the defensive in many places just to create offensive forces at critical locations. German losses had also been horrendous and everyone knew it: generals at every echelon by looking at statistics and frontline soldiers by looking around them at shrinking numbers of men and vehicles present for duty each morning.

On the eve of *Typhoon* Soviet leaders had many problems themselves. Losses of men, weaponry, territory, industrial capacity, and natural resources had been staggering. No European nation had ever sustained such devastation and survived. Gone were the massive mechanized corps; henceforth counterattacks would be conducted by small tank brigades and untrained infantry masses. Gone also was any semblance of combined arms formations; for ease of command and control infantry and armor fought alone while combat-support elements such as antiaircraft artillery and engineers were removed and consolidated in standalone outfits.

But also gone, due to the harsh realities of modern combat, were legions of old and incompetent interwar leaders. In the USSR's state of extreme emergency Stalin had few qualms about molding the country's top leadership in his image. Germany and the Wehrmacht suffered from many self-limiting effects and these would greatly assist the USSR. But Stalin and Zhukov would team up in November to actively halt *Barbarossa* in its tracks.

Tikhvin and Volkhov

As the final assault on Leningrad played itself out, Stavka took seriously the threat that Army Group North might attempt to link up with the Finns. To reinforce the 7th Independent Army now holding the Svir River, it established the 54th, 52nd, and 4th Armies in or around Volkhov. It shifted one tank and eight rifle divisions to the sector. German reinforcements during the same period consisted of the 254th Infantry Division at Volkhov and the 61st at Tikhvin. However, Hitler remained unmoved. Although he only had the battered XXXIX Panzer Corps left for such a mission, he ordered an attack northward. Stalin also urged his commanders to attack to reopen communications with Leningrad. Accordingly, Marshal G.I. Kulik assembled 63,000 men in eight divisions supported by 475 guns and 59 new KV tanks to attack on October 20.

Typically, the German commanders moved more quickly than the Soviets and struck on the 16th. While General Schmidt departed to temporarily replace the ill commander of the Second Army, the XXXIX Panzer, presently under General of Panzer Troops Hans-Jurgen von Arnim, split the boundary between the 52nd and 4th Armies. Both sides fought hard for small villages to gain some shelter at night. Freezing weather caused a holocaust of horses, breaking the hearts of hardened Landsers over the suffering of their equine companions. With 12th Panzer and 18th and 20th Motorized Divisions leading the way, the Germans captured Mal Vishera within one week. The German advance stopped and started as the weather in turn thawed and froze the mud and ice amid terrain cluttered with forests, lakes, and swamps. By October 25 any advance was basically over. On the following day von Leeb flew to Führer Headquarters in a vain attempt to squeeze additional support from the dictator. Henceforth, the field marshal described successive attacking forces simply as "new victims." Despite his negativity, he nevertheless managed to change Hitler's mind and won support for continuing the attacks. Somehow the Germans crawled forward against the collapsing defense. Finally the German forces occupied Tikhvin on November 8. Approximately 20,000 POWs, 179 guns, and 96 tanks fell into their hands.

From then on the 126th Infantry, 20th Motorized, and 8th Panzer Divisions (all very weak) attempted to defend 60 miles of front in an exposed salient. Although Luftwaffekommando Tikhvin (KG 77 and II/JG 54) provided some air cover, despite miserable weather, the German forces reaped no benefit from their brief occupation of Tikhvin's bauxite mines. To

Donbas to Rostov

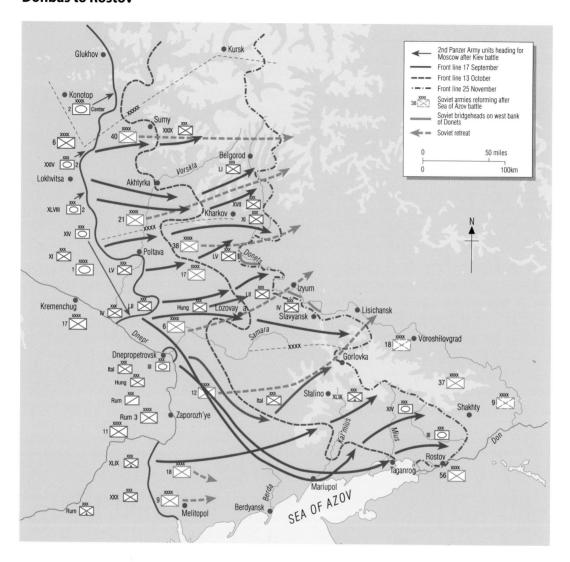

the northeast Group Boeckmann (I Army Corps, 11th and 21st Infantry Divisions, reinforced by the 254th) pushed to within 4 miles of Volkhov.

Tikhvin's beaten defenders fled and threatened to rout into the rear of the 7th Army facing the Finns. Kulik relinquished command and was soon executed. Stalin put 7th Army commander General K.A. Meretskov (just released from NKVD prison) in charge of the shaky 4th Army as well, with instructions to get positive control of the situation.

The Battles for Tikhvin and Volkhov

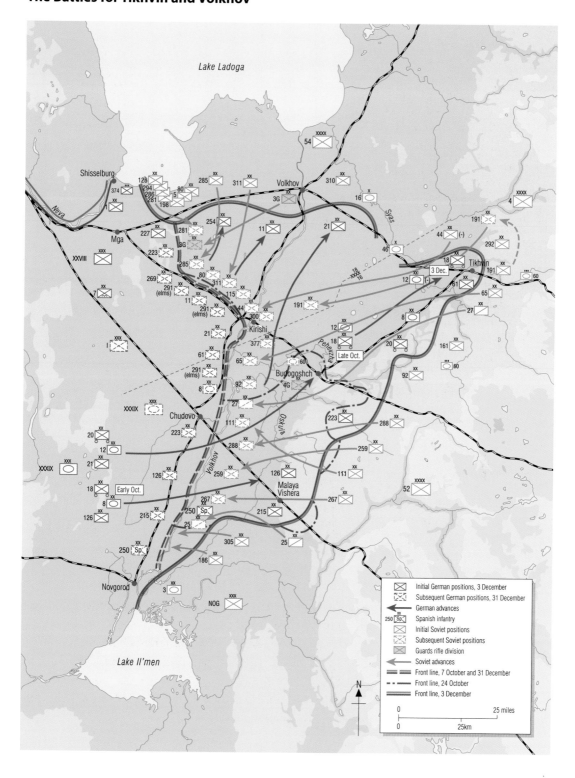

Lake Ladoga

Shisselburg

Neva

Mga

Volkhov

Syas

Tikhvin

3 Dec.

Kirishi

Pchevzha

Budogoshch

Late Oct.

Chudovo

Oskura

Malaya Vishera

Volkhov

Early Oct.

Novgorod

NOG

Lake Il'men

	Initial German positions, 3 December
	Subsequent German positions, 31 December
	German advances
250 Sp	Spanish infantry
	Initial Soviet positions
	Subsequent Soviet positions
	Guards rifle division
	Soviet advances
	Front line, 7 October and 31 December
	Front line, 24 October
	Front line, 3 December

N

0   25 miles

0   25km

The thick forests, wet marshes, and primitive infrastructure encountered during the latter part of Operation *Barbarossa* constituted ideal terrain for the Red Army's cavalry. Their 25th and 27th Cavalry Divisions actively participated in the Staraya Russa and Tikhvin operations. (NARA)

Stalin resolved to take the offensive along the entire front. With the Wehrmacht's main striking forces concentrated around Moscow, he would attack on the two flanks. Marshal Timoshenko would lead the assault in the south around Rostov. In the north the Germans' vulnerable salient at Tikhvin looked like a target of opportunity. According to Stavka's plan the 54th Army (Lieutenant General I.I. Fedyuninsky) would attack around Volkhov, the 4th under Meretskov would reduce the Tikhvin salient as the main effort, while the 52nd (Lieutenant General N.K. Klykov) plus the Novgorod Operational Group would advance in the south. Their overall goal was nothing less than reopening the Tikhvin–Leningrad railway and the destruction of all German forces east of the Volkhov River. At one point during the second half of October, Luftwaffe reconnaissance noted about 2,000 vehicles reinforcing the Volkhov Front.

The Red Army intentionally used staggered starts for its attacks. The 52nd Army began in the south on November 12, with Meretskov launching the primary assault on the 19th. The 52nd Army's attack produced meager results but forced the German forces to react by committing precious reserves. In the center Meretskov caused von Leeb the most concern. As the latter noted in his diary on November 22, "Tikhvin is more or less encircled." He knew he had to assemble a counterattack force and regain the town. The best he could do was rush in Haenicke's much-traveled 61st Infantry Division.

Some 28 German divisions faced 75 Soviet, many of the latter fresh. By December 3, XXXIX Panzer Corps reported it could no longer defend Tikhvin against the 4th Army. On the 6th Hitler still insisted the town be held, but the very next day von Leeb told the 61st Infantry to prepare to withdraw. That same night, December 7, he authorized the town's evacuation, telling the Führer over the phone of his "very painful duty to report that Tikhvin, over which we've fought and occupied for weeks, must regrettably be given up." Hitler approved the move *post facto* at 0200hrs the next morning.

Near Volkhov the Soviet 54th Army drove the I Army Corps south before it. A general withdrawal began as the Red Army hounded German rearguards. By mid-December Army Group North was back on the Volkhov River, where it had been two months earlier. Von Leeb tried to put a good face on his men's accomplishments during *Barbarossa* in his Christmas Order of the Day: 438,950 POWs, 4,590 guns, and 3,847 tanks captured or destroyed in five months. However, it was clear to all that the invasion, begun with such high hopes in June, had culminated without Army Group North accomplishing its objectives.

German army logistics elements lagged far behind combat units, and were often relegated to the worst "roads" – with dire consequences, given the Wehrmacht's heavy reliance on horse transport. It was not only the mud of the autumn and spring rainy seasons that imprisoned wagon wheels and wore down horses; the choking dust and deep, concrete-hard ruts of summer were also destructive. (HITM)

Operation *Typhoon*

In September, Army Group North arrived in the suburbs of Leningrad and severed the city from land communications. At Kiev, Army Group South, with the help of Second Army and Second Panzer Group, won history's greatest encirclement battle: two-thirds of a million men were trapped in a Kessel the size of Belgium and the Ostheer outnumbered the Red Army for the first and only time in World War II. The German forces had paid a price, but to most of the world it looked as if the campaign would continue to go their way; their victory at Moscow was assumed.

Planning for *Typhoon*

For once the German leadership anticipated events, and Hitler issued his order for the final assault on Moscow almost ten days before the trap around the Southwest Front slammed shut at Lokhvitsa. On September 6 his Directive No.35 stated that the successes of the flanking army groups had created the "prerequisites for conducting a decisive operation against Army Group Timoshenko, which is conducting unsuccessful offensive operations against Army Group Center's front." Hitler went on to instruct von Bock:

Landsers with mix of Kar-98 rifles and MP-38 machine pistols clear an intact village. (Topfoto)

launch an operation against Army Group Timoshenko as quickly as possible "so that we can go on the offensive in the General direction of Viazma and destroy the enemy in the region east of Smolensk by double envelopment… After destroying the main mass of Timoshenko's group of forces in decisive encirclement and destruction operations, Army Group Center will begin pursuing enemy forces along the Moscow axis.

The OKH staff added its Directive for the Continuation of Operations four days later with Halder in the uncommon (but insincere) role of team player. Von Bock's staff had shelved an earlier plan to attack Moscow because of the Kiev operation. On September 16 he issued his reworked *Typhoon* operations order for three panzer groups making three thrusts; in addition to the stalwart Hoth, Guderian would come back after concluding the Kiev operations, and from Army Group North he would later receive Hoepner's Fourth Panzer Group (XXXXI and LVI Panzer Corps, totaling three panzer, two motorized, and two infantry divisions). As on *Barbarossatag*, von Bock paired the panzer groups with field armies to ensure better coordination at the breakthrough points. *Typhoon's* mission was to destroy the West, Reserve, and Bryansk Fronts, and to prevent the enemy from retreating in good order to Moscow.

As usual, the German commanders could not complete their plan without debate. Von Bock wanted a deeper encirclement east of Viazma, while many favored a shallower one aimed at that city. For example Hoth argued against the deep option simply because he had so few panzers and trucks, so little fuel and Luftwaffe support. After closing the pockets Halder wanted to send the motorized units into Moscow, but Hitler wanted no part of urban combat, as he had made clear earlier at Kiev and Leningrad. Also, attempts to coordinate *Typhoon* with an attack by von Leeb toward Lake Il'men with Sixteenth Army, and with a movement by von Rundstedt on Kharkov with Sixth Army, met with mixed results.

For a month now Army Group Center had fought a relatively static battle, so it had accurate tactical intelligence on Soviet strength and dispositions; it identified 80 of the 83 Soviet rifle divisions to its front (typically, FHO identified only 54 of them.) Even in this static situation, German logistics were still unsatisfactory: despite large depots at Gomel, Roslavl, Smolensk, and Toropets they could only sustain a short burst towards Moscow. Panzer serviceability rates were also a problem: they stood at 50 percent for Guderian, 70–80 percent for Hoth, and 100 percent only for Hoepner. Prior to *Typhoon* 4th Panzer Division, for example, received as replacements only 30 PzKpfw IIIs and five PzKpfw IVs (creating a total of 110 operational tanks), and only enough fuel to travel 60 miles.

With von Brauchitsch, Halder, and Kesselring in attendance, von Bock hosted a conference on September 24 to wargame *Typhoon* with his six subordinate army and panzer group commanders. Fourth Army and Fourth Panzer Group in the center represented *Typhoon's* Schwerpunkt. Typically, logistics were falsely assumed to be adequate. The vaunted logistics pause that was supposed to precede the final Moscow offensive did not have the desired results because of near-constant fighting. However, Hitler's generals did convince him to release 60 PzKpfw38 (t)s, 150 PzKpfw IIIs, and 96 PzKpfw IVs panzers plus 3,500 wheeled vehicles from Führer reserve on September 15.

Most subordinate commands issued their orders on the 26th. For *Typhoon*, Army Group Center mustered 1,929,000 soldiers in 56 infantry, 14 armored, and eight motorized divisions; together they counted 14,000 indirect-fire weapons and 1,000 tanks, and the Luftwaffe contributed 1,390 aircraft. Not wanting to take any chances on the weather, Guderian obtained permission to begin his assault two days early.

Soviet Preparations

The Soviet leaders did not know it yet but they would soon regret expending so much energy and so many men assaulting von Bock in attacking during late summer. On September 10, four days after the issue of Führer Directive 35, Stavka ordered forces facing Army Group Center to halt their attacks and take up the defense. By then the average strength of many rifle divisions stood at only about 3,000 men. Since mid-July the Soviets had been building and improving works to defend their capital. The most important of these, Zhukov's anchor, the Mozhaisk Line, was 40–50 percent complete by September 30, and the same could be said for the other three Fortified Regions: Volokolamsk, Maloyaroslavets, and Kaluga.

The Soviet High Command had expected the "final assault" on Moscow around late August, and had allowed themselves to be lulled into a false sense of security since then. They would use a new defensive technique in the autumn, concentrating on roads and settlements, knowing that the German troops would need exactly those. But on the other hand, they also assumed, given the imminent *rasputitsa*, that Hitler would not launch a major offensive following the Kiev battle. Further, they thought that the Germans still had most of their panzers near Leningrad and Kiev. Red Army intelligence missed the movement of much of Fourth Panzer Group from von Leeb, and the return of Second

Panzer Group plus some of von Kleist's First Panzer Group from von Rundstedt.

Stalin's High Command knew that after Kiev there would be no more trading space for time before Moscow. However, with the correlation of forces all wrong it is no surprise that they also defended the wrong places. They expected the main thrust directly at Viazma along the Minsk highway. Von Bock's strikes on either side of the main defenses, and Guderian's thrust south of Bryansk, caught them completely off guard. As one blunt post-Soviet Russian history put it:

> Stavka failed to divine the German intentions... it issued its warning of an impending attack too late, and when it did, it never ordered the Reserve Front to prepare its defenses.[29]

From north to south, Colonel General Konev commanded the West Front (22nd, 29th, 30th, 19th, 16th, and 20th Armies) along a line 210 miles long. Budenny's Reserve Front (24th and 43rd Armies) guarded 60 miles of the front, while his 31st, 49th, 32nd, and 33rd Armies stood to the rear. On the southern flank, Yeremenko's Bryansk Front (50th, 3rd, and 13th Armies plus Operational Group Ermakov) covered 180 miles. Many of these armies had been fighting since June 22, and their headquarters, units, and men had been encircled and/or escaped encirclement many times. Owing to losses incurred at Viazma–Bryansk (see below) many of the defending units would be militia divisions, although some of these had been fighting since Yelnia.

Logistics problems plagued the Red Army also. Ammunition, transport and repair capacity, fuel, and aviation gas had all been used up during the "Timoshenko Offensive." Many *frontoviki* lacked winter clothing – it was not only the German forces who failed in this regard. However, while von Bock had literally no reserves for *Typhoon*, at least the "beaten" Red Army had husbanded some.

While Landsers in the foreground trudge past below a Panzer III, signal troops set up a radio with telescoping antenna. (HITM)

---

29   Hayward, *Before Stalingrad*, p.138.

Fully 40 percent of the entire Red Army between Leningrad and the Black Sea defended Moscow: 1,250,000 men (including 193,000 new soldiers) manned 83 rifle, 2 mechanized, one tank, and nine cavalry divisions plus 13 tank brigades. Sixty-six rifle divisions occupied the first echelon, with 17 rifle divisions and seven tank brigades behind them, and 12 rifle divisions and six tank brigades stood in reserve. They were supported by 7,600 guns, 990 tanks, and 863 aircraft (perhaps two-thirds of them operational).

On September 26, Konev reported that the German troops were preparing to attack across his front on October 1. This news completely surprised Stalin, who issued another defensive directive the next day. By the end of September the Soviet leaders were confident that their system could respond, survive, and probably not collapse. On the other hand, so far the German forces had always succeeded. By the end of the Moscow battle only one of these two statements would still be true.

Viazma and Bryansk

"Fast Heinz" Guderian lived up to his nickname when he moved out on September 30, two days before the rest of Army Group Center. Outside the ancient Ukrainian capital of Glukhov he hit the unprepared Operational Group Ermakov and scattered its five divisions, soon creating a 13-mile gap between Ermakov and 13th Army. Nevertheless Yeremenko called the attack "only a diversion" and "not critical." Ermakov rallied his forces to counterattack a day later, but he did not have much impact because of the usual failings: poor coordination, too few tanks, and no air support. However, by nightfall 3rd Panzer Division had its first experience with Katyusha rockets, dogs trained to run under tanks with explosives fixed to their backs, and almost undetectable wooden-cased, antitank mines.

Since the rest of the front seemed to be quiet, Yeremenko and the High Command considered Guderian's assault a diversion – fog and rain limited Luftwaffe activity, further deceiving the defenders. Nevertheless, Stavka began moving reserves toward the point of rupture, probably in homage to Guderian's reputation, but they were soon to find that the real danger lay to the north. To complicate matters they had no clear picture of events, since Luftwaffe raids soon cut Yeremenko's communications.

On October 2 (Paul von Hindenburg's birthday), Ninth and Fourth Armies created penetrations in the Soviet defenses in trench-fighting involving bayonets, hand grenades, sidearms, and spades; by the end of that day 260th Infantry Division alone had overcome 120 bunkers. The

Viazma and Bryansk

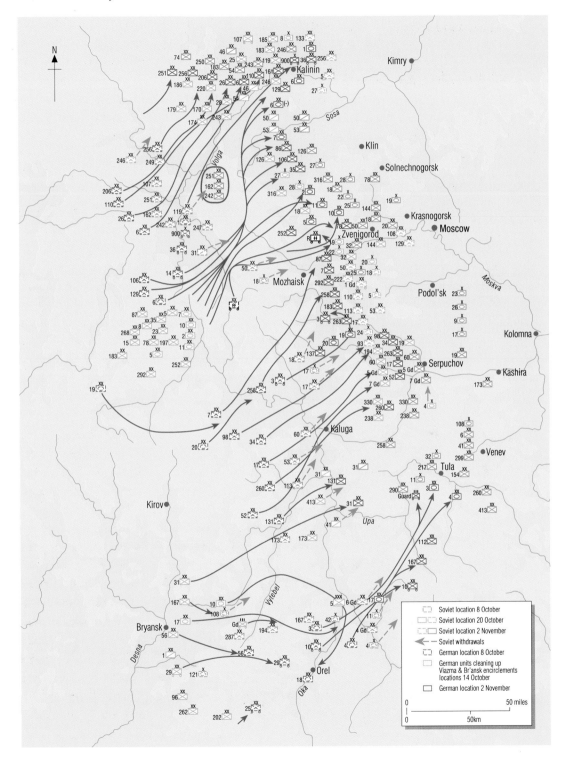

Map legend:

- Soviet location 8 October
- Soviet location 20 October
- Soviet location 2 November
- Soviet withdrawals
- German location 8 October
- German units cleaning up Viazma & Br'ansk encirclements locations 14 October
- German location 2 November

0 — 50 miles
0 — 50km

Locations labelled on map: Kimry, Kalinin, Klin, Solnechnogorsk, Krasnogorsk, Moscow, Zvenigorod, Mozhaisk, Podol'sk, Kolomna, Kashira, Serpuchov, Kaluga, Venev, Tula, Kirov, Bryansk, Orel

Rivers: Volga, Sosa, Moskva, Upa, Vytebel, Desna, Oka

A horse sunk up to its shoulders: what were these wagon drivers thinking? The horse will be lucky to get free and not die of exhaustion or hypothermia. (Nik Cornish at Stavka.org.uk)

infantry often reoccupied the same Yelnia battlefields that they had given up a month earlier.

Hoth's and Hoepner's armor exploited through the gaps; it took the latter only two hours to overcome the River Desna defenses. The 7th Panzer Division's artillery preparation amounted to 130 tubes per mile, while their 300 tanks spread across a 1½-mile front in two waves. On day one Third Panzer Group split 19th and 30th Armies apart, while the Fourth Panzer smashed 43rd Army in Budenny's first echelon and hit the 33rd Army behind it. Over Hoth's men flew four fighter and attack *Geschwader* (wings).

Konev ordered Boldin to counterattack against Hoth's right flank with the 126th and 152nd Rifle and 101st Motorized Divisions plus the 126th and 128th Tank Brigades (total tank strength approximately 300). Hoth was already miles to the east and Boldin's strike hit thin air. Yeremenko pleaded with Shaposhnikov to employ a mobile defense but the chief of staff ordered him instead to maintain a "stubborn defense of manned defensive lines." Naturally this played right into von Bock's hands. Since Stavka had already taken Guderian's bait and sent its reserves south it had nothing with which to counter the real danger.

Within 24 hours of launching *Typhoon* von Kluge began to interfere by ordering Hoepner, already 50 miles into the Soviet rear, to redirect XLVI Panzer Corps northward along the boundary of the Bryansk and Reserve Fronts in order to create a smaller encirclement west of Viazma. The field marshal tried to redirect XLVI Panzer Corps northward in order to create a smaller encirclement west of Viazma. This amounted to yet another dangerous dispersion of armor that was intended to be employed in mass. Kesselring, who had known Hoepner since the two had served together in World War I, considered the panzer general "shaken" and with "little confidence."

The bulk of Fourth Panzer Group, including 5th Panzer Division (new to the theater and originally earmarked for Africa – so many of its vehicles still wore their desert paint scheme), raced up the road toward Yukhnov. Soviet fighter pilots reported this movement, but Marshal Shaposhnikov demanded repeated confirmation, and by the time he was satisfied, the town had already fallen. Unsurprisingly, a couple of days later the same man, referring to the developing Viazma–Bryansk battles, said they were "…no basis for disquiet."

Logistics reared its ugly head when, after breaking into Konev's second-echelon 32nd Army, Hoth literally ran out of fuel on October 4 and his spearhead required Luftwaffe resupply. He could not move again until the 5th while Konev used that small pause to request permission to retreat from the quickly developing trap. Konev reported the potential danger to Moscow, "Stalin listened to me, but made no decision." He therefore ordered a relief assault toward Viazma against the German flanks, by Boldin from the north and Rokossovsky's 16th Army from the south. That night Stavka allowed Konev to begin retreating out of the encirclement. (In unrelated events, Hoth had now left for Army Group South to command Seventeenth Army; Reinhardt took command of his Third Panzer Group while Model in turn moved up to XLI Panzer Corps.)

The following morning Konev told 16th and 19th Armies to exfiltrate eastward, an order repeated to the rest of the West Front on October 7. He ordered Rokossovsky – unrealistically – to hold Viazma as the rear guard. These

Lieutenant General K.K. Rokossovsky, in a still from a Soviet propaganda film, at his 16th Army headquarters northwest of Moscow. He managed to survive torture during the Red Army purges of the 1930s to be recalled for service following the Winter War debacle. (Topfoto)

Meissen Porcelain struck this medallion to commemorate the Viazma–Bryansk Kessel: Left – An Iron Cross with an oak leaf wreath. The inscription reads: The German People Thank their Brave Soldiers. Right – A map of the battlefield framed by the count of captured booty: 657,918 prisoners, 1,214 tanks, eight Soviet armies, 4,396 guns. The inscription reads: Double Battle of Bryansk and Viazma in October 1941. (Author's Collection)

measures were too late: on the morning of the 7th, Reinhardt's 7th Panzer Division met Hoepner's 10th Panzer at Viazma. On that same day, October 7, Zhukov made a tour of the various Front headquarters and he could not have liked what he saw. Therefore General Lukin, who had only escaped from Smolensk two months earlier, was now placed in charge of forces inside the Viazma pocket, with the mission of breaking out through the weak 11th Panzer Division cordon toward Gzhatsk during the night of October 10/11.

Things did not go so well for the German troops in the south. The original mission of Second Army was to cover von Kluge's right flank and let Guderian trap Yeremenko. But, as before at Minsk and Smolensk, Guderian cared less about closing off encirclements than driving on Moscow. He remained focused on the city, without worrying about his exposed flanks – believing that the Southwest Front to his right was too weak after Kiev to mount serious resistance. Von Weich's slowness and Guderian's neglect conspired to slow the Bryansk (southern) half of the triple envelopment. Eventually Second Army picked up its pace and Guderian finally sent his XLVII Panzer Corps (17th and 18th Panzer Divisions) around the east side of Bryansk. On October 5 the panzers cut the rail connection from Moscow, the front's lifeline; the next day they almost captured the Bryansk Front headquarters (Yeremenko and his adjutant escaped). Two days later they linked up with Second Army north of the city. The second, incomplete Kessel had finally closed.

Reducing the huge encirclements bought the Soviet forces a breather and cost the Germans casualties and time. The outlines of the Kessels were often somewhat random and certainly not based on ideal defensive terrain. Breakout attempts were expected and violent: escapees climbed over mountains of their own dead. German soldiers stripped warm clothing off of Soviet dead and POWs. Conditions inside *Barbarossa*'s Kessels were horrendous. According to David Stahel those of Viazma–Bryansk were worst.

At Viazma and Bryansk the German forces destroyed seven of 15 Soviet armies, 64 of 95 divisions, 11 of 15 tank brigades, and 50 of 62 artillery regiments. They listed 6,000 guns and mortars and 830 tanks destroyed, killed approximately 332,000 Red Army soldiers – including three army commanders – and marched 668,000 into captivity. Soviet numbers do not significantly dispute these claims. However, the walls of the German trap were porous: approximately 85,000 men escaped from Viazma and another 23,000 from Bryansk. Although they had lost their heavy weapons, these men – plus another 100,000 escapees from 22nd, 29th, and 33rd Armies and Group Ermakov – lived to fight another day, and trickled east to occupy Moscow's various defensive positions. The German commanders wondered how the Soviet forces were able to find new units to keep throwing into the front lines. Their own casualties at Viazma–Bryansk amounted to 48,000 men.

Until November

Von Bock issued his order for the continuation of operations on October 7.[30] In the north, Ninth Army and Third Panzer Group would advance on Rzhev and Kalinin (in addition to moving toward Rybinsk and making contact with Army Group North); in the center Fourth Army would make for Maloyaroslavets and Kaluga, while Hoepner aimed for Mozhaisk; to the south, Guderian (his command now renamed Second Panzer Army) would drive on towards Tula with Second Army in support. However, all this had to wait until the two encirclements were cleared, a task requiring two-thirds of the army group and between one and two weeks. Additionally, Army Group Center's logistic woes prevented it from continuing sustained operations. So, just when von Bock had rent a 300-mile hole in the Moscow defenses, behind which the Soviet forces could muster scant reserves, he had to slow down to await reduction of the two pockets and to reconsolidate his army group.

---

30   On the same day Hitler ordered that no Germans were to enter Leningrad, Moscow, or other major city, casting doubt on his desire to actually occupy Stalin's capital.

Two Germans supporting each other in October. According to the caption, they are suffering shell shock following bombardment by Katyusha rockets. It is clear from the looks on their faces that *Barbarossa* possessed little glory for them. (Nik Cornish at Stavka.org.uk)

Stage II of *Typhoon* also had to contend with worsening weather. Rain began to fall in the southern sector on October 6 and elsewhere a day later. Luftwaffe sorties dropped 90 percent from 1,400 on October 6–7 to 139 on the 9th. Supplies could not come forward and the wounded could not be evacuated. Nevertheless, that same day Halder was optimistic about the chances of encircling Moscow. For a few hours those odds lengthened dramatically, as Hitler toyed with the idea of sending Guderian and von Weichs south toward Kursk. Although he scrapped the idea within hours, this is further proof of the minimal importance the dictator placed on Moscow – even at this late date, and the corresponding value he attached to destroying the Red Army. After all, many German commanders assumed that they had eliminated Soviet forces defending Moscow at Viazma and Bryansk, and should therefore concentrate on the flanks.

Simultaneously in the Kremlin, Zhukov told Stavka that "the chief danger is that all routes to Moscow are open and the weak protection along the Mozhaisk line cannot guarantee against the surprise appearance of enemy armored forces before Moscow." Having just arrived from Leningrad, he recommended massing all available forces along the Mozhaisk. The Soviet High Command therefore created the Moscow Reserve Front under Moscow Military District commander Lieutenant General P.A. Artemev, to hold the positions Zhukov suggested – now determined to be Moscow's principal line of defense.

Destined to play a critical role in the defense along the Moscow axis, General Zhukov (second from left) and staff doing the work of all good field commanders – planning with a map. (Elukka)

On October 10, Third Panzer Group moved toward Kalinin with the Ninth Army covering its left. Their mission was to join up, lever the Northwest Front off the Moscow–Leningrad railway, then turn southeast against the capital itself. The defending 22nd and 29th Armies put up a good initial defense, but 1st Panzer Division entered Kalinin on October 14. As had happened often during *Barbarossa*'s later phases, the German forces soon discovered taking a city and holding it were quite different. Now that Kalinin had been captured, Reinhardt could turn right and either initiate a deep encirclement of Moscow or roll up the Mozhaisk line from the north.

It took Northwest Front Chief of Staff N.F. Vatutin one day to organize a counterattack force of two rifle and two cavalry divisions plus a tank brigade, but fighting around Kalinin lasted two full weeks as both sides poured units into the battle. By the end of October neither had the energy to go farther. VIII Fliegerkorps occupied recently abandoned airfields around Kalinin, only to see its aircraft blasted by Soviet artillery. Meanwhile Zhukov dispatched Konev to command the new Kalinin Front, which basically connected that city with Moscow along the Volga.

"Stalin is with us!" A ski battalion marches through Moscow to the fighting front, late in *Barbarossa*. After Viazma–Bryansk few Germans believed that the Soviets could continue to put fresh units in their path. (Topfoto)

On the old Napoleonic battlefield at Borodino two regiments of the newly arrived Siberian 32nd Rifle Division plus 18th and 19th Tank Brigades tried to halt 10th Panzer and SS Reich Divisions (supported by half a company of Brandenburgers). On one night the commander of a company from 98th Infantry Division requested permission to attack. The regiment asked, "Attack where?" The lieutenant answered, "It doesn't matter where, we're freezing and need quarters!"

Due west of Moscow, as part of Operation *Schneesturm* (Snowstorm), Army Group Center assaulted the new Moscow Reserve Front, specifically 16th Army at Volokolomsk, 5th Army at Mozhaisk, 43rd Army at Maloyaroslavets and 49th Army at Kaluga. By October 16 all four had been defeated. These setbacks could have meant the end of the Moscow defenses, but instead the Soviet resistance stiffened. In about ten days during mid-October the forces defending the critical Mozhaisk positions grew from six rifle divisions, a like number of tank brigades and ten artillery regiments, to 14 rifle divisions, 16 tank brigades, and over 40 artillery regiments. These defenses were not simply a single thin line but reached in depth all the way to Moscow. With the Luftwaffe expending little effort on interdiction since mid-October, the capital's railway system provided an easy way to reinforce the Mozhaisk positions.

Part way through the battle Stavka merged Artemev's command with the West Front. On the southern flank, Guderian's progress slowed dramatically when XXIV Panzer Corps ran out of fuel and was then stopped completely at Mtsensk by the 1st Guards Rifle Corps. Earlier, in three days the Red Army Air Force airlifted 5,500 men to Orel under Stalin's express orders. After Kiev, parts of the Second Army, especially its rear services, were still struggling north during mid-October, so could not contribute fully in this sector. Luftwaffe Ju-52 transports refueled Guderian by dropping supplies since they could not land in the mud. At the end of the month 60 men from Grossdeutschland shot their way into Tula, but were thrown out within hours, never to return. The southern edge of that city marked the temporary limit of Guderian's advance.

As of October 14, von Bock still believed that there were no Soviet units defending Moscow. Inside the capital panic set in, despite directives signed by Stalin and Shaposhnikov on October 8 and 9. On the 12th the State Defense Committee put Moscow in a state of siege under NKVD control. Additional militia and "destroyer" units (local defense and security) were raised, and 440,000 workers were armed. Some government agencies evacuated the city for points east, and foreign embassies were advised to leave as well. However, on October 19 Stalin issued a directive meant to halt the panic once and for

The crew of a 2cm Flak gun build a fire to keep warm while guarding a bridge near Mozhaisk. As often happened, retreating Soviets demolished the original bridge, only for German engineers to build another right next to it. (Author's collection)

all. In mid-July Hitler had boasted that Moscow "must disappear from the face of the earth." Three months later, Stalin resolved to stay put and defend his capital. The dictator's determination heartened the *frontoviki*: "Stalin is with us!" Both dictators staked their all on the fate of the city.

Exhaustion set in on both sides, and the Mozhaisk line marked the end of *Typhoon*. After the encirclements at Viazma and Bryansk the Ostheer continued successfully to exert pressure on the Red Army defenses, but achieved no breakthroughs. A stalemate developed along the front, German morale rose a bit, and an unofficial truce between the two sides began, somewhat like in the trenches during Christmas, 1914. Hitler could not bring himself to assault Moscow frontally through its primary defenses, such as they were, and vainly sought a decision on the flanks.

In the north, although Third Panzer Group's occupation of Kalinin caused the Soviet leaders consternation, the maneuver represented just another dilution of German efforts; the distances from Viazma to Kalinin and Viazma to Moscow were the same 120 miles, but the effects of going in two different directions were enormous. In the south, for the third time during *Barbarossa*, Guderian had put personal goals ahead of organizational ones – on this occasion by his sloppy completion of the Bryansk Kessel, and still he could not get appreciably closer to Moscow.

At the time and since German commentators have used the autumn weather as an excuse for *Typhoon*'s failure, as if the *rasputitsa* was unpredictable. In fact, rainfall in 1941 was slightly below average for October and less than half an inch above average for November. The temperature in 1941 was even 2°(F) lower than the average for October, and only 3.5°(F) colder than average for November. Conversely, the frost came a little early in 1941, an advantage for the German troops. This does not mean that the wet and cold did not affect operations; they absolutely eliminated the possibility of a fast advance on Moscow after Viazma and Bryansk. But solid German staff work would have prepared the Ostheer better for the entirely predictable weather.

With predictable results at Viazma and Bryansk Stalin for the third time was going to throw the dice; he had already lost twice at Minsk and Smolensk. At each turn along the Moscow axis he had underestimated the speed and violence of the blitzkrieg, while overestimating the benefits of standing fast in immobile defenses. Likewise, after four months of hard lessons the Red Army still could not mount effective countermeasures against German armored spearheads.

Soviet defenses toughened noticeably by the time the Red Army occupied the Mozhaisk positions. Zhukov knew that thanks to the entirely unsurprising weather he could concentrate along the few all-weather roads. Rumors were reaching the *frontoviki* about the treatment of earlier Red Army captives at the hands of the Wehrmacht, so surrender became completely unattractive. In mid-October (the exact date is unknown) Stalin heard from his master spy in Tokyo, Richard Sorge, that Japan would not help Germany against the USSR, but was heading south toward the Philippines and Indonesia instead. Soon one division from the Soviet Far East was arriving near Moscow by rail every two days; by the end of the month an additional 13 rifle divisions and five tank brigades were present. German intelligence failed completely to identify this build-up. Rastenburg, OKW, and OKH simply could not believe that after Kiev, Viazma and Bryansk, and all its other disasters the Red Army had anything left to put in their path before Moscow.

The Crimea and Eastern Ukraine

With the Kiev Kessel no longer in doubt, on September 21 von Rundstedt received orders for continuing *Barbarossa* southeast of the Dnepr. Next stops: the Donbas and Crimea. Von Kleist would make for Rostov, the Eleventh Army would capture the Crimea, the Seventeenth was to aim for Voroshilovgrad via Kharkov while von Reichenau would cover its left flank to Belgorod and the Don River beyond.

The Crimea

In mid-September, with the Sixth and Seventeenth Armies and First Panzer Group at the Kiev Kessel and the Rumanian Fourth Army besieging Odessa, von Rundstedt dispatched the Eleventh and Third Rumanian Armies toward the Crimea. Geologically, a massive alpine fold created the 10,000-square-mile peninsula and its 5,000-foot mountains. It has a tradition of cultural uniqueness and dominates the Black Sea. Hitler wanted to eliminate this "aircraft carrier" targeted on Ploesti (though the USSR lacked strategic air capability) and gain a stepping stone to the Caucasus. He also wanted to woo Turkey into joining the Axis cause.

Meanwhile Tyulenev tried to re-establish a coherent defense in the wake of Uman. He had 20 rifle, one tank, and several cavalry divisions to hold the Dnepr line from above Dnepropetrovsk to its mouth at Kherson. On August 19 Stavka gave him the job of containing German bridgeheads at Dnepropetrovsk, Berislav, and Kherson. One week later D.I. Rybyshev replaced the wounded Tyulenev as Southern Front commander.

To Perekop

The Eleventh Army had progressed slowly for the entire campaign. It suffered isolation from the remainder of the army group, devoted much effort to keeping the Rumanians out of trouble and provided flank cover for the Seventeenth Army. Von Schobert kept his corner of *Barbarossa* advancing in as high morale as circumstances allowed. On September 9 von Rundstedt's headquarters ordered the Eleventh Army to seize the Crimea and cover the army group's flank along the Sea of Azov. The Eleventh had begun expanding its Berislav bridgehead days before.

Von Schobert, killed when his Fiesler Storch liaison aircraft landed in a Soviet minefield east of Berislav on September 12, never got a chance to carry out his new orders. That same day Rybyshev began pulling back to a shorter line running due south of Zaporozhe. The Reconnaissance Battalion of the LSSAH tried to capitalize on the confusion by dashing across the 50 miles to the Perekop Isthmus in a surprise move. It failed but in so doing discovered the Soviet defenses were much more sophisticated than expected.

Attending von Schobert's funeral at Eleventh Army headquarters in Nikolaev on September 17 was its new commander, von Manstein, newly arrived from the Leningrad Front. While he might have to work to match his predecessor's popularity he brought new energy to the Eleventh (and the Rumanian Third Army, under its operational control). Although it took weeks to implement, one of von Manstein's first tasks was to convince his superiors the army couldn't seize the Crimea and cover the army groups' flank, and that taking the Crimea had precedence. Penetrating the defenses of the Perekop represented his most immediate concern.

The isthmus has two narrow, easily defended chokepoints, one 5 miles wide near the town of Perekop and another near Ishun that, while technically wider, is broken up by numerous bitter lakes. The Russians had created a massive moat 150 feet wide and up to 60 feet deep with an earthen bank behind it. This was known as the Tartar Ditch. Two other routes connected the peninsula with the mainland but were not militarily significant.

The Soviet 51st Independent Army commander was Lieutenant General F.I. Kuznetsov (formerly facing Army Group North). He had four rifle and two cavalry divisions in his frontline with two rifle and one cavalry division to the rear. Defense lines were between 5 and 7 miles deep and were augmented by bunkers, minefields, and over 100 tanks. Field artillery, naval gunfire, and air support were in abundance. With Luftflotte 4 occupied at Kiev and Odessa, the Black Sea Fleet easily re-supplied the

ABOVE 46th Infantry Division assaults the Tartar Ditch, September 24, 1941. Pioneers advanced through barbed-wire entanglements and other obstacles with Bangalore torpedoes, improvised demolition charges (**1**), and wire cutters. Landsers advanced alongside the pioneers, providing covering fire but they took heavy casualties despite support from German artillery, Stukas (**2**), and assault guns. The squad shown here are equipped with a mixture of M1934 Karabiner 98k rifles (**3**), MP38 (**4**) and MP40 (**5**) sub-machine guns, and MG34 light machine guns (**6**). They are also supplied with the ubiquitous M1924 stick-grenade (**7**). Scaling the earthen rampart with assault ladders (**8**) the Pioneers got close enough to employ flamethrowers (**9**) and satchel charges against enemy bunkers and fighting positions (**10**) and defensive positions began to fall silent one by one. (© Osprey Publishing, Howard Gerrard)

defenders without interference. By contrast, von Manstein's railhead was way back at Pervomaysk (near Uman) and more to the point, the German forces were considerably outnumbered.

East of the Dnepr the Ostheer entered the legendary steppe. According to von Manstein's plan the XLIX Mountain and XXX Corps would chase the 18th and 9th Armies toward Melitopol while the LIV Corps was ordered to Perekop. In a move that presaged Operation *Blau* in 1942, General P. Dumitrescu's Rumanians would cover the army's extended left. After LIV Corps achieved its breakthrough, the Third Army would relieve the XLIX Mountain Corps, allowing the *Gebirgsjäger* to exploit into the Crimea's interior.

Cossacks with horse artillery in the age of mechanization. Troopers wear the *Kubanka* caps and *Cherkeska* caftans. As Soviet vehicle losses continued to rise, various cavalry forces had to provide the Red Army with a mobile capability. (NARA)

Storming the narrows fell to the 46th and 73rd Infantry Divisions backed up by all the combat support von Manstein could assemble: one assault gun and 20 artillery battalions plus *Nebelwerfer*. The Landsers attacked on September 24. The watchwords were infiltrate and bypass Soviet strongpoints. Within a day the men of Hansen's LIV Corps reached the Tartar Ditch. Punished by Stukas and counterbattery fire, Red Army artillery slackened. The German troops negotiated the moat and wall on September 26. It took two more days to break the first defensive belt.

Battle of the Sea of Azov

However, the final thrust into the Crimea would have to wait. In one of those coincidences of timing common in war, the Southern Front attacked against von Manstein's left during the last week of September. Between 10 and 13 Rifle divisions created a 10-mile gap in the Rumanian Third Army's lines, through which poured two tank brigades. Von Manstein moved his headquarters away from Perekop and north-eastward to reassure Dumitrescu. He also turned the XLIX Mountain Corps 180 degrees. Instead of punching into the Crimea it marched northeast to bolster the shaky Rumanian line.

Von Manstein personally intervened on numerous occasions as the situation became tense. Rain hampered the movement of German reserves. The Soviet attack soon stalled from a combination of poor coordination, limited objectives, and German resistance. Not actively involved at Kiev, von Mackensen's III Panzer Corps watched these developments from its Dnepropetrovsk bridgehead. A great opportunity arose for a decisive German counterstroke. On September 25 von Rundstedt issued Order No.9 directing von Mackensen south along with the XIV Panzer Corps driving out of the CSIR's Petrikovka salient to von Mackensen's northwest. After crossing the Oryol and Sarmara rivers, the panzers' objective was Berdyansk on the Sea of Azov.

They completely outmaneuvered the Soviet forces. Departing on October 1, XIV Panzer Corps on the right and III Panzer Corps swinging left cut Southwest Front's communications. Under blue skies von Kleist's men (he had lost XLVIII Panzer Corps to

Commander of the 1st Mountain Division, Major General Lanz, near Nikopol around the time of the Sea of Azov battle. The 1st Mountain performed masterfully on the flat steppe and consistently led the Seventeenth Army. (NARA)

Guderian after Kiev) put the 18th and to a lesser degree the 9th Armies in grave danger. By October 3 both armies were retreating and the Eleventh took up the chase. Two days later III Panzer Corps occupied Melitopol, the First Panzer Group became First Panzer Army, and Y.T. Cherevichenko took over Southern Front. On October 7, XIV Panzer Corps and the LSSAH joined hands at Berdichev and sealed the trap. The 9th and 18th Armies were crushed with a loss of over 106,000 POWs captured plus 212 tanks and 766 guns of all descriptions put out of action. The Germans buried 18th Army commander Smirnov with full honors. Von Manstein redirected his attention back to the Perekop.

Battle of the Sea of Azov

26 September–7 October 1941, viewed from the southwest, showing the abortive offensive by the Red Army's Southern Front and the devastating German counterattack that crushes the Soviet 9th and 18th Armies and captures over 100,000 men.

3. 26 September: Soviet 9th and 18th Armies attack Eleventh Army's north flank. Although some Rumanian units give way, the Red Army assault is too weak to threaten a major breakthrough.

5. 28–29 September: "LSSAH" and 1st Mountain Division halt the Soviet attack.

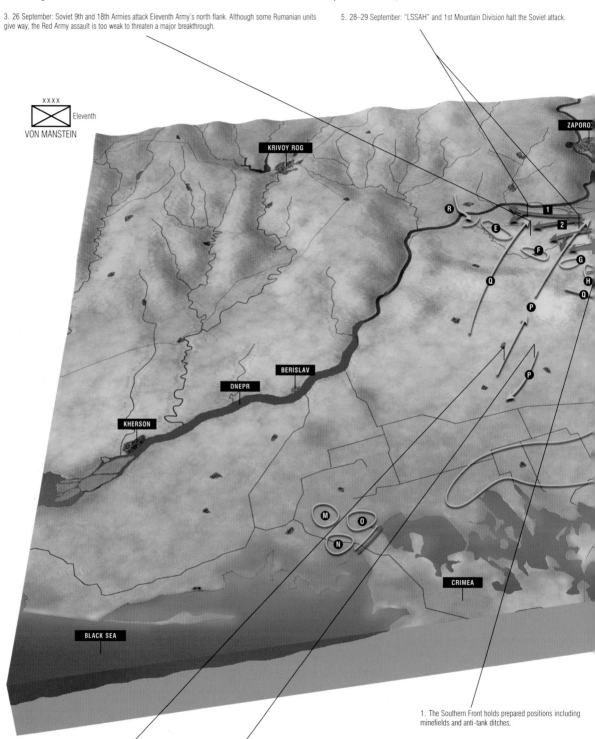

XXXX
Eleventh
VON MANSTEIN

KRIVOY ROG

ZAPORO

R
E
1
2
F
G
Q
H
Q
P
P

BERISLAV

DNEPR

KHERSON

M
O
N

CRIMEA

BLACK SEA

1. The Southern Front holds prepared positions including minefields and anti-tank ditches.

4. 27/28 September: Von Manstein orders 1st Mountain Division to about face to prepare to attack into the Soviet flank.

2. 26/27 September: Eleventh Army dispatches 1st Mountain Division to Perekop to act as an exploitation force in the Crimea. Rumanian Third Army relieves XLIX Mountain Corps in a supposedly "quiet" sector.

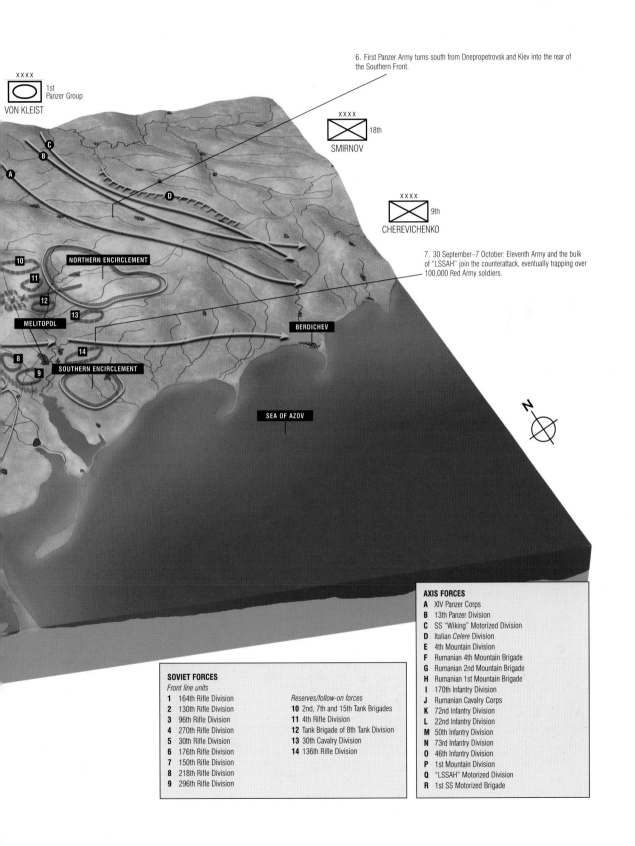

6. First Panzer Army turns south from Dnepropetrovsk and Kiev into the rear of the Southern Front.

xxxx
1st
Panzer Group
VON KLEIST

xxxx
18th
SMIRNOV

xxxx
9th
CHEREVICHENKO

7. 30 September–7 October: Eleventh Army and the bulk of "LSSAH" join the counterattack, eventually trapping over 100,000 Red Army soldiers.

NORTHERN ENCIRCLEMENT

MELITOPOL

BERDICHEV

SOUTHERN ENCIRCLEMENT

SEA OF AZOV

N

SOVIET FORCES

Front line units

1	164th Rifle Division
2	130th Rifle Division
3	96th Rifle Division
4	270th Rifle Division
5	30th Rifle Division
6	176th Rifle Division
7	150th Rifle Division
8	218th Rifle Division
9	296th Rifle Division

Reserves/follow-on forces

10	2nd, 7th and 15th Tank Brigades
11	4th Rifle Division
12	Tank Brigade of 8th Tank Division
13	30th Cavalry Division
14	136th Rifle Division

AXIS FORCES

A	XIV Panzer Corps
B	13th Panzer Division
C	SS "Wiking" Motorized Division
D	Italian *Celere* Division
E	4th Mountain Division
F	Rumanian 4th Mountain Brigade
G	Rumanian 2nd Mountain Brigade
H	Rumanian 1st Mountain Brigade
I	170th Infantry Division
J	Rumanian Cavalry Corps
K	72nd Infantry Division
L	22nd Infantry Division
M	50th Infantry Division
N	73rd Infantry Division
O	46th Infantry Division
P	1st Mountain Division
Q	"LSSAH" Motorized Division
R	1st SS Motorized Brigade

Conquest of the Crimea

Von Kleist took over responsibility for the Sea of Azov coast and von Manstein gave him XLIX Mountain Corps and the LSSAH as part of the deal. The Eleventh Army now had to conquer the Crimea with six infantry divisions and the promise of two more plus the small Rumanian Mountain Corps. His forces were half as strong as the 51st Army, now reinforced by the Odessa garrison (minus its heavy equipment left on the mainland). Von Rundstedt convinced Göring to provide three fighter and two Stuka *Gruppen* under Colonel Werner Mölders, the first Luftwaffe ace to both surpass the Red Baron and reach 100 victories. Mölders would land his Storch a few hundred meters behind the fighting and act as the forward air controller.

Kuznetsov had improved his positions during the battles around Melitopol. Meanwhile the flat, barren terrain offered no cover to von Manstein's men and any fighting positions they dug soon filled with salty water since the dry ground was barely above sea level. Hansen's LIV Corps again led the assault. The wider Ishun line allowed him to attack with three divisions, albeit at reduced strength because of the Perekop and Melitopol fighting. The XXX Corps would act as the exploitation force.

Artillery and *Nebelwerfer* opened up at 0540hrs on October 18 and Stukas joined in at sunrise. Without the additional CAS, Soviet fire would have obliterated the German forces as they worked through the nine defensive lines (6 miles deep) securing gaps between the saltwater lakes. After a day's progress on the east, that wing ground to a halt. Von Manstein therefore switched his Schwerpunkt to his right. About this time the weather turned wet, hindering German efforts to bring supplies forward while Odessa's displaced veterans continued to arrive and reinforce the defenses. By October 25 Hansen claimed his corps was combat ineffective. Von Manstein would not hear of it, "There's no such thing for a division to be finished."

Red Army forces had suffered as well, notably from Mölders' CAS. Kuznetsov's men finally broke on October 26. They had no more prepared positions south of the isthmus and the retreat turned into a rout. On the 29th Soviet authorities declared a state of siege throughout the parts of the peninsula they still controlled. By the next day the front cut through the Crimea's center. Kuznetsov lost coordination between his east and west. The 51st Army made for Kerch while the Coastal Army (formerly in Odessa) headed for Sevastopol. Since von Manstein now had no motorized units, surprise moves were out of the question. Accordingly his infantry kept marching until the Soviet forces decided to halt and face about. By early

November the XXX and LIV Corps stood in the foothills northeast of Sevastopol, which was defended by three divisions and the remnants of four others. At the Parpach Isthmus the newly assigned LXII Corps faced portions of five divisions. The Rumanian Mountain Corps held the partisan-filled mountains and coastline in between.

Soviet sailors near Kerch on the far eastern tip of the Crimea. Sailors and marines were in the thick of it whenever the fighting got close to a coastline, or especially, a naval base. (Corbis)

The 51st Army in the east simply could not organize effective resistance. By November 3 the XLII Corps had slipped around the defenders and captured the port of Feodosia. Denied that escape route, Kuznetsov tried to reach the larger port of Kerch at the far eastern tip of the Crimea. XLII Corps took the town despite heavy fighting on the 15th, preventing further Soviet escape. In eight weeks the Eleventh Army had captured over 100,000 POWs and 797 artillery pieces of every description. But with Sevastopol unbowed to the west von Manstein would not be crossing over to the Taman Peninsula to execute Halder's grandiose expedition to the Caucasus.

Sevastopol

Similarly to what the British did at Singapore, during the interwar period the USSR prepared Sevastopol for an attack from the sea. But in late 1940 and especially during the siege of Odessa they prepared for a land assault as well. They built three concentric defensive lines, respectively 1–2, 3–5, and 10 miles from the harbor. Over 3,000 bunkers interspersed with nearly 140,000 mines, antitank ditches, and trenches linked massive forts mounting naval caliber guns. Over 100 Red Army Air Force aircraft and the Black Sea Fleet made the defense a truly joint operation.

Not only did von Manstein's infantry lack any motorized units (except ad hoc formations created by consolidating vehicles from existing units), but steep mountains and deep ravines surrounding Sevastopol also slowed their advance. Attacker and defender prepared for the inevitable. It was vital that Eleventh Army utilize the available logistics as effectively as possible and von Manstein used economy of force elsewhere on the peninsula in order to concentrate against the fortress. LVI Corps represented the main effort coming from the north and northeast while the XXX Corps supported from the south.

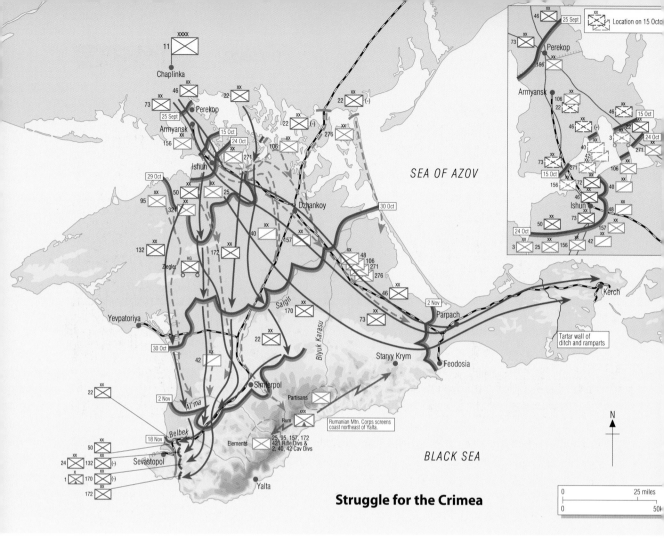

Struggle for the Crimea

Von Manstein planned to begin his assault at the end of November but terrible weather pushed the attack to 1942 – a date beyond the scope of this book. Von Manstein's infantry was in a weakened state after five months of campaigning plus German logistics between the Dnepr and Sevastopol, 400 miles distant, were in a shambles. Eleventh Army could not attack the fortress and fight partisan bands that sprung up everywhere, especially in the Yalta Mountains. His Luftwaffe support departed to first Moscow and then the Mediterranean. The USSR regained air superiority while the Black Sea Fleet proved capable of both resupplying the beleaguered garrison and conducting amphibious operations along the Crimean coast.

Having been denied the military honors of von Rundstedt's other armies the Eleventh finally had its chance to shine in September and October. Outnumbered on the ground it succeeded, with the help of von Kleist's panzers

in fending off an attack by two Soviet armies at Melitopol, with Luftwaffe assistance, in penetrating two well-prepared, narrow, and deep defensive positions at Perekop and, finally in clearing Red Army forces from the entire peninsula except for Sevastopol. If von Manstein had possessed even a single mechanized division with which to race into the fortress ahead of the marching Soviets, the battle for the Crimea might have been over much sooner.

Rear Admiral Oktyabrsky aboard the cruiser *Krasny Krym* (Red Crimea). The Black Sea Fleet commander was also in overall charge of the defense of the Crimea and Sevastopol and led numerous joint operations. (NARA)

Kharkov to Rostov

Processing and sending Kiev's 660,000 POWs into captivity took weeks and delayed Sixth and Seventeenth Armies. Their next objectives were the industrial areas of Kharkov and Stalino. Believing the Soviet forces would continue to defend every yard of territory Hitler expected other encirclements near these two cities. First Panzer Army aimed for Rostov. The Third Reich was already short of oil and the German High Command felt it had a good chance of reaching the Caucasus in 1941.

Meanwhile Stavka sought to stabilize its southern flank. The Soviet Union also depended on the steady flow of Caucasus oil and Western supplies now coming through Iran. Stalin had been anxious to regain the strategic initiative since *Barbarossatag*. With much of the Ostheer tied down in November facing Moscow's defenses he was keen to open offensives on either flank.

Sixth and Seventeenth Armies

Finally, on October 6 von Reichenau advanced with some difficulty through Achtyrka and Sumy while the Seventeenth Army moved south from Poltava with the Hungarian Fast Corps (now down to six battalions strength) as its mobile reserve. Shattered by the Kiev battles, the Soviet forces could not organize a coherent defense. Von Rundstedt fired von Stülpnagel, who in turn was replaced by Hermann Hoth. After some tough going near Krasnograd the new commander pushed the Seventeenth toward Lozovaya, which fell after two days' fighting. Hoth then split his army between the twin objectives of Izyum on the left and Stalino on the right. Again the fast-marching Seventeenth tried mightily to compensate for the fact that Army Group South had only one panzer army with only two panzer corps. The Sixth Army headed for Kharkov as the Soviet defenders struggled to offer more than token resistance. Von Reichenau's men likewise worked hard to maintain contact with Army Group Center on their left.

Late in the second week of October wet weather and poor logistics conspired to stop the Ostheer. Combat had destroyed all Dnepr bridges and now ice floes threatened pontoons erected by German engineers. European-gauge railroads would not reach far enough until the end of November. Hitler stepped in on October 14 and instructed both infantry armies to cooperate against Kharkov. While this might guarantee capture of Kharkov it simultaneously weakened the German effort in the Donbas and compromised Hoth's protection of First Panzer's lengthening northern flank. The Führer had lost confidence in von Reichenau, however, after the latter's uncertain leadership during *Barbarossa's* first months. It took three days of heated discussions before the generals convinced Hitler to allow the Seventeenth Army to continue toward the Don River undistracted and for the Sixth Army to capture Kharkov alone.

Von Kleist in an impromptu conference with Italian General Giovannelli, commander of the Pasubio Division. (Topfoto)

Stavka had no intention of allowing another massive encirclement at Kharkov and withdrew Red Army units. Improving weather in the third week of October meant increased mobility for the German troops. On October 19 German intelligence reported the enemy was "fighting without any enthusiasm and running away." While the German Seventeenth Army battled the Soviet 38th Army southeast of Kharkov, von Reichenau curled around the north, defeating the nine Soviet divisions defending the city on the 24th. Hoth labored with his army going in three directions and the Hungarian Fast Corps as his only mobile reserve. Soon bad weather intervened again to halt the German advance.

The Seventeenth Army crept forward. Their "pursuit detachments" consisted of infantry on native panje wagons. The Donbas defenders were a true Workers and Peasants' Red Army as 150,000 industrial and farm worker militia members joined regular army forces. Fighting was slow and costly in the heartland of prewar Soviet heavy industry. The German forces did manage to tap into the oil pipeline from Baku, acquiring many days of diesel fuel. Hoth eventually occupied most of the middle Don. The Sixth Army never made it much past Kharkov and Belgorod. For von Rundstedt's infantry the invasion ended.

The Battle for Rostov

17 November–3 December 1941, viewed from the southwest showing the see-saw battle around the strategic city of Rostov as German forces push forwards into an exposed salient and then, overstretched, are driven back to the line of the Mius River by Timoshenko's counteroffensive.

GERMAN FORCES

A	1st Mountain Division
B	Slovakian Motorized Division
C	SS "Wiking" Motorized Division
D	16th Panzer Division
E	60th Motorized Division
F	14th Panzer Division
G	"LSSAH" Motorized Division
H	13th Panzer Division
I	4th Mountain Division
J	138th Infantry Division
K	Italian *Celere* Division
L	IV and V Fliegerkorps
M	German airfields

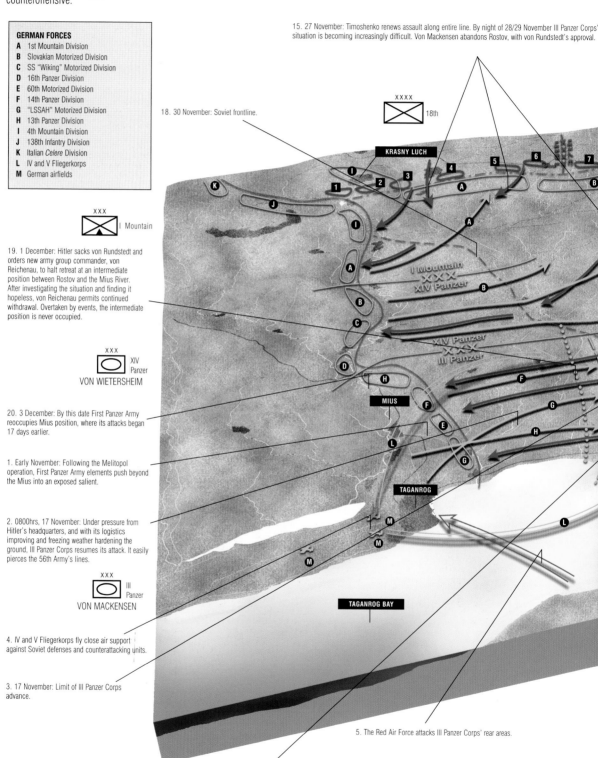

15. 27 November: Timoshenko renews assault along entire line. By night of 28/29 November III Panzer Corps' situation is becoming increasingly difficult. Von Mackensen abandons Rostov, with von Rundstedt's approval.

18. 30 November: Soviet frontline.

XXXX 18th

KRASNY LUCH

XXX I Mountain

19. 1 December: Hitler sacks von Rundstedt and orders new army group commander, von Reichenau, to halt retreat at an intermediate position between Rostov and the Mius River. After investigating the situation and finding it hopeless, von Reichenau permits continued withdrawal. Overtaken by events, the intermediate position is never occupied.

XXX XIV Panzer
VON WIETERSHEIM

20. 3 December: By this date First Panzer Army reoccupies Mius position, where its attacks began 17 days earlier.

1. Early November: Following the Melitopol operation, First Panzer Army elements push beyond the Mius into an exposed salient.

2. 0800hrs, 17 November: Under pressure from Hitler's headquarters, and with its logistics improving and freezing weather hardening the ground, III Panzer Corps resumes its attack. It easily pierces the 56th Army's lines.

XXX III Panzer
VON MACKENSEN

I Mountain
XXX
XIV Panzer

XIV Panzer
XXX
III Panzer

MIUS

TAGANROG

TAGANROG BAY

4. IV and V Fliegerkorps fly close air support against Soviet defenses and counterattacking units.

3. 17 November: Limit of III Panzer Corps advance.

5. The Red Air Force attacks III Panzer Corps' rear areas.

8. 18 November: 56th Army counterattacks 13th Panzer Division and "LSSAH".

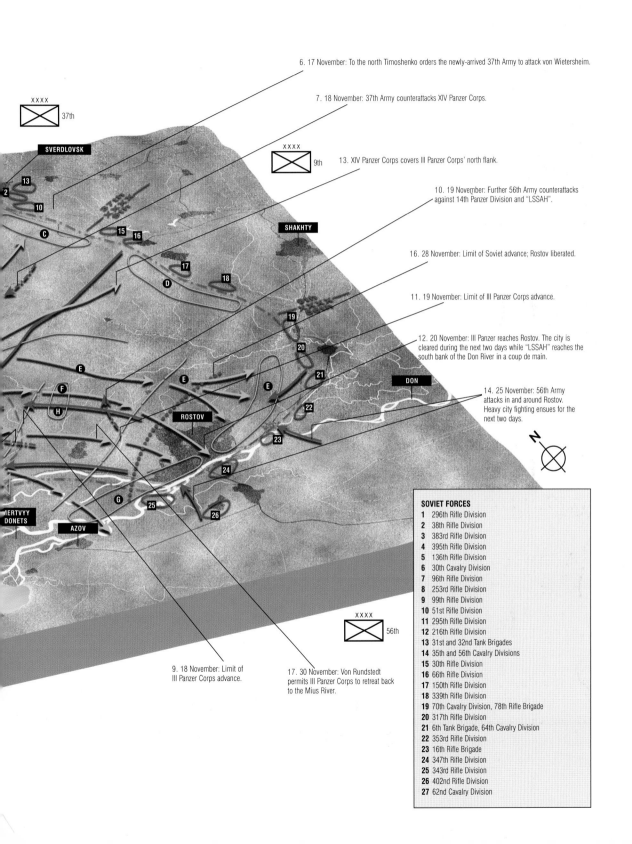

6. 17 November: To the north Timoshenko orders the newly-arrived 37th Army to attack von Wietersheim.

7. 18 November: 37th Army counterattacks XIV Panzer Corps.

13. XIV Panzer Corps covers III Panzer Corps' north flank.

10. 19 November: Further 56th Army counterattacks against 14th Panzer Division and "LSSAH".

16. 28 November: Limit of Soviet advance; Rostov liberated.

11. 19 November: Limit of III Panzer Corps advance.

12. 20 November: III Panzer reaches Rostov. The city is cleared during the next two days while "LSSAH" reaches the south bank of the Don River in a coup de main.

14. 25 November: 56th Army attacks in and around Rostov. Heavy city fighting ensues for the next two days.

9. 18 November: Limit of III Panzer Corps advance.

17. 30 November: Von Rundstedt permits III Panzer Corps to retreat back to the Mius River.

XXXX 37th

SVERDLOVSK

XXXX 9th

SHAKHTY

DON

ROSTOV

MERTVYY DONETS

AZOV

XXXX 56th

SOVIET FORCES

1	296th Rifle Division
2	38th Rifle Division
3	383rd Rifle Division
4	395th Rifle Division
5	136th Rifle Division
6	30th Cavalry Division
7	96th Rifle Division
8	253rd Rifle Division
9	99th Rifle Division
10	51st Rifle Division
11	295th Rifle Division
12	216th Rifle Division
13	31st and 32nd Tank Brigades
14	35th and 56th Cavalry Divisions
15	30th Rifle Division
16	66th Rifle Division
17	150th Rifle Division
18	339th Rifle Division
19	70th Cavalry Division, 78th Rifle Brigade
20	317th Rifle Division
21	6th Tank Brigade, 64th Cavalry Division
22	353rd Rifle Division
23	16th Rifle Brigade
24	347th Rifle Division
25	343rd Rifle Division
26	402nd Rifle Division
27	62nd Cavalry Division

Panzer Advance to Rostov

With First Panzer Army almost ineffective due to losses and lack of supply von Rundstedt recommended halting and taking up winter quarters.[31] No one in higher headquarters supported such a move. Von Kleist's role in the battle of the Sea of Azov ideally placed his panzer army for continued operations toward Rostov. With von Manstein now exclusively concerned with the Crimea, First Panzer had sole responsibility for the army group's right. After Kiev von Kleist reinforced Guderian's Second Panzer Army with the XLVIII Panzer Corps and in compensation received the XLIX Mountain Corps and the LSSAH. He arrayed his forces from north to south thus: CSIR, XLIX Mountain Corps, XIV Panzer Corps, III Panzer Corps, and finally the SS along the Azov coast.

Even before completing the Melitopol operation von Kleist consolidated all available fuel and pushed his right across the Mius River. Likewise, to conserve aviation gas the Luftwaffe flew only single-engine aircraft such as Bf-109s and Stukas. On the 20th the 1st Mountain Division captured Stalino, thoroughly ruined consistent with the Soviet High Command's scorched earth policy. Shortly afterwards the Italians took the Rykovo–Gorlovka area. On October 22 Army Group South issued its Directive No.10 for the final assault on Rostov.

The XIV Panzer Corps' tracked elements represented von Kleist's main effort. Von Wietersheim's men crossed the Mius at Golodayevka in early November. Aided again by bad weather commencing on November 7, the Red Army dug in south of the Tuslov River. In view of the increased resistance, the Schwerpunkt switched to von Mackensen. North Caucasus Front activated the 56th Independent Army under Lieutenant General F.N. Remezov to defend Rostov and the lower Don. The 37th Army commanded by A.I. Lopatin soon came alongside to extend Timoshenko's line northward.

Freezing weather returned on November 13, permitting resumed movement. Von Rundstedt planned to continue his advance four days later, but with Seventeenth Army incapable of covering the panzer army's north, von Kleist's advancing spearhead soon created an exposed 150-mile flank. Timoshenko saw this opportunity and planned to counterattack.

---

31   "Winter quarters" is a queer, almost 18th-century concept, considering that during *Barbarossa* both armies had caused massive destruction (i.e., scorched earth) throughout the German rear areas and the entire tactic implies contracting to inhabited locales and then surrendering vast areas between them to a dynamic enemy.

Von Mackensen massed his armor to the north alongside that of von Wietersheim. Together they attacked south of the Tuslov to take an indirect route to Rostov in a clockwise sweep. Both panzer corps moved out at 0800hrs on November 17 and quickly pierced the Soviet lines. Both air forces were extremely active: the IV and V Fliegerkorps providing CAS while the Red Army Air Force interdicted German supply lines between Mariupol and Taganrog.

The 37th Army's counterattack on the northern portion of the bulge presently attracted the attention of the XIV Panzer and XLIX Mountain Corps, leaving Rostov to III Panzer Corps. By November 19 von Mackensen's panzers reached Nachichevan, 4 miles northeast of Rostov, and his motorized infantry occupied Aksaiskoye 2 miles from the Don River. The next day III Panzer Corps entered the city while the LSSAH even fought its way across the Don and established a small bridgehead on the south bank of the massive, frozen river. Communist Party members and civilians fled before the panzer troopers. The Ostheer's furthest advance was reached on November 22 with the temporary occupation of Rostov. Von Kleist wanted to abandon the city after one day but von Rundstedt ordered him to stay.

Gaining the upper hand: emboldened by flagging German fortunes, and motivated to defend their capital, the Soviets increased their offensive activity in November and December. Here T-34/76 tanks accompany advancing Red Army infantrymen. (Elukka)

Final defense along the Don River by Leibstandarte SS Adolf Hitler, Rostov, November 25, 1941. On the south edge of Rostov overlooking the Don River the 300 men of LSSAH Motorized Division's reconnaissance battalion under Sturmbannführer Kurt "Panzer" Meyer held a 5-mile front. Early on November 25 Timoshenko loosed his 56th Army against the III Panzer Corps' defenses and at 0520hrs parts of three rifle and one cavalry divisions assaulted the German line. The mile-wide Don was frozen solid and supported all but the heaviest vehicles. T-34 tanks (**1**) provided support fire from the far bank. Soviet riflemen of the 343rd Rifle Division (**2**) attacked in battalion strength with bayonets fixed to their Moisin Model 1891 rifles (**3**). The German troops weaponry included the standard M1934 Karabiner 98k rifle (**4**) and MG34 light machine guns (**5**), with officers also carrying the Walther P38 sidearm (**6**), supported by a few Pak 38 50mm antitank guns (**7**). Some of the SS troops wore issued snow smocks (**8**), some improvised snow camouflage (**9**), while others had nothing but their standard wool uniforms (**10**). (© Osprey Publishing, Howard Gerrard)

Timoshenko's Counteroffensive

On November 9 Timoshenko briefed Stalin on his plan to use the Southern Front, now under Cherevichenko, to attack von Kleist's vulnerable left flank. With the bulk of the Red Army defending Moscow, Stavka could offer no additional help. The marshal assembled 12th (K.A. Korteev), 18th (V. Ya. Kolpatchy), 37th (Lopatin), and 9th (F.M. Kharitonov) Armies, in addition to Remezov's 56th Independent Army holding Rostov. Lopatin's 37th, assembling near Krasnodon, would be the main effort, with the confluence of the Tuslov and Krepkach rivers as its initial goal. The 9th and

18th Armies, hastily rebuilt following the Sea of Azov battle, covered his east and west flanks respectively.

Timoshenko's ultimate objective was Taganrog. His force consisted of seven armies, including 40 rifle and 13 cavalry divisions plus seven tank brigades and an airborne corps. The attack's size tested contemporary Soviet command and control, but drastic measures were required to secure Caucasus oil while keeping as many German units as possible distracted from Moscow.

Timoshenko launched his attack on November 17 and added over 100 tanks the next day. The Germans knew of the assault ahead of time but were too weak to offer much resistance along the lengthy flank. Lopatin struck portions of the Seventeenth Army, the CSIR, the XLIX Mountain Corps and, above all, the left flank of the XIV Panzer Corps. The boundary of these last two formations, held by the 1st Mountain and SS Viking Divisions, was breached. The T-34s overwhelmed von Wietersheim's panzers and the Soviet forces employed Katyusha rockets against Army Group South for the first time. Von Kleist dispatched Stukas and his last reserves, the Slovakian Mobile Division (a brigade's strength).

The threat to First Panzer Army's flank and rear was real enough, but not sufficient to keep the German forces out of Rostov. Despite losing the important city, Stavka remained fixed on eliminating von Kleist. The panzer general asked von Rundstedt for reserves and advice on stabilizing the dangerous situation. Oblivious, OKH vainly pressured Army Group South to execute Directive No.11 – a drive on Maikop in the Caucasus.

The XIV Panzer withdrew to the Tsulov River. Panzer Army headquarters pulled 13th and 14th Panzer Divisions out of Rostov in order to create a counterattack force. Hitler's personal promise for aerial resupply amounted to a mere 24 Ju-52s on November 24. Von Rundstedt's staff already considered retreating to the Mius when Timoshenko lashed out again.

At 0520hrs on November 25, men of the LSSAH saw battalions of Soviet infantry coming out of the fog. With arms linked and screaming "Urrah!" they stormed over the frozen Don. Without cover they fell to the German guns in their hundreds. With attack and counterattack supported by armor of both sides, the battle raged for two days. But the main differences between this attack and that of a week earlier were von Kleist's more exposed position and the absence of any support by the Seventeenth Army. By November 27 the Southern Front had assaulted the German defenses along its entire length. Luftwaffe CAS was out of the question due to the German Moscow offensive. Telephone lines hummed between army group headquarters and

Rostov, November 1941. Soviet riflemen advance through the "Gateway to the Caucasus". Rostov was the first Soviet city liberated, though the Germans recaptured it during Operation *Blau* the following summer. (NARA)

Rastenburg. On his own initiative von Kleist ordered III Panzer Corps out of Rostov during the night of November 28/29. His panzer divisions averaged 12–24 operational tanks and infantry companies numbered 50 men. Von Rundstedt approved moving to the Mius on the 30th. At 25 miles per day the retreat's pace matched that of the advance during *Barbarossa's* early days.

After hours of telephone calls between Hitler's and von Rundstedt's staffs (the field marshal refused to speak directly with higher headquarters), the Führer instructed First Panzer to halt east of the Mius along an intermediate line. With Luftflotte 4 flying overhead von Kleist's men pulled back all the way to the Mius anyway. They maintained a small bridgehead at Taganrog, mostly for its advanced airfields, but otherwise abandoned the river's east bank – a move sure to infuriate Hitler.

Von Rundstedt is Relieved of Command

At this juncture, with crucial battles taking place at Leningrad, Moscow, and Rostov, Hitler left his headquarters for head-of-state duties in Germany. Retreat to the Mius was practically an accomplished fact when he returned from the funerals of Luftwaffe aces Ernst Udet and Werner Mölders. Von Brauchitsch, who had suffered a severe heart attack on November 13, took the brunt of Hitler's wrath. The Führer demanded last-man defenses and counterattacks. Von Rundstedt would hear nothing of it and offered to resign, which Hitler immediately accepted.

In a teletype early on December 1 Hitler appointed von Reichenau joint army group and Sixth Army commander (both headquarters were in Poltava) and instructed him to halt von Kleist's withdrawal. Von Reichenau passed on the order to First Panzer headquarters and appealed to von Kleist's sense of duty. But the panzer commander knew better the disastrous implications of throwing his army back at the Soviet forces, and he had the wellbeing of his weary troops in mind. Von Reichenau relented late that day and confirmed the retreat order.

To personally investigate, Hitler made the unprecedented move of flying to the front on December 2. With von Reichenau and Lohr's chief of staff he flew to Mariupol to meet von Kleist and LSSAH commander Sepp Dietrich. Hitler could not ignore the two frontline leaders' unanimity. Dietrich's testimony of SS suffering and unstinted support of his Heer superiors impressed the Führer. Hitler left the next day, again flying via Poltava. There he met von Rundstedt, acknowledged the field marshal's service, and promised to reinstate him after some rest.

This was as close as Hitler ever came to admitting a mistake to one of his generals. By late November the army group's hopes rested on First Panzer Army. However, gravely weakened from five months of fighting, at the end of a feeble logistical tail and poorly supported by its northern flank units von Kleist could not hope to capture Rostov and hold it for longer than a week. Across the front the Soviet forces began to recover from *Barbarossa*'s initial shock, husband replacements, and develop operational skills of their own. Timoshenko's counteroffensive would not be the last time the Red Army exploited an overextended German thrust. Army Group South was fortunate von Rundstedt and von Kleist were as skilled in defense as offense.

Assault on Moscow

During the second half of October the German leaders hoped to build upon the momentum of the Viazma–Bryansk begun during the first half. Their own weaknesses, the weather and Soviet resistance made this impossible. Red Army forces along the entire front and in reserves close behind would grow from 269 divisions and 65 brigades totaling 2.2 million men at the beginning of November to 343 divisions and 98 brigades with over 4 million men a month later – and most of these new troops manned the Moscow sectors. On November 1 von Bock's forces fielded 136 divisions on paper, but with a real strength of 83, totaling 2.7 million men, and he would receive no reinforcements.

▼ EVENTS

1. By late September the Soviets were transitioning from offense to defense in anticipation of the German's final attack on Moscow. However, their lines are only one echelon deep and they have no reserves. Average per mile strength: 1,000 men, one tank, one and a half anti-tank guns and seven and a half indirect fire weapons (76mm or larger).

2. Hitler and Halder want shallow *Kessels* but von Bock wants deep thrusts. The Führer and Chief of Staff prevail.

3. 3-4 October: Group Boldin (three rifle divisions and two tank brigades) attack from developing Viazma *Kessel* against Hoth's right flank but accomplish little.

4. 6 October: The 7th Panzer from north and 10th Panzer from south (covering twice the distance) link-up at Viazma encircling elements of the 16th, 19th , 20th and 32nd Armies.

KEY TO UNITS 1ST OCT

GERMAN UNITS ■

1 Ninth Army
2 Third Panzer
3 Fourth Army
4 Fourth Panzer
5 Second Army
6 Second Panzer

SOVIET ARMIES ●

A 22nd
B 29th
C 31st
D 49th
E 30th
F 19th
G 16th
H 20th
I 24th
J 43rd
K 50th
L 3rd
M 13th

---

5. 6 October: The 17th Panzer Division captures Briansk from the east, including its Desna River bridges. This maneuver assists forward movement of the Second Army attacking to the north west. Near Trubchevsk elements of the 3rd and 13th Armies are trapped while elements of the 50th Army are encircled to the north east.

6. Soviet Mozhaisk defenses consist of two nearly parallel lines that include 225 miles of ditches and other antitank obstacles, 66 miles of dragon's teeth and 380 miles of wire obstacles.

7. 14 October: The 1st Panzer Division captured Kalinin and penetrates the Mozhaisk line. From here it can either roll-up Soviet defenses or threaten Moscow.

8. 18–22 October: Instead 1st Panzer and Lehr 900 Motorized Brigade make ill-fated attack to Mjednoye and AWAY from Moscow. Red Army counter-attacks quickly restore the situation.

9. 24 October: Soviet 29th Army attacks Third Panzer Army's left flank but is too weak and uncoordinated to be more than a nuisance.

10. Mid-October: Stavka creates Moscow Defense Zone roughly parallel to and behind the Mozhaisk lines.

11. 27 November: Major General I.V. Belov's 2nd Cavalry Corps (two cavalry and one rifle division plus equivalent to nearly two tank regiments) launches counter attack against 17th Panzer. Liberates Kashira and blunts Guderian's advance on Moscow.

12. In Moscow: 10 October: Stalin recalls Zhukov from Leningrad to take command of overall defense of Moscow; Mid-October: Soviet spy Richard Sorge in Tokyo reports to Stalin that Japan is definitely going to attack the US and UK interests in the Pacific. Therefore the USSR has freedom of action in Asia. By 1 December 70 divisions are transferred from the Soviet Far East to the Moscow region; 19 October: Stalin declares "State of Siege" in Moscow and appoints NKVD general to command defense of Moscow proper.

13. *Typhoon*'s ultimate objective: Second, Third and Fourth Panzer Armies meet at Nogisnsk and encircle Moscow.

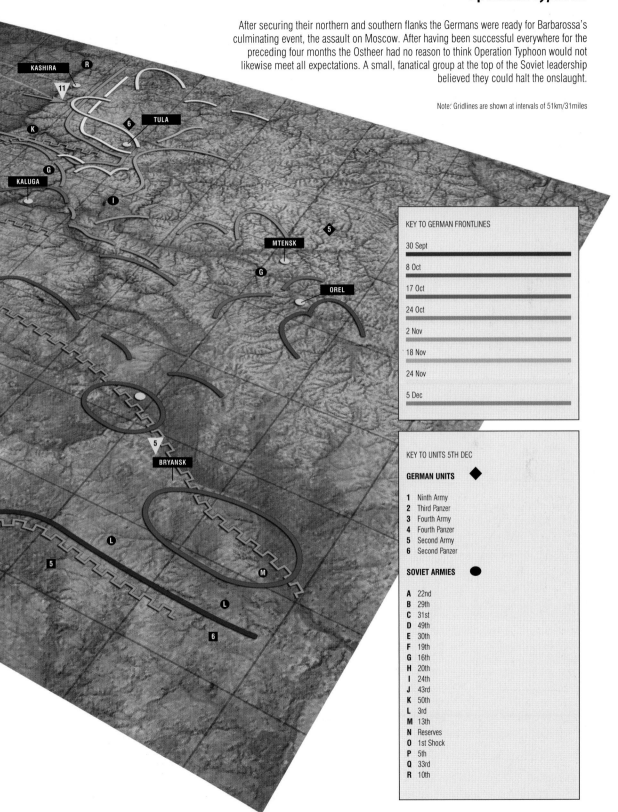

Operation *Typhoon*

After securing their northern and southern flanks the Germans were ready for Barbarossa's culminating event, the assault on Moscow. After having been successful everywhere for the preceding four months the Ostheer had no reason to think Operation Typhoon would not likewise meet all expectations. A small, fanatical group at the top of the Soviet leadership believed they could halt the onslaught.

Note: Gridlines are shown at intervals of 51km/31miles

KASHIRA
TULA
KALUGA
MTENSK
OREL
BRYANSK

KEY TO GERMAN FRONTLINES

30 Sept

8 Oct

17 Oct

24 Oct

2 Nov

18 Nov

24 Nov

5 Dec

KEY TO UNITS 5TH DEC

GERMAN UNITS ◆

1   Ninth Army
2   Third Panzer
3   Fourth Army
4   Fourth Panzer
5   Second Army
6   Second Panzer

SOVIET ARMIES ●

A   22nd
B   29th
C   31st
D   49th
E   30th
F   19th
G   16th
H   20th
I   24th
J   43rd
K   50th
L   3rd
M   13th
N   Reserves
O   1st Shock
P   5th
Q   33rd
R   10th

Landsers jump from a Panzer III during the fighting near Klin in December. (Topfoto)

On the last day of the month OKH issued yet another "Continuation of Operations Directive." It ordered Ninth Army to attack toward the Volga Reservoir while Third and Fourth Panzer Groups would slash toward Yaroslavl (nearly 200 miles northeast of the Volga) in the north. Second Panzer Army, with only 50 of its 600 tanks operational, was to aim for Gorky (over 200 miles distant), with Second Army covering its right while also making for Voronezh. Once again Fourth Army represented the army group's Schwerpunkt, with Moscow as its objective. The attack would begin on November 15. The other army groups received equally unrealistic missions: North was to link up with the Finns, while South was to push on to Stalingrad and Maikop!

Could Army Group Center reach Moscow? Many German soldiers were keen on the idea and willing to make the effort. Would accepting a personnel and material victory at Viazma–Bryansk followed by retreating back to the relative security of the Dnepr and other rivers as well as the prepared positions they had occupied before *Typhoon* be a better course of action than advancing into the unknown of the Soviet capital? No, von Bock had wanted to seize Moscow from the start, and now he would have his way. Like most German officers of that time, he was almost terminally optimistic: his soldiers would win the final battle, he would follow Hitler's orders, and he would capture the legendary city.

Preliminaries

On November 6, marking the anniversary of the 1917 Revolution, Stalin told soldiers marching from Red Square directly to the battlefield, "If they want a war of extermination, they shall have one." He feared the German forces could encircle Leningrad, Moscow, Rostov, and Stalingrad and perhaps even capture them. He therefore reinforced Zhukov's West Front, supported by Konev's Kalinin Front to the north and Timoshenko's Southwest Front in the south.

Zhukov wanted control of the entire battle for Moscow, and Stalin gave it to him. The West Front took command of 50th Army (from the disbanded Bryansk Front) on November 10, and 13th Army at Kalinin a week later. With fresh lessons from the defense of Leningrad in mind, Stalin ordered Zhukov to launch a series of pre-emptive assaults against the German positions. The general argued against this plan, but ultimately followed orders.

On the left, 49th Army (Lieutenant General I.G. Zakharkin) attacked on November 14 against XII and XIII Army Corps near Serpukhov. The 2nd Cavalry Corps tried to exploit but failed to have much impact. Two days later, near Volokolomsk, Rokossovsky led his 16th Army into the gap between 14th Motorized and 7th Panzer Divisions, likewise achieving little success. New units from the Far East had little time to prepare, were unused

German troops attempting to push a Krupp L2H143 1½-ton light truck along an icy Russian road. Most German wheeled vehicles did not perform well under these severe conditions. (Nik Cornish at www.Stavka. org.uk)

to combat, and lost up to one-third of their personnel and 157 of 198 tanks in ill-advised assaults. The follow-on charge of Major General L.M. Dovator's 3rd Cavalry Corps was essentially suicidal; his 44th Cavalry Division practically ceased to exist, and its sister 17th suffered 75 percent casualties. These attacks severely weakened Red Army forces that would soon desperately need all their available strength. However, merely taking the offensive bolstered Soviet confidence.

On the day before Zhukov's first attacks, Halder met with most of the Ostheer's army and army group chiefs of staff plus representatives of his own staff at Orsha. He had come to pass along Hitler's admonition for even greater efforts to achieve *Barbarossa*'s grandiose objectives. He arrived unable to imagine that the Red Army had any means left to stop von Bock before Moscow. Had they not just obliterated all the enemy's forces at Viazma–Bryansk? Unfortunately German intelligence was so poor they had no way to confirm or deny their assumptions. With Moscow now so close, the historic city was exerting an allure over many German leaders. Halder "hoped" for six more weeks of cool weather without much snow.

His hopes were dashed by the men who had just come from the fighting front. Representatives from Army Groups North and South wanted to stop where they stood. Von Bock's chief of staff, von Greiffenberg, echoed his commander when he said that Moscow could only be taken frontally and that Halder's pompous encirclement plans were out of the question. Halder conceded, and allowed the less ambitious army group plan to go forward. Kesselring spoke up to say that many of his Luftwaffe units had already left for the Mediterranean, and that his staff and "a substantial number of units" would depart on November 18. Von Richthofen's very much weakened VIII Fliegerkorps would take over the air support mission.

As usual, logistics concerns were soon being voiced. The OKH quartermaster representative said that they could not supply the army group; for example, fuel deliveries were one-quarter of requirements. Halder's response to this real problem was simply to announce that OKH was "not going to stand in von Bock's way if he thinks he can succeed; you also need a little bit of luck in war." Even though rail lines had operated to Gzhatsk by October 27 and to Borodino a few days later, von Bock's logistics remained under stress. Supply woes caused the staggered start of his final push. Nevertheless, Army Group Center wanted to start as soon as possible and not wait for its supply situation to improve; only Moscow justified this level of effort and risk.

Weather not fit for man nor beast: a small German supply column, including a "goulash cannon" field kitchen, makes its way past a knocked-out T-34. During winter raids, Soviet troops often targeted these trailers; in 1939–40 they had learned the hard way from the Finns that the combat potential of an isolated unit without the means to provide hot food and drink would degrade overnight. (HITM)

There would be few modifications to the plan of attack. Owing to the dire situation of von Leeb's Sixteenth Army to the north, Ninth Army's mission was limited. Reinhardt's Third Panzer Group would attack on November 15 and aim for the Volga–Moscow Canal. Three days later, Hoepner's Fourth Panzer Group (still the most powerful panzer group in the Ostheer) and Guderian's Second Panzer Army would move out toward Teryayevo and Kolomna respectively. Von Kluge, whose Fourth Army should have had major responsibilities, was left in limbo. The Second Army had to accomplish the impossible combination of covering the flanks of the Fourth and Second Panzer Armies, while maintaining contact with the Sixth Army of Army Group South, and also conducting its own attacks on Orel, Kursk, and Voronezh. The German High Command seemed completely divorced from reality.

Army Group Center received no reinforcements to make up its losses from combat and illness. Meanwhile, the Soviet forces around Moscow received 100,000 men, 300 tanks, and 2,000 guns during the first half of November alone. Among the new formations was an engineer army with three brigades of 19 pioneer battalions to help Zhukov dig in. Now, along the main front, 233,000 Germans, with 1,880 guns, 1,300 tanks, and approximately 800 aircraft were facing 240,000 Soviet soldiers, 1,254 guns, 502 tanks, and 1,238 aircraft. While Halder wrote on November 5 that "the Luftwaffe is slowly disintegrating" on its primitive frontline airstrips, most Red Army Air Force squadrons were operating from the well-equipped permanent airfields surrounding Moscow. In the meantime German troops had begun to talk openly about their fear of the enemy and the cold.

Von Bock Versus Zhukov: North

> The time for waiting is over. We can attack again. The last Russian defense of Moscow is destroyed. We must still the heart of the Bolshevik resistance in order to end the campaign for the year. The Panzer Group has the good fortune of leading the decisive stroke. Therefore all strength, our entire fighting spirit, the hard will… is required. Take hold of the enemy and destroy him. Retain your spirit! Your goal, a … conclusion to the difficult fight and your well-earned rest. Lead with courage! The battle gives you good luck!

So wrote Erich Hoepner to his troops as they began their final assault on Moscow.

Hitler had less interest in the Fourth Army and Fourth Panzer Group attacks in the center or Guderian's slow assault in the south; he cared most about the Third Panzer Group's operations in the north. Operation *Volga Reservoir* began on November 15, with Ninth Army's XXVII Army Corps joined by Third Panzer Group's LVI Panzer Corps and Hoepner's V and XLVI Army Corps a day later. (It took Strauss until the 20th to relieve Reinhardt's XLI Panzer Corps, which was still defending Kalinin and so the latter unit could not participate in the attack.) They made good progress, all things considered, and reached both the reservoir and the canal to Moscow on the 18th. When VII and IX Army and XL Panzer Corps threw their weight into the battle Rokossovsky's situation became desperate. Von Bock's special command train moved to his army group's northern flank in anticipation of continued progress.

The 16th Army commander requested permission from Zhukov to withdraw to the Istra River, but received a negative response. Rokossovsky then went over his front commander's head and made the same request of chief of staff Shaposhnikov, who authorized the retreat. Zhukov sent the following stinging telegram to his willful subordinate:

I am the one who gives orders to troops at the front! I overrule the order allowing troops to retreat to the Istra Reservoir. I order them to defend themselves where they stand and not retreat one step.

The closer the Germans got to Moscow, the farther they were from their supply sources, and the closer the Soviets were to theirs. Here two M1937 45mm antitank guns are manned by their well-equipped crews. (Elukka)

Thereafter Zhukov ruled with iron discipline. (He had the commander and commissar of 133rd Rifle Division executed in front of their troops for allowing an unauthorized retreat.)

Remnants of Dovator's cavalry corps managed to slow Hoepner, but Reinhardt made good progress against the boundary between 16th and 30th Armies. Third Panzer Group hit the right flank of 5th Army (now under General L.A. Govorov) near Zvenigorod on November 19–20. On the 21st, Zhukov sent Rokossovsky and the 16th Army deputy commander to personally shore up the situations at Solnechnogorsk and Klin respectively. Solnechnogorsk fell before Rokossovsky arrived, so both generals went to Klin, which likewise fell on the 22nd when the 30th Army retreated north rather than east.

Zhukov's right threatened to become unhinged with the 30th Army's swing north, creating a gap that Reinhardt soon exploited. Stalin dispatched all reserves, including all air assets, to the northern sector. The XLI and XLVI Panzer Corps crossed the frozen Istra Reservoir during the last days of November. Army Group Center's farthest advance north of Moscow occurred on November 27, when Colonel Hasso von Manteuffel of 7th Panzer Division (now down to 36 operational tanks) captured a bridgehead over the Volga at Yakhroma.

The 1st Shock Army, which the Soviet leadership had been secretly building for another mission out of seven rifle brigades and 11 ski battalions, was thrown into the breach between 16th and 30th Armies against the Third Panzer Group bridgehead. With only one very weak and unsupported panzer corps able to make it this far, the Germans gave up their Yakhroma outpost on the 29th. Another German outfit made it even closer to the Soviet capital when 2nd Panzer Division captured Krasnaya Polyana, only 12 miles from the Kremlin. The combination of 1st Shock and 20th Armies (the latter commanded by the brilliant but traitorous A.A. Vlassov) halted this threat as well. On December 3, Hoepner called for a three-day halt; but before the German forces could get started again the Soviet general counteroffensive had begun.

Von Bock versus Zhukov: South

A less serious threat developed to the south of Moscow when Guderian's Second Panzer Army attacked toward Tula on November 18. He initially made good progress, causing a 30-mile gap along the boundary of the West and Southwest Fronts, but his men soon came up against new Siberian divisions that Guderian described as "keen for battle and well trained." By the 22nd he wanted to stop on account of extended flanks, terrible weather, high casualties, poor logistics, and many other problems. The deplorable conditions made life difficult and the morale of Guderian's men, like that all along the Moscow fighting, constantly rose and fell. German field medical services, operating in the same ragged conditions, struggled against wounds, typhus, frostbite, fleas, and exposure. The following day von Bock flew to Guderian's headquarters to prop up his flagging subordinate and urge the Second Panzer Army to continue at least as far as Kolomna. But when Guderian hit Tula, "little Moscow," defended by a hodgepodge of workers' brigades and NKVD units, he came to a halt. Fighting there raged around Leo Tolstoy's old estate and German dead were buried right next to the great writer's grave.

137th Infantry Division assault through the Moscow defenses near Voronino, November 17, 1941. This scene shows infantry (**1**) and engineers (**2**) of the 137th Infantry Division negotiating the defenses near Voronino almost due south of Moscow, between Maloyaroslavets and Serphukov. The infantry first fought their way across a steep-sided antitank ditch and then through the primitive earthen field works beyond, losing many men to mines and machine-gun fire. The Soviets quickly launched counterattacks, often supported by tanks (**3**). Early on November 17, Soviet tanks overran two howitzers; the divisional commander, General Bergmann, asked for reinforcements, in this case 8.8cm Flak 36 guns of Corps Flak Abteilung 707 (**4**), pulled by their SdKfz prime movers (**5**) over a tactical bridge erected by the engineers (**6**). Overhead, *Nebelwerfer* rockets pound the Soviet lines (**7**).

In accordance with the blitzkrieg mentality the men of Second Panzer Army sidestepped Tula to the east, and somehow staggered on to Venev by the 24th and actually reached Kashira. There 17th Panzer Division handled Boldin's 50th Army roughly, drawing Zhukov's attention, and one of his last reserves, the 2nd Cavalry Corps. This formation, which was renamed 1st Guards Cavalry Corps on the 26th, received substantial CAS, and arrived in Kashira just hours before 17th Panzer. A sharp engagement developed around the town on the Oka River, the last natural obstacle in Guderian's way. But Belov's cavalrymen overran that division's scattered outposts – and then disappeared into Army Group Center's rear areas, for a five-month rampage.

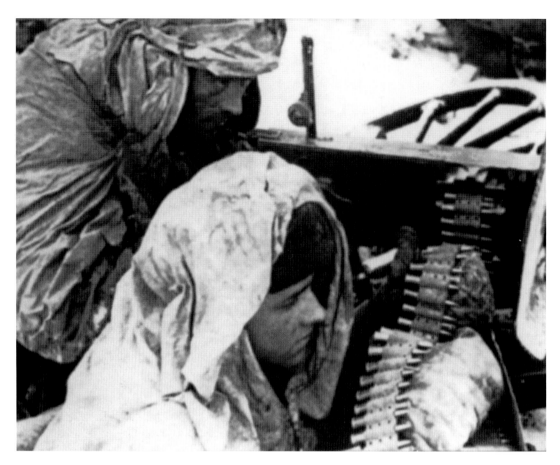

Unlike their relatively unprepared German counterparts, these warmly dressed and camouflaged Soviet troops – the two-man crew of one of the Red Army's ubiquitous Maxim M1910 machine guns – are well equipped for fighting in the snow. (Elukka)

Tula proved to be a very hard nut to crack as Boldin's men held on. On November 27–28 Guderian sent what remained of 3rd and 4th Panzer Divisions on a counterclockwise sweep north of the city. Their armor was consolidated into Kampfgruppe Eberbach, which numbered 110 tanks on the 17th but only 32 a week later. Guderian likewise ordered XLIII Army Corps to come clockwise from the south in an attempt to encircle this obstacle. Personally leading the advance, the panzer general experienced at first hand the difficulties faced by his men fighting in temperatures as low as -30° (F). The 340th Rifle and 112th Tank Divisions held open Tula's last corridor to the outside despite Guderian's efforts.

On November 27, Guderian added his voice to the growing chorus of Army Group Center generals frustrated at von Kluge's inactivity. Here is the downside of the *Auftragstaktik*, revealed at the most inopportune moment; the system trusted the judgment of the commander on the ground to make

A combination of ancient and modern: German supplies are offloaded from a Ju 52 trimotor transport aircraft and onto a horse-drawn panje sled. Distance, weather, terrain and partisan activity made aerial resupply essential on many occasions, but this was a task for which the Luftwaffe was inadequately equipped. Meanwhile, the Red Army was also using air transport: Stalin flew 5,500 men of 1st Guards Rifle Corps to Orel in just three days. (Podzun)

sound decisions, yet all could see that in having von Kluge lead the Schwerpunkt against Moscow this trust was grossly misplaced. Guderian said that he could not continue assaulting "if the right wing of Fourth Army for its part does not assume the offensive without delay." Von Bock told Guderian's chief of staff that such an attack was "out of the question." Meanwhile, on the army group's extreme right, the Second Army (with Colonel General Rudolf Schmidt replacing the ailing von Weichs) shoved aside the Soviet 3rd and 13th Armies and made for Voronezh. On von Bock's southern flank Guderian, aiming northward, and Schmidt, attacking to the east, could offer each other no mutual support. On top of that, the usual combination of terrible weather, weak logistics and Red Army resistance, plus poor coordination with the neighboring Sixth Army (Army Group South's left flank) conspired to bring Schmidt's men to a halt by the end of the month, well short of his objective.

While railcars full of undelivered winter clothing and equipment sit idle in Germany, these Ostfront soldiers have to make do with bed sheets and tablecloths. (Topfoto)

Von Bock Versus Zhukov: Center

Supposedly the Schwerpunkt in the critical Mozhaisk sector, the Fourth Army fought a defensive battle while the armor attacked on its flanks. With the motto "Moscow is behind us!" Zhukov felt secure about this critical sector. He would concentrate on the wings while keeping a wary eye on the expected attack up the middle.

While Third and Fourth Panzer Groups advanced early in the offensive, von Kluge launched some preliminary attacks with his left on November 18–19. However, according to von Bock, the right wing of Fourth Army was "very serious and precarious." Von Kluge paraded a series of excuses for his inaction, to the extreme annoyance of Halder. Von Bock discussed with the chief of staff the possibility of asking von Brauchitsch to give the balking Fourth Army commander a direct order to attack. For over a year the German Army had been anticipating the final assault against Stalin's capital, and now that the moment had arrived the commander of the main effort would not move.

Von Kluge finally stirred himself and attacked in earnest on December 1 in the direction of Naro–Fominsk, with XX Army Corps under the Austrian General Robert Materna flanked by LVII Panzer (total tank strength: 70) and IX Army Corps. Initial success against the 43rd Army offered a slight glimmer of hope when it looked as if 258th Infantry Division might achieve a breakthrough, hitting the second-echelon 5th Army defending the Minsk–Moscow highway.

A Red Army artillery firing position in the winter. During *Barbarossa*, Soviet artillery did not yet play the decisive and dominating role that it later would. During the summer and autumn of 1941 Zhukov husbanded his artillery for the battle that he knew would develop around Moscow. (Elukka)

Von Kluge correctly aimed his attack against the Mozhaisk line, but Zhukov anticipated the blow and had a counter. On the assault's second day 33rd Army (Lieutenant General M.G. Yefremov) attacked with the 5th and 11th Tank Brigades plus one tank and two ski battalions. T-34s and StuGs hunted each other through the villages, which Soviet aircraft bombed simply to deprive the invaders of any shelter. The German troops scattered in uncharacteristic panic and soon reoccupied their starting lines. Von Bock did not know what to think; on December 2 he told von Kluge, Hoepner, and Reinhardt that the Soviet forces were ready to break, but a day later he told Halder that he "doubted the success" of the Moscow operation.

Immediately following the battles for Viazma and Bryansk, Von Bock had had the defenders of Moscow reeling. When he did eventually resume offensive operations in mid-November, he could only do so in fits and starts. Having already given the Soviet divisions weeks to catch their balance, he now attacked sequentially over a period of weeks – which allowed Zhukov to parry in a corresponding fashion.

During the Ostheer's last lunge toward Moscow, Third and Fourth Panzer groups advanced between 50 and 60 miles, finally arriving 12–20 miles from the Kremlin. Their pressure near Yakhroma made November 27 a real day of crisis for Zhukov, although neither side was fully aware of the fact at the time. The relatively under-resourced Second Panzer Army never got as close

A miserable-looking German horse convoy braves a severe blizzard. (Corbis)

to Moscow and after Tula took no objective of even tactical value. Guderian, Hoepner, and Reinhardt all clamored to be designated as the assault's Schwerpunkt (the Wehrmacht could only resource one at a time), while the man given that distinction, von Kluge, did not know what to do with it. The three panzer commanders all complained about von Kluge, who in turn complained about them. Von Bock could not manage his unruly subordinates. Before Moscow he alternated between making analogies with the Marne in 1914 (where the younger von Moltke failed to take Paris at the last moment due to lack of nerves) and Verdun in 1916 (comparing the Soviet capital to the meat-grinder battle into which both armies fed more and more men).

Only at the Orsha conference did Halder finally realize the desperate condition of the Wehrmacht in Russia. In a juxtaposition of points of view, the chief of staff then decided that German forces must only threaten Moscow, not capture it. Hitler overrode Halder, stating that they needed to conquer the city. But how? This was the bizarre relationship between Germany's political leader and his generals. Hitler had his contradicting views; Halder had his cyclothymic moods. They made a study in despair that hamstrung Operation *Typhoon*.

By contrast, at the beginning of *Typhoon* the Red Army defense of Moscow suffered from apparent terminal disorganization. Six weeks later Zhukov had undisputed command of the entire theater and Stalin's full confidence. Only when it was far too late, by November 29 to judge from

Soviet cavalry in winter clothing. The cavalry arm was well suited for operations in the winter and Marshal Timoshenko used this to good advantage during his counteroffensive at Rostov. (NARA)

Von Bock's diary, did the German leaders acknowledge the USSR's "huge reserves." Stalin, Stavka, and the entire Soviet command structure had been waiting for *Typhoon* (and by extension, *Barbarossa*) to reach its culminating point so that they could begin their general winter counteroffensive. Between November 29 and 30, Zhukov briefed the dictator on the attack that would mark the end of both German advances and Moscow's danger. The anemic Army Group Center, with its long, indefensible lines of supply and uncovered flanks, was ripe for the taking.

Summary

It can be said that *Barbarossa* ended with a whimper rather than a bang; there was no deafening crescendo, just the dreaded *Flucht nach Vorn* (fleeing forward) because the two other options, stopping or retreating, were just too distasteful to the German commanders. Along the great mass of the front line in early November they dug in. At the northern and southern extremities, Tikhvin–Volkhov and Rostov, the Ostheer launched small, one-two corps sized attacks. Of course at Moscow they fought a huge offensive with six armies.

The campaign's fourth phase, Operation *Typhoon*, began with great promise. In a way, the starting lines looked eerily like those on *Barbarossatag* over four months earlier, with both armies drawn up face-to-face along hundreds of miles of front. Forces were greatly reduced due to the incessant

Pairs of well-clothed Soviet soldiers overcome a stout barbed wire obstacle. Under Zhukov the Red Army had little trouble transitioning from defense to offense. (Corbis)

fighting, but their relative qualities were very similar: a veteran Ostheer complete with mobile elites versus a relatively inexperienced Red Army soldiery (about the fourth completely new iteration to face the German forces). The main difference was at the top: the constant string of crushing German victories in battle had only confirmed the leaders' earlier hubris, while the equally constant string of crushing Soviet defeats had culled out their worst leaders. That left the Wehrmacht dreaming of objectives hundreds of miles *east* of Moscow on one side against hard-headed realists on the other.

The undeniable success of *Typhoon* gave *Barbarossa*'s final stage a look of invincible inevitability. Within ten days another million Soviets, dead and captured, were wiped off the Red Army order of battle. Propaganda Minister Goebbels, himself no military man, gushed with comparisons of Köningsgrätz and Sedan. But these battles, like *Typhoon*, had been operational victories. Hitler needed strategic success if he hoped to bring down the USSR, but, even with *Typhoon*'s relatively shallow Kessels and the German infantry all up close to the starting line, reducing and securing the pockets consumed valuable time. Exhaustion, poor logistics, and the *rasputitsa* would put the final bullets into the German leaders' plans to rush into an undefended Moscow.

Von Leeb, fighting his "poor man's war" in the north, predictably accomplished the least during *Barbarossa*'s finale. His already-smallest army group was made even smaller by the detachment of Hoepner's panzer group in mid-September. The northern theater's geography, always bad thanks to nature, got worse as the German troops settled in to besiege Leningrad. Here, all their advantages of mobility were negated. The attacks to Volkhov and Tikhvin were begun too late in the year, with too few forces and as too much of an afterthought to have any decisive success. Earlier in the year, with Hoepner's full panzer group and as a part of conscious and coherent plan, one can easily see the operation covering the last 40 miles to the Finns waiting along the Svir River.

Von Rundstedt also had to ante-up for *Typhoon*, although proportionally his losses were not as great as von Leeb's. Again reducing and securing their great Kessels, in this case Kiev's, took more time and resources that the German leaders would have liked. Formations not involved at Kiev, the Eleventh Army, or with the mobile flexibility to avoid Kessel cleanup duty such as First Panzer Group, pushed on to the southern Ukraine and Crimea. This was von Rundstedt's first and most significant exploitation of the Soviet's post-Kiev disorganization.

The Eleventh's successes on the confined Perekop isthmus demonstrated the German Landser's continued dominance over his Soviet counterpart. Meanwhile the Red Army had no meaningful counter to von Kleist's thrust into the Donbas. With the Kiev area subdued and occupied by early October, Sixth and Seventeenth Armies did reap some benefits from the emaciated Soviet defenses east of Lokhvitsa. Stuck in the relative no-man's-land between the more spectacular events of *Typhoon* and Rostov, these two infantry armies would have to be satisfied reaching Belgorod and Kharkov plus the middle Don River. The fleeting glory of Rostov turned out to be too exposed to be viable so von Kleist settled in along the more sensible Mius River.

During the awkward time between *Typhoon* and the penultimate assaults on Moscow, von Bock's men jockeyed for position from which to begin the latter when the final word came. With difficulty Hoth took Kalinin while Guderian only brushed with Tula. Despite tremendous losses sustained during *Barbarossa*'s

Adapt and overcome: the German 8.8cm Flak 18 gun changed roles and became famous throughout the European theater as the ultimate direct fire antitank weapon. (HITM)

previous five months of fighting and marching, German commanders believed they could carry Moscow. Since the beginning of *Typhoon* the Red Army had suffered the loss of 2 million men, including 750,000 dead. Add to that the additional million casualties from the battles in the Ukraine in September and there was no way the German High Command figured the USSR could possibly make up a 3 million-man shortfall. However the organizational prowess of the Soviet state did just that, to the astonishment of the Wehrmacht and much of the world. Of course it should be noted that the failure of Japan to threaten the Soviet far east did Stalin an immense favor in this regard.

Only Moscow was worth the all-or-nothing ultimate risk. Over a three-week period Army Group Center's Schwerpunkt shifted from Reinhardt/Strauss in the north to Guderian/Schmidt in the south to Hoepner/von Kluge in the center. Only in the first case was Zhukov's defense seriously tested. To the south Guderian's luck ran out while Schmidt's strength was dissipated on such improbable and widely separated objectives as Tula and Voronezh. In the

Reading *Barbarossa*

The literature of *Barbarossa*, and indeed the entire Nazi-Soviet War, has undergone many permutations since 1945. In the immediate post-war period mainly the Germans and Soviets themselves wrote about the Eastern Theater. Participants on both sides, mostly the generals, wrote their memoirs while the Soviets published voluminous official histories and campaign analyses. But the Eastern war's complexities, paucity of English language sources and the fact that few Americans or British served in the theater meant it initially received very little coverage in western literature.

Dividing Europe into NATO and Warsaw Pact camps, the rearming of Germans in both zones and other factors meant the histories soon fell under the spell of the Cold War. Especially in the West there was a need to prove that the Soviets could be beaten and the West Germans were the ones to help do it. Therefore, books at the time usually portrayed the Red Army as an unskilled mass which managed to win only due to its size, its willingness to accept casualties, and the amateurish interference of Hitler. Meanwhile the Wehrmacht supposedly fought a chivalrous war sullied only by Nazi Party hacks in the SS. After all, the captains and colonels of the Ostfront were soon the generals of the Bundeswehr. German

memoirs and histories by the likes of Paul Carell (himself a wartime Nazi propagandist) are examples of this genre. The US Army employed former Wehrmacht generals to write monographs about the East under the suspect supervision of Franz Halder. In 1960, the Soviets published the six volume, English version of their official *History of the Great Patriotic War of the Soviet Union, 1941–1945*. Today it seems dated and an ideological curiosity.

A third wave of "Russian Front" historians came along in the early 1960s. Using some official Soviet sources, British historians like John Erickson and Alan Clark helped redirect the Anglophone audience away from North Africa, Normandy, U-boats, strategic bombing, etc while beginning to correct the earlier, skewed impressions of the Nazi-Soviet War. Earl Ziemke added his two volume history, almost the official US Army version, ironically starting not with *Barbarossa* but with the war's later phases. In the early 1980s another American, Lieutenant Colonel David Glantz, began what can only be described as a one-man mission to set straight the record of the Nazi-Soviet War. Around the same time academic, as opposed to popular, German historians started to make serious contributions to the historiography.

center Hoepner practically went it alone against the teeth of Zhukov's defensive main effort. His nominal superior and the man on whom the Ostheer's forlorn hope rested, von Kluge, was nowhere to be seen. David Stahel believes that as reward for von Kluge's support during the German leader's July–August command meltdown, the Führer took it easy on the field marshal when it was clear that the latter had utterly failed at Moscow's gates.

In any event, at no time during *Barbarossa*'s last month do we see firm German leadership of the Moscow offensive. Halder was dreaming about Gorky and Stalingrad. Von Bock could neither control his subordinates nor coordinate the three main attack axes. By December 1 he evidently sensed the inevitable and requested either major reinforcements or permission to fall back to defensible lines. But hours later he then turned around and told Jodl he wanted to keep going on to Moscow! It is hard to see the hand of Hitler, the bogeyman in the generals' disingenuous postwar sniveling and excuse-making, in any of this nonsense.

The fall of the Berlin Wall and the collapse of the USSR ushered in a fourth generation with new access to former Soviet documents, intellectual freedom for Russian speaking historians, reduction of Cold War prejudices and advantages of the information age. Glantz continued to lead the way to the point of endangering his personal health. Israeli Omer Bartov demolished the myth of the squeaky-clean, apolitical Wehrmacht while American Geoff Megargee did the same for the vaunted German general staff. An invaluable addition to the literature came in 1998 with the MGFA (Military History Research Office now called ZMBW) series "Germany and the Second World War," which can be considered close to the Federal Republic's official history of World War II. Works by MGFA and BA-MA (Federal Military Archive) historians Boog, Förster, Müller, and Ueberschär are practically guaranteed to be excellent. Most recently (early 2013) Australian David Stahel is half way through his very in-depth study of *Barbarossa*.

Of course the historiography of the Nazi–Soviet War includes countless excellent authors and books not mentioned here. However, there are also completely discredited works like *Icebreaker* by Viktor Suvarov and those of doubtful analytical value such as Russell Stolfi's *Hitler's Panzers East*. Perhaps even more than most history, books on the Nazi–Soviet War should be read critically. Memoirs, books by authors like Carell and Haupt, or divisional histories published by veteran groups can probably be trusted for objective facts, such as the date a certain regiment was in a specific location, but should be viewed skeptically when discussing subjective judgments.

With the above caveats in mind, I would recommend any of the books in the present bibliography. Gabriel Gorodetsky's *Grand Delusion* gives an outstanding description of Stalin's behavior leading up to *Barbarossa*. Despite its title, *Stopped at Stalingrad* by Joel Haywood has excellent coverage of the 1941 campaign. For a unique German perspective, see Klaus Reinhardt, *Moscow, The Turning Point*. *The Wages of Destruction* by Adam Tooze set the new standard for economic history of the Third Reich and has much to say about *Barbarossa*. The examination of the campaign in H.P. Willmott's *The Great Crusade*, probably the best short, single-volume history of World War II, contains the excellent analysis of the fighting in 1941 we have come to expect from that prolific historian.

CONCLUSIONS

Army Group North

Whether Army Group North could have conquered Leningrad is unknown; Hitler ordered von Leeb's men to halt short of the city. Throughout the campaign, practically every time the army group, and more specifically Hoepner's panzers, was on the brink of success a higher headquarters halted them for the infantry or logistics to catch up. These pauses resulted in a fatal loss of momentum that allowed the Soviet forces time to recover.

As a result of losing the Byzantine battle for influence within Führer Headquarters over sending Guderian to Army Group South, Halder dug in his heels against sending Hoth's panzers north to von Leeb. Halder's "victory" undermined *Barbarossa* in the north. The decision to halt von Leeb outside of Leningrad doubtless saved his men from desperate and bitter urban warfare, but investing Leningrad tied down too great a proportion of the army group's strength and left it with no reserves.

Although in command at Leningrad for less than a month, Zhukov arrived at the critical point. He conducted an active defense, fired weak commanders, and forbade further retreat. For their part, the German forces were never able to completely seal off the city from the rest of the USSR. Bombing Lake Ladoga's winter ice in order to cut the supply road, for example, was an exercise in futility; Soviet truck drivers easily drove around any holes, which re-froze quickly. Even Spanish dictator Franco took better care to feed and clothe his *Guripas* than Hitler did his Landsers.

In common with other commanders von Leeb wielded an imperfect weapon. In his case he labored with an undersized contingent of panzers. At one point two-thirds of the Ostheer's infantry divisions considered significantly under-strength belonged to him. Logistically von Leeb was supposed to receive 34 supply trains per day but never took delivery of more than 18.

The VIII Fliegerkorps commander von Richthofen was very critical of von Leeb's campaign. The Luftwaffe flew without rest throughout the battles in the north: it supported the advance to the Dvina River, attacked Kronshtadt and Murmansk naval bases and mined numerous harbors, attacked the Stalin Line and the White Sea (Stalin) Canal, supported the Staraya Russa defense and

Strategic Overview – Army Group North

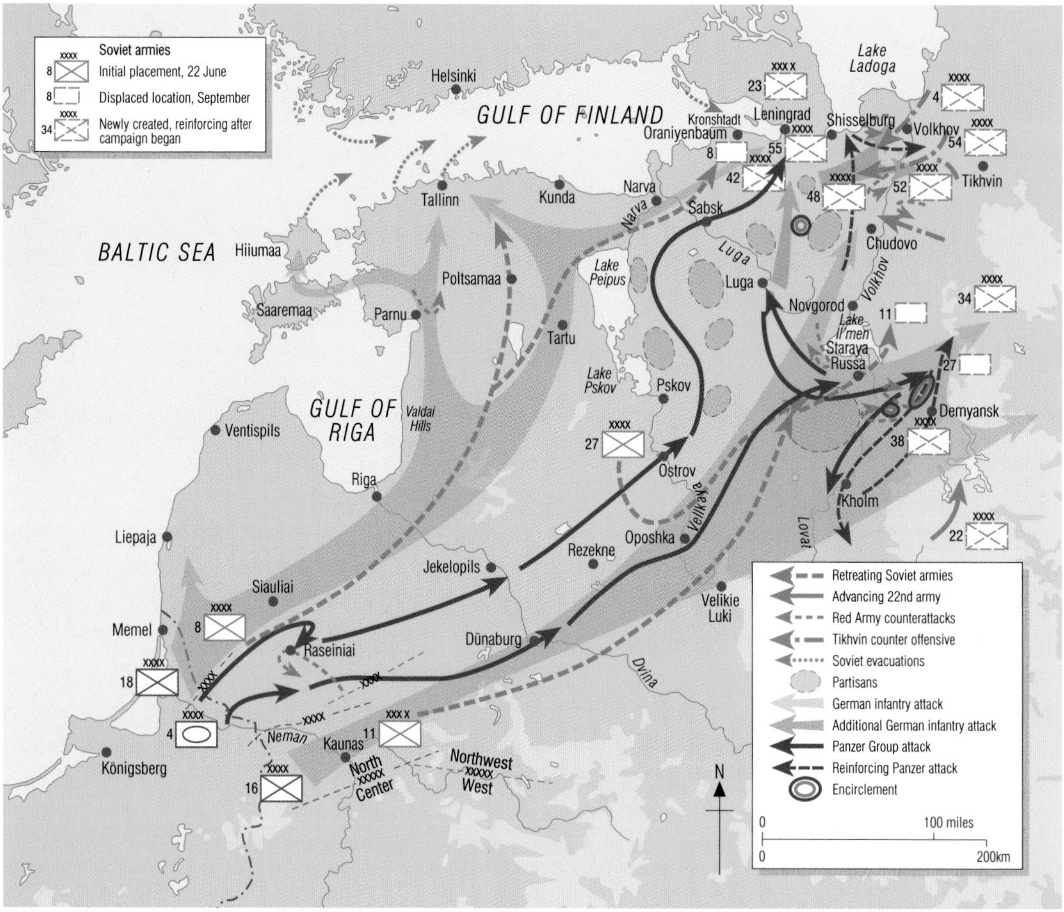

Soviet armies
- 8 | Initial placement, 22 June
- 8 | Displaced location, September
- 34 | Newly created, reinforcing after campaign began

Retreating Soviet armies
Advancing 22nd army
Red Army counterattacks
Tikhvin counter offensive
Soviet evacuations
Partisans
German infantry attack
Additional German infantry attack
Panzer Group attack
Reinforcing Panzer attack
Encirclement

0 — 100 miles
0 — 200km

counterattack, the advance on Leningrad, amphibious operations against the Baltic Islands, and the defense at Tikhvin, all the while interdicting Soviet rail lines throughout the theater. The Red Army Air Force and its antiaircraft artillery ruled the skies over the city while "almost the entire generation of [Luftwaffe] prewar trained officers was lost in combat."[32]

Nevertheless Army Group North began the invasion very well; in fact Führer Headquarters viewed its initial reports with disbelief. But von Leeb could not manage conflicting reports from below and orders from above. Mismanaged victories, such as at Dünaburg, were frequent. Neither was von

PREVIOUS PAGE:
While undoubtedly still very cold, well-clothed Red Army infantry march across open terrain. In these near whiteout conditions the horizon where earth and sky meet is indistinguishable. (Elukka)

32   Bergstrom, *Black Cross, Red Star*, p.222.

Leeb the right man to command the Leningrad effort during the leadership vacuum represented by the Hitler–Halder duel in mid-summer. Von Leeb eventually received two panzer corps from Hoth, separated in time and space. Lacking the mass of a similar reorganization sending Guderian southward, the impact of the additional panzers on Army Group North was significantly less. The former maneuver created the largest encirclement battle in history while the latter is nearly forgotten.

In Finland the Axis tried in vain to fight an effective campaign in a poorly-resourced strategic backwater. Von Falkenhorst constantly worried about Hitler's emphasis on defending Norway and fought with too little directed from too far away. Hitler had no respect for the 50 miles Dietl had to cover to reach Murmansk. Mannerheim's Finns outclassed the Soviet troops at every turn but were not fighting a war of world domination like Germany.

Finland always had limited objectives for the war and Mannerheim took a dim view of the German forces' demonstrated weakness in front of Leningrad. When the Red Army drove Army Group North away from Tikhvin and Volkhov after only a month,

Strategic Overview – Finland

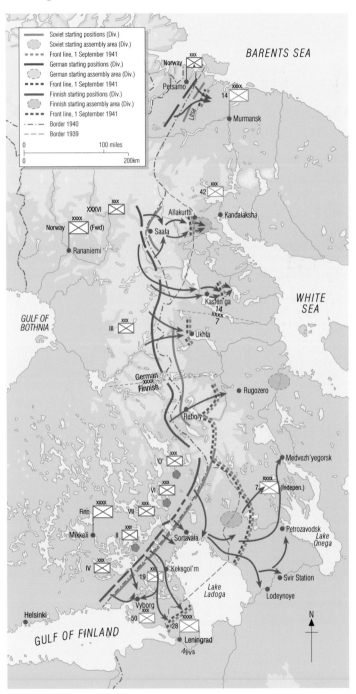

Approximately 30 miles west of Moscow, reasonably well-clothed German infantry present a contrast with the usual image. A number of photographs of men from SS Reich, in the Istra river sector during the mid-November actions against Rokossovsky's 16th Army, show them wearing white hooded smocks and trousers as well as the more common, long, snow-camouflage coats. Such clothing would not become general issue until the second winter of the Nazi–Soviet War. Right up to the gates of Moscow, Paul Hausser's men could be found in the thick of the fighting at von Bock's center. (Podzun)

the prospect of the two "co-belligerents" linking up receded even further. In the final analysis, the Wehrmacht's half measures at Tikhvin and Volkhov only drained valuable resources from the Ostheer's Moscow Schwerpunkt. More German resources employed earlier might have made a union on the Svir River a reality. The possibility of Finland fighting an unlimited war completely changes the complexion of *Barbarossa* in the north but properly belongs in the contra-historical category.

The poor leadership of first Kuznetsov and then Voroshilov presented von Leeb with every opportunity to succeed in the early going. While the Red Army may have collapsed along the northern front, the Soviet state held strong everywhere; Stalin's USSR was internally stable. The Northwest Front may not have halted Army Group North, but it did cause von Leeb to swerve more than once. Counterattacks at Soltsy and Staraya Russa might have failed tactically or even operationally but succeeded on the strategic level.

The battle for Leningrad magnified differences in leadership on both sides. Von Leeb could not focus his strength on a single, decisive Schwerpunkt. Across the frontlines however, Zhukov brought superior command to bear. Even though the German troops cut off Leningrad from overland communication with Russia eight days before Zhukov's arrival this did not signify the end of the city's struggle. The fact that Leningrad did not surrender when basically surrounded (and never would surrender) was probably a bad omen for Germans hoping Moscow would soon give up. Both huge cities were central to the Soviet state and cities they would die fighting for.

Von Leeb told the postwar Nuremberg tribunal he "hardly hoped ever to reach the gates of Leningrad." General Günter Blumentritt, writing after the war, compared Hitler's decision to halt before taking the city to a similar decision at Dunkirk 16 months earlier. Blumentritt believed that Leningrad "probably would have fallen." However, as Hitler would do weeks later when he declared the battle for Moscow over following the twin encirclements at Viazma and Bryansk, Hitler declared victory too soon.

Field Marshal von Leeb conducted a flawed campaign. His own plan did not take into account the fact that with such a small panzer group its only hope of encircling and destroying major portions of the Red Army would be to trap the enemy against the Baltic Sea. As he said later he had "very limited experience in the use of panzer formations on a large scale." This was quite obvious as at numerous critical junctures he halted Hoepner or refused to accept risks essential to blitzkrieg success. He failed to stand up to his higher headquarters' demands that he divide Fourth Panzer Group into non-mutually supporting corps. As Army Group North commander the lion's share of its failings rests on von Leeb's shoulders.

Army Group Center

Von Bock's army group began the invasion with almost every advantage, while Pavlov's West Front could hardly have been in a worse position. In a matter of days von Bock's men had trapped a third of a million Red Army soldiers at Minsk. Two weeks later they were on the verge of closing another, larger, and more significant Kessel at Smolensk. Everywhere, Soviet countermeasures came up short due to a combination of effects.

Nazi poster comparing POW totals for World War I, the Polish Western and Balkan campaigns of World War II, as well as during the first four months of *Barbarossa*. Unfortunately for them, massive numbers of POWs did not equate to strategic victory over the USSR. (Corbis)

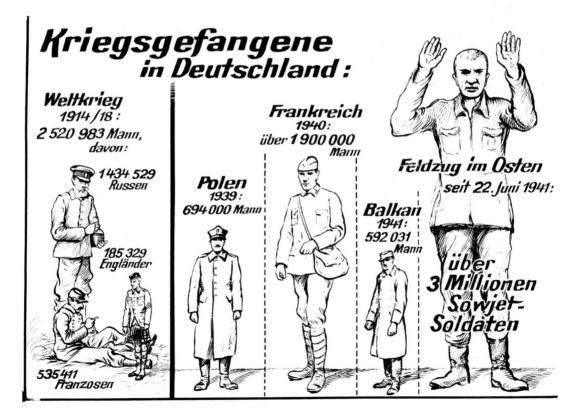

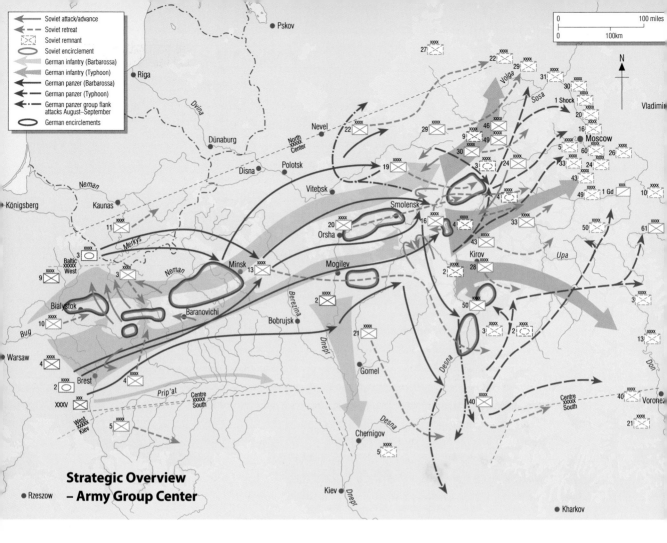

**Strategic Overview
– Army Group Center**

The drive on Moscow looked unstoppable. However, Moscow did not rate high on the list of *Barbarossa*'s objectives. In the various campaign orders, in Hitler's pronouncements, and in other pertinent documents Stalin's capital is mentioned almost as an afterthought. Consistent with the Prussian-German orientation on the destruction of the enemy, the Ostheer concentrated on exterminating the Red Army.

All did not go perfectly for Army Group Center, but initial successes concealed *Barbarossa*'s flaws from both combatants and the wider world. Logistics represented a limiting factor from its earliest days. Various Kessels took longer and required more mechanized forces to reduce than planners expected. Leaders like Guderian pursued individual goals. Organizations like Third Panzer Group were expected to accomplish too much relative to its resources: to continue the advance eastward, reduce encirclements and close the northern flank with von Leeb.

Many German generals at the time thought in terms of taking Moscow, chief among them Franz Halder. But even he was far from consistent in this as he changed his mind often. Many commentators have taken the German leadership to task for not capturing the city. While taking the enemy's capital has the false ring of sound military judgment, there is no proof that occupying Moscow would have led directly to the collapse of the USSR shopworn clichés about the "seat of centralized Soviet power" or the "hub of the Soviet transportation net" notwithstanding.

In fact, it seems clear that the closer the German forces got to Moscow the more *Barbarossa* lost its compass. After Smolensk they surrendered the initiative in the center to regain it on the flanks. Guderian's turn south reaped a huge harvest at Kiev. The half measure of sending only part of Hoth's Third Panzer north did not have nearly the same impact.

Meanwhile, first Timoshenko and later Zhukov gladly picked up the initiative dropped by the German commanders. Their counterattacks achieved little more than the temporary liberation of Yelnia; a place it turns out not that essential to the assault on Moscow, and, therefore, not justifying costly German efforts to hold it.

On the eve of *Typhoon* Goebbels thought Hitler looked healthy, full of confidence and energy. By this time both dictators knew Japan would not enter their war. The speed and ferocity of the final assault surprised the Soviet leadership once again. However, first exhaustion and logistic weakness, and then the *rasputitsa* terminally slowed the advance. On October 8 Hitler hinted at a speech to Party faithful at Munich's *Löwenbraükeller* that the war in the east might even last until 1942. With the Kremlin practically in sight Hitler diluted the Moscow offensive by attacking Voronezh and stripped away much of von Bock's air support in favor of the north African sideshow. During *Typhoon* the Soviet defense crumbled as before but it did not devolve into a confused rout. As Timoshenko told the Supreme Defense Council:

> If Germany succeeds in taking Moscow that is obviously a grave disappointment for us, but it by no means disrupts our grand strategy; that alone will not win [them] the war.

As throughout *Barbarossa*, at Moscow the Red Army took advantage of every German pause and weakness.

For more than two years, through the battles of Viazma–Bryansk, the German forces had prevailed everywhere they chose to create a Schwerpunkt.

The Germans seriously underestimated the Communist Party's ability to mobilize the Soviet population to repel the invader. Here men and women dig an antitank ditch in front of Moscow. (Elukka)

However, in November and December 1941, it was not to be; the Germans failed this time. *Barbarossa's* weaknesses, principally the failure to set clear objectives east of Dnepr–Dvina River line, lack of consensus among the national leadership, sanguine planning, and simply the realities of a relatively small country (allied with even smaller countries) invading the world's largest nation all conspired to bog down the campaign at this late date. When these factors are balanced against the ruthless Soviet leadership, the tenacious never-say-die Red Army defense, terrible weather and terrain, plus a new and talented generation of generals led by Zhukov, one can see that the German forces had to perform flawlessly if they were to win in Russia.

Army Group South

Of the three army groups von Rundstedt's came closest to achieving its *Barbarossa* goals: it crossed the Dnepr, occupied most of the agrarian and industrial areas of the Ukraine, neutralized the Crimea as a threat to Rumanian oil, captured over 1 million Red Army troops, and killed again as many. As with the rest of *Barbarossa*, all of these operational victories did not equal strategic victory over the USSR. After five months the Führer had driven the army group's commander into temporary retirement, begun to micromanage even the smallest frontline units, and handed the German generals their biggest defeat since 1806.

Battles on the frontier were brutal. Von Reichenau mismanaged the First Panzer Group (initially under Sixth Army control) from the time it was jammed-up behind the German start line until von Kleist received his freedom of action on June 26. Kirponos counterattacked but could not concentrate his mechanized corps. With his riposte at an end both armies raced east to see which one would occupy the Stalin Line first. Von Kleist's panzers did and they soon reached the gates of Kiev. But so far Kirponos had avoided encirclement and destruction plus kept Army Group South behind schedule. This permitted Stavka to reinforce the Western and Reserve Fronts fighting on the Moscow axis.

While the Soviet military leaders expected von Rundstedt to turn northeast against their capital at any time (many German commanders expected the same thing), instead he pivoted his panzers southward to Uman. Kirponos had too few tanks left after the frontier battles to halt such a maneuver. In place of a modest Kessel at Vinnitsa the Seventeenth Army and First Panzer scored a major victory at Uman, the army group's first significant encirclement. The victory was tarnished, however, when von Kleist lost time clearing the Dnepr bend instead of racing for bridgeheads over the massive river. As Paulus wrote after the war, securing these crossings "proved to be very prolonged and costly."

On the far south flank the Eleventh Army and two Rumanian armies moved out along the Black Sea coast. Some German units had marched all the way from Greece. Soldiers of the Rumanian Mountain Corps marched "barefoot for two or three weeks." By mid-August, however, they achieved von Rundstedt's first operational objective when they encircled Odessa.

Von Reichenau on the army group's extreme left continued to struggle. The Sixth Army had won no big victories, was stuck near the Rokitno Marshes against the pesky 5th Army and watched as First Panzer and Seventeenth Army grabbed all the glory. Hitler blamed many of the army group's delays on "that egoist von Reichenau" and Halder likewise never forgave him.

Some Soviet armies migrated to their destruction inside the trap while Stavka ordered others to die in place there. The Kiev battle had four phases: 1) securing bridgeheads over the Dnepr and Desna rivers, August 21 –

A Ukrainian woman laments the destruction of her village. Civilians paid a brutal toll during the fighting all around them. (NARA)

September 9; 2) pushing toward Lokhvitsa, September 4–16; 3) fighting for Kiev proper, September 13–19; and 4) clearing the pocket, September 14–27.

The issue of the Kiev encirclement is one of the most contentious of Operation *Barbarossa* and indeed World War II. Many see forfeiting the potential capture of Moscow as the worst example of Hitler's desire for the quick reward in an ultimately futile operational-level conquest. Two facts support the German leaders' actual course of action: 1) the simultaneous threat to von Bock's left and von Rundstedt's right posed by unvanquished enemy forces ignored at Kiev and around the Rokitno Marches and 2) the resilience and will to survive of the USSR. Soviet plans to continue fighting beyond the potential loss of Moscow are well documented. The real issue surrounding Kiev is a month wasted on indecision and bureaucratic infighting within the German leadership.

Army Group South suffered a serious dispersion of effort following Kiev. It gave von Bock's drive on Moscow nine divisions, including two panzer and two motorized. Luftflotte 4 likewise could not concentrate but supported the Crimean operation and pursuit to the Don, fought the Black Sea Fleet,

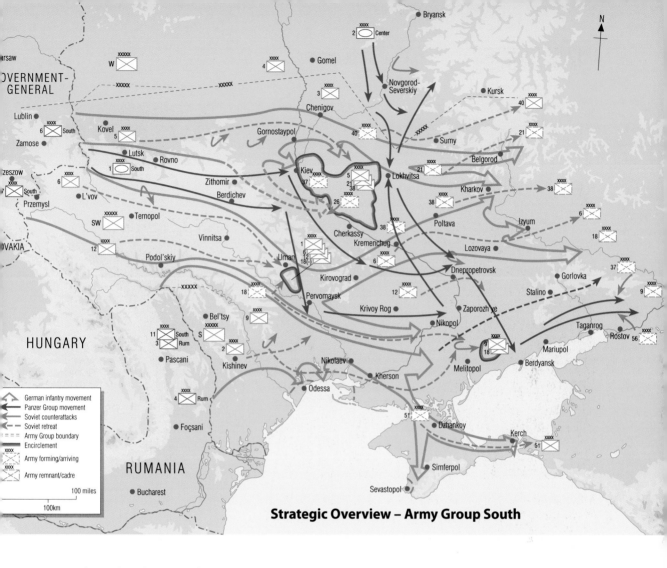

Strategic Overview – Army Group South

and interdicted Soviet railroads and rear areas. It expected 724 trains to reach its bases on the Dnepr in September but received only 195. Von Rundstedt's troops in the field starved while five trains per day shipped food from the "Ukrainian breadbasket" back to the Reich. Soviet recuperative powers continued to amaze the German leaders.

Meanwhile, on October 21 the OKH vainly ordered the Sixth Army to Voroshilovgrad, the Seventeenth to Stalingrad, and the First Panzer to Maikop! Even refueled with oil siphoned off the Baku–Stalino pipeline von Kleist barely made it to Rostov. Timoshenko fortified the resurrected Soviet defenses there, looked for any opportunity to sting the German troops and chased von Kleist back to the Mius River. Within a week the momentum switched back to the Red Army, Hitler cashiered von Rundstedt and *Barbarossa* ended on the southern wing.

Within strategic and political constraints first Kirponos and Tyulenev and later Timoshenko worked defensive wonders in the Ukraine. Nevertheless von Rundstedt's men performed masterfully. His army group alone conquered an area larger than France. It is appropriate to quote at length his Order of the Day for August 15, following the battle of Uman:

> … I am proud to stand at the head of an army group whose troops execute all their tasks with the highest devotion and battle readiness and meet the enemy in fierce daily combat… I repeatedly express my thanks and unreserved appreciation for all those outstanding efforts… However, the campaign has not yet been won. We must keep pressure on the enemy and allow him no quarter, for he has many more reserves than we… I request that all command authorities find the means to create short recuperation breaks for their exhausted formations, during which they can be removed from the front and, for one day get the rest they need. During these recuperation breaks don't harass the troops with training. They should get their fill of sleep, dedicate time for personal hygiene and mending clothes and equipment, and if possible, further refresh themselves with increased rations…

Personnel losses were horrendous. One fifth of the German casualties were killed in action while another 5 percent went missing. The remaining three-quarters were wounded who might eventually return to duty or were POWs. The figures given below detail the damage caused to the Southern and Southwestern Fronts by the III Panzer Corps plus von Mackensen's own losses:

III PANZER CORPS LOSSES

Theater, dates	Soviet POWs	Tanks Dest/ Capt	Guns Dest/ Capt	KIA (Off)	MIA (Off)	WIA (Off)
Frontier, June 22–July 10	14,500	868	472	806 (65)	388 (3)	2,426 (124)
Kiev, July 11–22	16,800	932	622	1,294 (95)	448 (4)	3,846 (194)
Uman Flank, July 23–Aug 12	28,900	940	759	1,642 (120)	500 (6)	5,095 (233)
To Dnepropetrovsk Aug 13–25	62,100	1,281	1,350	2,015 (135)	508 (6)	6,442 (439)
Dnepropetrovsk Bridgehead Aug 26–Sept 29	96,300	1,304	1,509	3,215 (178)	625 (7)	11,097 (439)
Melitopol–Mius, Sept 30–Nov 5	118,400	1,423	1,856	3,805 (204)	667 (8)	13,517 (548)
Rostov, Nov 6–Dec 2	137,900	1,506	2,116	4,214 (223)	814 (10)	15,356 (638)

One can see that the German forces' heaviest losses came during two periods: 1) the initial 18 days breaking through fresh Soviet units and holding off Kirponos' counterattacks; and 2) while defending their bridgehead at Dnepropetrovsk. When advancing their casualties were noticeably lighter.

The Southern and Southwestern Front leadership suffered no catastrophic breakdown as occurred elsewhere along the battle lines. Major disasters happened when they were caught by a surprise German move (Uman), when their actions were dictated by Stavka (Kiev), or when they were ordered to execute desperate measures (Sea of Azov).

Operationally and tactically von Rundstedt was in the stronger position. This won him engagements and battles but not the war. The field marshal himself was caught between a rock (in this case both Hitler and Halder) and a hard place (too few, under-motorized forces in a huge country bitterly defended). But he performed well and is guilty of few mistakes.

Operation *Barbarossa* was not an event *per se*, it was much more of a process. As each battle or maneuver occurred, new opportunities arose or disappeared; *Barbarossa* was not about certainties but about possibilities. At its start Hitler told an aide, "At the beginning of each campaign one pushes a door into a dark, unseen room. One can never know what is hiding inside." The campaign in the East was Hitler's war; without Hitler there is no *Barbarossa*. Planning by both combatants was strikingly similar in that each appeared to be divorced from reality. After the war one German general wrote that the campaign's planning "rested upon the assumption that German military power was and would continue to be irresistible."

Many of *Barbarossa's* senior leaders had served on the Russian Front during 1914–17, and knew that even the Tsar's bungling army had still fought that of the Kaiser to a stalemate. Yet these same men believed a force smaller than that required to subdue France in 1940 would only need a couple of months to conquer the earth's largest nation and army. The Wehrmacht's leadership might have gained some valuable tactical lessons from the 1940 Western campaign, but it had learned all the wrong operational and strategic ones. Unlike the campaigns in Poland and France, the Soviet Union's vastness dissipated the blitzkrieg's shock value. Meanwhile, Soviet leaders naively expected to be counterattacking deep into the German rear within days or weeks of an invasion.

A scene repeated countless times during Operation *Barbarossa*: a *frontovik* who has given his all defending the motherland. The ordinary German and Russian junior rank – the Landser and *frontovik* – fought and tried to survive in very similar conditions. Both served regimes led by dictators of boundless wickedness and violence. Both fought boldly in the attack and tenaciously in defense. Summer heat and winter cold affected them equally; the dust or mud were just as bad on each side of the lines, and poor food, inadequate medical care, lack of home leave, and abundance of vermin made life miserable for the fighting men of both armies. (Elukka)

By the spring of 1941 each military had evidently developed more respect for the other; Germany essentially doubled the number of divisions it considered necessary, while the USSR mobilized an additional half-million men the month before *Barbarossa*. Not wanting to test wartime German civilian morale as had happened a generation earlier, Hitler maintained domestic goods manufacture over ordnance production until well past 1941. For his part, Stalin discounted unmistakable signs of the German build-up as just another skirmish in the war of nerves that had dominated Europe for five years.

Following long tradition, the Ostheer concentrated on destroying enemy formations rather than seizing terrain objectives common in many other armies. This doctrine made it very difficult to judge success, especially in view of the Wehrmacht's pitiable strategic intelligence capabilities. As for logistics, *Barbarossa* devoured materiel at a rate unanticipated by all but the most dire estimates.

The whole world did indeed hold its breath on June 22, 1941. The one bright spot for Stalin that day was Churchill's promise of unconditional support (although many conditions were added later). Shortly after *Barbarossa*

began, Stalin complained that he had lost Lenin's proletarian state and went silent. German soldiers heard rumors that he had escaped to China, Iran, or Turkey or had been assassinated. Judging by his diary entries, German successes surprised even Halder. The Wehrmacht assaulted in strength everywhere along the lengthy front. This massive effort confused the Soviet leadership to the extent that the Red Army could not discern its main effort, thus complicating the defense immensely. In a couple of days the German forces snatched up the Dünaburg bridgehead, were closing the Minsk Kessel, and had fended off determined Soviet counterattacks in the Ukraine.

The less glorious side of war. Germans pause to bury their dead in a ceremony repeated often by both sides. During *Barbarossa* the advancing Germans could at least honor their fallen comrades, the retreating Soviets usually could not. (NARA)

By the first half of July, panzer groups were within striking distance of Leningrad, Smolensk, and Kiev. Soviet counterattacks following prewar plans all failed due to a pattern of poor command and control, inexperience, and German operational and tactical acumen. By then, however, first lieutenants commanded some battalions. The Red Army initiated a second wave of countermoves along the Moscow axis, most notably those bearing Timoshenko's name. These attacks signaled that the Soviet forces would not give up the Dvina–Dnepr line without a fight.

Not even a coffin lid for shelter... Doubtless trying to share body warmth, these German soldiers froze to death in their sleep beside a road. (Podzun)

By the first week of August the Uman and Smolensk pockets marked victories by Army Groups South and Center. In the north, however, operational triumph eluded the German forces. Von Leeb ordered the costly and time-consuming assault across the upper Luga River. Although Army Group North eventually cut off the USSR's second city from overland communication, von Leeb's attack essentially culminated at this point.

With Paulus admittedly concerned about purely military issues, that left Hitler to be his "own Ludendorff" and run the political and economic aspects of the Nazi–Soviet War. However, key generals, like Halder, would not accede to the Führer's primacy and constantly interjected their own ambitions and goals. In addition to fighting the stubborn Stalin, Hitler had to fight his own general staff while the Red Army essentially bled white and de-mechanized the Ostheer. By the end of July, exactly one year after Hitler announced his Eastern crusade at Berchtesgaden, the campaign had stalled as the Führer argued with his generals over the prosecution of the war's second half. *Barbarossa* moved forward, albeit rudderless, until Hitler resolved the matter in late August. But despite the month delay at German headquarters, the Ostheer still operated well within the Boyd Loop of the Soviet's decision-making cycle.

Never in favor of a direct attack on Moscow, Hitler had strategic reasons for taking decisive action on *Barbarossa*'s wings. Success at either extreme could possibly bring Turkey into the war or motivate Finland to redouble its efforts. Anyone even slightly familiar with Germany's tremendous economic problems knows it needed every last resource of the Ukraine (at the same

Civilians and soldiers formed many militia divisions for the urgent defense of large Soviet cities. It is likely that these men, photographed in the shadow of Moscow's Kremlin walls, are heading directly out to the fighting line; note their mixture of uniform and civilian clothing. (Elukka)

The battlefield today; the author seated before an SU-152 assault gun at the Chernigov war memorial in July 2005. Casual historian beware: the map in the background shows the 1943 liberation of the city, but no mention is made of its loss on September 7, 1941. (Author's collection)

time the Soviet Union was proving that it could survive without them). Jodl considered turning Guderian south the "perfect solution" to getting von Rundstedt on schedule.

Once the decision to go to Kiev had been made, Guderian moved south quickly. Stalin, focused on Moscow and distracted by Luftwaffe bombing of the capital, missed the move. Von Kleist's panzer group sought the line of least resistance and occupied most of the middle Dnepr. Their two armored jaws slamming shut at Lokhvitsa represented the zenith of German operational art, but victory at Kiev was soon offset by superior Soviet force generation.

While Army Group Center had been fairly static on either side of Yelnia, the Soviet forces took the offensive and proved that they were not beaten. Von Bock's last great victory came at Viazma–Bryansk. He was then abruptly slowed by weather (first in the form of mud and later by sub-zero cold) combined with the "four horsemen" of Nazi strategic overstretch: troop exhaustion, personnel and materiel attrition, anemic logistics, and the continuing inability to settle on attainable objectives.

Toward the end of November, von Bock's men stumbled toward Moscow in the infamous *Flucht nach Vorn*. Von Leeb at Tikhvin and Volkhov, and von Rundstedt at Rostov, did the same. Capturing Moscow, seen by many as the

Brobdingnagian checkmate of the Soviet state, never occurred. Encircling the city represented an orthodox but equally impossible solution (as subsequent events at Leningrad and Stalingrad would indicate).

In the skies above, initial Luftwaffe victories amazed friend and foe; Göring did not believe estimates of Red Army Air Force aircraft destroyed on the ground during *Barbarossa*'s first days until an actual count of captured airfields revealed the claims were low. Like many German assets, the Luftwaffe was stretched too thin. It tried to prosecute a reduced war against Britain, sent training units into combat as a short-term solution to its small size, thus eliminating any reserves, and soon lost hard-to-replace specialists. It concentrated its efforts only twice during *Barbarossa*. The Luftwaffe's premier CAS unit, VIII Fliegerkorps, deployed only when approved by Göring and Hitler.

In closing, even with the advantages of hindsight, at no point before about mid-November 1941 is *Barbarossa*'s conclusion clear. If one concentrates on operations and ignores German logistics and the disparity in force generation, it may seem that until the end of that month the Ostheer might have had a chance of winning. Strategically the USSR held the best cards, small comfort to Red Army generals and soldiers facing the German forces. In the end the two sides were just too unevenly matched.

In June the balance sheet seemed to favor the invaders as clearly as it appeared to favor the defenders in December. Did the German High Command cling too long to the anachronistic concept of the Napoleonic decisive battle when planning *Barbarossa*? None of their spectacular list of victories at Minsk, Ivanskoye, Uman, Smolensk, Kiev, Viazma–Bryansk, Melitopol, the Crimea, and elsewhere delivered the hoped-for knockout blow against the Red Army.

German victory required operational success in destroying the Red Army and capturing Leningrad, Moscow, and the Ukraine, not just one or two of these objectives. That was clearly beyond their capabilities. The constant Soviet counterattacks, the death-by-a-thousand-cuts technique, eventually saved the USSR. As *Barbarossa* went on, wherever Zhukov showed up, German fortunes faded. However, *Barbarossa* also had to demolish the Stalinist state, even more difficult than achieving the required battlefield victories. When the Nazi–Soviet War transitioned from one of maneuver to one of attrition, victory moved decisively beyond Hitler's grasp. Ultimately, for all who wore the *Feldgrau* the prospect of *Barbarossa* was much brighter than its reality.

APPENDIX

These matrices are meant to assist the reader in tying together the complex and massive campaign, especially for those readers new to Barbarossa. At each stage they show the engagements within the various larger battles as well as the eastern limit of the German logistics on the key central axis. They are provided to demonstrate the inter-relatedness of German and Soviet moves, both within each stage and among the various stages. The reader may want to refer to the appropriate matrix while reading the combat narrative.

THE FRONTIER BATTLES

Legend

Offense

Defence

Army Group	Battle	Engagements
North	*Lithuanian Frontier (Jun 22–29)*	Dubysa, Kaunas, Liepaja, Siauliai
	Dvina Bridgeheads (Jun 27–Jul 1)	Dunaburg, Jekolopils
Soviet Defense		Kelme, Raseinai
Center	*Bialystok/Minsk (Jun 22–Jul 10)*	Baranovichi, Brest, Grodno, Novogrudek
	Mogilev (Jul 12–19)	
Soviet Defense		Brest, Grodno
South	*Galicia/Volhynia Frontier (Jun 22–Jul 12)*	Lutsk, L'vov, Ostrov, Proscurov, Ternopol
Soviet Defense		Dubno
Arctic & Finland	*Platinfuchs, Polarfuchs,*	
Eastern limit of German logistics base in AGC:	Vilnius, Minsk (June 30)	

THREE STEPS FORWARD, ONE STEP BACK

Legend

Offense

Pursuit

Defence

Army Group	Battle	Engagements
North	***Dvina Breakthrough (Jul 2–12)***	Dorpat, Riga
	Estonia (Jul 4–Sep 5)	Tallinin
	Russian Frontier/Lake Il'men (Jul 8–Sep 23)	Ivanovskoye, Narva, Pskov, Ostrov, Sabsk
Soviet Defense		Stolsy
Center	*Mogilev (Jul 12–19)*	
	Smolensk (Jul 8–Aug 15)	Vitebsk, Yartsevo
Soviet Defense		Bobruisk
Soviet Offensive	"Timoshenko Offensives"	
South	*Bessarabia (Jul 2–25)*	Bel'tsy, threaten Odessa
	Western Ukraine/Stalin Line (Jul 2–25)	Berdichev, Kiev (I)
	To the Dnepr (Jul 25–Oct 5)	Berislav, Cherkassy, Dnepropetrovsk, Garnostoypol, Uman
Soviet Defense		Kiev (City)

Arctic & Finland	*Karelia*	
Soviet Defense North		Stolsy
Soviet Defense Center		Bobruisk
Soviet Defense South		Kiev (City)
Soviet Offensive	Timoshenko Off VII–VIII	
Eastern limit of German logistics base in AGC:	Nevel, Orsha (July 22)	

BARBAROSSA IN THE BALANCE

Army Group	Battle	Engagements
North	Staraya Russa (10–24 Aug)	Kholm, Lovat River, Stoltsy
	Advance on Leningrad (Jul 12–Sep 25)	Dudergof, Luga Line, Neva River, Novgorod, Petergof
	Baltic Islands (Sep 8–Oct 15)	
	Leningrad Siege (start Sep 26)	
	Transition (Sep 26–Oct 15)	Valdai Hills
Soviet Defense		Staraya-Russa
Center	*Berezina-Dnepr (Jul 28–Aug 11)*	
	Velikie Luki (Aug 22–27)	
	Roslavl (Aug 1–9)	
	Timoshenko Offensive (Jul 26–Oct 1)	
	Yelnia (Aug 10–1 Oct)	
	Gomel/Krichev (Aug 9–20)	
	Desna River (21–30 Aug)	Novgorod-Severskiy
	Kiev (Aug 21–Sept 27)	Chernigov, Konotop, Romny
Soviet Defense		Smokensk, Roslavl, Yelnia
Soviet Offensive	"Timoshenko Offensives"	
South	*Kiev (Sep 14–27)*	Lokhvitsa, Kremenchug, Poltava
	To the Donets (Oct 1–Nov 21)	Izum, Stalino
	Sea of Azov (Sep 26–Oct 11)	
	Perekop/Isthmus (Aug 31–Oct 27)	Ishun
	Black Sea Coast	Odessa
Eastern limit of German logistics base in AGC	Smolensk, Gomel (Sep 1)	

Legend

Offense

Transition

Defence

END GAME

Legend

Offense
Transition
Defence

Army Group	Battle	Engagements
North	*Leningrad Siege (start Sep 26)*	
	Tikhvin/Volkhov Offensive (Oct 16–Dec 7)	
Soviet Defense		Tikhvin, Volkhov
Soviet Offensive		Tikhvin, Volkhov
Center	*Viazma-Bryansk (Sep 30–Oct 20)*	Gshatsk
	Moscow Offensive (Oct 4–Dec 5)	Kaluga, Kashira, Malayaroslavets, Mozajsk, Tula, Voronezh
	Kalinin (Nov 18–Dec 5)	Klin
	Orel (Oct 21–Nov 18)	Yefremov
Soviet Defense		Kalinin, Moscow
Soviet Offensive		Kalinin, Moscow
South	*Kharkov (start Oct 26)*	Belgorod, Donbas
	Crimea (start Oct 28)	Kerch, Sevastopol
	Rostov (Nov 17–28)	
	Winter Defense (start Nov 22)	Mius River
Soviet Defense		Rostov
Soviet Offensive		Rostov
Eastern limit of German logistics base in AGC:	Rzhev, Bryansk (Oct 30)	

GLOSSARY

Abwehr   German counterintelligence service

Attentat   The July 20, 1944 assassination attempt against Hitler by German military leaders

Auftragstaktik   The German doctrine of giving subordinates broad "mission type" guidance rather than specific orders, figuratively a doubled-edged sword

Axis   The alliance of Germany, Italy, and Japan, sealed by the Tripartite Pact of September 1940, numerous smaller nations joined later

Bersaglieri   Italian fast light infantry

BSMD   Baltic Special Military District

Barbarossatag   Barbarossa Day, the day of the German invasion of the USRR, June 22, 1941

Boyd Loop   USAF Colonel John Boyd's decision-making model used to evaluate leadership, especially in stressful situations like those found in war. Also known as the OODA Loop, the key components are Orientation, Observation, Decision, and Action. The side that cycles through this loop faster will usually be successful

CAS   Close air support

CSIR   Italian Expedition Corps in Russia

DP 41 (Soviet)   State Defensive Plan 1941

Einsatzgruppen   Special Task Forces; SS- and SD-manned mobile death quads that operated in German-occupied Eastern Europe

FHO   *Fremde Heere Ost*; Foreign Armies East, section of the General Staff responsible for intelligence on the Red Army

Freikorps   Non-official military organizations raised by right-wing former German Army officers after World War I, active in Germany and points east, i.e., the Baltic States

frontovik   Soviet frontline soldier

Führerprinzip   Lit. "leader principle," the German doctrine that the Führer's word was absolute and that ultimate responsibility lay with him. Later included other party and military leaders

Gebirgsjäger   German mountain infantry

Heer   German Army

Igel   Lit. "hedgehog," German all-round defensive position

Kessel   Lit. "cauldron," German encirclement battle or pocket

Kriegsmarine	German Navy
KSMD	Kiev Special Military District
Landser	Lit. "man of the land," German infantryman
LOG	Luga Operational Group (Soviet)
LSSAH	*Leibstandarte SS Adolf Hitler*; SS unit originating as Hitler's personal bodyguard
Luftwaffe	German Air Force
MP 41 (Soviet)	Mobilization Plan 1941
NCO	Non-commissioned officer
NKVD	Soviet People's Commissariat for Internal Affairs, responsible mainly for internal security
OKH	*Oberkommando des Heeres*; German Army High Command
OKW	*Oberkommando der Wehrmacht*; Supreme High Command of the German Armed Forces
Ostheer	Lit. "Eastern Army," German forces fighting against the USSR
panje	panje horses, native to Poland and Russia, can also refer to the carts they pulled
POW	prisoner of war
rasputitsa	Russian spring and autumn rainy season
Reichsbahn	German national railway
Schwerpunkt	The main, overriding objective of a mission, offensive or defensive. All other efforts are secondary to it. As Paul von Hindenburg said, "An operation without a *Schwerpunkt* is like a man without character."
Stavka	Headquarters of the Soviet High Command
Strosstrupp	Lit. "Storm troop," German infiltration technique used by highly-trained, independent units developed late in World War I to break stalemate in the trenches on the Western Front
Sturmabteilung	The original paramilitary wing of the Nazi party, the SA
Volk	German people
Wehrkreis	Lit. "Military District," one of 17 army administrative divisions of Germany, responsible for mobilization, recruiting, etc
Wehrmacht	German Armed Forces, comprising the Heer, Kriegsmarine, and Luftwaffe. The SS, while technically a Nazi Party organ, fell under the operational control of the Wehrmacht
Wolfsschanze	Wolf's Lair; Hitler's military headquarters for the Eastern Front near Rastenburg, Prussia (today Poland), built for Operation Barbarossa
WSMD	Western Special Military District (USSR)

BIBLIOGRAPHY

Andrew, Christopher, *The Sword and the Shield,* Basic Books, 1999.

Bartov, Omer, *Germany's War and the Holocaust,* Cornell U., 2003.

Baumann, Hans, *Die 35 Infanteriedivision,* G. Braun, 1964.

Bergstrom, Christer, and Andrey Mikhailov, *Black Cross, Red Star,* Pacifica Military History, 2000.

Beyersdorff, Ernst, *Geschichte der 110 Infanteriedivision,* Podzun, 1965.

Blakemore, Porter, *Manstein in the Crimea,* PhD. Dissertation, University of Georgia, 1978.

Blankenhagen, Wilhelm, *Im Zeichen des Schwertes,* Giebel, 1982.

Bock, Fedor von, *The War Diary,* Schiffer, 1996.

Boog, Horst, ed., *Germany and the Second World War,* Vol. IV, "Attack on the Soviet Union," Clarendon Press, 1998.

Buxa, Werner, *Weg und Schicksal der 11. Infantrie-Division,* Podzun Verlag, 1963.

Carell, Paul, *Hitler Moves East,* Ballantine, 1971.

Chales de Beaulieu, Walter, *Der Vorstoss der Panzergruppe 4 auf Leningrad-1941,* Scharnhorst, 1961.

Chales de Beaulieu, Walter, *Generaloberst Erich Hoepner,* Vowinckel, 1969.

Chickering, Roger and Jürgen Förster (eds.), *Shadows of Total War,* German History Institute, 2003.

Childers, Thomas and Jane Caplan (eds.), *Reevaluating the Third Reich,* Holmes & Meyer, 1993.

Citino, Robert, *The German Way of War,* University of Kansas, XXXX

Clark, Alan, *Barbarossa,* William Morrow, 1965.

Creveld, Martin van (ed.), *Airpower and Maneuver Warfare,* Air University Press, 1994.

Creveld, Martin van., *Supplying War,* Cambridge University, 1977.

Davis, C.R., *Von Kleist,* Lancer Militaria, 1979.

Dieckhoff, Gerhard, *Die 3. Infanterie-Division,* H.W. Blick, 1960.

DiNardo, R.L., "The Dysfunctional Coalition", *Journal of Military History,* Oct. 1996.

Dunn, Walter, *Hitler's Nemesis,* Greenwood, 1994.

Ellis, John, *Brute Force,* Viking, 1990.

English, John, *On Infantry,* Praeger, 1984.

Erickson, John, and David Dilks (eds.), *Barbarossa,* Edinburgh University Press, 1994.

Erickson, John, *Road to Stalingrad,* Westview Press, 1984.

Fugate, Bryan, *Operation Barbarossa,* Presidio Press, 1984.

Glantz, David, *Barbarossa,* Tempus, 2001.

Glantz, David, *Before Stalingrad,* Tempus, 2003.

Glantz, David, *Colossus Reborn,* University of Kansas, 2005.

Glantz, David, ed., *The Initial Period of the War on the East Front, 22 June–August 1941,* Frank Cass, 1993.

Glantz, David, *Stumbling Colossus: The Red Army on the Eve of War,* University of Kansas, 1998.

Glantz, David, and House, Jonathan, *When Titans Clashed*, University of Kansas, 1995.

Glantz, David, numerous self-published booklets and atlases.

Goerlitz, Walter, *Paulus and Stalingrad*, Greenwood, 1974.

Gorodetsky, Gabriel, *Grand Delusion*, Yale University, 1999.

Guderian, Heinz, *Panzer Leader,* Ballantine, 1957.

Hagen, William W., *German History in Modern Times,* Cambridge University, 2012.

Haupt, Werner, *Army Group Center*, Schiffer, 1997.

Haupt, Werner, *Army Group North*, Schiffer, 1997.

Haupt, Werner, *Army Group South*, Schiffer, 1998.

Haupt, Werner, *Die 260 Infanteriedivision,* Podzun, 1970.

Haupt, Werner, *Die Deutschen vor Moskau,* Podzun, 1996.

Haupt, Werner, *Kiev*, Podzun, 1964.

Haywood, Joel, *Stopped at Stalingrad,* University of Kansas, 1998.

Hillgruber, Andreas, *Hitlers Strategie*, Bernard & Graefe, 1993.

Hitchins, Keith, *Rumania, 1866–1947,* Oxford, 1994.

Hertlein, Wilhelm, *Chronik der 7 Infanteriedivision,* Bruckmann, 1984.

Hossbach, Friedrich, *Infanterie im Ostfeldzug,* Giebel, 1951.

Hoth, Hermann, *Panzer Operationen,* Vowinkel, 1956.

Hubatsch, Walter, *Die 61. Infanterie-Division*, Podzun, 1983.

Hull, Isabel, *Absolute Destruction,* Cornell University, 2005.

Jacobsen, Otto, *Erich Marcks*, Musterschmidt, 1971.

Jentz, Thomas (ed.), *Panzertruppen*, Schiffer,1996.

Kaltenegger, Roland, *Krieg am Eismeer*, Leopold Stocker, 1999.

Kershaw, Ian, *Hitler: Nemesis,* Norton, 2000.

Kleinfeld, Gerald and Lewis Tambs, *Hitler's Spanish Legion*, Southern Illinois University Press, 1979.

Knoblesdorff, Otto von, *Geschichte der niedersachsischen 19 Panzerdivision,* Podzun, 1958.

Kokoshin, Andrei, *Soviet Strategic Thought 1917–91,* MIT Press, 1998.

Komar, Gary, *Operation Barbarossa – The Case Against Moscow*, unpublished MS.

Koral, V.E., et al, "Tragic 1941 and Ukraine," *Journal of Slavic Military Studies*, March 1998.

Kozhevnikov, M.N., *Command and Staff of the Red Army Air Force*, USAF, 1977.

Laffin, John, *Jackboot*, Cassell, 1966.

Lanz, Hubert, *Gebirgsjaeger*, Podzun, 1954.

Lewis, S.J., *Forgotten Legions*, Praeger, 1985.

Loeser, Jochen, *Bittere Pflicht*, Biblio Verlag, 1988.

Lossberg, Bernhard von, *In Wehrmachtführungsstab*, H.H. Noelke, 1950.

Lüttichau, Charles von, unpublished manuscript, Ft. McNair, Washington, DC.

Mackensen, Eberhard von, *Vom Bug zum Kaukasus*, Vowinkel, 1967.

Magenheimer, Heinz, *Hitler's War*, Arms & Armour, 1998.

Mann, Chris and Jorgensen, *Hitler's Arctic War,* Thomas Dunne, 2002.

Manstein, Erich von, *Lost Victories*, Presidio, 1984.

Manstein, Ruediger von, *Manstein*, Bernard & Graefe, 1981.

Mazower, Mark, *Hitler's Empire*, Penguin, 2008.

Megargee, Geoffrey, *Inside Hitler's High Command*, University of Kansas, 2000.

Megargee, Geoffrey, *War of Annihilation*, Rowman & Littlefield, 2006.

Merker, Ludwig, *Das Buch der 78 Sturmdivision*, Kameradshilfswerk, n/d.

Messe, Giovanni, *Der Krieg im Osten*, Thomas Verlag, 1948.

Meyer, Georg (ed.), *Generalfeldmarschall Wilhelm Ritter von Leeb*, Beitrage zur Militaer und Kriegsgeschichte, 1976.

Meyer-Detring, Wilhelm, *Die 137 Infanteriedivision*, Kameradschaft, 1962.

Mierzejewski, Alfred, *The Most Valuable Asset of the Reich*, University of North Carolina, 2000.

Mitcham, Samuel, *Men of the Luftwaffe*, Presidio, 1988.

Moynahan, Brian, *Claws of the Bear*, Houghton-Mifflin, 1989.

Müller, Rolf-Dieter, Gerd Ueberschär, and Bruce Little, *Hitler's War in the East, 1941–1945: A Critical Assessment,* Berghahn Books, 1997.

Muller, Richard, *German Air War in Russia*, Nautical and Aviation Publishers of America, 1992.

Muller-Hillebrand, Burkhart, *Germany and its Allies*, University Publishers of America, 1980.

Murphy, David, *What Stalin Knew*, Yale University, 2005.

Nafziger, George, *German Order of Battle, Infantry in World War Two*, Stackpole Books, 1999.

Neumann, Joachim, *Die 4 Panzerdivision*, Bernard und Graefe, 1957.

Newton, Steven, *German Battle Tactics on the Russian Front*, Schiffer, 1997.

Niehorster, Leo, *The Royal Hungarian Army, 1920–1945*, Axis Europa, 1999.

Oehmichen, Hermann, *Der Weg der 87 Infanteriedivision*, Selbstverlag, 1969.

Overy, Richard, *Russia's War*, TV Books, 1997.

Paul, Wolfgang, *Brennpunkte*, Hoentges Verlag, 1977.

Paul, Wolfgang, *Geschichte der 18 Panzerdivision*, Preussische Militär Verlag, 1989.

Plato, Anton von, *Die Geschichte der 5 Panzerdivision*, Walhalla, 1978.

Pleshakov, Constantine, *Stalin's Folly*, Houghton Mifflin, 2005.

Plocher, Hermann, *German Air Force versus Russia*, Arno Press, 1968.

Pons, Shivo, *Stalin and the Inevitable War*, Frank Cass, 2002.

Reinhardt, Klaus, *Moscow, The Turning Point*, Berg, 1992.

Ruge, Friedrich, *Soviets as Naval Opponents*, US Naval Institute Press, 1979.

Scheibert, Horst, *Die Gespenster Division*, Pallas, 1981.

Schmidt, August, *Geschichte der 10 Division*, Podzun, 1963.

Schueler, Klaus, *Logistik im Russlandfeldzug*, Peter Lang, 1987.

Seaton, Albert, *Battle for Moscow*, Stein & Day, 1971.

Seaton, Albert, *Stalin's War*, Combined, 1998.

Sharp, Charles, *Soviet Order of Battle in World War Two*, Nafziger, 1996.

Snyder, Timothy, *Bloodlands,* Basic Books, 2010.

Spahr, William, *Stalin's Lieutenants*, Presidio, 1997.

Stahel, David, *Kiev 1941*, Cambridge University, 2012.

Stahel, David, *Operation Barbarossa and Hitler's Defeat in the East,* Cambridge University, 2009.

Stahel, David, *Operation Typhoon,* Cambridge University, 2012.

Statiev, Alexander, "The Ugly Duckling of the Armored Forces," *Journal of Slavic Military Studies*, June 1999.

Stephan, Robert, *Stalin's Secret War*, University of Kansas, 2004.

Sterrett, James, *Southwest Front Operations, June–September 1941*, MA Dissertation, University of Calgary, 1994.

Stoves, Rolf, *1. Panzer Division, 1939–45*, Hans-Henning Podzun, 1961.

Tarleton, Robert, "What Really Happened to the Stalin Line?" parts 1&2, *Journal of Slavic Military Studies,* June 1992 and March 1993.

Taylor, Brian, *Barbarossa to Berlin, Vol. 1*, Spellmount, 2003.

Tooze, Adam, *The Wages of Destruction*, Viking, 2007.

Topitsch, Ernst, *Stalin's War*, St Martin's, 1985.

Toland, John, *Adolf Hitler,* Knopf, 1976,

Ueberschar, Gerd (ed.), *Unternehmen Barbarossa*, Schoeningh, 1984.

Warlimont, Walter, *Inside Hitler's Headquarters*, Presidio, 1991.

Weinberg, Gergard, *World at Arms*, Cambridge University, 1994.

Willmott, H.P., *The Great Crusade*, Free Press, 1989.

Winters, Harold, *Battling the Elements*, Johns Hopkins University, 1998.

Wuorinen, John (ed.), *Finland and World War Two*, Greenwood, 1983.

Zaloga, Stephen, and Leland Ness, *Red Army Handbook, 1939–45*, Sutton Publishing, 1998.

Zhukov, Georgi, *Marshal Zhukov's Greatest Battles*.

Zhukov, Georgi, "The War Begins: The Battle of Moscow," in *Main Front*, Brassey's, 1987.

Ziemke, Earl and Magda Bauer, *German Northern Theater of Operations, 1940–45*, US Army, 1959.

Ziemke, Earl, and Bauer, Magda, *Moscow to Stalingrad*, Military Heritage Press, 1988.

INDEX

References to illustrations are shown in **bold**.